A PSYCHOLOGIST'S CASEBOOK OF CRIME

A PSYCHOLOGIST'S CASEBOOK OF CRIME

FROM ARSON TO VOYEURISM

Edited by

BELINDA WINDER

Reader in Forensic Psychology, Nottingham
Trent University, UK

and

PHILIP BANYARD

Reader in Psychology, Nottingham Trent
University, UK

palgrave
macmillan

First published 2012 by
PALGRAVE MACMILLAN

Palgrave Macmillan in the UK is an imprint of Macmillan Publishers Limited,
registered in England, company number 785998, of Houndmills, Basingstoke,
Hampshire RG21 6XS.

Palgrave Macmillan in the US is a division of St Martin's Press LLC,
175 Fifth Avenue, New York, NY 10010.

Palgrave Macmillan is the global academic imprint of the above companies
and has companies and representatives throughout the world.

Palgrave® and Macmillan® are registered trademarks in the United States,
the United Kingdom, Europe and other countries.

ISBN 978–0–230–24273–9 hardback
ISBN 978–0–230–24274–6 paperback

This book is printed on paper suitable for recycling and made from fully
managed and sustained forest sources. Logging, pulping and manufacturing
processes are expected to conform to the environmental regulations of the
country of origin.

A catalogue record for this book is available from the British Library.

A catalog record for this book is available from the Library of Congress.

10 9 8 7 6 5 4 3 2 1
21 20 19 18 17 16 15 14 13 12

Printed in China

This book is dedicated to Lynn Saunders (Governor of HMP Whatton), Karen Thorne, Kerensa Hocken, Clare Breed and all of the psychologists and other staff at HMP Whatton who work with such dedication and commitment to reduce reoffending; they combine professionalism and empathy in their drive to prevent further victims of sexual crime.

This book is also dedicated to Laura Hamilton, Rebecca Lievesley and Nick Blagden – my 'partners in crime' in forensic research.

Dr Belinda Winder

CONTENTS

TABLES

FIGURES

BOXES

ACKNOWLEDGEMENTS

We are extremely grateful to all the authors who contributed to this book and would also like to thank our colleagues in the Division of Psychology at Nottingham Trent University for their continual support, friendship and good humour.

Belinda Winder would also like to thank a number of other animals, human and otherwise, who have in some way contributed to the book and/or to life generally; thanks to Dave (tolerance and understanding), Gollie and Tiny (fraud and proofing), Jumble (all-round cuteness), Charlie Elf (indexing), and Somnium, Sloggi, Om and Wyatt (who have slept through most of it).

Phil Banyard would like to acknowledge the tolerance and efforts of his co-author and the diverting and always interesting company of Christian Adey.

The publisher and authors would also like to thank the organisations and people listed below for permission to reproduce material from their publications:

- Refuge for Figure 3.1, Box 3.4 and Figure 3.5
- Women's Aid for Box 3.1 adapted from Women's Aid *Survivors' Handbook* and Figure 3.2
- Domestic Abuse Intervention Programme for Figure 3.4
- ManKind Initiative for Figure 3.6

Material is acknowledged individually throughout the text of the book.

Every effort has been made to trace all copyright holders but, if any have been inadvertently overlooked, the publisher will be pleased to make the necessary arrangements at the first opportunity.

NOTES ON CONTRIBUTORS

Philip Banyard is a reader in psychology at Nottingham Trent University, UK. He is the author of many texts in psychology, including *Introducing Psychological Research* (with Andy Grayson) and *Ethical Guidelines in Psychology* (with Cara Fanagan). His main focus of research is the impact of digital technologies on behaviour and in particular on education. He is a season ticket holder at Nottingham Forest as a penance for the bad things he has done in his life.

Dr Nicholas Blagden is a lecturer in forensic psychology at Nottingham Trent University, UK, and a chartered psychologist. He has taught undergraduate and postgraduate courses in psychology, forensic psychology, criminology and policing. He has been involved in training new police officers, and has worked and researched within the Criminal Justice System and HM Prison Service.

Clare Breed is a chartered and registered forensic psychologist based at HMP Whatton, UK, and has been involved in the assessment and treatment or sex offenders for the last 16 years.

Joanna Cahall MA is a PhD student in clinical forensic psychology at John Jay College/the Graduate Center of the City University of New York, USA. She is currently working under the supervision of Dr Barry Rosenfeld and Dr Michele Galietta as a therapist on a randomised controlled trial evaluating the effectiveness of two empirically validated treatments with stalking offenders.

Joanne Clough is a senior lecturer in law at Northumbria University, Newcastle upon Tyne, UK, and a practising solicitor specialising in criminal defence work. Her teaching and research focuses on criminal law, litigation and evidence.

Andrea Daykin is a forensic psychologist in the Nottinghamshire County Community Forensic Service. Over the last 11 years she has worked in various settings, including the Dangerous and Severe Personality Disorder Programme and the Personality Disorder Service at Rampton High Secure Hospital, low secure and community services, and prison. Her clinical interests include personality disorder, cognitive analytic therapy, clinical supervision and fire setting. In the past she has co-facilitated the Arson Treatment Programme for male in patients at Rampton High Secure Hospital.

Heather D. Flowe PhD is a lecturer in forensic psychology at the University of Leicester, UK. Her primary research interests include eyewitness memory, aggression, and the social endocrinology of risk taking.

Mélodie Foellmi MA is a PhD student in clinical forensic psychology at Fordham University, New York City, USA. Working under the supervision of Dr Barry Rosenfeld, she is a therapist, intake clinician, and coordinator at Project SHARP, a randomised controlled study evaluating the effectiveness of two empirically validated treatments with stalking offenders. Her research focuses on assessing the validity and reliability of stalking risk assessment instruments.

Professor Liz Gilchrist is a registered forensic psychologist and Professor of Forensic Psychology at Glasgow Caledonian University, UK. Her primary research interest is in the area of domestic violence, with a particular focus on risk assessment. Since 1996 she has been involved in training postgraduate forensic psychologists and has been a member of various forensic and professional committees within the British Psychological Society. She is currently the Division of Forensic Psychology (DFP) representative on the Partnership & Accreditation Committee in the British Psychological Society and Chair of DFP-Scotland. Liz is recognised as an expert in the area of domestic violence and child protection. She is a member of the violence network within the Scottish Centre Crime and Justice Research, a member of the Research Advisory Group and a recognised training provider for the RMA, a part-time psychologist member of the Parole Board for England and Wales, and a lay member of the Parole Board for Scotland. She has recently undertaken training of prison psychologists with the Council for Europe in Turkey and presented her research in the USA and China.

Laura Hamilton is a registered forensic psychologist and course director for the MSc in forensic psychology at Nottingham Trent University, UK. She has worked in a range of forensic settings, most recently at Rampton High Secure Hospital on a unit specialising in the assessment and treatment of offenders with severe personality disorders.

Kerensa Hocken is a registered forensic psychologist based at HMP Whatton, UK. She is the clinical lead for the sex offender treatment programmes and specialises in the assessment and treatment of sexual offenders. She is a national trainer for the prison service's Sex Offender Treatment Programmes and the Structured Assessment for Risk and Need for Sexual Offenders. She is undertaking doctoral research on the development of a risk assessment for use with intellectually disabled sexual offenders.

Anthony McNally is currently undertaking a PhD in the Psychology Department at Nottingham Trent University, UK, and in collaboration with HMP Whatton. Previously he worked at Rampton Hospital and his current research involves studying the collecting behaviour of Internet sex offenders who download and save child abuse images.

Gerard Milano Detective Chief Inspector is a serving police officer with Nottinghamshire Police, UK. He has managed a number of specialist crime investigations, including some concerned with the sexual exploitation of children and other vulnerable groups, as well as heading up investigations into more mainstream and performance-driven aspects of police service delivery, such as volume acquisitive crime and major crime. He has also worked in various regional and national crime agencies.

Wendy Morgan is a chartered forensic psychologist who specialises in the risk assessment and management of violent and sexual crimes. She has worked with HM Prison Service, the Parole Board of England and Wales, the police, schools and charities that work with the victims of domestic violence. She is Course Director of the MSc in forensic psychology at London Metropolitan University, UK, and is affiliated with Marymount University, Virgina, USA.

Sarah Pemberton is Lecturer in Criminology at Birmingham City University, UK. She has recently completed a PhD, undertaking a critical discursive psychological study of convicted adult rapists' offence accounts.

Dr Dave Putwain is a senior lecturer in psychology at Edge Hill University, UK. His research interests focus on how socio-cognitive models can be applied to education and offending.

Dr Barry Rosenfeld is Director of Clinical Training and Co-Director of the Forensic Specialization at Fordham University, New York City, USA. His research encompasses a range of forensic psychology topics but has focused significantly on the assessment and treatment of stalking offenders. In addition to his academic position and clinical practice, he has developed and serves as Executive Director of Project SHARP, the first treatment programme developed specifically for the treatment of stalking offenders.

Dr David Rowson is a chartered accountant and is employed as a forensic investigator with the Solicitors Regulation Authority (SRA), UK. The SRA is the independent regulator of solicitors, the firms in which they operate and all those working within those firms.

Elizabeth Scowcroft is currently working for Samaritans as a researcher. The main function of the research team within the charity is to conduct action-based research to provide evidence for the Samaritans service in order to support its callers better. Prior to this she completed an MSc in psychological research methods at Nottingham Trent University, UK, where she conducted research into the experience of being involved in, and living, around gangs.

Kerry Sheldon was previously a research fellow at Rampton High Secure Hospital, UK. She has worked for the probation service in sex offender treatment and as a lecturer in psychology and criminology. She is currently undertaking clinical training.

Dr Gillian W. Smith is a senior lecturer in psychology at Nottingham Trent University, UK. Her research centres on alcohol and drug use with a particular focus on patterns and consequences of polydrug use.

Melanie K. Takarangi PhD is a lecturer at Flinders University in Adelaide, Australia. Her primary research interests include memory distortion in forensic and legal settings, and cognitive processes related to aggression and violence.

Karen Thorne is a chartered and registered forensic psychologist and is the East Cluster Manager for East Midlands Forensic Psychology Service, Public Sector Prisons, UK. Until recently she was the Head of Interventions at HMP Whatton, an establishment specialising in the treatment of sex offenders. She has 17 years' experience in the assessment and treatment of violent and sex offenders.

David Wilson is Professor of Criminology at Birmingham City University, UK, and Director of the Centre for Applied Criminology, one of the university's research centres of excellence. He is regarded as one of the country's leading experts on murder and serial murder, and his most recent book is *A History of British Serial Killing* (2010. He is Editor of *The Howard Journal of Criminal Justice* and Vice Chair of the Howard League for Penal Reform.

Dr Belinda Winder is a reader in forensic psychology at Nottingham Trent University, UK, and heads the Sexual Offences, Crime and Misconduct Research Unit in the Division of Psychology at the university. The unit works collaboratively with HMP Whatton (Europe's largest sex offender prison) to conduct applied research on issues surrounding sex offenders and sexual crime.

PROLOGUE

DETECTIVE CHIEF INSPECTOR GERARD MILANO

Crime, quite simply, matters. It touches everyone in a way that is matched by little else and, as a consequence, has been the subject of innumerable academic studies as well as the topic of many popular fictional works over the years. It would be fair to say that, in general, all forms of the media are happy to satisfy the voracious appetite that exists for crime-related matters amongst the general public.

Whilst official crime rates continue to fall, the fear of crime is still a very tangible thing for many, including those people (the majority of the population, in fact!) who have not been directly affected by it. Views are often expressed regarding the impact of offending on individuals and communities. This is then usually followed by a range of opinions outlining what the relevant authorities should do more effectively to tackle the issue. Evidence of the fundamental relevance of crime in all aspects of British life can be gauged by the fact that every UK post-war general election has had law and order as one of its main policy topics.

There can be little doubt that the national debate around crime can only benefit from it becoming a more informed one. To this end, I hope that this book will go some way towards helping its readers to explore different aspects of offending behaviour, challenging some of the prevalent preconceptions about the subject and dispelling some of the more common myths that persist.

This book represents a comprehensive look at crime – from examining the current policing priority of tackling volume serious acquisitive crime to looking into the very emotive and difficult subject of paedophilia. Ask yourself the following questions: What mental pictures do you have when you think of a burglar? How does this differ from the image that your mind creates when you think of a paedophile? In many cases, the two pictures conjured by your mind will be very different, but do you know what factors have influenced your thinking and why?

The majority of the general public that I have worked with during my policing career have been heavily conditioned by what they have seen and read (often somewhat unhelpfully in fiction) and are therefore predisposed towards certain assumptions can often be detrimental to the investigative process. It also shows just how much potential there is for some people, to varying degrees, to be almost pre-programmed by their own core values to be prepared to accept a number of preconceptions and assumptions as facts in a subject that they regard as being very important to them.

The most commonly held views about crime-related matters are based on a perceived emotional understanding of what the offence is about, as opposed to a logical and fact-based assessment of the impact of the offending behaviours in question, the motivation to offend and the environmental factors that provide (or, I hope, more often negate) the opportunity for the offending behaviour to take place in the first instance. An appreciation of these crucial components of criminal behaviour is the key towards then attempting to design effective solutions to the challenges that crime presents to its victims, the perpetrators and society at large.

Although crime itself, as well as the myriad different contributing factors to be considered, can often be complex, it is my view that there is one issue that needs to be acknowledged as being at the core of the matter. This is that the victims of crime deserve to be placed at the heart of how any civilised society aims to deal with crime. Often, attempts to prevent further crimes from taking place or gaining an understanding as to why the offender committed a crime in the first place become the focus of much of the work and the efforts of the various statutory and other agencies involved. While this is all very valid activity, it is still my view that not enough emphasis is being placed on helping victims to come to terms with what has happened to them in a way that would truly be indicative of a victim-centred approach to tackling crime.

In conclusion, I very much hope that besides being useful and rewarding for the purposes of your studies, this book also goes some way towards igniting a real desire for you to get the most out of your time learning about this key subject matter. After all, perhaps one day, this knowledge and understanding of the subject will better equip you in your working life to play a key role in helping society to prevent and fight crime more effectively.

Enjoy the book!

Gerard Milano
Detective Chief Inspector
Nottinghamshire Police

INTRODUCTION

BELINDA WINDER AND PHILIP BANYARD

The original idea of this book was to produce an A–Z of crime and look at the contributions of forensic psychology to all of them. These contributions include our understandings of the crime and the interventions that are used to discourage repeat offending. In putting together this book, we have been fortunate in persuading some excellent expert authors to outline what forensic psychology can bring to the area in which they specialise. Of course, it was not possible to cover all the categories of crime in one text, but we have made a selection that covers a wide range of offences and includes the most prominent of crimes.

Some crimes attract a higher profile than others, and this attention to certain crimes changes over time and across cultures. One constant high-profile crime is murder, which has always attracted a lot of interest by both professional workers and the general public, who, it seems, can't get enough of it. Murder is the staple diet of television drama, suggesting our preoccupation with it, although interestingly, the UK murder rate is currently the lowest for 20 years (http://www.guardian.co.uk/uk/2009/jul/16/crime-figures-recession-impact) and fewer than 700 die in this way each year compared with 3000 who die on the roads.

Other crimes have achieved greater prominence in recent years. For example, crimes against women have only recently been acknowledged as crimes. Until 1991 it was not possible for a woman to bring a charge of rape against her husband and, to this day, there remain concerns that rape is seriously underreported and with very low conviction rates in respect to rape perpetrated by a partner, ex-partner or acquaintance (the Fawcett Society website). Domestic violence is another set of crimes that predominantly – but not exclusively – affect women, and a recent change in attitude towards them has resulted in better understanding of the issues and more convictions.

The major moral panic of the moment concerns sex offenders, where the general view is to see the main danger as being from stranger assaults although, in fact, the most dangerous place for a child is their own home. We include chapters on a number of sexual offences, including paedophilia, Internet sex offences (not 'just' looking at pictures – see Winder & Gough, 2010), adult rape and exhibitionism, dogging and voyeurism. This partly reflects our own interest in sexual crime at the Sexual Offending Crime and Misconduct Research Unit (SOCAMRU), which is based in the Division of Psychology at Nottingham Trent

University, UK; it is also a reflection of the importance of understanding these crimes given the horrific consequences for victims. Of course, all crimes can leave tragedies and fatalities behind them, and individuals chapters discuss the impact of each crime on the victims; Chapter 5 on fraud makes it clear that even so-called 'victimless' crimes do, in fact, cause damage to others.

What is crime?

Before we launch into our A–Z of crime we need to define what it is that we are looking at. When we think about crime, we most commonly see it as something that other people do. Not me, I don't do crime. I'm not a criminal. This sense of the criminal as 'the other' gives us a clue as to the nature of crime in a society. At one level we hold up the criminal as an example of something we are not, and this is reassuring and confirms our position as a paid-up member of society. This scapegoating aspect of crime becomes clear when we honestly consider our behaviour throughout our life. Have you ever gone over the speed limit in a car, or used your phone while driving, or taken 'souvenirs' from a pub or hotel or been in possession of cannabis, or added a few pounds to your expenses claim? We all break some of the rules some of the time. You might say that it is a matter of degree and that some people habitually do these things, and much worse, compared with your own minor errors. But crime seems something more than merely breaking the threshold of naughtiness.

The more you consider what crime is, the more you realise that a hard and fast definition is not possible. Depending on your view of the world and people, you might believe that the act of crime comes from individual wickedness or that it comes from the way a society socially constructs rules of behaviour. For example, without ownership there can be no theft. Although this may sound nonsensical to Western ears, it is not a universal for all members of a community to regard objects, people and places as something over which they have exclusive rights. In a society that didn't all want to own their own lawnmower, dishwasher and plasma television there would be no theft. Likewise, in a society where people didn't wear clothes there would be no flashers. Crime is a social construction, although we have to admit that this is not something you want to hear just after you find someone has stolen your hubcaps.

Because it is socially constructed, it means that not everyone buys into the same definitions of what constitutes criminal activity. It also means that crime will always be with us because it is part of any society's way of setting limits and ensuring that some people are excluded. What we can be sure of is that crime matters to people and fear of crime is a major concern. We also know that our view of crime is different in different times and different cultures and 'there is no behaviour which is always and everywhere criminal' (Phillips, 1971, p. 5).

In this book we focus on the behaviours that are currently seen as crimes in this country and how we can explain and limit these behaviours. As such we are taking a legalistic definition to describe these crimes and suggest that crime is 'behaviour which is prohibited by the criminal code' (Michael & Adler, 1993,

p. 5). This straightforward approach says that no act can be considered as criminal until a court has found the person guilty. And if we take this approach a number of conditions must be met before an act can legally be considered a crime:

- The act must be legally prohibited at the time it is committed (*actus rea*).
- The perpetrator must have criminal intent (*mens rea*).
- The perpetrator must have acted voluntarily.
- A punishment has been legally prescribed for committing the act.

Our A–Z of crime takes through a range of serious offences that come before the criminal courts and largely fit this definition. Each chapter includes statistics on both the *incidence* of crime (number of crimes committed) and the *prevalence* of crime (number of people committing offences) and, in order to put these data in context, the next section gives a very brief overview of the types of crime data that are available to us.

Crime data

When analysing how much crime is committed, we can focus on three different streams of data about offences, victims and perpetrators.

Offence data

The police collect data about the crimes that are reported within their jurisdiction, and the Ministry of Justice compiles these data and make them available to the public through their website, http://www.justice.gov.uk/publications/statistics-and-data/.

These police-recorded data cover crimes that are reported to and recorded by the police and are a good measure of trends in well-reported crimes, as well as of the less common but more serious crimes. They are also an important indicator of police workload. One of the problems with police-recorded data is that they will, of course, include only crimes that have been reported to the police and will not therefore include many less serious crimes (such as petty theft, criminal damage to property).

Victim data

The best source of data we have in the UK is from the British Crime Survey (BCS). This is a large survey of a representative sample of people aged 16 and over resident in households in England and Wales. The survey is conducted every year; it asks about people's experiences and perceptions of crime and includes questions on people's attitudes towards crime-related topics (e.g. anti-social behaviour, the police and the criminal justice system, CJS). It also allows us to assess people's fear of crime, and to see how this compares with actual levels of victimisation. The BCS provides the most reliable measure of the extent of victimisation and of national trends over time. One of its strengths is that it is not affected by whether the public report crime to the police (i.e. it will include offences which were not reported to the police).

Offender (perpetrator) data

Offender data are typically collected through Her Majesty's Prison Service and comprise information about the individuals serving time in prison. They can also include surveys of offenders conducted inside or outside prison. In both of the latter, there may be ethical problems with asking people about what offences they have committed (i.e. what happens if they tell you about an offence they have committed for which they have never been charged? Under our professional codes of conduct as forensic psychologists, we would need to pass this information on to the authorities. However, we would also need to make sure that we had told the offenders *before* we started the interview or testing session that, if they told us about 'new' offences, we would have to pass this information on).

Offender data include both quantitative data (perhaps about their offences and psychological characteristics, such as their level of empathy) and qualitative data (e.g. about their experiences and accounts of their own offending). When we collect offender data, these are typically to help us 'intervene' or treat these offenders. The treatment of offenders is a critical issue in forensic psychology – and this is the subject of the key debate in Chapter 9 (paedophilia).

How to read this book

This text comprises 14 specialist chapters, each dedicated to a particular crime. There are probably three main ways in which you might approach reading this book – the really 'nerdy' might like to read the whole thing, straight through, without stopping. We wouldn't recommend that, however. Other readers might like to pick and choose specific chapters, finding more of interest in drugs and voyeurism (for example) and less of interest in burglary (though this is a really good chapter ...). Finally, readers might like to take advantage of the highly structured nature of the chapters (see below for framework) and compare, for example, information on the investigation and detection (section A.6 of each chapter) across various crimes.

Each chapter is structured into three main parts (A, B and C).

Part A gives us definitions, facts and figures about the offence, information about the perpetrators, and any links between the offence and mental illness, substance abuse and personality differences. This section also contains a fascinating section regarding misconceptions about the crime – things you hear repeatedly proffered by the media or the general public, but which are wrong (how many of these did you think were true?). Part A also contains information about the investigation and detection of the offence, as well as information on the sentencing of perpetrators and their punishment, rehabilitation and the probability of reoffending. Finally, this part gives information about the victims of the offence – who they are likely to be and how they might be affected.

Part B of each chapter details explanations and theories as to why people commit the offence in question.

Part C gives the reader some suggestions for further reading, together with the contact details of organisations for further information and/or voluntary work.

The aim of the book

The book aims to give an up-to-date review of how forensic psychologists are thinking about and dealing with crime in the UK. Forensic psychologists are interested in finding out more about the psychology of crime. That means they want to look at the differences between people who commit crimes and those that don't, the risk factors that enhance criminal behaviour and the explanations that offenders give for their own behaviours. Why does someone assault, sexually abuse or defraud someone else? Do they enjoy what they do? Do they regret it? How do they justify it to themselves or others? Forensic psychologists are also interested in the ways that people who commit crimes can be discouraged from repeat offending: What make them stop (desist) from committing crimes? Is it punishment? Treatment? Or because they learn to recognise the harm that they have done to others?

We hope that you enjoy this book and that, for some of you, it is a step along the path to becoming a Registered Forensic Psychologist.

chapter

1

ARSON

ANDREA DAYKIN AND LAURA HAMILTON

PART A: The offence – Who, what, when, why?

A1.1. Introduction

Fire is intertwined in our history, serving many human functions. Fire is central to survival, providing warmth, a sense of reassurance and comfort. Fire is also part of our folklore, history and cultural experiences, for example, the Great Fire of London in 1666, 'Bonfire Night' to mark the anniversary of the Gunpowder Plot in 1605, cremation and in movies such as '*Backdraft*' and '*Towering Inferno*'. Fire has been employed as a punishment, for example, in the case of Joan of Arc who was burned at the stake in France. Fire is also the weapon of choice for some offenders and terrorists, with arson causing death, property damage and serious injury. The powerful and destructive force associated with fire is evident in devastation of entire landscapes in the case of the American and Australian bushfires. For instance, across Australia, major bushfires are estimated to have cost $2.5 billion Australian dollars in the period from 1967 to 1999, corresponding to an average annual cost of $77million (BTE, 2001) and resulting in 223 deaths and 4185 injuries with a total cost of $654 million (Australian Institute of Criminology, 2004). The UK government estimated the direct financial costs of arson are well over £2.4 billion a year (Office of the Deputy Prime Minister [ODPM], 2004).

A1.2. Definitions

Fire and its causes are often classified into five types:

Type of fire	Causes
Natural	as a result of lightning, for example
Accidental	as a result of faulty electrical equipment

Unknown	unable to identify the cause
Suspicious	likely that an individual has deliberately set the fire
Incendiary	deliberately set by petrol bombs, for example.

Suspicious and incendiary fires are classified as crimes of arson, and although legal definitions of arson vary from country to country (Geller, 1992), English common law (the basis for our legal system) defines arson as 'the wilful and malicious burning of a building or property'. The key criteria that define fire setting as arson are wilful and malicious motive and intent (Gaynor & Hatcher, 1987; Ritchie & Huff, 1999). The police record arson as defined by the Criminal Damage Act 1971 and offences in the Act are summarised below in Box 1.1:

Box 1.1. Categories of arson recorded by the police

Section	Offence
Section 1	Destroying or damaging property
	1. Intentional or reckless damage to property
	2. Damage or destruction endangering life of another
	3. Damage caused by fire is termed arson
Section 2	Threats to damage or destroy property
Section 3	Possession of objects with the intent of damaging property

Source: Criminal Damage Act 1971.

Section 1(1) of the Act covers the intention to destroy or damage property or reckless damage to property. Section 1(2) of the Act covers damage to property that endangers the life of another individual. Section 1(3) of the Act specifies that when damage to property has been caused by fire, the offence is charged as arson.

In addition to arson, other terms have been used in the literature such as fire raising, fire setting, pyromania and pathological fire setting (Prins, 1995). Fire raising is the term favoured by Prins (1995) given its breadth in encompassing all other terms relating to this behaviour. Fire setting has been described as the 'intentional setting of fire' and has been considered to represent a progression of increased fire-related activity within three stages, starting with fire interest followed by fire play and fire setting (Gaynor, 1996). Pyromania has been described as 'repetitive fire-raising without obvious causes, such as revenge or clear mental disorder' (Prins, 1995, p. 272). The term pyromania is classified as an impulse control disorder in the *Diagnostic and Statistical Manual of Mental Disorders IV* (APA, 1994), and this diagnostic classification refers to individuals who 'receive pleasure, gratification or relief when setting fires' (p. 615). It has been reported that individuals diagnosed with pyromania do not present with any signs of a significant mental disorder and the fire-setting behaviour does not appear to be driven by motives such as gain or revenge (Prins, 2001).

A distinction has been made in the literature between pathological and non-pathological arson (Jackson, 1994) which is useful for aiding our understanding of fire setting. Based on earlier work, Jackson offers a pragmatic approach to a definition of pathological arson that incorporates five key criteria (Jackson et al., 1987a) including:

- recidivism;
- fire to property rather than fire against persons;
- fire setting alone or repetitively with a single accomplice;
- evidence of psychiatric, psychological or emotional problems;
- absence of financial or political gain as a motive.

The term fire setting will be employed in this chapter as it goes beyond the legal definition of arson to refer generally to the behaviour of deliberately setting fires.

A1.3. Who?

There is no specific profile of an arsonist and indeed an examination of the literature highlights that they are quite a diverse group. The research clearly tells us that arson is committed by males and females, with individuals under the age of 18 years being responsible for around half of all property arson and around one-third of recorded vehicle fires (Home Office, 2000, 2002).

A number of psychological and clinical features are noted in those who engage in chronic fire setting:

- **Substance misuse:** Arsonists are reported to experience problems with alcohol and drugs (Rice & Harris, 1991) and indeed from our own forensic experience of working with arsonists, many described problems with alcohol and drug dependency.
- **Intellectual functioning**: There is some evidence for arsonists being of below-average intellectual ability, which may be attributable to mild learning disabilities (Lewis & Yarnell, 1951; Bradford, 1982; Murphy & Clare, 1996) and/or limited schooling (Bradford, 1982).
- **Employment difficulties**: Arsonists often have poorer employment histories, with a large number having unskilled jobs (Bradford, 1982).
- **Social skills:** They are also likely to lack social skills and/or perceive themselves as ineffective socially (Jackson et al., 1987a).
- **Emotional expression**: Arsonists seem to have difficulty identifying and expressing their emotions, preferring less direct expressions of their desires, frustration, pain, sadness or feelings of hostility (Jackson et al., 1987a; Geller, 1992; Haggert, 2001). Some arsonists have been identified as seeking thrills or attention or recognition or in a minority of cases gaining sexual satisfaction from fire setting (Douglas et al., 1997).
- **Childhood trauma:** There is evidence of unstable childhoods and serious psychological difficulties in fire setters (Prins, 1995). Based on our own experience of working with arsonists in forensic settings, many arsonists report that their childhoods were characterised by instability and some form of physical, sexual and/or emotional abuse. In addition, many

arsonists reported how they experienced problems with peer relationships, often feeling rejected along with multiple incidents of bullying.

- **Physical disability**: A high level of mild facial disfigurement has been noted in arsonists (Lewis & Yarnell, 1951). The relevance of this to fire setters is that disfigurements can impact on how individuals compare themselves with others. This can lead to a reduced self-esteem and subsequent difficulties in interpersonal relationships. Indeed, based on our professional experience of working with arsonists in prison and high secure settings, we have observed arsonists with Klinefelter syndrome (Eytan et al., 2002), facial disfigurement, physical disability and hearing impairments. Whilst these characteristics would not constitute the defining features of an arsonist, they are important in that these features can make them vulnerable to rejection and bullying by their peers.

- **Self-harm**: Official statistics indicate that males and females use fire in institutional settings, such as prison and secure hospitals. Individuals may set fire to their cells and belongings as a protest. In addition, some offenders use fire to harm themselves and the most extreme form of this is when individuals set themselves on fire as a means of committing suicide. Interestingly, the use of fire against the environment and against the body can be seen as a way of communicating personal distress, such as highlighting difficulties with a cell mate, self-hatred and so on. Clinical experience suggests that many individuals who harm themselves with fire also utilise other forms of self-harm, particularly cutting.

- **Mental health**: For those arsonists who are transferred into the psychiatric system (in the USA) the most common diagnoses are schizophrenia, personality disorder, various forms of mental handicap, substance abuse and mood disorders (Koson & Dvoskin, 1982). It has been noted that when females commit acts of fire setting and have even a minor degree of mental disorder, they are more likely to be diverted into the psychiatric system than males (Prins, 1994).

A1.4. Misconceptions

Arson is not a violent offence

Some individuals would argue that as arson is not an act directed at another individual it does not constitute violence. Indeed many of the arsonists with whom we have worked would argue this, particularly as many of them do not engage in physical violence, opting for indirect means. Fineman (1995) states that *'though usually an act of indirect aggression against property, fire setting can be directed against people also. In either case, it is an act of violence'* (p. 32).

Arson is not a serious offence

The offence of arson can carry a maximum prison sentence of life and this reflects the serious nature of this offence.

Arson is a sexually motivated offence

Arson has been associated with sexual satisfaction (Prins, 1980). Indeed some researchers have said that setting fires serves the purpose of releasing sexual tension, but whilst this may be a motivating factor it is not a major causative factor (Gold, 1962).

A1.5. Facts and figures

How big is the problem of arson? Many factors make it difficult to establish the size and impact of arson in the UK. These include a lack of consistency in recording and measurement practices by the fire and rescue services and the terminology used (Office of Deputy Prime Minister, 2005). For example, asking the police and the fire service how many arson offences were committed within the previous year, the numbers provided would be somewhat different. The police have to comply with the Criminal Damage Act 1971 and so have to prove an individual behaved 'recklessly' or 'intended to damage property' before recording an incident as arson. The fire service categorises non-accidental fires as malicious, deliberate or doubtful (when the fire is considered to be suspicious), and they have only to suspect that ignition was deliberate to record the incident as arson.

Although official statistics should be interpreted with caution due to inconsistent recording procedures, they nevertheless provide useful data regarding trends in arson attacks. The most recently published UK Fire Statistics Monitor (2010) and Police Recorded Crime (Flatley et al., 2010) suggest there was an upward trend in the recorded number of deliberate primary fires/arsons in the UK between 1997 and 2003 and downward trend from 2004 onwards. Fire statistics suggest a fall of 15% in the total number of deliberate primary fires (including vehicle and dwelling fires) between 2008 and 2009, with police statistics suggesting an 11% fall in arson offences over a similar period. This decline in deliberate fires was noted in most locations across the UK, with deliberate fires remaining more prevalent in city areas. Fire fatalities in the UK are also declining, with 421 fire fatalities recorded in 2008/09, 57 (13%) less than in 2007–8, but 35% fewer than ten years previously (645 in 1998/9) and 56% fewer than 25 years earlier (963 in 1983/4).

A1.6. How are offenders caught?

The Arson Prevention Bureau (APB) (2003) outlines how arson offences are investigated in their paper 'Detecting and convicting the arsonist: Lessons from the United States'. In the first instance, a suspected or serious fire is referred to a fire investigation officer in the fire service who will usually attend the scene. However, in smaller services there may not be a dedicated fire investigation officer and in larger services the fire investigation officer may not be available for reasons such as sickness, holidays or shift work. When this happens a fire officer will attend in their place, and they are likely to have variable knowledge and experience of fire investigation. A paper produced by the ODPM (2004) states that since 2001/2 various initiatives have been put in place to improve fire investigation, such as modernising the syllabus for Fire Investigation work, increasing the provision of equipment for use by fire investigators and greater use of hydrocarbon detector dogs to detect the use of accelerants at fire scenes.

The APB (2003) highlights the fact that if the fire officer considers the cause of fire to be arson the matter is handed over to the police, who will then investigate the possible crime. The purpose of an investigation is to determine whether an offence has taken place and this process will involve obtaining witness statements and interviewing suspects. Crime scene investigators are employed to obtain forensic evidence and they may ask for assistance from the forensic science service. Elements in establishing the cause of a fire are detecting the seat of the fire, the use of any accelerants (e.g. petrol), activation of fire alarms, method of spread of fire and blockage of any exits. When sufficient evidence has been gathered that allows the police to charge an individual, the matter is handed over to the Crown Prosecution Service (CPS) who then decides whether to prosecute. If a prosecution is going to take place, a CPS solicitor is allocated to the case. If the case goes to trial, the solicitor may refer the prosecution to a barrister.

Obtaining successful detections and convictions can be problematic as those who become involved in the investigation and prosecution of a case may have limited expertise in fire science. This ultimately leaves society with offenders who get away with their crimes (APB, 2003). Indeed the UK has a poor record of detecting arson cases with an equally poor rate of successful prosecutions.

Fire statistics categorise fire incidents into primary and secondary. Primary fires include all fires in non-derelict buildings and outdoor structures, non-abandoned vehicles or any fires involving casualties or rescues or any fires attended by five or more appliances. Secondary fires are the majority of outdoor fires including grassland and refuse fires unless they involve casualties or rescues, property loss or if five or more appliances attend. A Fire Statistics Monitor (2010) report recorded a total of 199,573 deliberate fires in the UK in 2008–9, with 51,583 being recorded as primary fires and the remainder as secondary fires. According to police statistics arson offences accounted for 4% of all police-recorded criminal damage offences in 2008–09. A total of 34,826 arson offences were recorded, and under the new police recording classification introduced from 1 April 2008 these were separated into arson endangering life ($n = 3629$) and arson not endangering life ($n = 31,197$). The number of detected arsons which resulted in a sanction was 962 for arson endangering life and 2146 for arson not endangering life, representing a detection rate of 27% and 7%, respectively. These statistics indicate that police detection rates are better for more serious arson attacks. Nevertheless the vast majority of deliberate fires and arson attacks are not investigated or solved by the police, consequently any account of arson and arsonists based on convicted offenders is likely to be limited and speculative.

A1.7. What happens to offenders?

Sentencing

Arson is defined in the UK under the Criminal Damage Act 1971 as a reckless or intentional act to damage or destroy property by fire, or (the more serious charge) as reckless or intentional damage to property in which the life of another individual is recklessly or intentionally endangered. With this offence there are three stages of seriousness (Gilyeat, 1994):

(i) arson – damage destruction;
(ii) arson – reckless as to whether life would be endangered;
(iii) arson – with intent to endanger life.

The courts treat arson cases seriously and approximately one-third of disposals are custodial (Soothill et al., 2004). An individual who is guilty of arson under Section 1 of the Criminal Damage Act is liable to life imprisonment, the maximum penalty imposed. A charge under Section 3 of the Act is appropriate when intent can be established, so for example, the individual may be stopped with petrol and the means of lighting a fire before s/he has had the opportunity to set fire to anything.

When sentencing offenders, the court considers any aggravating or mitigating factors, so intent and motive are important features of the offence (Gilyeat, 1994). For example, consideration is given to whether the offender wanted to instil fear into the victim as well as cause harm and whether the victim has been forced to move or has been made homeless as a result of the fire. Other aggravating factors include the extent of the damage caused (however, whilst the damage caused may be minor the intent could have been deemed to be high); the use of accelerants; the dwelling attacked by fire; and the risk of fire spreading. In our clinical experience, some arsonists have used fire to instil fear into a victim with the result of their behaviour being the tragic loss of life.

High levels of mental disorder have been found in fire setters (Puri et al., 1995) which is in contrast to Home Office research which suggests that less than 25% of those arrested for an offence of arson have a mental disorder (Arson Prevention Bureau, 1998). In some cases a psychiatric report is made available to the court, and this can be used to inform sentencing and disposal decisions. The literature highlights that courts request psychiatric reports in nearly all cases, even in seemingly straightforward ones where the motive for arson is insurance fraud because there may be an underlying psychiatric disorder (Prins, 2005).

Preventative measures and treatment approaches

Fire setters are not a homogenous group of offenders and as noted in the literature, given the complexity of their presentation, no single form of management is likely to be effective (Prins, 2001). As fire-setting behaviour is diverse and its motive is not always apparent, the subsequent management of these offenders is not a straightforward process. Whilst punishments such as fines and imprison-ment may be deemed to be appropriate for those who commit arson mainly for profit, there are other offenders for whom therapy would be more appropriate, for example those who are mentally disordered. It is important that interven-tions take into account an individual's cognitive capacities so that treatment programmes are tailored appropriately to ensure they can access and benefit from them. In our clinical experience, some offenders lack the ability to assimi-late information and lack basic literacy skills. Programmes need to be adapted to ensure these offenders can participate in and benefit from the intervention.

Researchers have attempted to examine what interventions are available in England and Wales for arsonists and young fire setters (Palmer et al., 2007). They found that the majority of interventions for arsonists were provided by the fire and rescue service, youth offending services and forensic mental health units; with interventions including arson education, stress management and coping skills, social skills, alcohol and drug programmes, anger management and psychotherapy to address underlying personality and relationship difficul-ties. Palmer et al.'s (2007) excellent review highlighted that fire and rescue services favoured an educational approach, while forensic mental health units favoured a cognitive-behavioural approach.

Fire service interventions

The fire service operates educational programmes for children to highlight the dangers of lighting fires. For example, the fire and rescue service in Merseyside aims to work with children and young people in order to reduce fire crime and antisocial behaviour in addition to accidental injury and death. Based at local fire stations during school holidays, they offer a five-day programme called LIFE (Local Intervention Fire Education). This programme helps children who are at risk to understand fire safety and to prevent arson, provide positive role mod-els and help the school fire liaison officers spread the message of fire safety to children.

Public awareness campaigns may go some way to highlighting the extent and cost of arson to the community. The media have promoted other cam-paigns to raise public awareness of the dangers and risks of engaging in certain behaviours, for example drink-driving. Campaigns raising awareness in relation to arson may help the public to become more proactive and alert to arson (Kocsis, 2002).

National offender management (prison and probation service)

Palmer et al. (2007) found that there was no provision of accredited programmes for arsonists in the prison or probation services, with no reported plans to pro-vide such programmes in the future. However, they reported in their survey that since 1998 HM Prison Liverpool has been implementing an adapted version of the Fire Awareness Child Education UP (FACE UP) programme which was devised by Merseyside Fire and Rescue Service for young offenders. This pro-gramme was initially established for young offenders (aged 10–25 years) with the aim of confronting, challenging and changing an arsonist's underlying neg-ative attitudes underlying their fire-setting behaviour. This programme has not yet been evaluated to determine its effectiveness in reducing recidivism with this adult population (Palmer et al., 2007).

Forensic mental health services

In relation to adult arsonists, the majority of work is carried out with mental health populations, although there was no single, systematic approach used with arsonists and there have been no large-scale evaluations of these interventions (Palmer et al., 2007). Given that arsonists are such a heterogeneous group, it is difficult to offer a standardised assessment approach. Based on our experience of working with arsonists, we recommend that in the first instance a compre-hensive assessment is carried out in order to evaluate the individual's treatment needs. This assessment information would then be used to develop a formula-tion or working model that attempts to explain why the individual engaged in fire-setting behaviour. This formulation will then guide the clinicians' decisions about treatment recommendations. Jackson (1994) suggests the following areas as a starting point for any in-depth exploration:

- personal demographic characteristics (physical/psychiatric disorders; psy-chological disorders; social/family problems; offending history; fire-related factors);
- family characteristics (number of siblings, highly expressed emotion, emotional neglect in the family, poor conflict resolution in the family);
- fire-related behaviour (development history of larger fires, solitary fire setting, emotional states preceding fire).

Palmer et al. (2007) reported a small number of cognitive-behavioural interven-tions being used for intellectually disabled forensic populations. One example of such work is that carried out by Taylor, Thorne and Slavkin (2004), who delivered a group-based intervention for fire setters with mild learning disabil-ity in low secure settings. The Arson Treatment Programme (RATP) at Rampton High Secure Hospital was developed in the early 1990s by Michael Haggett, a nurse consultant. This programme drew on Jackson et al.'s (1987a) model for recidivistic arson and Fineman's (1995) dynamic behavioural model, and both these models will be outlined in Part B. The RATP programme incorporates four modules:-

- Module One: The Dangerousness of Fire (12 weeks);
- Module Two: Coping and Social Skills (24 weeks);
- Module Three: Self-esteem and Self-awareness (12 weeks);
- Module Four: Relapse Prevention (12 weeks).

The structure of the RATP is such that group sessions took place once per week over a period of about 18 months, and these were supplemented by individual sessions which took place on a fortnightly basis to ensure that facilitators could work equally with all patients undertaking the group. The overall aims of the RATP programme are to look at the individual's interest and experience with fire, provide education and coping strategies, to improve self-esteem and self-awareness and to develop prevention strategies to reduce the likelihood of further incidents.

KEY DEBATE: Are arsonists violent offenders?

Researchers have attempted to explore why arsonists may not exhibit the same level of interpersonal aggression that typically characterises violent offenders. Arsonists are often not perceived as a management problem in prison and secure settings in relation to expression of interpersonal conflict and aggression.

Tentative findings from one study suggest certain features are characteristic of both arsonists and violent offenders (e.g. levels of depression, alcohol use, suicide attempts), whereas there are two main differences.

Differences: arsonists perceive themselves to be less assertive and so experience more problems in conflict resolution. This may lead to a direction of hostility towards property rather than an individual. Violent offenders have better defined constructs of person versus property offences compared with arsonists – but there was no bias to rating person offences as more serious than property offences.

Results are limited: small sample size and specific population of offenders (high secure). Further research is required. Antecedents to arson are varied and complex.

References:
Jackson, H.F., Hope, S. and Glass, C. (1987). Why are arsonists not violent offenders? *International Journal of Offender Therapy and Comparative Criminology*, 31, 143–2.

Relative effectiveness of treatment

Most of the literature evaluating treatment programmes for arsonists has focused on young arsonists and as such there is a dearth of literature evaluating interventions for adult arsonists. Additionally some of the examples in the treatment evaluation literature relate to individual case studies. For example, Clare et al. (1992) adopt a cognitive-behavioural approach; Swaffer et al. (2001) provide a case study of a mentally disordered patient who had completed a group intervention of fire setting; Taylor, Thorne and Slavkin, (2004) provide case descriptions of male arsonists with mild intellectual disabilities who had completed group treatment in forensic hospital settings. More large-scale and tightly controlled evaluations are clearly required to determine the effectiveness and efficacy of treatment interventions with adult arsonists.

Recidivism

Recidivism is a term used in the literature to include the setting of multiple fires (Rice and Harris, 1991) and reconviction for arson (Soothill and Pope, 1973). Given that conviction rates for arson are low and many offences go undetected, it follows that it would be difficult to offer any accurate rates of recidivism. Indeed, fire-setting recidivism rates have varied widely in the literature from 4 to 60% depending on where studies have been conducted, namely the criminal justice system (CJS), forensic psychiatric settings or psychiatric hospitals (Brett, 2004).

Dickens et al. (2009) noted the characteristics of recidivistic arsonists (those who set more than one fire as evidenced from case notes) and related these to recidivism risk factors noted in previous research:

- younger;
- single;
- started their criminal careers earlier (Rice and Harris, 1991; Repo et al., 1997; Lindberg et al., 2005);
- spent longer in prison and had more extensive history of other property crime (Rice and Harris, 1991);
- poor school adjustment (Rice and Harris, 1991);
- childhood enuresis (Repo et al., 1997);
- mental health needs: learning disability (Lindberg et al., 2005) and personality disorder were common in multiple fire setters (Rice and Harris, 1991; Lindberg et al., 2005) and psychosis was more common in first-time fire setters (Repo et al., 1997).

This research suggests that recidivistic arsonists are likely to have developmental difficulties and an entrenched pattern of antisocial behaviour combined with complex clinical needs. However, drawing conclusions on this research must remain tentative and speculative, as the research is based on convicted offenders and the study by Dickens et al. (2009) involves a retrospective review of case notes and criminal records for those offenders referred for psychiatric assessment (a highly specialised sample of arsonists).

A1.8. And the damage done . . .

The crime of arson can leave a trail of devastation in that entire families can be left traumatised when their homes are destroyed, physical injuries can be permanent and psychological damage can be difficult to deal with (Weiner, 2001; DTLR, 2000). At its worst, arson can lead to the death of individuals. There are also further implications of arson, businesses can be destroyed which can lead to the loss of employment opportunities. In the case of bush fires in Australia for example, entire landscapes can be destroyed along with the wildlife living in these areas. The UK national weekly statistics suggest that each week there are 2213 arson attacks with two people being killed and 53 injured. Additionally each week 20 schools and colleges are damaged or destroyed by arson, along with 262 homes, 360 businesses and public buildings and 1402 cars (Arson Prevention Bureau, 2010).

The financial impact of arson is far reaching. There is the cost of physical damage to property, costs in terms of the disruption caused, cost to the National Health Service (NHS) for treating injuries, and cost to the fire service and the police for attending fires. Canter and Almond (2002) draw our attention to the fact that in the UK the direct financial costs of arson are in excess of £2.1 billion per year.

PART B: Theories and explanations

The case of Tom (described in Box 1.2) is characteristic of individuals who set fires, but how do we attempt to make sense of why individuals such as Tom set fires? Researchers have attempted to provide explanations for this behaviour and these have included devising typologies and offering theoretical models. These will be considered in turn.

Box 1.2. Case notes of an arsonist

Tom sits on the prison wing quietly reading a book. The officers on his wing say that he doesn't present them with any problems, as he keeps himself to himself. He has an extensive history of fire setting and is serving a sentence for arson with intent after setting fire to a residential home. He describes himself as fascinated with fire and sees it as a powerful means of expressing his feelings. He started setting fires with his peers when he was a child and this included setting fires to fields, dustbins and old settees. However as he got older and found he could not deal with his problems as well as other people he started to use fire to vent his anger, to gain the attention he wanted and to feel powerful.

Tom had a childhood that was characterised by physical and sexual abuse, and his subsequent antisocial behaviours brought him into contact with the police. He was eventually taken into care. Tom says he has never been able to deal with interpersonal conflict, and he has struggled to be assertive and find appropriate ways of getting his needs met. Tom has tried to have relationships with women, but he has never been able to maintain his relationships. When these have broken down he has set fires to communicate his distress. He has made use of sub-stances including alcohol to manage his emotions, but he says that this increased his risk of setting fires and so made his problems worse. He is anxious about his release back into the community.

B1.1. Typologies of fire setters and fire-setting behaviour

Researchers have attempted to devise descriptive subgroups of fire setters often based on characteristics such as age, gender, and psychiatric diagnosis. More commonly researchers have attempted to devise classifications of the motives for setting fires. Such classifications are typically referred to as typologies. One of the earliest typologies was offered by Lewis and Yarnell (1951), and subsequent ones have been developed by Inciardi (1970) and Levin (1976) who classified major categories of fire setters. Whilst the following does not represent an exhaustive list, it provides a snap shot of those to be found in the literature.

Rider (1980) proposed a typology to capture the perceived motivation of the fire setter and this was based on interviews conducted with convicted offenders. Rider's typology comprises four categories that are not mutually exclusive:

1. Jealousy-motivated adult males who set fires in response to events that threaten their vanity or self-esteem;
2. Would-be-heroes who rush to the scene of the fire they have set as they wish to be perceived to want to save lives. In such cases they will call the emergency services and remain at the scene. Sometimes these fire setters are 'fire buffs' wanting to be firemen and hang around the fire station;
3. Excitement fire setters who require personal excitement and achieve this when watching fires. These individuals are likely to stay at the scene and watch the fire. Rider argues that there is no sexual component to the excitement;
4. Pyromaniacs, described as compulsive personality types, who are compelled to set fires. These individuals feel a release of tension, some pleasure and gratification. For some there may be a sexual component and they may masturbate whilst watching the fire, although there is no evidence to suggest that this is the major motivation of this group.

Prins, Tennent and Trick (1985) proposed the following classification based on the examination of parole dossiers of 113 imprisoned arsonists:

1. Arson for financial reward.
2. Arson to cover up another crime.
3. Arson for political purposes (e.g. terrorist activity).
4. Self-immolation as a political gesture.
5. Arson for mixed motives (e.g. in a state of reactive depression, as a cry for help, under the influence of alcohol).
6. Arson due to the presence of an actual mental or associated disorder:
   a) severe affective disorder;
   b) schizophrenia;
   c) organic disorders (e.g. brain tumour, injury, temporal lobe epilepsy);
   d) mental subnormality (retardation), impairment.
7. Arson due to motives of revenge
   a) against an individual or individuals (specific);
   b) against society or others more generally.
8. Arson committed as an attention seeking-act (but excluding those set out under (5) above), and arson committed as a means of deriving sexual satisfaction/ excitement (pyromania).
9. Arson committed by young adults who are 16 years and older (vandalism).
10. Arson committed by children.

Prins (1999) notes a limitation of this classification is that it is based on retrospective data and collates behavioural characteristics and motives of various types of fire setters. Other researchers have suggested that focusing on the context in which fire setting takes place would be more informative (Canter & Fritzon, 1998).

Douglas, Burgess, Burgess and Ressler (1992) categorised arsonists on two levels. Level one is related to the frequency of fire-setting behaviour and level two is related to the arsonist's motivation. At the first level, they identified the following:

- Serial arsonist. This would involve three or more separate fire-setting episodes. The victims tend to be selected.
- Spree arsonist. This would involve the setting of fires at three or more locations with no 'cooling off' period between them.
- Mass arsonist. This would involve the setting of three or more fires at one location during a limited time period.

At the second level, they identified the following motivations:

- Vandalism whereby offenders tend to be young, act in groups and target educational buildings, are from a lower class background and live close to the scene of the crime. They tend not to use alcohol or drugs, flee from the scene or may watch from a distance.
- Excitement. This is subdivided into Thrill Seeker, Attention Seeker, Recognition Seeker and Sexually Perverted. These individuals tend to set fires and watch from a safe distance, or attempt to blend in with bystanders. They typically set fires alone or with one other individual and usually have an offence history.
- Revenge. The goal here is to gain revenge for an actual or perceived injury.
- Profit. Arson is committed purely for material gain.
- Concealment of a crime. The offender is not interested in fire but uses it as a means to destroy any evidence from another offence such as murder or burglary.
- Extremists set fires to advance some political or religious objective.

Typologies such as those above are useful heuristics that may aid crime investigation and highlight the heterogeneity within this group of offenders. However, these typologies can be misleading as there is no robust evidence to suggest that these typologies represent discrete categories of arson offenders. Based on our experience of working with arsonists in prison and high secure settings, we would argue that fire-setting behaviour cannot be reduced to one single factor to explain the motivation underlying the act. Whilst those arsonists we have worked with share commonalities, attempting to reduce why they committed acts of fire setting to one factor dismisses the complexity of the issues with which an arsonist can present. A more meaningful way of understanding fire setters would be to incorporate all those factors associated with fire setting, in other words antecedent factors, the behaviour itself and the consequences.

B1.2. Psychodynamic theory

Whilst psychodynamic theory is one of the earliest attempts to explain fire-setting behaviour, its weakness lies in the lack of empirical support. It has been argued that this theory drew on myths and symbols for which fire is used (Vreeland & Waller, 1979). Freud (1932) interpreted the Greek myth of Prometheus (*in which Prometheus steals fire from the gods and gives it to mortals. As a result of this the top god – Zeus – punished Prometheus by chaining him to a rock and had a eagle eat his liver every day. No namby-pamby sentencing in those days*) and took the view that fire setting was linked to sexual desire and urination. Sexual feelings were seen as the primary drive for the ignition and extinction of fire. Later explanations have focused on instinctual drives such as aggression and anxiety to explain this behaviour (e.g. Macht and Mack, 1968).

One of the most comprehensive studies of arsonists (Lewis and Yarnell, 1951) examined the histories of over 1100 adult male fire setters and found only 40 reported sexual arousal associated with fire setting. Since this study, Rice and Harris (1991) found that only 6 out of 243 male fire setters derived sexual pleasure from setting or watching a fire. The evidence to support a psychodynamic explanation is therefore limited.

B1.3. Interaction theories

With the influence of social learning theory, researchers have attempted to develop models that incorporate several factors to explain and predict fire-setting behaviours. The two main theories providing are Fineman's (1995) dynamic-behavioural model and Jackson et al.'s (1987a) functional analysis model. These theories propose that there is an interaction between individual characteristics and features of the environment that leads to fire setting.

A functional analysis of recidivistic arson (Jackson et al., 1987a)

Jackson et al. (1987a) developed a functional analytical approach to understanding recidivistic arson, which was later developed into the Only Viable Option Theory (Jackson, 1994). Jackson's model was based on clinical experience of working with arsonists in a maximum-security hospital, views pathological arson as the only resolution to a problem and considers it to be an attempt to change an individual's conditions (both internally and externally) when all other options have been unsuccessful. This theory includes a developmental element that acknowledges the transition from fire play in childhood to later pathological arson. Within this theory, fire-setting behaviour is argued to be positively reinforced by consequences such as an increase in self-esteem and perceived effectiveness, distress reduction, a change in the individual's environment and increased arousal. Reinforcement can create an intense interest in fire setting, and entrenched automatic associations between fire and positive states of being.

Jackson et al. stress that fascination and experimentation with fire is a common feature of normal child development. How significant others such as parents, peers and authority respond to this behaviour are important features in its subsequent development.

Antecedent events consist of three types:

1. General setting conditions including psychosocial disadvantage, which is reflected in their unfavourable social conditions and personal inadequacies; general dissatisfaction with life and the self, which is reflected in feelings of depression and low self-esteem and unsuccessful social interaction (actual or perceived) because of social skills deficits.
2. Specific psychosocial stimuli that direct the individual to the use of fire include previous experience of fire (personal or vicarious) and the inhibition of behavioural alternatives.
3. Triggering events leading to fire setting vary between arsonists and can be categorised into external and internal factors. We have noted that many arsonists describe a range of emotions including anger, fear, anxiety, loneliness and frustration that can act as an internal trigger to an urge to set a fire in order to change their circumstances, channel their emotions and therefore provide them with a sense of control over their situation.

Behaviour. Arsonists generally choose similar targets for their fire setting. Of significance to the fire setting is an examination of the emotions and behaviours preceding the setting of the fire. Following the fire, individuals may choose to stay at the scene and they may call the fire brigade. Most fire setting is a solitary activity and, in our experience, the majority of pathological arsonists set fires alone in contrast to fire play in childhood, which tends to occur in groups.

Consequences of fire setting can be either positive or negative, which then serves as reinforcement for the behaviour. For example, for a child fire may provide a powerful way of gaining attention from peers or parents when feeling isolated or rejected. Setting a fire can change this state of affairs and increase the contact they have with their parents. As this behaviour increases, the individual receives additional attention from various professionals. Negative reinforcement can result from fire setting whereby the child is deemed to be experiencing emotional difficulties and is therefore protected from the source of the stress; for example, this may involve moving school if being bullied. For adults, being placed in an institution such as a prison can provide the individual with an escape from an environment that is difficult to manage. We have experience of arsonists who have stated that they set fires in order to get back into prison because this was a place of safety for them.

The functional analytic model has provided a useful organising framework in our clinical and forensic experience of working with arsonists in both prison and high secure settings, particularly when reflecting on those experiences that are deemed to be disadvantageous to the arsonist. We have observed that they describe difficulties in resolving problems in socially acceptable ways and in managing their emotions effectively. Specific psychological factors predisposing an individual to fire setting include a lack of assertiveness, a fear of negative evaluation and a lack of experience in resolving conflict.

Dynamic behaviour theory

Fineman (1995) proposed a dynamic–behavioural model to improve our understanding of why individuals set fires. He was of the opinion that for a model to have any practicality it should reflect both the literature as well as the clinical impressions of those professionals working in the fire service and in clinical settings.

Fineman (1995) studied the behaviour and characteristics of children who set fires and identified two types, namely pathological fire setters (those who set fires with intent) and non-pathological fire setters (those who set fires out of curiosity). Fineman (1995) states that pathological fire setters have a tendency towards engaging in various types of antisocial behaviour, with fire setting being one example. An interest in fire develops in childhood, either as a result of poor parental supervision or from punishment through their activity with fire. Furthermore, children who are not exposed to appropriate role models fail to develop the appropriate skills enabling them to deal with daily problems. Fire setting can then become a means of expressing emotions such as anger or frustration when individuals are faced with a problem that they feel unable to manage effectively. Fire setting is usually preceded by a crisis or trauma and it has been argued that this event increases impulsiveness and reduces the ability to manage the resultant stress. Examples of crisis or trauma, include school exclusion, parental divorce or rejection by a significant other. The individual will often generate a fantasy of successfully setting a fire and as such obtains a desired reward. A decision is then made to set a fire and during this phase the individual will obtain materials to ignite the fire and decide on where the fire will take place. Following the setting of the fire, certain factors reinforce the behaviour. It has been suggested that fire setting can be externally reinforced by rewards such as money or internally reinforced by peer attention for example.

This model conceptualises fire setting as a result of the interaction between the following three psychological determinants:

1. personality and individual characteristics such as demographic, physical, emotional, motivational and psychiatric variables;
2. family and social circumstances including family, peer and social variables;
3. immediate environmental conditions or events that occur immediately before, during and after the fire-setting behaviour.

This model has generally been applied to juvenile fire setting and has yet to be tested empirically with adults, although Fineman (1995) argues adult fire setters typically have a history of childhood fire setting. Our observations of working with arsonists would support Fineman's view that adult arsonists have a history of childhood fire setting in addition to reported incidents of vicarious experiences of fire.

Evaluation of interaction models

These two approaches share some common features. For example, both suggest that certain features predispose an individual to fire setting. These include psychosocial disadvantage, social skills deficits, previous experience of fire and emotionally significant events triggering a fire-setting incident (Jackson et al., 1987a). Overall, we would argue that Jackson et al.'s model provides the most comprehensive explanation of adult fire setting because it identifies antecedent events to fire setting, the behavioural features associated with the act – for example, staying at the scene or calling the fire brigade – and the consequences that reinforce and maintain fire-setting behaviour. In addition, Jackson's model offers an explanation for the re-occurrence of fire-setting behaviour.

PART C: Further information

C1.1. Further reading

Arson Prevention Bureau website (www.arsonpreventionbureau.org.uk) provides advice and information to help address the problem of arson nationally in the UK. This website provides statistics on arson trends, measures to protect oneself, information about arson and arson prevention, in addition to detailed research reports.

The Arson Control Forum was established in April 2001 and is a government-led body aiming to reduce arson-related deaths, injuries and damage. Their website (www.arsoncontrolforum.gov.uk) contains information on research, arson statistics, and links to other arson resources on the web.

The Arson Toolkit is an excellent resource outlining how the crime of arson can be reduced and brings together information on recent developments. The Arson Control Forum helped to produce this Toolkit, and it can be found on the following website: www.crimereduction.homeoffice.gov.uk.

chapter

2

BURGLARY

DAVE PUTWAIN

PART A: The offence – Who, what, when, why?

A2.1. Introduction

Burglary represents one of the most common and serious domestic crimes accounting in 2004 for 6–8% of all crime committed in the UK (Dodd et al., 2004). It can have a traumatic effect on victims, who are then at greater risk of being a repeat target, and also represents a substantial economic cost (estimated at £2.7 billion in 2000; Brand and Price, 2000). In this chapter we will explore some of the major features of burglary including its legal definition, which is not limited to theft, rates of offending as measured from police records and victim surveys and psychological research on why offending occurs and how it can be reduced. Although the majority of research has focused on domestic burglary, commercial burglary is no less important in terms of its personal, social or economic costs. As we work through the chapter, I will attempt to highlight the relevant work to commercial burglary where it complements or differs from the more prevalent work on domestic burglary.

A2.2. Definitions

Under English Common Law, burglary refers only to theft from a residential property during the night. The 1968 Theft Act is a much broader definition, includes both domestic and commercial burglary and makes a distinction between the seriousness of the offence and whether the offence included violence or the threat of violence. There are two categories of offence: burglary and aggravated burglary.

- A person can be convicted of burglary if they enter a building or part of a building as a trespasser and attempt to steal anything in the building, inflict grievous bodily harm (including rape) on any person in the building or cause unlawful damage to the building or its contents.

- A person can be convicted of aggravated burglary if the perpetrator has possession of a firearm, imitation firearm, any weapon of offence or explosive.

It is clear from this expanded criterion that conviction for burglary need not include an actual theft. The Theft Act was updated in 1978 and 1996 to include obtaining money by deception, dishonestly retaining wrongful credit and making off without payment, but from 2006 these monetary aspects of theft have been covered under the Fraud Act (see Chapter 5 on fraud).

A2.3. Who?

Burglary targets include residential dwellings and commercial properties. Domestic properties include houses, caravans, houseboats and also buildings permanently attached to houses such as garages. Commercial properties include manufacturing premises such as factories, retail premises such as shops and large out-of-town stores found in retail parks, hotels, farms and businesses that are primarily office based (such as call centres). Burglars are therefore provided with a diversity of potential targets located in different geographical areas and containing very different kinds of items. As we shall explore later, the distribution of burglary offences is not evenly spread across locations and types of house. It therefore becomes an important question in understanding the psychology of burglary and in crime prevention why certain premises may be targeted and not others, and whether certain premises are targeted by a particular type of burglar.

First we will turn our attention to the question of whether there are many individual differences in burglars. In order to identify differences in offender characteristics, Farrington and Lambert (1997) analysed data from 345 burglars collected at the time of arrest from Nottinghamshire Police Criminal Record Office case files. Information was collected about gender, physical (e.g. height and eye colour) and demographic background (such as ethnic background and place of birth), marital status and so forth. Few differences emerged; the typical offender was male (95.4%), white (only 7.7% were from an Afro-Caribbean background) and born locally (82.1% were born in Nottinghamshire). Clearly, factors such as the proportion of offenders from distinct ethnic backgrounds could change along with the demographic of the local area, but on the basis of this research it would seem there are few differences between individual physical characteristics of burglars. A more fruitful approach might be to examine individual differences in the targets or modus operandi of burglars.

Distinctions between different types of burglars have been made by researchers, by the police and by burglars themselves. For instance, one crude distinction is made between 'professionals' and 'amateurs' (Shover, 1973); however, a more detailed typology elaborating individual differences in burglars can be found in the work of Maguire (1982) based on police records and interviews with convicted offenders, police officers and victims in the Thames Valley.

Maguire (1982) distinguished between three types of burglar: 'professional', 'persistent' and 'impulsive' based on the degree of planning in the offence, the type of properties targeted, the value of goods and access to criminal networks for handling stolen goods. *Professional burglars* had access to criminal networks for handling stolen goods (also known as 'fences'). Thefts were carefully planned in order to steal valuable items to order or which could be sold to collectors (such as silver, artwork or antique items). As a consequence, target premises were carefully selected and could involve travelling some distance. Entry to premises depended on the exact circumstances, but could involve disabling electronic security measures. Violence was used where necessary to gain access to premises or items.

Persistent burglars did not have access to fences to handle stolen goods and so they targeted the theft of lower-value items (such as televisions or jewellery) that could be readily sold for cash. Suitable premises were targeted from areas that were regularly visited and known as part of established daily routines. Entry to premises was forced (such as breaking through doors and windows) and relied on slow responses to electronic alarms from police and private security.

Impulsive burglars would steal low-value items for personal use (such as shoplifting cigarettes or stealing cash from a neighbour) and did not have access to criminal fences. Targets were chosen impulsively and opportunistically and burglars did not rely on prior planning. Unlike professional and persistent burglars, impulsive burglars placed greater value on the excitement associated with the offence, sometimes by juveniles as a 'risk' or 'dare' to impress peers, rather than the value of the stolen goods. Where entry to premises was forced, it was done with little finesse.

The distinction between types of burglars based on the degree of planning is one supported by Bennet and Wright (1984), who identified three types of offenders from interviews with 128 convicted offenders: 'searchers', 'planners' and 'opportunists'. *Searchers*, who represented the majority of interviewees, would travel to a chosen area and then 'search' for a suitable target based on previous experience of risk, rewards and ease of entry. This group would seem to correspond to Maguire's (1982) *persistent* group. *Planners* would engage in a more detailed degree of preparation prior to the offence and opportunists in little prior preparation, and would seem to correspond to Maguire's (1982) *professional* and *impulsive* groups, respectively. Nee and Meenaghan (2006) found that some searchers were starting to use specialist fences to dispose of stolen goods and Palmer, Holmes and Hollin (2002) reported burglars using more planning in general. These findings suggest that burglars are becoming more sophisticated and the distinction between *professional* and *persistent* burglars or between *planners* and *searchers* may no longer be so clear-cut.

Maguire's (1982) analysis of different types of burglars also helps to provide some clues as to why different types of residential properties may be targeted. Because professional burglars had access to specialist criminal networks to dispose of stolen goods through fences they would target high-income properties.

Persistent burglars did not have the same access to fences, so were more limited in what stolen goods they could dispose of and would target middle-income properties. Impulsive burglars also did not have access to specialist fences and would typically engage in petty theft from lower-income properties. Taken as a whole, these findings suggest that crime prevention needs to understand that different types of burglars will have different types of targets and operate in different ways.

A2.4. Misconceptions

Perhaps some people hold a stereotype of a burglar as someone breaking into a residential property at night to steal personal belongings. This is possibly due to the origins in English Common Law and reflected in the meaning of the word burglary in old English, which can be broken down into 'burgh' meaning *house* and 'laron' meaning *thief*. As we noted in the legal definition of burglary (in Section A2.2), burglary can be targeted at commercial as well as residential property and is not limited to theft but can also involve personal injury or damage to buildings. Furthermore, domestic burglary is actually most popular during the daytime when occupants are at work, whereas it is commercial burglary that takes place at night when premises are empty (Butler, 1994). One final misconception refers to the burglar as someone who is opportunistic, unskilled and indiscriminate. As we noted in Section A2.3, this may refer to only one type of burglar, and this is a theme we will take up later in the chapter in Section B2.2. The approach promoted by Rational Choice Theory (Cornish and Clarke, 1986) and the research that followed suggests that burglars can be highly discriminating in their choice of targets and follow an intelligible decision-making process typical of skilled performance.

A2.5. Facts and figures

The incidence of burglary can be established from several sources of official statistics, including The British Crime Survey (BCS), official recorded crime figures (PRC) and Commercial Victimization Survey (CVS). The Home Office produces an annual report in July summarising the incidence of domestic burglary from both the BCS and PRC. In 2009/10 there were 659,000 burglary incidents reported in the BCS, a drop of 9% from 2008/9 and consistent with a drop of 6% according to PRC (Murphy and Eder, 2010), and 2.2% of households were victims of one or more burglaries, with a higher risk in urban (2.5%) than in rural areas (1.1%). Statistics for the period 1981–2010 are reported below for the BCS (Figure 2.1) and PRC (Figure 2.2). Even when changes to the way in which police recorded burglaries are taken into account (see Murphy and Eder, 2010), both sets of data show a similar trend. Burglary showed a steady increase throughout the 1980s before peaking in the mid-1990s and gradually reducing in 2000s.

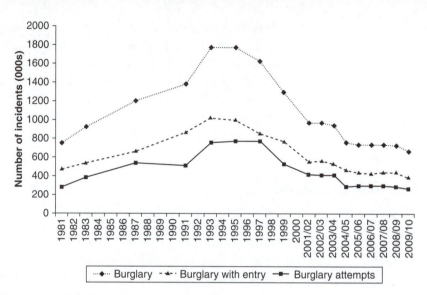

Figure 2.1 *British crime survey, 1981–2010*
Source: Reproduced from Murphy and Eder (2010, p. 81).

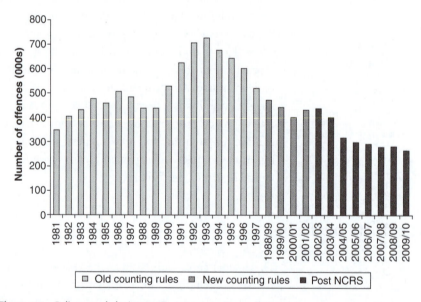

Figure 2.2 *Police recorded crime, 1981–2010*
Source: Reproduced from Murphy and Eder (2010, p. 82).

It is difficult to establish the incidence of commercial burglary from these data. The BCS does not include commercial burglaries, and the non-domestic category included in police-recorded crime includes non-commercial buildings (garages and sheds unconnected to houses). The CVS, conducted in 1994 and 2002, collected data about crimes committed against small and medium commercial premises and so provides more specific details about commercial burglaries than either the BCS or PRC. Findings from the 2002 survey are summarised in Shury et al. (2005). As with domestic burglary, they indicate a reduction since the early 1990s.

- 16% of retailers reported burglary (down from 24% in 1993); 58% occurred at the weekend and 82% occurred in the evening or at night.
- 16% of retailers reported repeat burglaries, which was lower than fraud (18%), vandalism (23%) and customer theft (43%).
- 14% of manufacturers reported burglary (down from 24% in 1993); 60% occurred during the week, 73% in evening or at night.
- 14% of manufacturers reported repeat burglaries, the second most common form of repeat victimisation after vandalism (16%).

KEY DEBATE: Is burglary an opportunist crime?

For:
Some convicted residential burglars report themselves as opportunists, entering properties that have left windows open or have poor security measures, and choosing times when they believe that the occupants will be out.

Against:
Other convicted burglars report a high degree of planning in choosing target properties, how to break in, what escape routes are available, what would be stolen and how to dispose of stolen goods.

Conclusion:
It may be the case that there are different types of burglars depending on their level of skill. Opportunists tend to be less skilled and engage in less planning, whereas non-opportunists can be highly skilled and plan their crimes in great detail.

References:
Palmer, E.J., Holmes, A. and Hollin, C.R. (2002) Investigating burglars' decisions factors influencing target choice, method of entry, reasons for offending, repeat victimisation of a property and victim awareness. *Security Journal*, 15, 7–18.
Wright, R., Logie, R.H. and Decker, S.H. (1995) Criminal expertise and decision making: An experimental study of the target selection process in residential burglary. *Journal of Research in Crime and Delinquency*, 32, 39–53.

A2.6. How are offenders caught?

In an analysis of 404 burglaries, Farrington and Lambert (1997) reported that the most common way of apprehending a burglar was when they were caught mid-burglary (14.5%), through an informant (12.5%), caught near to or leaving the crime scene (12%), traced when disposing of stolen goods or through items left at the crime scene (10.5%), acting suspiciously (7.7%), confessing to burglary when apprehended for another crime (7%) or from a witness description (6.7%). Given the proportion of burglars apprehended at or near the crime scene, it is not surprising that the majority of burglars are arrested within one hour of the offence (43%), a further 6% within one day, 13.3% between 2 and 10 days and

14.5% 11–30 days after the offence. Only 16.2% were arrested after more than 30 days.

A2.7. What happens to offenders?

According to Ministry of Justice (2010) figures 23,651 persons were convicted of burglary in 2008, which represents a reduction of 24% since 1998. Four percent were first-time offenders, which is much less than for some other offences such as fraud, and 38% had 15 or more previous convictions (but not necessarily for burglary). A further 110,348 were convicted of the associated offence of theft and handling stolen goods. The maximum Crown Court sentence for a domestic burglary is 14 years' imprisonment, 10 years' for commercial burglary and life imprisonment for aggravated burglary. Maximum sentences are rarely used, however, and courts may impose non-custodial sentences such as community sentences and/or rehabilitation programmes and fines for less serious offences or first-time offenders. A minimum custodial sentence of 3 years' imprisonment is given for third-time burglars over the age of 18 years.

In 2008, 70.8% of persons convicted of burglary in a dwelling by a Crown Court were given a custodial sentence with an average length of 24.9 months, and 13.2% given a community sentence. Sixty-eight per cent of persons convicted by a Crown Court of burglary in a dwelling other than a building were given a custodial sentence with an average length of 17.4 months, and 13.6% given a community sentence. Clearly, the burglary of a dwelling is considered the more serious offence. Antisocial behaviour orders (ASBOs) have been used if a defendant is found guilty in a civil case requiring a lower burden of proof (on balance the accused *probably* committed the act, unlike criminal cases which require a higher burden of proof, the accused *must be guilty beyond reasonable doubt*), resulting in behavioural restrictions such as exclusions from a particular geographic area or a nightime curfew. ASBOs have not been specifically targeted at burglars, but evidence suggests that many youths targeted for behavioural contracts (similar to ASBOs) have had prior contact with police over burglary, suggesting that they may have potential (Bullock and Jones, 2004). The UK Government announced in 2011 that ASBOs would be replaced by *Criminal Behaviour Orders* and *Crime Prevention Injunctions* in an attempt to simplify and streamline the process. Time will tell.

One form of offender rehabilitation used with convicted burglars by the prison and probation services in the UK is the *Reasoning and Rehabilitation Programme* (Home Office, 2001; Joint Prison Probation Accreditation Panel, 2002). The *Reasoning and Rehabilitation Programme* (R&R) is a form of cognitive-behavioural training originally developed in Canada by Ross, Fabiano and Ewles (1988) which aims to change the thinking and attitudes of the offender so that decisions which lead to planning and committing an offence will be replaced with pro-social decisions. Although this type of programme may seem well suited to the rehabilitation of burglars for whom the decision to offend and choice of target seems to follow a predictable pattern of decision making (see Section B2.2), evaluating the effectiveness of R&R for burglary is difficult. Many evaluation studies do not differentiate between different types of offences, include interventions other than R&R and cannot randomly allocate participants to intervention (R&R) and control groups, as participation in the programme may be included in sentences passed by courts.

Wilkinson (2005) reported findings from an evaluation of a community-based R&R programme in which 105 adult offenders (including 39 burglars) who attended the programme were compared to a group of 98 adult offenders (including 37 burglars) matched on the previous number of sentences who did not. After two years those who attended the programme were as likely to be reconvicted as those who did not (reconviction rates were 68% for both groups). Mitchell and Palmer (2004) compared 31 young offenders (aged 15–18 years) voluntarily attending an R&R programme with a comparison group of 31 young offenders matched by length of sentence, type of offence, age of release and number of previous convictions while on a waiting list for the programme. The most common offence for the young offenders was burglary, but violence and drug-related offences were also included. There were no significant differences in rates of reoffending or re-imprisonment between the treatment and comparison groups: 80.6% of the treatment group had reoffended within 18 months of release and 83.9% of the comparison group; 58.1% of the of the treatment group were re-imprisoned within 18 months of release and 64.5% of the comparison group.

Notwithstanding the methodological difficulties of conducting evaluation studies, these findings suggest that R&R is not an effective way of rehabilitating convicted burglars when judged solely in terms of reconviction rates. It is not possible for the existing research to determine whether this failure is due to the specific protocols involved in R&R programmes or whether any attempts to reduce burglary by employing cognitive-behavioural strategies to change beliefs or attitudes are ineffective. Nee and Meenaghan (2006) suggest that any successful rehabilitation programme would have to take into account the decision-making chain of events that leads to burglary, in particular how automatic processes may be triggered by offence-related stimuli and the heightened ability of expert burglars to recognise these stimuli. It may be the case that R&R protocols to date have simply not paid sufficient attention to these important antecedents of burglary.

Anecdotal evidence reported in the popular press (e.g. Asthana and Doward, 2010) where convicted burglars meet or have correspondence with victims of burglary as part of 'restorative justice' schemes has apparently resulted in offenders 'seeing the error of their ways'. It would be prudent, however, to treat these claims with scepticism until the findings of independent evaluation research (e.g. the European Commission-funded *Mediation and Restorative Justice in Prison Settings Project*) have been reported.

A2.8. And the damage done...

Victims of burglary

The experience of burglary is traumatic for many victims, even if they did not come face to face with the offender. Some experiences are in common with other psychological consequences of victimisation, such as feelings of anxiety, helplessness, anger, vulnerability and mistrust of others (Kahn, 1984). Interviews with the victims of burglary suggest there are individual differences in responses to burglary across gender and age (Maguire, 1980). The most common response for men was anger and for women was fear and shock: 65% of respondents felt these emotional effects remained for up to ten weeks after the burglary and 15% were frightened to be alone in their house; the effects were more severe in the elderly.

Once a property has been burgled, there is a greater likelihood that it will be targeted again, a phenomenon known as 'repeat victimisation' and, according to Ainsworth (2000), its influence should not be underestimated. A greater understanding of repeat victimisation can help to target police resources more efficiently and assist in crime prevention by helping to identifying repeat offenders and concentrate efforts in areas of highest crime. Repeat victimisation is not limited to domestic burglary, Wood, Wheelwright and Burrows (1997) reported that 69% of burglaries to small businesses in Leicester were suffered by only 17% of the businesses surveyed.

The interviews with offenders conducted by Bennett and Wright (1984), briefly reviewed in Section A2.3 (also see Bennett, 1995) suggested two possible reasons for repeat victimisation in burglary, known as 'boost' and 'flag explanations'. *Boost* explanations suggests that the same offender returns to the same property again because it is a known target, perhaps due to ease of access or because the burglar knows it contains valuable property or that items are likely to have been replaced following an insurance claim and so newer and more valuable items can be stolen (Ashton et al., 1998). The repeat offence can be planned in more detail and/or colleagues can be enlisted to help steal more bulky items. A variety on this *boost* explanation is where a different offender targets the house because information has been passed on by a previous offender.

The alternative *flag* account suggests that something about the property flags it up as vulnerable (perhaps as a soft target) to potential offenders, leading it to being targeted on more than one occasion. Being able to differentiate between these different explanations would undoubtedly help in crime prevention, but it is not possible to provide a definitive answer. Pease (1998) suggests that most evidence supports the first explanation, but it is difficult to establish the exact proportion of repeat victimisation attributable to the same perpetrator.

PART B: Theories and explanations

In the following section we will explore in more detail the prevailing psychological approach of explaining burglary, based on rational decision making, and attempts to reduce crime known as *Situational Crime Prevention*. Building on the seminal work of Maguire (1982) and Bennett and Wright (1984), Rational Choice Theory and the subsequent research it has promoted have largely relied on using convicted burglars as research participants. This practice is not without its critics and so it is also important to frame the main points in the methodological debate over how best to research the psychology of burglary. Reducing crime has been the focus of many Home Office initiatives over the last 30 years resulting in a plethora of reports, evaluations and statistics. Untangling this evidence also brings a whole host of complex and thorny methodological issues and, in the latter part of this chapter, we will examine the main findings and conclusions from the literature.

B2.1. Explaining and reducing burglary

Why do people commit burglary?

According to 'routine activities theory' (Cohen and Felson, 1979) burglaries occur from the interplay of factors when the motivated perpetrator locates a suitable target in the absence of a suitable deterrent. Burglary targets are not distributed evenly across geographical locations, resulting in 'hot spots' of enduring high levels of burglary. This can be partly explained by how burglars choose suitable targets. Bennett and Wright (1984) showed offenders convicted of residential burglary films of different types of residential property from a pavement view and asked them to identify potential targets and explain their reasons. The three most important factors reported were risks, rewards and the ease of entry. Burglars would avoid houses with alarms, dogs (for fear that the dog barking might alert someone, rather than fear of being bitten), where people appeared to be at home, whether access could be gained without being easily visible to neighbours and whether there would be valuable property in the home. Ease of entry risk was identified as the most important factor in choosing a target.

Targets are also determined by the *usual routines* of the offenders: where they live, the areas they routinely visit and are familiar with (Brantingham and Brantingham, 1984). Findings from the *Statistical House Offender Profiling* database used by the Northumbria Police indicate that most serial burglars repeatedly reoffend within half a mile of their home (Stevens, 1997). Although the majority of work into the choice of burglary targets has focused on residential offenders, evidence suggests that targets for commercial burglaries are also selected in the same way. Stores in out-of-town retail parks are more at risk than city centre stores for the ease of entry, ease of escape, size of likely reward and as it is easier to disable silent alarms (Burrows and Speed, 1996). Non-retail theft is targeted at industrial estates rather than single, isolated premises for similar reasons (Wiersma, 1996).

Bennett and Wright (1984) also highlighted how around half of the burglars they interviewed (the 'searchers' – see Section A2.3) followed a rational decision-making process in making the decision to offend at a location away from the crime scene, travelling to a location previously identified as having suitable targets and then selecting a particular target based on visual cues including those which indicated wealth, occupancy, access and a lack of security. According to Nee and Meenaghan (2006), these findings suggest that burglars are not driven by some inexorable urge to commit crime, but are rational decision makers relying on speedy 'rules of thumb' based on prior experience. Accumulated evidence suggests that burglars are more skilled in identifying cues to identify and recognise targets for burglary than police officers, householders and other types of offenders (Nee and Taylor, 1988, 2000; Taylor and Nee, 1988) and that this was even the case with juvenile burglars aged 15–17 years (Logie et al., 1992).

Wright and Decker (1994) refer to this rational and habit-driven decision-making process to target selection as following a 'cognitive script'. Once entry to a house had been gained, offenders would follow a fixed pattern and head straight to the main bedroom to search for guns (this was a North American study), cash and drugs, exiting within 20 minutes. Other bedrooms would only be visited if time allowed. In a study of 50 convicted burglars, Nee and Meenaghan (2006) report how 45 followed a predictable search strategy once a domestic property had been entered and 37 described their search as automatic rather than deliberate. This type of automaticity is typical of expertise in a particular domain (you can do something well without having to think about it too much), allowing a task to be conducted in a speedy, methodical and efficient fashion (Palmeri et al., 2004). Furthermore, 15 participants described listening attentively for auditory cues which might signify the presence of the occupiers while conducting their search. This again is indicative that search strategies were automatic, allowing cognitive resources to be directed to other tasks such as listening.

Many of these types of decisions are captured in the *Rational Choice Theory* (Clarke and Cornish, 1985; Cornish and Clarke, 1986), which suggests that the decision to offend is driven by the same choice-making processes that govern decisions in other areas of one's life. They suggest an eight-stage model in the decision to commit a burglary in a middle-class location (see Figure 2.3). Stages 1–3 refer to background, cognitive and learning factors and stages 4 and 5 to decision points. Before the final decision is made to offend (stage 8), however, the person needs to be ready to satisfy his or her needs through burglary (stage 7) and be precipitated through some chance event (stage 6).

According to Nee and Taylor (2000), the consistency of findings in relation to the sequential nature of the decision-making process in burglary, the environmental cues used by burglars to target properties and the cognitive processing strategies and resulting behaviour used by offenders once they have gained entry to a property provide clear support for the position set out in Rational Choice Theory that burglars are driven by a habitual and previously successful decision-making process. The model is not without its critics (see Feldman, 1993); for example, it has been questioned whether offenders who are intoxicated or in a high state of arousal can actually be considered to be rational, whether offenders are really *choosing* to offend or whether they are driven by a combination of personality, adverse home background and education. Furthermore, given the distinctions between different types of burglars set out in Section A2.3, we must also question whether this approach applies only to those types of burglars

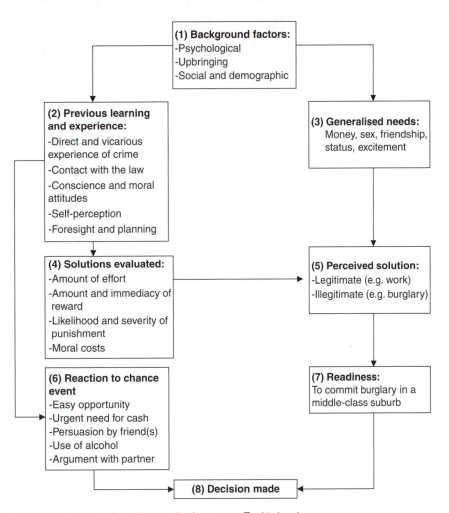

Figure 2.3 *Rational Choice Theory: The decision to offend in burglary*
Source: Adapted from Clarke and Cornish (1985, p. 168).

who do rely on planning (Wright and Decker, 1994), and most burglars will still exploit unplanned opportunities (Wiles and Costello, 2000). Even when burglars do plan, the extent to which relying on 'rules of thumb' for identifying and assessing targets represents a rational decision-making process can be questioned (Cornish, 1994; Cromwell et al., 1991).

B2.2. Advantages and disadvantages of using convicted burglars as research participants

The methodological approach of using convicted burglars as research participants was popularised in North American research from the early 1970s using field interviews with incarcerated offenders (e.g. Scarr, 1973; Shover, 1973; Reppetto, 1974). Maguire (1982) and Bennett and Wright's (1984) research from the UK also used convicted offenders as interviewees (as well as in other more experimental-type tasks), along with police records and interviews with police officers and victims. Nee (2010a) suggests that research has progressed by employing ethnographic and grounded theory approaches in which it is the burglars themselves who are viewed as the experts, allowing for a greater insight into the perceptions, understandings and decision making of the burglar. Early researchers tended not to approach particular projects with predefined hypotheses and theories but immersed themselves in the life world of the burglar. Gradually, as hypotheses emerged, later work incorporated quasi-experimental and experimental approaches using slides of potential target properties to be burgled or simulated residential neighbourhoods to test specific hypotheses about burglars' decision making and memory.

The counter-argument goes that using incarcerated burglars as research participants may reduce validity as this group represents 'failed' criminals who may be reconstructing events from memory in a biased manner, and there are also likely to be more younger or first-time offenders who may have had non-custodial sentences (Ainsworth, 2000). However, since the nature of burglary means that most burglars are likely to serve time in prison at some point, if researchers interview active burglars it is only a matter of time before they become incarcerated. Furthermore, research participants can be recruited in prisons who are serving time for other offences. Since they have not been convicted of burglary, it does not necessarily follow that they are 'failed' burglars just because they are incarcerated (Nee, 2010b). There are also reasons to suggest that incarcerated burglars may provide a better quality of data. Prisoners, unlike active burglars, have plenty of time to spare, are often bored and have less to lose from engaging in research. Active burglars, on the other hand, are most likely to have a drug dependency, making them less cooperative and reliable participants. Nee (2010b) concludes that rather than viewing one type of sample as inherently superior it is better to view both as having specific advantages and disadvantages.

B2.3. Situational crime prevention

The Situational Approach to Crime Prevention (SCP) was developed in the 1970s and 1980s by the Home Office (Clarke, 1983). It has several notable characteristics based on practical measures which can be taken to reduce crime, modify the environment to discourage criminal behaviour and focus on the specific offence rather than the offender. The basic idea is to identify and reduce opportunity for crime. Specific Home Office initiatives to reduce burglary have been based on SCP, including the *Safer Cities* targeted at reducing all crimes in cities with the highest rates of crime from 1988 to 1995 (Ekblom et al., 1996) and the *Reducing Burglary Initiative* running from 1998 to 2002 (Homel et al., 2004). There are three principal elements to SCP (Clarke, 1992):

1. *Increase the amount of effort required to commit the crime.* Strategies can include making it physically more difficult for an offender to access targets through target-hardening strategies, alley gating, fences and barrier

plants. Target-hardening strategies include security enhancements to doors and windows such as locks or grilles over windows. Alley gating is where the access to the rear of houses (popular in Victorian terraces) is reduced. Fences and barrier plants (large prickly bushes such as holly) are often used in conjunction with alley gating to help reduce access points to premises.

2. *Increase the perceived risk of committing the crime.* Strategies can include fitting burglar alarms, enhanced lighting and CCTV. Burglar alarms can provide a visible deterrent to potential offenders and audible alarms used in domestic properties may alert bystanders. Commercial properties may have silent alarms which directly alert the police or a private security firm. Enhancing street lighting or security lighting can increase the risk of surveillance and therefore act as a deterrent. CCTV can provide covert surveillance.

3. *Reduce the likely rewards of crime.* Strategies include the marking of property (using stickers or UV pens whose ink is visible only under ultraviolet light) and covert tracking devices. In principle, the marking of property allows the police to recover stolen property and arrest persons handling stolen goods; however it is an effective deterrent only if the marking of property is publicised, such as placing a sticker in the widow to indicate that property has been marked (Laycock, 1991). The use of tracking devices involves fitting hi-tech tracking technology to high-value items likely to be stolen. Such approaches require specifically trained staff and are intended to provide intelligence on and then reducing the opportunity for selling on of stolen goods.

The success of reducing burglary and repeat victimisation in the Kirkholt Estate in the Rochdale area of Greater Manchester is often held up as an example of the effectiveness of the SCP. The Kirkholt Estate was an area of Local Authority Housing consisting of 2280 dwellings. The *Home Office Burglary Prevention Project* ran in Kirkholt from 1986 to 1990 at a total cost of £298,000 for intervention and evaluation (Welsh and Farrington, 1999). The main features of the project included (1) upgrading the security on recently victimised dwellings, property marking and the removal of gas and electricity meters that took cash (this was the SPR part of the project); (2) probation service community programmes for offenders; and (3) school-based programmes for youth. Between 1986 and 1990, recorded residential burglary fell by 75% and repeat victimisation fell to 0% (Forrester et al., 1990).

These findings would suggest the project was a success and that situational crime prevention can form part of an effective burglary reduction; however, some of these effects might also have been attributable to the larger *Kirkholt Development Project* which started in 1984 and also included improvements to dwellings, community development and youth work (Hope, 2002). This point highlights the difficulties facing researchers responsible for evaluating the impact of interventions taking place in real-life environments. When there are multiple causes for burglary, multiple burglary reduction strategies and

Table 2.1 *Summary of results from evaluation studies*

Strategy	Evidence for success
Increase the effort:	
Window and door locks to all houses in a whole area	Strong evidence for success
Window and door locks on houses that had been previous targets of burglary	Moderate evidence for success
Alley gating	Strong evidence for success
Fencing	Some evidence for success
Barrier plants	Mixed evidence for success
Increase the risks:	
Street lighting	Some evidence for success
Alarms	Some evidence for success
Reduce the rewards:	
Property marking	Some evidence for success
Covert tracking	Mixed evidence for success

Source: Adapted from Hamilton-Smith and Kent (2005).

multiple interventions being implemented simultaneously, pinpointing the exact reason(s) for a reduction in burglary is not an easy matter (see Hope, 2002).

The *Reducing Burglary Initiative* was also subject to a number of evaluation studies from independent teams based in the South, Midlands and the North of England. Hamilton-Smith and Kent (2005) summarised results from the evaluation studies, which are presented in Table 2.1. CCTV was not included in the evaluation; however, other evidence suggests it is not a particularly effective deterrent for burglary partly because offenders believed that police would not be able to respond quickly enough to apprehend them (Gill and Loveday, 2003).

SCP assumes that offenders are making a rational decision to offend by weighing up the risks and benefits of exploiting a particular opportunity, so that if the perceived costs can be manipulated in such a way that they outweigh the perceived benefits for the perpetrator, then they will make the decision not to offend. The success of some of the SCP strategies can also be taken as further indirect support for Rational Choice Theory. SCP is also highly practical and allows both police and potential victims to take realistic steps to reduce the likelihood of burglary (Crawford, 1998). This may have important psychological benefits by helping people feel in control (Ainsworth, 2000). One potential disadvantage of SCP is that it may simply be displacing crime from one target (individual property or whole neighbourhood) area to another; the burglar chooses an alternative target where costs are lower and rewards are higher (Heal and Laycock, 1986). This argument suggests that SCP would not be helpful in the long term, but providing evidence for displacement is difficult. Just because burglary reduction in one discernible geographical location is matched by a corresponding increase in another, it does not necessarily follow that burglary is being displaced. There are many other factors to take into account, such as offenders switching from domestic to commercial burglary (or vice versa) and other geographical locations containing suitable alternative targets.

In summary, the predominant psychological view of burglary is that of a rational decision based on prior expertise in assessing risks, rewards and ease of entry. Questions remain, however, over the use of convicted offenders as research participants, the rational status of the decisions made, the degree of choice involved and whether this approach can apply equally to all burglars. Situational Crime Prevention used by the Home Office is based on increasing effort (i.e. reducing the ease of entry), increasing the risks and reducing the rewards. Some strategies have proved useful in reducing burglary although evaluating crime reduction programmes is difficult and there may be a risk that burglaries have been displaced to other locations. The success of these burglary reduction initiatives provides additional, if indirect, evidence for the rational decision-making approach to burglary.

PART C: Further information

C2.1. Organisations to contact for information and voluntary work

www.victimsupport.org

(the website also includes an online enquiry form for volunteering)

The national volunteering helpline number is 0800 840 4207

Victim Support is a registered charity (no. 298028) that gives free information, emotional support and advice for the victims of crime, their families and also witnesses of crimes. Victim Support does not solely help victims of burglary, but does provide specific advice for victims of burglary and has a 2005 report *Investigating the Practical Support Needs of Burglary Victims* available to download on the website. There are multiple ways to volunteer for Victim Support, including working with victims in the community, supporting witnesses in court and working on the Victim Supportline.

Safer Lancashire

www.saferlancashire.co.uk

Safer Neighbourhood schemes are run in conjunction with local authorities and local police forces to support community-led crime reduction. There are different ways of volunteering for the Safer Neighbourhoods scheme to assist the police in identifying the key local issues through becoming a panel member, mentoring ex-offenders or participating in a Neighbourhood Watch scheme. The details of individual schemes can be found from links on individual constabulary websites or alternatively by searching on the Internet for 'safer neighbourhood' and then the particular area you are looking for such as 'Lancashire'. The exact schemes and the different types of voluntary opportunities differ from one scheme to another.

C2.2. Further reading

For further reading into the psychology of burglary, I would recommend looking at one of the two classic texts, either Bennett and Wright (1984) or Maguire (1982). Although somewhat dated, they provide valuable insight into many aspects of burglary and will help the reader understand the foundation on which much subsequent research has been based. An excellent example of more recent follow-up work can be found in Nee and Meenaghan (2006).

Bennett, T., and Wright, R. (1984) *Burglars on Burglary: Prevention and the Offender*. Aldershot: Gower.

Maguire, M. (1982) *Burglary in a Dwelling: The Offence, the Offender and the Victim: Cambridge Studies in Criminology*. London: Heinemann.

Nee, C. and Meenaghan, A. (2006) Expert decision-making in burglars. *British Journal of Criminology*, 46, 935–49.

For further reading about crime reduction, I would recommend the following two chapters. Hamilton-Smith and Kent (2005) provide a detailed analysis of the Home Office *Reducing Burglary Initiative* evaluation studies, which we have only had space to summarise here. The chapter by Hope (2002) provides a particularly good review of the methodological difficulties in designing and interpreting evaluation studies.

Hamilton-Smith, N. and Kent, A. (2005) The prevention of domestic burglary. In N. Tilley (Ed.) *Handbook of Crime Prevention and Community Safety*. Collumpton: Willan.

Hope, T. (2002) The road taken: evaluation, replication and crime reduction. In G. Hughes, E. McLaughlin and J. Muncie (Eds.) *Crime Prevention and Community Safety: New Directions*. London: Sage.

chapter

3

DOMESTIC VIOLENCE

WENDY MORGAN AND ELIZABETH GILCHRIST

PART A: The offence – Who, what, when, why?

A3.1. Introduction

Domestic violence (DV) is often described as being a hidden crime because it is often not reported and therefore it is commonly underestimated. Worldwide, as many as 2 out of 3 women have been abused by their partners (World Health Organization [WHO], 2005). Within the UK, one in five of us will be the victims of domestic violence during our adult lifetime (approximately 1:4 women and 1:7 men), and in 2010 31 men and 101 women in England and Wales were killed by their current or former partners (Coleman and Osbourne, 2010, Figure 1). In this chapter we will look at the risk factors for domestic violence and the response of the justice system to the perpetrators and the victims.

A3.2. Definitions

There is considerable variability in attempts to define domestic violence (DV) (Paradine and Wilkinson, 2004). For example, some definitions of DV focus on the most serious forms of violence (Dekeseredy and Schwartz, 2001) and others reference the pattern of abuse between partners (see www.refuge.org). The Ministry of Justice takes a broad view (of both behaviours and victims) and defines DV as:

> any threatening behaviour, violence or abuse between adults who are or have been in a relationship, or between family members. It can affect anybody, regardless of their gender or sexuality. The violence can be psychological, physical, sexual or emotional. It can include honour based violence, female genital mutilation, and forced marriage. (www.justice.org.uk)

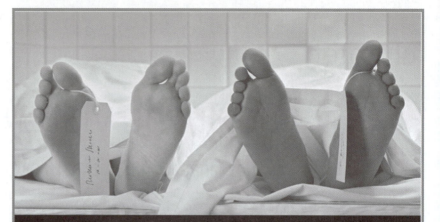

Every week, another two women escape domestic violence.

According to the Home Office, two women in England and Wales are killed by their partner or ex-partner every week.

At Refuge, we've learned in our 37 years that what starts as a slap or shove can escalate into a pattern of frequent brutal beatings, and can even lead to death.

We've learned that far from being about losing control, domestic violence is actually about men taking control.

And we've learned that emotional abuse can do a huge amount of harm.

Forewarned is forearmed, so Refuge would like to alert you to some of the early warning signs of domestic violence.

- Is the man in your life charming one minute and terrifyingly aggressive the next?
- Is he excessively jealous and possessive?
- Is he stopping you from seeing your family and friends?
- Is he constantly criticizing you and putting you down in public?
- Does he control your money?
- Does he tell you what to wear, who to see, where to go, what to think?
- Does he pressure you to have sex when you don't want to?
- Are you starting to walk on eggshells to avoid making him angry?

Refuge

For women and children.
Against domestic violence.

Don't ignore the early warning signs. www.refuge.org.uk

Registered charity no: 277424

Figure 3.1 *Refuge campaign to highlight the extent of domestic violence (© Refuge, Warning signs campaign, www.refuge.org.uk).*

This definition recognises that both men and women can be victims of DV. In 2004, it was agreed that this definition would apply to all UK government departments. However, some writers feel that DV experienced by women at the hands of men should be defined differently and that *family violence, mutual aggression* or *partner abuse* should be used to refer to abuse between couples (Reed et al., 2010). Because broad definitions of DV can refer to any abuse within the home (e.g. violence by and against fathers, mothers, siblings, partners), the term intimate partner violence (IPV) is more commonly used within the *psychological* literature to refer to abuse between current or former intimate partners. It is this form of DV that will be the predominant focus of this chapter.

The types of behaviours generally considered as evidence of DV between intimates are summarised in Box 3.1.

Box 3.1. What is domestic violence?

While physical abuse is often the most 'obvious' form of abuse between couples, a range of other behaviours are also relevant.

- *Destructive criticism and verbal abuse*: e.g. shouting, mocking, accusing, verbally threatening;
- *Pressure tactics*: e.g. sulking; threatening to withhold money;
- *Disrespect*: e.g. persistent put-downs in front of other people;
- *Breaking trust*: e.g. lying; withholding information; being jealous;
- *Isolation*: e.g. monitoring or blocking telephone calls; dictating movements;
- *Harassment*: following; checking;
- *Threats*: making angry gestures; destroying possessions; threats to kill or harm family pets;
- *Sexual violence*: using force, threats or intimidation in relation to sexual acts;
- *Physical violence*: punching; slapping; biting; kicking;
- *Denial*: denying the abuse happened; blaming the victim.

Source: Adapted from *The survivor's Handbook*, Women's Aid Federation of England, 2005. Revised 2009 (reproduced with permission).

A3.3. Who?

Because of the pervasiveness of DV, some researchers have suggested it is not helpful to explore individual risk factors – rather we need to look at the social structures that support abuse (see Part B). However, studies have shown that there are some individual factors that are associated with risk of violence towards partners.

Psychopathology

There is evidence that in some DV perpetrators personality dysfunction is relevant – specifically *borderline personality disorder traits* (Dutton, 2007a). Some offenders have *antisocial personality disorder* because they have a wider pattern of problematic behaviour, both inside and outside of the home.

Drugs and alcohol

Misuse of drugs and alcohol has been identified as a risk factor for DV (Stith et al., 2004), and many episodes occur following the consumption of alcohol by either or both partners. There is considerable debate about the true nature of this risk factor. For example, it is not clear whether the consumption of substances increases risk of DV through the physical effects, the psychological *expectancy effect* or whether it is used as an excuse to justify behaviour (Klostermann and Fals-Stewart, 2006).

Mental health and trauma

Studies have found that a *minority* of DV perpetrators have experienced problematic childhoods and, as a result, have developed trauma symptoms. Such individuals tend to have a chaotic and unstable personality style and have problematic intimate relationships (e.g. being over-attached or particularly fearful of abandonment). A history of depression or suicide attempts is commonly found with these individuals (see Dutton, 2007b, for a review of this area).

Individual differences

There is a great deal of variability among DV offenders. For example, while some offenders have risk factors associated with general violence, others, who demonstrate violence only within the home, have fewer generalised risk factors. When findings of 85 studies of DV risk factors were combined (using a *meta-analysis*), Stith et al. (2004) found that anger/hostility, distortions about the use of violence as a problem-solving strategy, *traditional sex-role ideology*, poor marital satisfaction and career/life stress were predictive of physical DV.

A3.4. Misconceptions

It only happens to women

Men and women can be the victims of violence by their partner. For example, the most recent British Crime Survey (BCS) found that 6% of women and 4% of men (aged 16–59) had, within the past year, been the victims of domestic violence (Roe, 2010).

It only happens to poor women who live on council estates

Cattaneo and DeLoveh (2008) found that violence reported to the police by women of higher socio-economic status (SES) was of greater severity than that reported by other women. And while studies have found higher rates of DV among women of lower SES (Campbell, 2002; Finney, 2006), conclusions from these data are not easy to draw. For example, some victims of DV may live in temporary accommodation and have low incomes as a consequence of leaving an abusive relationship (Finney, 2006). Also, greater economic freedom in SES groups may 'mask' rates of DV. For example, such individuals may have the potential to leave a relationship at the point at which it becomes abusive, thus reducing apparent prevalence rates in this group.

Victims should just leave

Victims may remain in the relationship out of fear – risk of homicide increases when women are trying to, or have just left, an abusive relationship (Campbell, 2007). In addition some abusive behaviours (e.g. isolation from friends, limited access to money) or specific barriers, such as disability or other forms of disadvantage, may make it difficult for victims to leave (Finney, 2006; see Figure 3.2).

He only does it because he was abused himself

While studies have found that *some* offenders have a history of abuse (Dutton, 2007b), this is not a characteristic associated with all DV offenders

Figure 3.2 *Some domestic violence victims may face barriers to their leaving the relationship (reproduced with permission)*

(Gilchrist et al., 2003). Furthermore, many individuals who are victims of abuse do not themselves go on to perpetrate abuse against others (Cannon, 2001). Thus a history of abuse as a child is best conceptualised as a potential risk factor but not the sole cause of later domestic violence.

A3.5. Facts and figures

Domestic violence accounts for one-quarter of all recorded violent crime and, on average, one incident of domestic violence is reported to the police every minute (Stanko, 2001). In England and Wales, half of all female and 7% of male homicide victims are killed by their current or former partner (Coleman and Osbourne, 2010). It has been estimated that domestic violence costs the English and Welsh economy over £23 billion a year (see Box 3.2 for a breakdown).

Box 3.2. Estimated costs of domestic violence for England and Wales in 2001

Criminal justice system: £1 billion. This includes costs related to the police (the main component), prosecution, probation, prison and legal aid.

Health care: £1.2 billion for dealing with physical injury (e.g. GP or hospital treatment) and £176 million for mental health care.

Social services: Almost quarter of a billion pounds per year – mainly associated with providing services to children who have been affected by DV.

Housing: Cost of emergency housing, dealing with homelessness as a result of DV and refuges = £160 million

Civil legal costs: Over £1.3 billion – this includes specialist legal action (e.g. injunctions) as well as actions related to the breakdown of marriages (e.g. divorce and child custody hearings).

Lost economic output: The cost of time off work due to injuries = approximately £2.7 billion. Half covered by employers, half by victims (i.e. lost wages).

Pain and suffering: The human and emotional costs are estimated at over £17 billion.

Source: Walby (2004).

A3.6. How are offenders caught?

Detection and Prosecution

Despite the established identity of the perpetrator, this form of abuse has a relatively low detection and prosecution rate (Harwin, 2006). Due to the nature of DV, it relies more upon victim reporting of the offences rather than police investigation. This raises several relevant issues: (1) many victims erroneously think they have not been the victim of a crime – a trend more noticeable among men (Finney, 2006); (2) victims may be unwilling to disclose abuse (social embarrassment, financial dependence) unless systems have been set up to support them; (3) other witnesses (e.g. neighbours) may be reluctant to report the abuse and; (4) the attitude of the criminal justice system (CJS) has been a historic barrier to prosecution – although in recent years strenuous efforts have been made to improve this and to support victims through the court process (Hester and Westmarland, 2005; Crown Prosecution Service, 2009).

Conviction

Hester et al. (2008) studied the progression of DV incidents through the CJS across two police forces. Attrition occurred at every stage of the criminal justice system and fewer than 6% of incidents resulted in a conviction (see Figure 3.3).

The low conviction rate reflects a number of factors. Victims may be unwilling to press charges, police may lack *powers of arrest*[1] (POA – see Figure 3.3) and the circumstances under which DV occurs (e.g. lack of witnesses, the only witnesses being children, witnesses being unwilling to testify) may make it difficult to obtain a conviction (Hester and Westmarland, 2005). In an effort to address these concerns, legislation has been implemented to assist the police and courts to manage DV cases. However, there are concerns about using conviction rate as a sole measure of success.

1. Not all incidents of DV are legislated against – for example, financial or emotional abuse (see Box 3.1).
2. Prosecution may not be helpful for the victim. Sometimes victims call the police because they want immediate assistance – the effects of prosecution (e.g. financial distress caused to the family) may be ultimately unhelpful (Itzin, 2000).

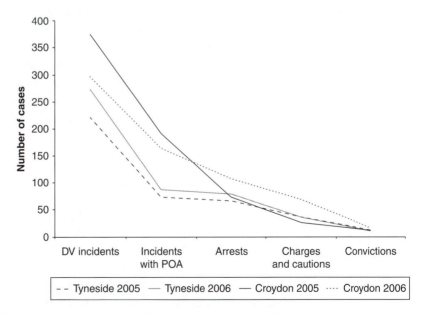

Figure 3.3 *Domestic violence incident progression through the Crown Prosecution Service*

A3.7. What happens to offenders?

Information on sentencing

Within the UK (unlike in other jurisdictions) there is no specific criminal offence of domestic violence; instead, perpetrators could be charged with a number of offences (e.g. criminal damage, assault, sexual assault, harassment). This makes it difficult to research sentencing trends. There has been some concern that the courts were not viewing DV offences as seriously as stranger violence (Gilchrist and Bisset, 2002), although the Sentencing Guidance Council (SGC) is clear this should not be the case.

Aggravating factors (which are likely to result in a harsher sentence) include a history of DV, the impact of the offence on children, abuse of a vulnerable victim and breaches of previous court decisions. Being of 'good character' is generally a mitigating factor at sentencing, but this is complicated in DV cases because some perpetrators are violent only in the home (Holtzworth-Munroe et al., 2003). Therefore having a job, absence of criminal record and being of good standing in the community should not be seen as mitigation within DV cases if these factors mask the offending (and risk) pattern.

Treatments typically offered

There are currently no specific treatment interventions for female DV perpetrators. Male offenders can be offered treatment in both custodial and community settings. Gilchrist et al. (2003) found that perpetrators who had higher drug and alcohol dependence and were more 'antisocial', 'sadistic' or emotionally volatile were most likely to be ordered to attend domestic violence programmes.

There are two main DV intervention approaches. *Duluth* interventions adopt a psycho-educational approach and teach men about the need to accept responsibility and learn the consequences of their behaviour. The alternative *cognitive behavioural therapy (CBT)* approach aims to break patterns of dysfunctional learning through teaching skills to interrupt inappropriate thoughts and attitudes, thereby enabling respondents to have different emotional and behavioural responses to conflict (Bowen, Gilchrist and Beech, 2005).

Relative efficacy of treatments

A recent meta-analysis concluded that overall DV treatment effectiveness is low (Stover, Meadows and Kaufmann, 2009). It is possible that some offenders will do worse in treatment that others and that a general analysis masks treatment effects. For example an analysis of a UK sample of treated participants suggested that those individuals who had greater contact with the police for DV had committed theft prior to treatment and had higher levels of interpersonal dependency and were more likely to reoffend following treatment (Bowen et al., 2005).

Recidivism

Domestic violence has a high repeat victimisation rate (Roe, 2010). However, because so many instances of DV do not result in a prosecution (see Figure 3.3) reconviction is not a particularly helpful measure of reoffending. Instead, measures of police call-outs or victim reports are often used (Bowen et al., 2005). Stover et al. (2009) found partner reports suggested recidivism rates of between 20 and 30% for those men completing treatment. However, it is possible that partners are more willing to disclose incidents of abuse because of the support they receive when their partners are in treatment.

Co-occurrence or progression to other crimes

Domestic violence is a broad category of offences that includes physical and sexual violence, harassment and stalking, and homicide against adult family members. In addition, there are high rates of co-occurrence of child abuse and neglect (Hester et al., 2007) and violence against strangers or acquaintances (Holtzworth-Munroe et al., 2003).

Prognosis (life course information)

Early models of DV (e.g. Walker, 1979 – who focused on male-perpetrated abuse) concluded that DV escalated in severity and frequency over time. However, more recent research has suggested there is significant variability in abusive behaviour. Overall there is a general trend for violence to decrease with age (Stith et al., 2004), although some offenders increase or remain constant in their levels and patterns of abuse towards partners (Holtzworth-Munroe et al., 2003).

A3.8. And the damage done . . .

Who are the victims?

DV is widespread – it is committed against individuals of different classes, cultures, ages and backgrounds (WHO, 2005). However, abuse is more prevalent in countries where gender inequality is more pronounced (Archer, 2006). Within the UK, individuals with a limiting illness or disability are at higher risk of becoming victims of DV (Finney, 2006). Children within DV households are also victims of DV. Most are aware of the abuse and many directly witness it. Children may be physically harmed either as part of a wider pattern of abuse, or when they trying to protect their parent (Hester et al., 2007).

Cost of crime

Most of the research on the consequence on DV has been on female victims – in part because of the prevalence of serious health outcomes. Worldwide, between

40 and 70% of female murder victims are killed by their current or former partner (WHO, 2002), and DV is the leading cause of non-fatal injuries to women in the USA (WHO, 2009). Physical effects (chronic pain, deafness, reduced physical functioning) and sexual and reproductive difficulties (unwanted pregnancy, sexually transmitted disease, infertility) are common within DV victims (Campbell, 2002). The impact of DV on children is also significant. Children who grow up in DV households are at greater risk of adjustment difficulties (including overprotectiveness of parent and siblings, poor school performance) and psychological concerns (depression, eating disorders, self-harm) (Hester et al., 2007).

Fear of crime, changes in attitudes and behaviours

Laroche (2005) found within a large community sample that over 75% of the male and female victims who experienced the most severe forms of abuse feared for their lives. Golding's (1999) meta-analysis found that rates of depression, suicidality and alcohol/drug use and dependence were higher in samples of battered women than in the general population. Rates of post-traumatic stress disorder (PTSD) were greater in DV populations than within samples of women who had experienced childhood abuse.

PART B: Theories and explanations

B3.1. Introduction

Despite the widespread prevalence of DV, this area of study has only relatively recently been the subject of scientific investigation. The field is still rapidly expanding and subject to much controversy. For example, there is much debate about the extent to which individual factors (such as, alcohol use, experience of abuse), as opposed to wider issues (e.g. societal structures), are relevant in explaining DV. However, perhaps the biggest controversy is whether DV should be considered a crime that has particular meaning when perpetrated by men against women or if the focus should be on the act and not the gender of the perpetrator. The arguments put forward by advocates on both sides are briefly summarised in the key debate below. For a fuller discussion and for some sense of the strength of feeling surrounding this debate, see Section C3.2.

> **KEY DEBATE: Is DV gender-specific or gender-neutral?**
>
> *The case that DV is gender-specific*
> This case is based on the premise that relationship violence against men is not the same (in nature or degree) as violence against women (Gondolf, 2002). For example, many studies show women experience higher rates of all forms of DV

(sexual, emotional, physical) and are more likely to suffer a physical or psycho-logical injury or need to take time off work as a result of the abuse (Walby and Allen, 2004; Laroche, 2005). Police, court and emergency room data consistently identify greater numbers of women than men needing agency support as a result of DV (Johnson, 2008), and women are more likely to be the victims of domestic homicide (Coleman and Osbourne, 2010). It is argued that when men are violent this is often part of a systematic pattern of abusive behaviour that leads to women feeling terrorised and trapped in the relationship, but when women are violent this is generally in self-defence or in a different form than male-perpetrated violence, because 'while many couples may have an exchange of slaps or minor blows at some time, and this is unfortunate and regrettable, this does not nec-essarily constitute a pattern of systematic and sustained abuse meant to harm, intimidate, terrorise, and brutalise', with the latter predominantly experienced by women (Dobash et al., 2000, p. 4). The gender-specific theorists argue that this systematic pattern of abuse is 'rooted in historic and enduring inequity' (Reed et al., 2010).

The case that DV is gender-neutral
This case is based upon the premise that any violence within relationships is a cause for concern. Furthermore, it is argued that female-perpetrated violence is not as asymmetrical as the gender-specific theorists propose. For example, in community samples women report slightly more use of physical aggression within relationships than men (Archer, 2002). And, while male victims of DV are less likely to call the police or seek help for the abuse that they suffer (e.g. Walby, 2004; Laroche, 2005), they can suffer serious injuries and can feel controlled and fearful as a result of partner abuse (Laroche, 2005). A review of the literature on female-perpetrated DV by gender-neutral researchers came to the following conclusions: '(1) women are injured more than men but (2) men are injured as well and are not immune to being seriously injured. Simply because the injury rates are lower, men should not be denied protection' (Carney, Buttel and Dutton, 2007, p. 110).

B3.2. Radical feminism

The early DV researchers were part of the women's movement which highlighted the need to consider abuse within the family as a serious public health issue. They concluded that the widespread prevalence of abuse towards women (and the failure to consider this as a serious problem) was because social structures, specifically patriarchy, supported, justified and, in some cases encouraged, DV.

Patriarchy is a socio-political system in which being male is associated with being of higher status and 'in charge'. Accordingly, male violence can be jus-tified, and in some cases necessary, in order to maintain good order (especially within the family). There is much historical support for this interpretation; many religious texts refer to a man's duty to discipline his wife (Dobash and Dobash, 1978). While in Western Society such views may no longer be openly expressed, radical feminism suggests that men are exposed to a number of subtle messages that they have special status (see Box 3.3).

Box 3.3. Patriarchy and male privilege in action?

How often do we hear references to the 'head of the household' applying to women or girls?

The UK royal family (and many others) has a male line of succession. The crown is not passed down through birth order; males take precedence over females.

It is more common for women to change their names upon marriage than men. Few husbands adopt their wives' names.

It was only in 1991 that marital rape became illegal in England and Wales. Prior to this there was a legal assumption that upon marriage the wife had 'consented' to sex within the relationship.

DOMESTIC ABUSE INTERVENTION PROJECT

202 East Superior Street
Duluth, Minnesota 55802
218-722-2781
www.duluth-model.org

Figure 3.4 *The power and control wheel (reproduced with permission)*
Source: Domestic Abuse Intervention Programme.

Therefore, the radical feminist interpretation of DV (and many other forms of violence) is that within the home a man is violent not because he loses control but is using violence in an attempt to gain control of his partner and family (Reed et al., 2010). This interpretation is supported by the results of interviews with women in DV shelters that led to the development of the Power and Control Wheel (Pence and Paymar, 1993 – see Figure 3.4). At the hub of the wheel is the notion of dominance, and this desire underpins the abusive behaviours. Sexual and psychological violence act as the rim of the wheel – these may only be occasionally used because a range of other behaviours allow the perpetrator to have control within the relationship. This conceptualisation of DV remains hugely influential and determines much work conducted with DV perpetrators in the USA and UK (see Part A). Interventions that stem from this model are often referred to as the Duluth interventions, after the US town where this research was first conducted (see text Box 3.4).

Box 3.4. Interventions – The Duluth model

Because wider attitudinal patterns and social norms are believed to affect men's views of relationships, a range of community, legal and agency approaches are required.

Psycho-educational programmes that hold men who are abusive accountable for their behaviour, and explain the role of power and control within abuse are essential for perpetrators.

Community education that emphasises that DV is not acceptable. Women's Aid 'Real Men' and 'Act' campaigns are examples of this intervention strategy within the UK (see Figure 3.5).

Figure 3.5 *Examples of community education programmes (© Refuge, Don't Ignore Domestic Violence campaign, www.refuge.org.uk).*

Mandatory arrest: The criminal justice system response is vital in enforcing messages about the unacceptability of violence in the home. Therefore the assumption of mandatory arrest is supported; when the police become aware of abuse within the home the suspected perpetrator should be arrested without the need for the victim to press charges (thus avoiding some of the issues).

Evidence to support the role of patriarchy within the aetiology of DV has emerged. For example, countries that have more gender inequality have higher rates of DV (Archer, 2006). Adinkrah (1999) found that Fijian communities with higher patriarchal systems had greater rates of all levels of DV, including domestic homicide, than those Fijian communities with less patriarchal structures (thus suggesting this model also applies at the community level). Finally, Stith et al.'s (2004) meta-analysis identified traditional sex role ideology (a measurement of the extent to which individuals tend to accept patriarchal views of men and women) as predictive of physical DV.

However Stith et al.'s (2004) analysis also identified a range of predictors including those that did not reflect patriarchal factors (such as depression, career or life stress). Even in countries that have very high gender inequality and patriarchal views, not all women are abused (Archer, 2006). And not all offenders present the same level of risk (e.g., not all DV offenders present a lethal risk [Campbell, 2007]). Taken as a whole, the data suggest that while highly patriarchal views contribute to DV, other factors may also be relevant. Furthermore, as the radical feminist model does not attempt to explain the use of violence by females within relationships (other than when it is used in self-defence), or violence within homosexual relationships, it does not explain all aspects of DV.

B3.3. Family violence models

Researchers in this field focus on the characteristics (including prevalence and frequency) and causes of violence within the family as a whole (Gilfus et al., 2010). Violence between partners is conceptualised as part of a continuum of conflict resolution strategies used to resolve arguments or disputes within the family. The poor conflict resolution skills that underpin abuse can also be reflected in wider issues of abuse within the home (such as child or elder abuse). Violence may occur more frequently with the home because of the complex dynamics and pressures within families (e.g. poverty, stress); however, individuals with the propensity to use inappropriate conflict resolution methods may also demonstrate this tendency outside of the home.

Support for this conceptualisation comes from *longitudinal studies*. For example, Connolly et al. (2000) found that childhood bullies were likely to be aggressive within dating relationships. Serbin et al. (2004) reported that women who were aggressive as children are likely to be hostile to their own children. Moffit, Robbins and Caspi (2001) found that the strongest risk factor for male and female perpetration of partner abuse (PA) was a history of violent delinquent behaviour. Because DV is therefore believed to reflect more general patterns of poor conflict resolution, a wide range of intervention strategies – which can apply to various members of the family – are suggested (see Box 3.5).

Box 3.5. Interventions – The family violence model

Interventions suggested by this model address underlying risk factors for aggressive conflict resolution and wider family problems as well as partner abuse.

Family interventions: Through the adoption of the family systems approach (where the wider pattern of family dynamics is considered) child abuse, as well as parental aggression towards each other, can be addressed.

Couples therapy: Whereas the feminist model explicitly rejects the use of joint marital therapy (given the inherent power balance), this theory proposes that (following rigorous screening) such interventions may prove useful in helping couples to explore the issues that have led to the violence.

Gender-neutral support: Family violence theorists firmly believe that support should be available for all victims of partner abuse (see Figure 3.6).

Figure 3.6 *Example of gender-neutral support (reproduced with permission)*

Preventative work: As individuals who are at high risk of behaving violently with the family can be identified by risk markers, support programmes can be designed to prevent violence – for example, group therapy programmes for at-risk mothers.

Source: Hamel and Nicholls (2006).

The family violence approach has contributed much to our understanding of patterns of abuse (by both genders) within a range of family relationships (including same-sex couples). However, this model does not account so well for those individuals who abuse for reasons other than for conflict resolution. It does not account for the high rates of partner violence within those countries with higher gender inequality and does not account for why many more women than men are killed by their partners even in countries where weapons such as guns are relatively easily available (Brookman and Maguire, 2003). Feminist researchers argue that this is because the measures of PA that family violence researchers commonly use (see Box 3.6) are not truly tapping into the controlling behaviours associated with the most serious forms of DV (e.g. domestic homicide) (Campbell, 2007).

Box 3.6. The conflict tactics scale

Asking individuals whether they have experienced domestic violence often results in under-reporting. Therefore many studies use the conflict tactics scale – CTS (Straus, 1979, later revised as the CTS2, Straus et al., 1996) to identify abuse within relationships. This self-report questionnaire asks respondents about the extent to which they have engaged in, or been the victim of, specific conflict resolution behaviours, allowing for objective comparisons across studies to be made.

Physical violence	Psychological aggression	Sexual coercion
Threw something that could hurt	Shouted	Made my partner have sex without a condom
Twisted arm or hair	Said something to spite	Insisted my partner have oral or anal sex (but did not use force)
Choked	Destroyed partner's belongings	Used force to make my partner have oral or anal sex

The CTS has, however, been widely criticised by feminist researchers. It has been suggested that it is unhelpful in assessing the patterns and meanings of the abuse – for example, that it does not explore the behaviours noted in the power and control wheel (Figure 3.4) and the emotional impact these have upon the victim (Johnson, 2008).

B3.4. Typology approaches

There is a considerable psychological literature base to suggest that DV offenders are heterogeneous and have distinct behavioural patterns, treatment needs and risk factors. For example, Gilchrist et al. (2003) investigated the criminogenic needs of over 300 convicted male offenders attending DV courses in the community. From victim reports they were able to identify particular types of abuse behaviours associated with different psychological tendencies (See Table 3.1)

Johnson (2008) suggested that exploring individual patterns of abuse may be helpful in resolving the questions over the DV gender debate. For example, women in shelters (the clinical samples that inform much of the work of the radical feminist movement) may be experiencing a different pattern of abuse from that which men and women in community samples describe (which features in the work of family violence researchers). Based on a re-analysis of predominantly North American data, he proposed three main patterns of abusive behaviour – each associated with different risk factors and gender distributions.

Intimate terrorism (IT) is associated with the controlling behaviours noted in the power and control cycle (Figure 3.4). This abuse is often chronic, severe, extensive and extremely damaging for the victim. While this form of violence can be perpetrated against men by women, Johnson concludes that this is overwhelmingly a form of violence suffered by women at the hands of men. When these women defend themselves with violence this is termed *violent resistance*.

However, not all violence by women falls within this category. Johnson proposed that the most common form of violence within relationships (and one that is frequently identified within survey samples using the CTS) is *situational couple violence (SVC)*. This is characterised by an absence of coercive control, and reflects a tendency for couples to use violence as a conflict resolution strategy. Situational triggers would be important in identifying risk factors for this violence, so issues such as poor communication skills and drinking would be important to consider. In contrast, situational factors would be largely irrelevant in Intimate

Table 3.1 *Types of behaviour reported by partners of offenders*

Abuse type	Antisocial perpetrators	Emotionally volatile perpetrators
Emotional abuse	Very emotionally abusive	Only at time of assault
Male privilege	Expects gratitude – does not do much about the house	Takes an active role in the home if for his own reasons – e.g. shopping to prevent her leaving the house
Intimidation	Smashes property, uses children or looks to create fear	Limited use of intimidation
Economic abuse	Limited desire to have control over money	Very controlling about money

Source: Gilchrist et al. (2003).

Terrorism (IT) to avoid confusion abuse as this reflects entrenched inappropriate attitudes.

There is general support for these different patterns of abusive behaviour (Laroche, 2005). However, this model remains a descriptive typology, and as such does not fully explain why some individuals become abusive and others do not. Furthermore, the gender distribution of abusers has not been entirely supported (Ross and Babock, 2009). For example, Laroche (2005) found a number of female intimate terrorism (IT) abusers within his community study. Finally, gender equality rates differ between the UK and USA and therefore, while the patterns of behaviour described by the Johnson typology may be applicable to the UK, the gender distribution may not (thus suggesting limits to the generalisability of this model). However, the Johnson typology is widely cited within the DV literature, as is that of Amy Holtzworth-Munroe. Her typology, based on theoretical constructs and later supported by empirical validation (Holtzworth-Munroe and Stuart, 1994) suggests that male DV offenders can be differentiated on three dimensions: (1) generality of violent behaviour; (2) severity of violence; and (3) psychopathology. Combining these three elements three distinct clusters of DV offenders emerge.

Generally antisocial violent offenders have a generalised history of abuse and commit offences inside and outside of the home. They tend to have experienced family-of-origin violence and have learnt to use violence as a general conflict resolution method. The violence they inflict upon their partners tends to be of moderate to severe levels. Such individuals are likely to show evidence of antisocial personality disorder.

Family-only offenders do not have a history of violence or criminality outside of the home. They commit the least serious forms of partner violence and demonstrate little or no psychopathology (e.g. no history of substance abuse or childhood trauma).

Borderline/dysphoric offenders demonstrate the highest levels of psychopathology (e.g. history of depression, substance misuse). They are emotionally volatile and tend to be jealous of, and highly dependent upon, their partners (see Section A4.7). They tend to engage in moderate to severe levels of violence within the home but show no generality of violence. Some authors suggest these DV offenders require distinct assessment and treatment that considers the causes and consequences of their personally style (Dutton, 2007b).

B3.5. Personality disorders and traits

Generally DV offenders do not have personality disorders (i.e. chronically dysfunctional behaviours, cognitions or emotions). Even many of the borderline/dysphoric offenders described above do not warrant a clinical diagnosis of *borderline personality disorder*. However, their behaviour does reflect some of the characteristics of this disorder, such as poor emotional control and changeable behaviour (Dutton, 2007a). While their erratic moods may be detected by others, such as work colleagues, their emotional difficulties are largely contained within intimate relationships and this is where they demonstrate violence. Such individuals react badly to fears over abandonment and may be constantly seeking to check on their partners (see Chapter 13 on stalking). Their abusive behaviour may appear cyclical in nature see Section B3.6; they are intermittently but chronically abusive (Dutton, 2007a).

The source of the interpersonal and emotional difficulties within these offenders is believed to stem from background experiences. Such individuals have often experienced rejection, alienation and sometimes trauma as children (Holtzworth-Munroe and Stuart, 1994; Dutton, 2007b). A growing body of work has suggested that such early experiences can result in the development of neurological pathways which predispose individuals to act in a fearful or panicked manner when exposed to threat of rejection by significant others. When this emotional reaction is combined with acceptance of violence as a means of problem solving, aggression or abuse may be the result (Mitchell and Gilchrist, 2006). These findings have significant implications for treatment. For example, in addition to enabling individuals to be aware of their patterns of behaviour and learning alternative conflict resolution skills, this model proposes that attention should also be paid to the trauma symptoms and the resultant emotional regulation problems that such individuals have (Dutton, 2008).

While this theory may offer an explanation for some DV, it is not comprehensive. Many individuals who commit DV show no signs of dysphoric behaviour. Many individuals who have dysphoric traits and problematic adult relationships do not become domestic abusers. Finally, although borderline personality disorder is diagnosed at much higher rates in women than men, lethal assault in response to a partner threatening to leave is a pattern overwhelmingly seen in men and not women (Brookman and Maguire, 2003). Thus, while it appears that in some individuals dysphoric traits contribute to DV propensity, other aspects such as attitudes play a key role.

B3.6. Walker's cycle of abuse

Leonore Walker (1979) described how abuse may be experienced as cyclical in nature. In the *tension-building phase* the perpetrator is moody and looking to find faults. They may be drinking heavily or using drugs. They are verbally abusive towards their partner who may feel like they are 'walking on eggs'. The tension ends with the commencement of the *battering phase*. During this time the victim may suffer physical and sexual abuse, and in response may leave.

Following this the perpetrator may appear to show genuine *contrition*; they apologise, cry, send flowers and buy gifts. They beg forgiveness and offer to attend treatment (such as Alcoholics Anonymous (AA) or counselling). Frequently, the victims feel hopeful and return to the relationship, or stop legal proceedings. However, eventually tensions emerge and the cycle of abuse starts again.

While this pattern of abuse may not apply to all DV incidents, or may not be stable over time, Walker's work was a key study in helping us explore the behaviours of both abusers and victims within violent relationships.

B3.7. Nested ecological model

All of the theories outlined above have contributed to our understanding of DV. The early feminist theories identified the role of attitudes at both societal and community level and highlighted that DV can reflect a systematic pattern of abuse designed to control family members. Family violence researchers have identified that DV is often associated with other inappropriate conflict resolution strategies, and that individuals potentially at risk of committing family abuse can be identified at an early state. The typology research reminds us that not all forms of DV are the same and suggests that different risk factors may be associated with different forms of abuse. Personality and neurobiology work has identified one mechanism by which childhood experiences may result in DV in some offenders. However, none of these theories offer a complete explanation; none of them identify why some people become abusive and others do not; none of them can account for all the variances associated with this phenomenon and many of them offer competing as opposed to integrated theoretical perspectives.

One model that has attempted to integrate a range of different variables associated with DV is the nested ecological model (see Table 3.2). This model suggests that individuals can be exposed to risk factors that operate at societal,

Table 3.2 *The nested ecological model*

Individual level	Situational level	Social structure level	Societal level
Witnessing marital violence as a child	Male dominance within the family	Unemployment/ low socio-economic status	Notion of masculinity linked to dominance, toughness and honour
Being abused as a child	Male control of wealth within the family	Isolation of the woman and the family	Rigid gender roles
Absent or rejecting father	Marital conflict	Delinquent peer associations	Sense of male entitlement/ownership over women
–	Use of alcohol	–	Approval of physical chastisement of women
–	–	–	Cultural ethos that condones violence as a means of solving interpersonal difficulties

Source: Heise (1998).

community (social structure), situational and individual levels. The number and extent of risk factor exposure suggests different abuse potential. For example, an individual could live in a society that condones violence, engenders a sense of ownership over women and has rigid gender roles. If, however, this individual is not exposed to social or situational factors that support abuse they may not engage in DV.

This model suggests that interventions are required at multiple levels (in keeping with the Duluth model) but that individual psychopathology is also vital to consider (in keeping with neurological research). Different patterns of risk factors may result in different abuse patterns (thereby allowing the typology work to be considered).

However, while promising, this model does not yet represent a comprehensive explanation of DV. It summarises the range of factors that have been correlated with increased rates of DV but does not clarify the direction of the relationships. For example, unemployment may create stress within relationships, which increases the risk of poor conflict resolution (and DV), or generally poor interpersonal skills (including conflict resolution and stress management) may have contributed to the employment problems. It has not yet been sufficiently developed to offer a holistic theoretical explanation of how the various factors identified combine to produce risk of DV at the individual level. The considerable body of evidence that suggests that typologies of abusive behaviour exist has not been fully incorporated into this model – for example, there are no suggestions as to how different risk factors may combine to produce different offence pathways. Finally, this model has been proposed to explain only male-perpetrated DV.

B3.8. Final words

In general, theoretical explanations of DV are less developed than for other forms of offending and still have some way to go before they could be considered comprehensive explanations. For example, Ehrensaft (2008) has criticised current DV theories because many of them do not consider the crossover with other forms of family abuse (such as child abuse, stalking and sexual abuse). Wider patterns of criminal behaviour are also overlooked – many DV offenders share criminogenic needs with other types of offender. Antisocial personality disorder is regularly reported within DV samples, yet none of the current theories address the role of this beyond descriptive levels. Single-factor theories that have been found to be largely unsatisfactory explanations of other forms of offence behaviour still dominate the DV field. Set against this background it is therefore not surprising that currently DV interventions are largely unsatisfactory and recidivism for DV remains high. Future directions could usefully look to integrate models that have been used to explain related forms of offending (murder, child sex offences, rape, stalking and violent crime) so as to assist with both risk assessment and treatment strategies.

PART C: Further information

C3.1. Organisations to contact for information and voluntary work

Women's aid: Support for women experiencing domestic abuse (www.womensaid. org.uk/).

Refuge: Support for women and children experiencing domestic abuse (www. refuge.org.uk/); Refuge and Woman's Aid National Domestic Violence Helpline, 0808 2000 247 (24-hour helpline).

Scottish Women's Aid: http://www.scottishwomensaid.org.uk/ 0800 027 1234 (24-hour helpline).

Broken Rainbow: Support for lesbian, gay, bisexual and transgender people experiencing domestic violence (www.broken-rainbow.org.uk/ 03009995428) (not 24 hours).

Mankind Support for Male Victims of Domestic Abuse and Domestic Violence: (http://www.mankind.org.uk/); National helpline 01823 334244 (not 24 hours).

C3.2. Further reading

www.duluthmodel.org: This is the website of the Domestic Abuse Intervention Programme. The information is clearly presented but does reflect the feminist philosophy underlying the programme.

Sex Roles (2010) Volume X, Issue 62: This issue contains a number of papers presenting alterative perspectives on the gendered nature of DV. It includes contributions from a number of leading DV researchers, including Johnson.

Dixon L. and Browne, K. (2003). The heterogeneity of spouse abuse: A review. *Aggression and Violent Behavior*, 8, 107–30: This literature review summarises research studies that have explored male-perpetrator typologies, identifying similarities and differences among the different themes that have been detected.

Home page for Professor Murray A. Strauss (http://pubpages.unh.edu/~mas2/): Professor Strauss is a leading family violence researcher. He has written extensively about partner and other forms of family violence, and a large number of papers are available to download from his website. He strongly believes that DV is a gender-neutral offence and hence writes from this perspective.

Notes

1. For example, prior to the Domestic Violence, Crime and Victims Act (2004) police could not automatically arrest individuals for breaching a 'non-molestation order' (a court order designed to protect victims from harassment); there were also limits on arresting individuals who had committed common assault if they had left the scene (Ward and Bird, 2005).

chapter

4 DRUG OFFENCES

GILLIAN W. SMITH AND JOANNE CLOUGH

PART A: The offence – Who, what, when, why?

A4.1. Introduction

Drug offences tend to fall into three main categories: drug-defined offences, drug-related offences and drug-related lifestyle offences. Drug-defined offences relate to criminal activity regarding possession, use, distribution or manufacture of drugs. Drug-related offences broadly encompass those arising either from pharmacological effects of drugs (e.g. interpersonal violence) or those committed to support the use of illicit drugs such as theft. Drug-related lifestyle offences relate to participation in an illegal economy, or arise from the exposure to criminal networks and involve racketeering, tax evasion, violence over hierarchy, territory, punishment or debt collection. They may occur within the prison system or in the community.

This chapter deals primarily with issues from the UK where the primary law governing drug-defined offences is the Misuse of Drugs Act 1971. Drugs regulated under the Act are usually referred to as 'controlled drugs'. These are categorised into three classes dependent on their perceived harmfulness to the user and society, although the classifications have raised controversy (Nutt et al., 2007). Class A controlled drugs include those considered most harmful including heroin, cocaine, crack, ecstasy and LSD. Class B drugs include amphetamines, barbiturates and cannabis, with Class C including tranquillisers and mild stimulants. Whilst the relationship between drugs and crime is difficult to categorise, this chapter aims to break down some common misconceptions and outline a number of the key issues prevailing within the criminal justice system (CJS) in the UK today.

A4.2. Definitions

Possession: Possession is difficult to define legally. Someone may be considered to have possession if they have something in their custody or under their control and have knowledge of both the nature of the substance (i.e. that it is an illegal drug of some kind) and the knowledge it is in their custody or control.

Supply: Supply requires passing substances from one person to another, and it does not require any form of commercial benefit such as payment or reward. Note that where a controlled drug is handed to a person with the intention that the custodian will return it to the person who had deposited it, then the custodian has intent to supply. The depositor would also be guilty of supply.

Drug rehabilitation requirement: This is one of the requirements that can be imposed as part of a community order or suspended sentence order. It is designed to provide the offender with drug treatment should the offence be considered motivated by drug use, with the aim to reduce further offending.

Controlled drug: Any substance or product specified in Part I, II and III of Schedule 2 to the Misuse of Drugs Act 1971. Drugs are 'controlled' in that their use and distribution is regulated so as to prevent, eliminate or minimise harmful effects of their use. The Secretary of State is vested with wide powers under statute to make such regulations as are necessary from time to time and, most recently, used powers to make the substance mephedrone and other similar drugs illegal.

A4.3. Who?

Psychopathology

Drug-defined offences are not typically considered to be pathological; however, motivations behind some drug offences may be perceived as part of an addiction spectrum. Typically, this may involve either drug abuse or drug dependence. Drug abuse is considered to reflect drug use in the context of significant impairment or distress. It is characterised by one or more of the following symptoms: failure to meet role obligations, repeated use in hazardous situations (e.g. driving), repeated legal problems arising from use or continuing to use despite recurring social or personal problems.

A definition of drug dependence requires three criteria from the following list in a 12-month period. These symptoms include needing more drugs to have the desired effect; withdrawal symptoms when drug use ceases; consumption of greater amounts or over a longer period of time than desired, a desire to cut down (or unsuccessful attempts to do so); spending too much time acquiring, using or recovering from use; reducing important activities due to use; or continuing to use despite health problems caused by use. However, not all drug use relating to offences may be considered an 'addiction' and not all of those who have either drug abuse or dependence commit crimes to support their addiction. This is explored later in Part B.

Mental health and trauma

It is difficult to disaggregate drug use, mental health, trauma and criminal behaviour to explore the links. However, drug use and drug use disorders such as abuse or dependence are known to co-occur with other mental health problems. In a US population sample, Grant et al. (2004) found 48% of those with a drug use disorder had a co-morbid personality disorder such as antisocial, histrionic or dependent types. Personality disorders are also considered to be associated with criminal behaviour (see Hammersley, 2008 for a more thorough explanation); however, the presence of drug use, of crime and/or of mental health disorders does not imply causation. Traumatic experience (particularly in childhood) may affect personal adjustment and psychological development, and increase the like-lihood of substance use and crime; however, again, it is not a simple causal relationship between these factors. McMurran (2008) notes that the interactions between substance use, mental health and offending may reduce effectiveness of treatments or rehabilitation strategies. Individuals with complex needs should therefore be identified and appropriate treatment given.

Individual differences

There are some similarities in the personality traits associated with substance use and offending. Extraversion and sensation-seeking are said to relate to drug use or disorders (Sher, Bartholow and Wood, 2000) and offending (Knust and Stewart, 2002). There is also some evidence to link traits like nervousness, neuroticism, disagreeableness and impulsivity with drugs and crime (Hammersley, 2008; Samuels et al., 2004). Gudjonsson and Sigurdsson (2004) note the role of excitement in the motivation to commit drug-defined offences, but state it was less likely that drug-defined offences were committed in response to peer demands.

A4.4. Misconceptions

Racial misconceptions

Home Office (2006) data on race in the CJS indicated that those of Black ethnic origin were considerably more likely to be stopped and searched than other ethnic groups under the Police and Criminal Evidence Act 1984 (PACE). Note the most common reason to be stopped under PACE is for suspected drug activity. Offenders of Black ethnic origin sentenced at Crown Court for both drug and drug-related offences were also more likely to get an immediate custodial sentence than other ethnic groups. In mid-2005, black and minority ethnic (BME) groups accounted for 24% of the male prison population (disproportionate to their numbers in the general population).

A range of studies have found variation within the CJS in patterns of drug use amongst ethnic groups. For example, an Arrestee Survey (Boreham et al., 2006) showed that arrestees who had taken heroin, crack or cocaine (the drugs tested for in the Drug Interventions Programme (DIP)) within the previous 12 months were more likely to be White and less likely to be Black or Asian than other arrestees. Surveys among prisoners show the prevalence of drug dependence prior to imprisonment to be higher among White prisoners than BME groups. Note that BME groups are not homogenous; however, the size of groups in most studies can be too small to analyse them separately. There is a need to better understand how drug activity, drug offences and drug use relate to ethnicity, and in particular the role of race in raising suspicion and creating reasonable grounds for searches.

There are no drugs in prison

Drugs get into the prison environment by five main routes: from being thrown over the prison fence, by post or brought in by visitors, prisoners or staff. A recent report by the Ministry of Justice (2008b) noted that disruption of one of the routes can raise the use of others. Smuggling drugs into prisons can involve considerable resourcefulness. Some means for smuggling include the concealing drugs on the person, sewing drugs into the lining of clothes to be sent to prisoners for court appearances, and throwing concealed drugs over the walls of prisons (e.g., in mobile telephones, dead pigeons, tennis balls or even encased in ice).

A4.5. Facts and figures

Prevalence rates

There are a number of primary sources of official statistics in the UK on drug offences, including the British Crime Survey and the Police Recorded Crime Statistics. This section will provide estimates of the prevalence of drug-defined, drug-related and drug-related lifestyle offences using data collected in the period 2009/10 from these sources (Flatley et al., 2010).

In 2009/2010, police in England and Wales recorded 38,262 incidents of possession of controlled drugs, excluding cannabis. Figures for cannabis possession were considerably higher, forming a substantial percentage of all drug-defined offences in the year at 162,610. Trafficking in controlled drugs increased in 2009/10 from the previous year, with 33,009 recorded incidents in this period. Overall, the figures suggested there were 234,998 drug-defined offences recorded in the year 2009/10.

Regarding drug-related offences, one in five violent incidents reported in the year 2009/10 were perceived by the victim to be committed by an offender under the influence of drugs. In all, this accounted for approximately 396,000 offences. Note that these were based on opinion and are not objectively verified (e.g. through drug testing). Other alcohol- or drug-related offences included 35 cases of death by dangerous driving where the offender was on alcohol or drugs. The British Crime Survey asked the perceptions of the public on the role of drugs in criminal activity. Drugs were considered to be the primary reason for crime by 26% of the sample, but considered by 69% of the sample to be one of a number of reasons for crime.

Statistics on drug-related lifestyle offences are difficult to obtain. However, statistics for 2009/10 suggested that 26% of those surveyed believed that drug use or drug dealing were problematic characteristics of their neighbourhood.

Crime statistics relating to drug use should always be interpreted with caution. Proactive policing and changes in detection strategies can affect statistics. For example, changed priorities may reflect a higher vigilance of drugs as relating to criminal behaviour. Additionally, many more drug offences do not come to the attention of the police; this is particularly evident in recreational drug users, who may pass drugs amongst friends. This would still be considered distribution, but is unlikely to be high on the policing agenda. As noted later, offences may also remain undetected in the absence of suspicion.

A4.6. How are offenders caught?

Detections and prosecutions relating to Class A drugs are a high priority for the police, as it is seen to be a strong cause of societal problems and other crime (South, 2007). Different methods exist to detect and investigate those in possession of controlled drugs compared with those who supply.

Detection

Detection depends to a large extent upon the behaviour of the drug offender. Suspicious behaviour by a drug offender noticed by a police officer or other person may lead to detection. For example, those involved in an acquisitive crime may be searched upon arrest and any substances found seized as evidence. In these circumstances, the police are often less interested in prosecuting for the drugs offence than the acquisitive offence for which the person was originally arrested. Instead, the drugs will be an indication of the motivation behind the offending and may play a role in sentencing.

Behaviour of recreational drug users may display body language indicative of drug consumption and this may be considered 'reasonable grounds' necessary to warrant a search. Under section 23 of the Misuse of Drugs Act 1971, police officers have the power to search any person who they suspect to be in possession of a controlled substance and detain the person for the purposes of a search. The police also have the power to stop and search a vehicle or vessel for the same purpose. A driver under the influence of a controlled substance, or someone who is carrying a controlled substance in their vehicle is not immune from being searched. Evidence perceived to relate to a drug offence found during a search under the Act can be seized, to assist the police in making a case against the offender.

It is an offence for an owner or manager of premises to permit production or supply of controlled substances to take place on those premises. Where the police have suspicion that premises are being used for such a purpose, they can apply to the local Magistrates' Court for a warrant to enter and search (by force if necessary) those premises under the Misuse of Drugs Act 1971. Anyone found within the premises can also be searched at the same time. Once again, suspicious activity raises awareness of potential drug-related offending, and police rely on surveillance and intelligence information to detect offenders.

In the prison environment, the watchful eye of the prison guards and those who control the closed-circuit security systems (CCTV) within the visitation areas will be important in detecting visitors who supply controlled drugs. Prisons have systems in place to detect visitors supplying drugs, such as the use of security scanners, pat-down searches of all visitors, fully trained drugs dogs (sniffer dogs) and requirements for visitors to leave all property behind before entering the visitors' area.

To detect the most serious drug offences, including drug-related lifestyle crime, most police forces have dedicated drug enforcement units. Specialist agencies also exist in order to detect high-level supply and manufacture. The Serious Organised Crime Agency (SOCA), established in 2006, primarily aims to reduce harm caused by serious organised crime. They rely predominantly on intelligence in order to detect those involved in serious drug offences. Such surveillance need not be confined purely to obvious drug-related activities. Frequent cash transfers for large amounts between the UK and countries linked to drug production raise suspicion. Police can also conduct undercover operations; an officer might pose as a user to catch dealers in the act of supplying drugs, or they may befriend dealers to gain personal access to their activities and contacts.

Investigation

The investigation process for those in possession of personal amounts of controlled drugs is straightforward, as offenders will usually have a small amount of the illegal drug on their person, in their home or in their vehicle. Investigations for street-level dealing or drug trafficking are more complex. Police will build a portfolio of evidence against the offender; this may comprise evidence from searches of the offender's home and vehicles, surveillance of their day-to-day pursuits or monitoring of financial activity. Police are now able to work with other agencies such as Revenue and Customs in order to monitor offenders' spending habits, on the assumption that those spending more money than declared as legal earnings may well be involved in criminal (possibly drug-related) activity. At the start of a financial investigation (which usually runs alongside the criminal investigation), the investigating authority can request an asset-freezing order under the Proceeds of Crime Act 2002, to prevent the suspect from disappearing out of the country. Monitoring orders (under the same legislation) can also be granted in order to trace transactions. SOCA have the power to work with national and international agencies (such as Interpol) in order to investigate large-scale drug crime, but these investigations can take a number of years to complete.

Conviction

Common to all drug-related prosecutions is the requirement to prove that the substance which is the subject of the charge is a controlled drug, and expert testimony will usually be required. Such evidence will usually consist of an opinion on the street value of the drugs seized and purity of the substance (Archbold, 2010). Where the case involves a larger amount of controlled substance, the prosecution will usually suggest this is indicative of intent to supply the substance rather than possession.

For those charged with supply offences (including possession with intent to supply), the prosecution will rely upon other circumstantial evidence such as large amounts of cash (see Box 4.1 for what may become of the cash recovered) or evidence of an extravagant lifestyle. The seizure of items from a suspected dealer's property may also assist the prosecution case, such as electronic scales (used to weigh the drug for deals), mixing agents, rolls of cling film, lists of names and telephone numbers (a dealer's list of customers) or unregistered pay-as-you-go mobile phones (quite often a dealer will have multiple unregistered phones to avoid being traced). Telephone triangulation can be useful in linking a particular mobile phone seized from the suspected dealer's property to the location of a known drug deal, but the prosecution would have to prove that the suspect before them was responsible for making the calls.

Box 4.1. Community cashback

Community cashback is a recent scheme where £4 million from the proceeds of crime are fed back into community improvement initiatives. Funding can be sought by community groups to reduce criminal activity or antisocial behaviour in one or more neighbourhoods and must have a demonstrable value for money and community impact. Some of these can be particularly tailored to drug-related initiatives; for example, in Humberside 'The roundabout' provides street-based advice and support for alcohol and drug users by former users or offenders.

For more information, see http://www.direct.gov.uk/en/Nl1/Newsroom/DG_178917

Convictions for all levels of drug offences can also rely on eye witness testimony. As high-level drug dealers can be involved in gang culture and are capable of serious violence, witnesses in the most serious drug cases can be fearful of assisting in the prosecution of these offenders. Measures are available to protect these witnesses as it may be crucial to securing a conviction.

Conviction rates

According to the Ministry of Justice, 229,000 drug offenders were either convicted or cautioned (which requires the offender to admit guilt in police interview) in 2007–8 and this accounted for 16% of all offences brought to justice in the same ways that year (Ministry of Justice, 2008a). Of these drug-defined offences brought to justice, 45% were warnings for cannabis use, a tool used frequently following the 2004 declassification from Class B to Class C as an alternative to starting court proceedings. The number of offenders cautioned or convicted of drug offences in 2007–8 demonstrated a 14% increase from the previous year, although it is unclear whether this was due to better detection rates, more offences or better conviction rates.

A4.7. What happens to offenders?

Information on sentencing

In possession or supply offences, sentencing will depend on two main factors: the class and amount of substance involved. Generally, the higher the class of substance and the greater the amount, the more punitive the sentence will be. Where the drug-defined offence occurs within prison, whether simple possession by a prisoner, or supply/intent to supply by another, this is likely to result in sanctions (Archbold, 2010).

The maximum period of imprisonment for offenders found guilty of possession of a Class A drug is up to seven years. Dealing in Class A substances can attract up to life imprisonment. Those caught in possession of Class B substances are liable to serve up to five years' imprisonment; however, dealers of these substances could face up to 14 years in prison. For Class C substances, possession can secure imprisonment of up to two years, and dealing up to 14 years' imprisonment. These are the maximum penalties that can be imposed, but the courts do not usually resort to this extent in sentencing offenders. Of the 11,402 drug offenders sentenced in the Crown Court in 2007 (i.e. for the most serious drugs offences) 61.5% were sentenced to an immediate custodial sentence. The average period of imprisonment was 36.9 months (Ministry of Justice, 2009).

Repeat offenders convicted of possession risk imprisonment, but those committing their first possession offence may undertake a community-based sentence designed to rehabilitate the offender and deter them from further drug offending. In 2007, 23% of all drug offenders were given such an opportunity (Ministry of Justice, 2009). These sentences could comprise probation supervision and drug treatment in order to assist the offender in refraining from drug abuse.

Drug dealing – and particularly drug-trafficking offences– attract the most serious of penalties. A minimum prison sentence of seven years must be imposed on a person over the age of 18 who is convicted of a third class A drug trafficking offence, unless the court finds that it would be unjust under all the circumstances to impose it (section 110 of the Powers of Criminal Courts (Sentencing) Act 2000). This power was exercised eleven times during 2007 and this is a steady increase since the provision came into force in 2000 (Ministry of Justice, 2009). The main purpose of custodial sentences is deterrence from further offending, but as serious drug-related crime can be associated with criminal lifestyle offences, it does not always work on its own. The Courts therefore have a number of additional measures available to them in order to deal effectively with such offenders.

The main tool employed by SOCA is post-conviction asset recovery. Reducing financial resources is one effective way of damaging an offender's ability to operate, and may serve as a greater deterrent than a prison sentence (SOCA, 2010). The first step in the process is to assess the offender's finances, and determine any financial benefit gained from their offending. Courts can make a confiscation order to recover the value of the defendant's proceeds from drug offences, which may include surrender of money or property. In 2007, 1100 such confiscation orders were made with the average amount seized in that year being £7900 (Ministry of Justice, 2009). Offenders may also be required to report their financial details at regular intervals for up to 20 years where they have been sentenced to life imprisonment for a drug offence (a Financial Reporting Order), or they can have their movements restricted by way of a Travel Restriction Order if convicted of a drug trafficking offence that attracted at least four years' imprisonment. Serious Crime Prevention Orders can be imposed to prohibit, restrict or require certain behaviour from an offender – for example, to prohibit going to a certain area where drugs are available. The aim of all these orders is to act as a control on an offender's behaviour with a view to prevent further offending. In all cases where drugs have been seized from an offender the court will make a forfeiture order, to retain and destroy the controlled substances.

Treatments typically offered

In 2008, the Government launched a new ten-year drug strategy (2008–18) aimed at reducing the availability of, and minimising demand for, illegal drugs. Part of this strategy was an effort to deliver new forms of drug treatment to users (Home Office, 2008a). Treatment goals for drug offences involving users aim to rehabilitate an addict and prevent reoffending.

Throughout the UK, there are a number of key public sector stakeholders involved in providing treatment to those who clinically require it, including the Department of Health who have overall responsibility for treatment availability and the National Treatment Agency (NTA), a specialist health authority who aim to improve access to, and effectiveness of, treatment. On a local level, treatment is coordinated by the Drug (and Alcohol) Action Team partnerships (D(A)ATs) who work with partners such as the police, the probation service, the prison service, housing and education agencies and the National Health Service (NHS) in order to provide treatment to those who need it most. Funding for treatment is available through a specialist budget which is supplemented by NHS funding and local authorities.

Therapeutic treatment for drug use includes counselling, psychotherapy, cognitive behaviour therapy, family/relationship therapy, detoxification, 12-step programmes and motivational enhancement therapy. Equally, there are medical options available such as drug substitution using methadone (maintenance prescriptions) or antagonist prescriptions. Typically, drug users will prefer a combination of options as part of a residential or other programme. Irrespective of the choices available, it is necessary that the drug user engages fully with the treatment to improve the likelihood of a successful outcome.

The DIP is part of the Government's strategy to reduce drug-related criminal behaviour (for those in the CJS). The aim of the DIP is to identify Class A drug users involved in criminal activity (particularly at the detection stage) and use interventions to engage them in treatment and disengage from criminal behaviour. An offender can also be offered treatment in a community or a suspended sentence order. Often this is only available to offenders involved in low-level drug-defined offences, or those who have not frequently come before the courts for drug offending, or those who have demonstrated a willingness to avoid use following convictions for drug-motivated acquisitive crime. This drug rehabilitation requirement (DRR) has been available since 4 April 2005 (previously the stand-alone community order, Drug Treatment and Testing Order). During the period specified in the community or suspended sentence order, the offender must submit to treatment under the direction of an experienced drug health care professional. The purpose of the order is to reduce or eliminate the offender's dependency on drug use with a view to reducing offending. The overall progress of the order is monitored by the Probation Service, but this order cannot be imposed unless the offender is willing to undergo agreed treatment. The DRR is one of the key ways in which the DIP engages with a convicted offender within the community. In prison, offenders will also have access to treatment. The Counselling, Assessment, Referral, Advice and Throughcare Service (CARATS) team are key workers responsible for providing treatment and support to those prisoners who are assessed as drug users upon their reception in prison. The CARATS team will be involved in detoxification of offenders, as well as providing advice on drug misuse and referring offenders to other agencies to assist with coping upon release into the community. The team can refer prisoners to drug treatment rehabilitation programmes. Prisoners will regularly be tested for the presence of drugs in their system throughout their sentence.

Relative efficacy of treatments

The Home Office (2008a) state that every £1 spent on treatment saves at least £9.50 in crime and health costs and, in doing so, assert the link between drug use and criminal activity. The motivation and personal circumstances of the drug user is paramount to treatment success, and thus conclusions about the impact of available treatments can be difficult to draw. It may be that the treatment works better when the offender is getting weary of the drug lifestyle or maturing out of drug habits (South, 2007). Certainly, treatment for an offender will have the greatest impact if there is an obligation to remain in treatment, where there is mandatory drug testing attached and the treatment is due to last at least 60 days (Bean, 2008). Some of the treatment methods within the CJS fail as such methods are often imposed on the offender rather than the treatment being a personal choice.

The overall reported impact of the DIP appears to be positive, with the Home Office reporting that approximately half of the drug users who came into contact with the DIP at the detection stage of proceedings had showed a decrease in offending in the following six months (Home Office, 2008b). A study conducted in Liverpool indicated that following treatment through the DIP, money spent on drugs and involvement in offending behaviour were reduced; in addition, an improvement in family relationships was found (Home Office, 2008b). The use of methadone maintenance or other drug substitution practices have been seen to decrease acquisitive crime (Perry McDougall and Farrington, 2006). Furthermore, Jones et al. (2009) highlighted a number of positive outcomes following contact with treatment. Seventy-six per cent of all eligible treatment seekers and 89% of those starting treatment were either retained for at least 12 weeks or until they completed their programme. However, those with no experience of the treatment system were much less likely to be retained in this way. Following treatment, employment levels increased for the participants, the stability of living arrangements improved and those with dependent children were more likely to have their children living with them. Overall, all drug types were used by significantly lower proportions of the participants than before treatment, with numbers of those using heroin, crack, cocaine and amphetamines halving. In prisons, boot camps and group counselling are seen as the least effective solutions (Pearson and Lipton, 1999); however, detoxification, therapeutic communities, Cognitive Behaviour Therapy or (CBT) which helps people think about what they do and make positive changes to their life and prescription substitution have been seen to bring success in reducing drug use in offenders.

Co-occurrence or progression to other crimes

Drug-related crime may be acquisitive and non-violent in nature (e.g. shoplifting, theft, forgery or prostitution). Researchers have suggested that links with crime are highest amongst street heroin users than for any other group of users or for any other drug (Bean, 2008), with the exception of alcohol (Bennett and Holloway, 2005). There is a link between those who misuse heroin and crack cocaine and acquisitive crime to fund their addiction (Bennett et al., 2001); however, not all those using these (and other drugs) commit crimes.

The link is clearly recognised by the CJS. When sentencing for drug-motivated acquisitive crime, the offender's addiction to a drug will be treated as a mitigating factor. For the offences of theft and non-dwelling burglary, the Sentencing Guideline Council (2009, p. 103) recommends that 'where an offence is motivated by an addiction (often to drugs, alcohol or gambling) this does not mitigate the seriousness of the offence, but a dependency may properly influence the type of sentence imposed. In particular, it may sometimes be appropriate to impose a drug rehabilitation requirement . . . as part of a community order or a suspended sentence order in an attempt to break the cycle of addiction and offending, even if an immediate custodial sentence would otherwise be warranted'. The offence of robbery usually attracts a custodial penalty, but if there is evidence to suggest that drug dependency motivated the crime, this may attract a drug rehabilitation requirement if it is considered that this would tackle offending behaviour (Archbold, 2010).

Prognosis

The prognosis for those committing drug offences can be a function of a multitude of different factors such as future plans for life, involvement in the criminal underworld, work-based factors, school activities and family or social networks (Topalli, Wirgy and Fornanfo, 2002). Aromaa and Järvinen (1989) suggest that there are three types of criminal careers stretching across many criminal subtypes. First there are peripheral careers (very little involvement in crime), which may be typical of many experimental or recreational drug users, who may just purchase and consume illicit substances but do not involve themselves in other crime. Second, those who are mid-career active will play some role in the criminal 'underworld' and activities, having some contact with others in legitimate society. This could potentially involve drug users who perhaps occasionally commit supply offences to friends, or those who commit occasional crime, usually acquisitive offences. Third, professional offenders usually have few tangible relations with legitimate society and command power and respect within underworld hierarchies. These may be either street- or higher-level suppliers, traffickers or those who prepare drugs. These people may be employed, and are likely to be participating in, the illegal economy.

A4.8. And the damage done . . .

Who are the victims?

Victims tend to be associated with drug-related offences or drug-related lifestyle offences. For example, victims of acquisitive crimes are the owners of property, from persons to large multinational companies. They may also be drug users themselves, as high levels of crime and drug use can often occur in the same area (Bean and Wilkinson, 1988) or intoxication may increase vulnerability to being a victim of a crime. Victims may also be family members or friends who have additional emotional costs. However, it is noted by Hammersley (2008) that crimes can have benefits through the employment of criminal justice personnel, stimulation of the insurance market or through the purchasing of new replacement items from local businesses.

Drug-related lifestyle offences arise as drug markets operate outside the law, with no legal protection. Protecting transactions and territory mean that violence is a key tool for negotiation and protection (Dorn, Murji and South, 1992). There may be victims exploited within wider criminal networks, for which drug dealing may be a component part, such as prostitution or terrorism (McEvoy, McElrath and Higgins, 1998). There may also be impact beyond the UK, such as environmental damage linked with the Colombian cocaine trade or simply through the sustenance of criminal networks in other countries.

KEY DEBATE: Should we decriminalise drugs?

Should we take the lead from Portugal and decriminalise the use and possession of illicit drugs? Note decriminalisation refers to removal of criminal sanctions, but allows for the possibility of administrative sanctions (such as treatment or civil fines)

For:
Evidence has consistently argued that harsh penalties against drug users do not affect levels of drug use. These harsh penalties have important consequences for the offender. Criminal sanctions do not necessarily decrease use or possession, and decriminalisation recognises human rights and both social or societal impacts. Portugal in particular noted the failure of punitive policies in the decision to change the legal consequences of drug use, and changes in their policy across all drugs (not just cannabis) have not led to rises in drug use, have taken pressure off the criminal justice system and led to social and health benefits for the user and society. Note that this does not include possession with the intent to supply.

Against:
Changes like these send the wrong message that drugs and their use are acceptable. Some researchers suggest that if there are not criminal penalties, drug use will increase and in particular harm the most marginalised, deprived communities. Politically, this is unlikely to be a popular policy amongst voters in the UK (and in other countries), and consequently the likelihood of 'going soft' on drugs is unlikely. Community orders can have requirements to attend treatment as a component of the sentence.

Action:
Debates on Drug Policy, the severity and effectiveness of criminal justice sanctions continue to be debated in Parliament, the Advisory Council for the Misuse of Drugs (ACMD) and the Home Office being the main drivers and advisors for change. Recent changes to the severity of consequences included the reclassification of cannabis to Class C from Class B in 2004 and then back to Class B in 2008.

References:
McKeganey, N. (2007) The challenge to UK drug policy. *Drugs: Education, Prevention and Policy*, 14: 559–71.
Hughes, C.E. and Stevens, A. (2010) What can we learn from the Portuguese decriminalization of illicit drugs. *British Journal of Criminology*, 50: 999–1022.

Cost of crime

A report by Gordon et al. (2006) suggests the cost of Class A drug use in England and Wales was estimated to be around £15 billion. It suggests that the cost per year, per problem Class A drug user is approximately £44,000, the majority of which is considered to be associated with crime. Hammersley (2008) stresses a key point that not all problem drug users engage in criminal activity. Health and social functioning may also be considered a key cost of drug offences, and an estimate of the cost to England and Wales is in the region of £5 billion (Gordon et al., 2006). Consumption arising from drug offences is considered to reduce the health of the nation and increase demands on health services.

Fear of crime

In areas of high levels of drug-defined offences or use, fear or violence in communities can reduce cohesion and affect social norms and behaviours in the area (Blumstein, 1995). This may further result in increased criminal activity (even if unrelated to drugs). Prohibition approaches to drug use are considered potentially to decrease community relations and increase violence (Rasmussen and Benson, 1999), but harm-reduction strategies are considered to have better utility (White and Gorman, 2000). Goode (1997) notes that drug markets bring violence and fear of crime; this tends to be directed more at the drug-related and drug-related lifestyle offences as consequences of consumption or drug-defined offences.

Changes in attitudes or behaviours

There is a lot of misunderstanding about drug use and its effects, much of which has been helpfully summarised by Drugscope (see links in Part C). Prevention strategies to such as those included in UK policy arise from four main strands: reducing drug-related crime, reducing the supply of illegal drugs, preventing new users and supporting existing users to quit through treatment and support (Home Office, 2008a).

PART B: Theories and explanations

B4.1. Introduction to theories and explanations

There are five main ways to categorise the relationship between drugs and crime. These relate to whether drug use causes crime, whether criminal behaviour causes drug use, whether drug use and crime cause each other, whether links between crime and drugs are caused by common factors or whether there is no link between the two. Each of these will be considered in turn.

B4.2. Reasons for drug crimes

Drug use causes crime

In some ways this is inevitable as the use of illicit drugs involves criminal activity, and this is a popular representation of drug use in the media and in drug strategies (Bean, 2008). However, there are three ways in which this might be explained, through the pharmacological properties of the drugs or combinations of drugs, through economic compulsive reasons and for systematic drug-related lifestyle reasons (Goldstein, 1985).

The pharmacological explanation suggests that the consumption of specific drugs in isolation or combination or states of withdrawal post-drug(s) consumption may increase the irritable, excitable, impatient or irrational nature of the user and increase the likelihood of criminal behaviour (Goode, 1997). White and Gorman (2000) further highlight the role of 'disinhibition, cognitive-perceptual distortions, attention deficits, bad judgement and neuro-chemical change' (p. 170) as influential on a proposed causal link of drug use and violent crime. However, pharmacological properties can also reduce the likelihood of criminal activity through excessive intoxication or the effects of the drugs themselves (Hammersley, 2008). Drugs such as cannabis can relax the user, reducing the motivation to engage in a criminal act, or fear of heroin withdrawal associated with the beginning of a prison sentence may reduce motivation to commit crime (Maruna, 2001). Drug use is unlikely to be sufficient to cause criminal activity – social and environmental factors also play a vital role (White and Gorman, 2000). These may include characteristics of users like sex or personality, or situational factors like group norms, provocation or interactions with others.

Economic models to explain drug use causing crime suggest that addicts are enslaved by their drug use. Goldstein (1985) suggests that economic necessity to fund drug use fuels other crime. Individuals may resort to acquisitive crime to raise cash to sustain use, if unable to do so through legitimate activities. Turnbull et al. (2000) noted that the approximate median spend on drugs for an addicted person was around £21,000 per annum. Not all addicted individuals will commit crime even in the event of low financial resources, as some may choose to substitute drugs, stop, cut down on their use or fund through other means.

Drug-related lifestyle offences also support the hypothesis that drugs cause crime. Drug distribution is connected with additional crimes including money laundering, racketeering, violence over organisational hierarchy and territories, punishment violence, aggressive debt collection or other violent acts (Goode, 1997). Deviant social networks may also play a role. In particular areas, dealers may be perceived as successes in their neighbourhood. This would be apparent where culture may not openly challenge use, where criminal activities provide the basis for legitimate life or where there may be sharing of profits with friends, family or neighbourhood projects (McKeganey and Barnard, 1992).

Crime causes drug misuse

Pharmacological explanations for the link include the celebration of criminal success in a similar way to which alcohol may also be used to celebrate (Menard, Mihalic and Huizinga, 2001). Those with an aggressive disposition may use drugs as an excuse or explanation for committing aggressive crimes for which they have made a prior, sober decision to engage in (Collins, 1993). Economic models suggest that the proceeds of crime make it possible to engage in drug use and to be in a place where drug use may be more likely (White and Gorman, 2000).

Drug-related lifestyle explanations suggest that if drug use was removed, crime may still occur (Goode, 1997). Chaotic lifestyles as a function of criminality – such as erratic working conditions, free time between jobs or lack of things to do or involvement in parties with time to recover – might support drug use (Collins and Messerschmidt, 1993). White (1990) notes that involvement in criminal activity increases the exposure to other deviant behaviours, including drug use.

Reciprocal models

Reciprocal models suggest that the link is bidirectional based on need and opportunity (White and Gorman, 2000). Hough (1996) considers this to be a key explanation for the drug–prostitution link, with prostitution providing the means to fund drug use and the drug use providing the need for prostitution. Menard et al. (2001) suggest that stage in drug-using career is important, with those that recreationally use less likely to commit criminal activities, but those in an 'addiction' may be more likely to continue with both drug use and criminal activity. For this, perhaps the crime causes drug use and drug use causes crime. Allen (2005, p. 356) suggests that 'participation in acquisitive crime (which mainly involves petty shoplifting) tends to precede the first use of drugs such as heroin and crack cocaine', but that 'participation in more serious crimes, such as street crime' may occur after the start of regular use. This theory suggests that neither necessarily comes first.

Common causes of the link

This model suggests that another variable causes both drug use and crime (Bennett and Holloway, 2005). This could reflect shared causes including mental health status, biological or genetic explanations, personality traits, poor social relations, erratic upbringing and poor relationship with parents (White, 1990). It may also relate to environmental causes, such as poor social capital or investment in a neighbourhood. It may also reflect interaction between drug use, crime, social deprivation and social disorder, particularly in urban areas, but it must be noted that drugs and crime can be found in rural areas.

No connection

The final hypothesis suggests there is no causal link – the link is just a coincidence of problem behaviours. This may reflect drug offences where the offender's lifestyle is broadly deviant, and drug offences and drug use are just two components of that lifestyle. This seems particularly applicable in areas of community disorganisation where there may be a general context for drug use and criminality.

C4.1. Organisations to contact for information and voluntary work

- www.drugscope.org.uk: This is a useful resource, primarily for thoughtful consideration of drug use and drug policy. It also hosts an interesting media guide to drug use, and debunks a number of drug myths. There is also an extensive list of places to search for volunteering opportunities relating to the drugs field.

C4.2. Further reading

- www.ukdpc.org.uk: The UKDPC was launched in April 2007. Its objectives are to provide independent analysis of drug policy in the UK and to provide the government, the media and the public with this analysis in order to promote informed debate. The UKDPC Commissioners conduct independent research and produce papers on drug issues, and they include individuals from a wide base of expertise covering drug treatment, medical research, policing, public policy and the media.
- www.talktofrank.com: This is an independent, government-funded website providing facts about drugs, details about ongoing debates and useful links for those who need help with their own addiction or in relation to someone else.
- *Drugs and Crime* by Phillip Bean: This provides a thorough and interesting analysis of issues relating to drug-related offending, including sentencing, theories and suggestions for the way forward.
- *Understanding drugs, alcohol and crime* by Bennett and Holloway: This provides further reading by illustrating the role of alcohol in addition to drug use in criminal activity.

References

Aromaa, K. & Järvinen, S. (1989). The Criminal Career as a Series of (Rational) Choices. In M. Junninen (2006). *Adventurers and Risk-Takers: Finnish Professional Criminals and Their Organisations in the 1900s Cross-Border Criminality. HEUNI: Monsey, USA.*

chapter

5 FRAUD

DAVID ROWSON AND BELINDA WINDER

PART A: The offence – Who, what, when, why?

A5.1. Introduction

For a long time fraud as a crime was relatively ignored and consequently was able to prosper relatively undisturbed. It is seen as a typically economic crime and does not invoke the same moral outrage as most other crimes. Although methods and resources for assessing and combating fraud have become more effective in recent years, the crime still remains difficult to quantify and fraud persists and flourishes worldwide. New types of fraud constantly emerge as technology evolves (the scam in Box 5.1, a form of advance fee fraud, is not original in nature as it appeared in the 1980s but was sent by fax rather than e-mail) and, in addition, the problem of fraud is exacerbated by increased opportunities for transnational crime. Davia (2000, p. ix) remarks, 'the world of fraud . . . is so vast and so hidden that it defeats any attempt at empirical study'.

Box 5.1. The plausible e-mail

Many people have received an e-mail similar to the one below:

Attn:
I am Barrister Daniel Tete, a solicitor at law, personal attorney to Mr. J.C. Wilmot, a national of your country, who used to work as a contractor in Lome, Togo. On the 30th of April 2000, my client, and their only daughter were involved in a fatal accident. Since then I have made several enquiries here to locate any of my clients relatives, this has proved unsuccessful. After these several unsuccessful attempts, I decided to search through with his name which motivated me to contact you. I have contacted you to assist in repatriating the fund valued at US$20.5 million left behind by my client before it gets confiscated by the Security Finance (bank) where this huge amount were deposited. The said Security Finance Bank has issued me a notice to provide the next of kin or have

---

his account confiscated within the next 21 official working days. Since I have been unsuccessful in locating the relatives, I seek the consent to present you as the next of kin to the deceased since you have the same last name, so that the proceeds of this account can be paid to you. Therefore, on receipt of your positive response, we shall then discuss the sharing ratio and modalities for transfer. I have all necessary information and legal documents needed to back you up for this claim. All I require from you is your honest co-operation to enable us see this transaction through and an administration fee of US$1,000.00 to enable the completion of various documents to release the funds. I guarantee that this will be executed under legitimate arrangement that will protect you from any breach of the law. Best regards. Daniel Tete (esq)

Do you respond to Daniel Tete?

The example shown in Box 5.1 is a typical advance fee fraud, based on blinding the victim with the prospect of a sudden windfall of an unexpected fortune in order to trick them into paying a considerable amount to the fraudster in advance of the proposed transaction. It is likely that further funds will be requested in addition to the administration fee by the fraudster, such as 'legal bills' and 'local taxes'. The victim never receives the promised but non-existent fortune.

A5.2. Definitions

Definitions of fraud

There is no accepted universal definition of fraud and there was no legal definition of fraud until the Fraud Act 2006. The Act introduces a criminal liability for fraud and obtaining services dishonestly. The Act categorises fraud into three areas: fraud by false representation (Box 5.2), fraud by failing to disclose information and fraud by abuse of position.

Box 5.2. False representation

A representation is false if it is untrue or misleading and the person making it knows that it is, or might be, untrue or misleading.

A person is in breach of failing to disclose information if s/he dishonestly fails to disclose to another person information which s/he is under a legal duty to disclose.

A person is in breach fraud by abuse of position if they occupy a position in which they are expected to safeguard, or not to act against, the financial interests of another person and dishonestly abuse that position.

Source: Fraud Act, 2006.

Prior to the Fraud Act there was no specific criminal offence of fraud and the courts relied on other laws such as those on deception to prosecute fraudsters. Not only has the Fraud Act dealt with this anomaly, but such a definition of fraud brings more specifically the breach of some professional rules, such as those governing solicitors and accountants, into the area of defined crime and should make it easier to prosecute errant professionals than was previously the case (Rowson, 2009).

Box 5.3. Other definitions of fraud

Fraud must have two elements: deception or concealment and deprivation or loss to the victim.

Buckley J's comments in Re London and Globe Finance Ltd
(cited in Huntington and Davies, 1994)

All those activities involving dishonesty and deception that can drain value from a business, directly or indirectly, whether or not there is personal benefit to the fraudster.

Davies (2000)

The deliberate misrepresentation of circumstances or the deliberate failure to notify changes of circumstances with the intent of gaining some advantage.

Benefits Fraud Inspectorate (cited in Jones, Lewis and Maggs, 2002)

Any behaviour by which one person intends to gain a dishonest advantage over another.

Comer (1985)

Fraud is generally considered to include acts of deception and persuasion, with the principal aim of cheating people out their property and/or money.

Fraud Advisory Panel (2006)

The lack of a comprehensive or universally accepted definition of fraud is a real problem in drawing an accurate picture of the nature and extent of fraud. Perhaps the main reason that fraud is difficult to define is that there are many different types of fraud, diverse in nature, which are also difficult to categorise.

Classification of fraud

Albrecht, Wernz and Williams (1995) postulate that there are six main categories of fraud: employee embezzlement (direct or indirect); management fraud; investment scams; vendor fraud; customer fraud; and miscellaneous frauds.

The National Fraud Authority, set up by the government in 2008, have categorised types of fraud under the main headings of Individual fraud, Corporate Fraud, Internet Fraud and Advance Fee Fraud to be specific to current fraudulent activity. However, within each major category of fraud there are a number of different types of fraud that include both the new and traditional.

Levi et al. (2007), in a report for the Association of Chief Police Officers (ACPO), defined the most common types of fraud (see Box 5.4). Levi et al. (2007) do not include identity fraud as a separate category of fraud, preferring to incorporate such behaviour within other types of fraud. Identity fraud can be defined as the impersonation of another person for financial gain. Fraudsters steal your personal identity and/or financial information and use it to purchase goods and services or to access facilities in your name (Fraud Advisory Panel, 2008).

Box 5.4. Common types of fraud

Benefit fraud: Frauds of various kinds upon the social security system, ranging from widespread 'working and drawing' by employees to the more common (by volume) failure to notify benefit officials of changes in circumstances that disentitle claimants to benefits.

Charity fraud: Frauds in which donations are stripped from entirely fictitious or unregistered charities, or are embezzled from registered charities.

Cheque fraud: Most frauds on individuals' cheques are covered by guarantees up to a particular limit, depending on the card type (£50–200) if presented at the time; beyond that losses accrue to the firm that accepted them unless bank negligence can be demonstrated.

Consumer frauds: A broad category including lottery/prize scams; rogue dialling and other communications-based frauds; 'dishonest' mis-descriptions of products and services and purchases of goods and services that are not sent by the supplier.

Counterfeit intellectual property and products: A broad set including medicines, vehicle parts, art and antiques sold as genuine and believed by consumers to be genuine. Thus, few people buy viagra or antibiotics or genuine Microsoft software expecting them to not work. This should be distinguished from, say, Rolex watches bought for £10 in a street market, which almost no one is deceived about or regards as genuine; these do not usually involve some actual financial loss to Rolex or other branded goods firm, but can do so in addition to reputational loss.

Counterfeit money: A direct loss to the individuals/business people given counterfeit money.

Data-compromise fraud: Frauds on companies and on individuals (sometimes called 'phishing' and 'pharming') arising from website manipulations; these frauds include the manipulation of corporate websites to make the target believe that the firm they are dealing with is the genuine business. 'Phishing' attacks occur when the public receive a bogus e-mail claiming to be from a legitimate site, asking the target to click on links within the e-mail (to provide, say, access to an Internet bank account password, which is then abused). 'Vishing' involves the same scam but it works over a 'voice-over Internet protocol' (voip) phone line.

Embezzlement: Frauds against all businesses, government departments and professional firms by staff, ranging from junior clerical staff to directors and officers of the company or partners of the unincorporated firm. This normally involves either accounts manipulation or the construction of false invoices.

Gaming frauds: This refers to 'fixed' races and other forms of sport upon which spread-betting and other gaming wagers have been made. This has an effect on the profits of the gambling industry as well as on the chances of winning for individual consumers.

Insider dealing/market abuse: This affects the general integrity of the market but may not have any directly attributable victims or – in any given individual case – even affect people's confidence in the market. It involves an 'insider' using 'inside' information to profit from the sale or purchase of shares.

Insurance fraud: Insurance companies may be victims of a variety of frauds by businesspeople (e.g. arson for profit, maritime fraud) and by consumers who may inflate claims from a house burglary or make fictitious claims.

Investment frauds: These include advance fee fraud, as shown in the introduction, and boiler room frauds which are basically share scams. The operator of the boiler room fraud will sell to investors, at inflated prices, worthless shares that are impossible to sell.

Lending fraud: This category includes a variety of frauds involving lending funds and lending credit for goods and services. It includes fraudulent bankruptcy (sometimes referred to as long-firm frauds), where goods and services have been ordered and received in advance of payment with the knowledge that they will be unable to pay; and mortgage frauds (which can involve the manipulation of property prices, at one extreme, or the overstatement of applicants' income to get a loan that otherwise would not be granted, at the other).

Payment card fraud: Frauds on issuers and merchants. Some debt, credit and charge card purchases that are made without authorisation by the acquirer are charged back to the merchant (e.g. computers bought remotely with stolen/counterfeited cards and that are not delivered to the cardholder's billing address).

Procurement fraud: Frauds and corruption in the purchasing process, including price-fixing rings and abuse of inside information in the construction of tenders or in their application.

Tax fraud: This involves failure to pay direct, indirect or excise taxes. This encompasses income tax and corporation tax fraud, ranging from individuals failing to declare income to large schemes involving corporate manipulation; excise tax fraud primarily encompasses alcohol and tobacco and motor oil tax evasion, from small-scale smuggling to large bonded warehouse frauds; and some tax frauds also arise at the local government level, in relation to council taxes.

Source: Adapted from Levi et al. (2007).

Internet fraud

With evolving technology, new opportunities and new methods of fraud have also evolved. The Internet has created a whole new and international market for fraud, and innovation has resulted in the repackaging of traditional frauds. Internet fraud is the use of the Internet to present fraudulent solicitations to potential victims; to conduct fraudulent transactions; and to transfer funds of fraudulent activity. Many of the common types of fraud (Box 5.4) can be conducted using the Internet, but new frauds have also arisen as a result of the Internet, such as phishing (obtaining sensitive information such as credit card details and passwords by masquerading to be a trusted person or organisation) and pharming (redirecting traffic from a legitimate website to a fraudulent website that can be used to obtain sensitive information).

A5.3. Who commits fraud?

Anyone can commit fraud; this idea has been reinforced by Romney, Albrecht and Cherrington (1980), who conducted a study of fraud over a period of several years illustrating the similarities between white-collar criminals and non-criminals; perpetrators of employee embezzlement cannot be distinguished from other employees on the basis of demographic or psychological characteristics (Albrecht, Wernz and Williams, 1995). Fraud by employees is a major area of fraud against organisations, and Cressey (1953, p. 12) points out that 'the differential in behaviour indicated by the fact that some persons in positions of financial trust violate that trust, whereas other persons or even the same persons at a different time, in identical or very similar positions do not so violate it'.

Employee fraud

Frauds resulting in the largest financial loss are committed by insiders, whether employees or management (Ernst and Young, 2000), and the main perpetrators of organisational fraud are internal perpetrators working alone (Barnes and Sharp, 1999). Internal fraud has increased recently due to 'bonus culture fraud'. A link has been established between performance-related pay for senior executives and the levels and types of economic crime their organisations suffer. Globally, one survey found that among companies that do not pay executive performance-related bonuses the incidence of fraud in the previous 12 months was 26%; for the rest the figure was substantially higher. In the UK, 33% of companies with no bonuses reported accounting frauds, but among companies who paid the highest bonuses (i.e. 50% or more of total executive pay) this rose sharply to 56%. The survey found that all of the main types of fraud are more likely to occur in companies where executive pay is heavily skewed towards bonuses (Fraud Advisory Panel, 2009).

The demographics of fraud

Some researchers have studied possible links between social demographic factors (age, gender, culture) and fraud. Ramage (2005) reported that, in a four-year survey in the UK of the perpetrators of serious frauds, there was a far greater percentage of older people relative to non-fraud crimes. These findings indicate that the more serious frauds are carried out by older individuals, which is not surprising in that the opportunity to execute serious fraud is far more likely to be available to more senior (and therefore older) individuals. Tax fraud offenders are usually older and theft at work increases with age (Croall, 2001a).

Culturally, there are undoubtedly issues related to differing social norms (and laws) across cultures. Where an individual has not fully immersed themselves in the expectations and laws of the land in which they are living and working, then some fraud due to cultural differences may be expected (Ramage, 2005).

Males commit the majority of fraud offences (Association of Certified Fraud Examiners, 2010). However, most crimes are heavily skewed towards male perpetrators but, in respect of fraud, particularly lower level fraud, this is not as apparent (Croall, 2001a). Albrecht, Wernz and Williams (1995) noted that, whilst 2% of property crime offenders were female, 30% of white-collar criminals were female.

Fraud occurs globally, with organisations throughout the world reporting fraud. In a global economic crime survey (PricewaterhouseCoopers, 2009), the countries where respondent organisations reported most fraud were Russia (71%), South Africa (62%), Kenya (57%), Hong Kong (13%), the Netherlands and Turkey (15%), with the lowest being Japan (10%). The UK was the sixth highest country, at 43%.

There is also an increase in organised crime fraud, particularly technology based. Organised criminals are increasingly exploiting the Internet, in particular its use in commerce and finance, to develop new crimes and transform traditional ones. Criminals at all levels are able to buy compromised private data, often to access bank accounts and payment card details (SOCA, 2010).

The fraudulent personality

Given the various types of personality disorder, that of a psychopathic personality disorder is the most likely general disorder of personality to manifest in fraudsters. Of course, the lack of conscience exemplified by individuals with psychopathic tendencies may equally manifest in other forms of crime and thus psychopathy may be seen as just another measure of criminality per se (Ramage, 2005).

Common personality traits of fraudsters are narcissism, being power-hungry and the need to be in control, but these characteristics would also describe many people who were not prolific white-collar criminals (Croall, 2001a).

A5.4. Misconceptions

A number of misconceptions exist regarding individual and corporate victims of fraud.

Fraud is a victimless crime

It is widely considered that fraud is a victimless crime; that no one is losing out. However, as with other crime there is always a victim. Fraud affects individuals, organisations, communities and society as a whole. Fraud directly against the individual can result in both financial loss and emotional distress, particularly with regard to frauds such as identity theft and credit card frauds.

The victim is to blame

Victims of fraud are often apportioned some of the blame for their victimisation. For example, that they were 'greedy', 'stupid' or 'gullible'. Similar assumptions for other types of crime have been gradually refuted over time.

Businesses can afford the cost of fraud

Businesses are often perceived to be able to afford the cost of fraud. The effect of corporate fraud upon the business, its suppliers, employees and customers is largely unrecognised but nevertheless it does cost business financially, which can have a number of outcomes affecting the business, its staff, its suppliers and its customers.

Victims of fraud only lose money

Victims of fraud can lose much more than just money. Fraud can lead to health problems, suicide, depression and the disintegration of the family unit through divorce or estrangement. Corporate victimisation can lead to loss of customers, public confidence in their products and/or reputational damage (Fraud Advisory Panel, 2006).

The vulnerable are more likely to become victims

Members of society often perceived to be the most vulnerable, such as the elderly and young, may not be more likely to become the target of fraudsters; however, when they do become victims of fraud, the effects may be more severe.

A5.5. Facts and figures

Prevalence of fraud

The number of fraud and forgery offences recorded by the police in 2009–10 was 152,348, which represents 4% of all recorded crime (Home Office, 2010b).

Although this is a decrease from the previous year the historical trend is upwards, as demonstrated by the Home Office statistics going back over 100 years: the number of incidences reported in 1982 was 123,101; in 1962, 51,954; and in 1898 it was just 3055 (Home Office, 2010a).

Furthermore, as noted in the British Crime Survey 2010, the measurement of fraud is challenging for several reasons. Incidents are known to be substantially under-reported to the police. There are also difficulties with using surveys like the British Crime Survey to estimate the extent of fraud because, for example, victims are often businesses, which are not covered by the British Crime Survey, and respondents might not be aware that the deception has taken place or may mistakenly believe a bank error represents fraud.

Due to the method of compiling the figures for the British Crime Survey, plastic card fraud is not included within the recorded offences of fraud and forgery. Plastic cards (i.e. credit, debit or bank cards) that are stolen are included in the main British Crime Survey crime count under the relevant offence, such as burglary or theft from the person, but subsequent fraudulent use of stolen cards is not included within the main crime count since plastic card ownership was low and there was little evidence of related fraud when the survey first started (Home

Office, 2010b). In 2009/10, 6.4% of credit, debit or bank card users were aware that they had been a victim of card fraud in the previous 12 months and there was 2.7 million fraudulent transactions on UK-issued credit cards in the UK in 2009/10, a decrease of 2% on the 2.8 million recorded in 2008 (Home Office 2010b).

Doig (2006) also makes the point that the Home Office statistics do not cover the numbers of fraud cases that fall outside their remit – which relates only to cases reported to and recorded by the police. Thus, the other agencies with prosecuting powers, such as the Department of Work and Pensions and HM Revenue and Customs, do not have their figures included.

Furthermore, there is also ample evidence from the disparity between official statistics and victim surveys (Putwain and Sammons, 2002) to suggest that many instances of fraud are not reported or even detected by the victims. Certainly, the official statistics on fraud have been criticised as understating the problem to a greater extent than with other crimes, with many frauds occurring that are not reported, or even suspected, by the victims of these crimes (Shover and Wright, 2001).

A5.6. How are offenders caught?

Investigation

There are number of units that investigate and gather intelligence regarding fraud, such as individual police force fraud squads and Economic Crime Units; the Serious Fraud Office (SFO); the Serious Organised Crime Agency (SOCA); the National Fraud Intelligence Bureau (NFIB); and the National Fraud Authority (NFA). Investigations will also be carried out by organisations with prosecuting powers and by various professional bodies such as the Financial Reporting Council (accountants) and the Solicitors Regulation Authority (solicitors), who will carry out investigations within their remit and, where the results of the investigation warrant criminal proceedings rather than just disciplinary proceedings, the case will be referred to the police. Insurance companies, financial institutions and many large businesses will also have fraud investigation and detection departments that will refer any fraudulent activity to the police for a criminal investigation.

Box 5.5. Example: Mortgage fraud

A solicitor acted in connection with the acquisition of the interest in a property with joint owners for £179,000.00, discharging an order for mortgage arrears to a lending institution and the remortgage of the property with a different lending institution. The solicitor also acted for the second lending institution in connection with the mortgage advance of £144,000.00 to be secured on the property. It was noted by the forensic investigator that this mortgage was in arrears from its inception. The property was eventually repossessed and sold by the lending institution as mortgagee in possession.

The following further facts were discovered by the forensic investigator, identifying that the solicitor and their client had committed mortgage fraud: the solicitor did not report to the lending institution that the purchaser was also one of the joint owners of the property; and the solicitor recorded in the Report on Title that the purchase price was £179,000.00, despite the actual purchase price being only £144,000.00 as recorded in the Land Registry transfer form. This resulted in the purchaser improperly being able to obtain a 100% mortgage. The vendors did not receive any money for their interest in the property and no mortgage payments were made.

It transpired that the sole purpose of the transaction was to obtain £144,000.00 from the lending institution, by deception.

Source: Rowson (2009).

However, despite the extent of fraud, it is not an area of crime that attracts substantial resources for police investigations.

Doig (2006) sums up some of the problems of dealing with fraud: 'even allowing for the volume of cases, fraud does not itself fall into an obvious category, ranging from the high-volume low-cost crime of card fraud or benefit fraud to multi-million pound swindles. Even though it records more offences than some other crimes, the public and political concerns over the nature of the numerically smaller categories, such as sex crimes or drugs, means that fraud is less likely to receive significant police resources, be the subject of media campaigns, or the attention of governments' (p. 43).

Detection

Of all crimes, fraud is perhaps the most difficult to detect due to lack of resources and also often with no clear evidence that a fraud has been committed. Organisations cannot solely rely on the police to detect fraud. Some companies have introduced fraud prevention management techniques; larger businesses have employed fraud investigators to guard against both opportunist and sophisticated fraudsters; and these investigators are trained to attempt to combat the problem of fraud in a proactive, and not simply reactive, way (Davia, 2000).

The strength of the internal control structure of an organisation plays an important role in fraud detection and prevention (Matsumura and Tucker, 1992). However, internal controls can be strong yet may frequently be overridden by management (Caplan, 1999), and organisations and individuals will lose money from fraud despite robust internal control systems. Internal audit is the method by which most frauds are detected in organisations followed by tip-offs (internal source); fraud risk management; tip-offs (external source); by accident; whistle-blowing system; suspicious transaction reporting; corporate security; rotation of personnel; with law enforcement being the least likely method of fraud detection (PricewaterhouseCoopers, 2009).

A5.7. What happens to offenders?

Conviction rates

The police sanction detection rate for all fraud and forgery offences in 2009 was 24%, down from 28% in 2008 (Home Office, 2010).

Box 5.6. Sanction detection

Sanction detections include offences that are cleared up through a formal sanction, i.e. when an offender has (where applicable to fraud and forgery offences):

- been charged or summonsed;
- been cautioned, reprimanded or given a final warning;
- had an offence taken into consideration.

Source: Home Office (2010b).

The detection rate is not the same as the conviction rate, since the Crown Prosecution Service may not take forward proceedings or a defendant maybe found not guilty at Court. Convictions in fraud cases are fraught with difficulty as it is a crime that is problematic to prove in a court of law.

Even once a crime and culprit have been established for fraud offences, securing a prosecution may be difficult. It has often been successfully argued that any (mis)conduct under scrutiny was not deliberate; for those investigating the fraud to prove otherwise can sometimes be impossible, and there are indeed a number of strategies that defence lawyers adopt in order to minimise the chance of conviction (Mann, 1985). Levi (1991) states that it 'remains true that people have a much greater chance of being detected, reported, and prosecuted for petty theft offences than for serious fraud' (p. 277), whilst Higson (1998), writing about fraud by company directors (but true of most types of fraud) reported that there was a reluctance to both report and prosecute fraudulent activity. Another complication is that the regulation of fraud is complex and fragmented involving government agencies, self-regulatory bodies and commercial bodies as well as the police (Levi, 1992).

In addition, fraud trials are typically long, expensive and complex processes; the group of ordinary men and women who form the jury are liable to have problems understanding the evidence (Nelken, 2002) – this view was promulgated by the Roskill Report (1986), which articulated the difficult task faced by the juries of complex fraud trials. Some observers believe that jurors are inadequate when it comes to complex cases and a change in the justice system is required. The depth of understanding required by ordinary people in juries and the seemingly innocuous nature of fraud have probably impacted on conviction rates; some of the jurors may well have failed to appreciate the difference between good business and fraud.

One of the problems with obtaining convictions for fraud is the ambiguity of the law towards fraud. As Heerden, Blignaut and Groenendijk (1999) state, in most legal systems 'an antiques dealer who sells a fake chair for, say, R10,000 is considered to commit fraud. On the other hand, a buyer who pays R10 for a chair in a flea market, knowing it is worth R10,000, does not commit fraud, even though the deal would never have been agreed upon had the seller been correctly informed of the chair's value' (p. 210). Also, the distinction is blurred between what is, and what is not, defined as criminal activity in law. For example, it is not illegal to use another person's identity until it is used to obtain goods and services by deception, yet a victim of identity theft may consider themselves a victim of fraud, regardless of whether a crime has actually been committed in the eyes of the law (Fraud Advisory Panel, 2006).

Despite these difficulties, conviction rates for fraud have been increasing, especially for serious fraud. The Serious Fraud Office achieved a conviction rate of 91% in 2009/10 (78% in 2008/9) (SFO, 2010).

It is generally considered that convicted fraudsters receive too short a prison sentence in the UK. On average a sentence for fraud is between three and four years, with the maximum sentence under the Fraud Act 2006 being ten years. Many fraudsters do not serve a prison sentence at all but are punished by community service orders. This can be contrasted with the USA where fraudsters are often given prison sentences of 20 years or more. Reoffending of fraudsters is relatively low compared with other offences at approximately half the reoffending rate of all crimes (Ministry of Justice, 2010). There is no formal prison treatment programme for convicted fraudsters.

Regulatory sanctions for professionals

Where a fraudster is a professional such as an accountant or solicitor, there will often be regulatory sanctions against them including orders to pay compensation to their victims and/or being disbarred. The burden of proof required by a professional tribunal is much lower than that required by criminal courts, and therefore a professional can be struck off from their professional body yet not be convicted of fraud.

A5.8. And the damage done . . .

Who are the victims?

Economic crime has a widespread effect on business, on economies, on communities and on individuals (Croall, 2001b). Different types of fraud result in different types of victims but cover the full spectrum of society. For example, identity fraud will affect individuals financially and emotionally; certain forms of investments scams will be targeted to defraud pensioners' retirement savings; mortgage fraud will result in losses for financial institutions; money laundering may finance other crimes such as terrorism or drug dealing; businesses and shareholders will be the victims of employee, management and customer fraud; and probate fraud can mean beneficiaries such as charities do not receive legacies bequeathed to them.

Private individuals are often ignored as victims of fraud, with businesses being perceived as the usual victim, but often frauds are aimed at the individual with devastating results.

Box 5.7. Barlow Clowes investments

Peter Clowes was the fraudster behind a £17 million investment fraud that took place in the mid-1980s. His business, Barlow Clowes Ltd, attracted private investors (predominantly retired people) to buy gilt-edged securities promoted as being secure. The scheme was a fraud from the start. His claims and promises were false. He simply stole investors' funds. Initially he made returns to investors from further funds received from new investors, therefore giving the impression that his business was a success and thus attracting further investment. After a trial at the Old Bailey in 1992 in which 113 witnesses appeared for the prosecution, he was sentenced to ten years' imprisonment.

SFO (2010)

Practical Property Portfolio Ltd:
Buy-to-let developed as an alternative to more conventional forms of investment. Based in Gateshead, Practical Property Portfolio (PPP) Ltd was one such business, attracting investors from around the UK through its national press advertising. It sold around 4000 residential properties in the north of England to over 1750 investors, taking in funds of around £80 million. Though mostly from small private investors for single properties, there were also some investment companies who would multi-buy.

The PPP scheme was that properties, typically urban 'Coronation Street'-type houses, would be offered at a package price of £25,000 to include refurbishment and letting to vetted tenants to provide rental income as well as profit on eventual resale.

However, what started seemingly as a genuine commercial venture sank into one of deliberate fraud and misrepresentation. Buyers, many of whom did not inspect the properties, were receiving some rental income but it was coming from new money put into the PPP scheme by other investors. Properties were not being refurbished or let. The shocking standard of some houses was filmed by an investor who had used her pension savings and wanted to see what she had bought. Instead of an asset upgraded to provide her with an income she saw a burnt-out, derelict shell in a row of houses vandalised and graffiti marked.

An investigation culminated in five people being charged in 2007. When the case came to trial, all five pleaded guilty to conspiracy to defraud investors. Investor claims when the company was wound up totalled £16 million. It is thought that almost £65 million of funds was providing no real return on investment.

The chief offenders were John Potts, PPP's chairman and Peter Gosling, managing director. They and the three others used PPP funds for their own extravagant use: luxury cars, racehorses, a villa, antiques, art and high salaries. All were given prison sentences (Potts five years and a 15-year directorship ban).

SFO (2010)

The effects of fraud can be particularly devastating for vulnerable victims such as the elderly, the socially isolated and the disabled. It is amongst these groups that the emotional and financial impact can be the greatest. For some, the betrayal of trust can be the same or worse than the actual loss itself. The impact of fraud can be equally great for corporate victims, particularly small- to medium-sized businesses which may be unable to recover from the financial and/or reputational damage caused. The physical, psychological, financial and social effects of fraud can be the same for business owners as individual victims. Even large multinational organisations feel the impact of fraud through the increased costs of doing business. One of the wider ramifications of fraud is that it can undermine public confidence in legitimate businesses or industry sectors, particularly those that sell products or services known to be targeted by fraudsters, such as timeshare properties, lotteries and Internet shopping websites. There is likely to be a level of fraud where it becomes too risky for people to engage in certain activities. For example, Internet fraud may make people too afraid to shop online, or timeshare frauds may make people apprehensive about purchasing legitimate timeshare properties. Fraud can also have a knock-on effect. For example, credit card fraud affects not only the individual victim but also the bank that issued the card, the shop in which the card was used and other consumers through higher fees (Fraud Advisory Panel, 2006).

The financial cost of fraud

Wachman (2005) believes that British businesses are failing to accurately evaluate and effectively manage the risk of fraud, pointing out that this affects us all, manifesting as a hidden tax on everyone, since it raises the cost of goods and services, decreases investment values for small and corporate shareholders, reduces the future value of private pensions, threatens jobs and lowers confidence in the reputation of the financial institutions and other businesses both in the UK and abroad. Fraud damages development, innovation and investment (Fraud Advisory Panel, 2000).

The fraud world can be subdivided into three main groups: the first group comprises fraud that is exposed and in the public domain, and this accounts for approximately 20% of the total frauds; the second group consists of fraud that is known by a few, but not made public, and is said to account for 40% of all frauds; whilst the third group (undetected fraud) accounts for the final 40% of all frauds committed (Davia, 2000).

It is estimated that in 2009 fraud cost the UK £30.5 billion, with £17.6 billion of that relating to public sector fraud, £9.3 billion to private sector fraud and £3.5 billion to individual and charity sector fraud (NFA, 2010).

KEY DEBATE: Should complex fraud trials be conducted without a jury?

For:
Failed complex court cases cost the taxpayer tens of millions of pounds every year and the failures are due to cases for serious fraud being too complex for jurors to fully comprehend. An alternative proposal is that in such cases a single judge

will replace the jury. Under the current system convictions are gained for simple, petty frauds but more complex cases either have to be abandoned or never get to court, as a conviction is considered unlikely due to the complexity involved.

Against:
Defendants have been entitled to trial by jury for over 800 years, and this is a fundamental right in the legal system. Failures in complex fraud cases are due to prosecution incompetence and not to inadequacies in the criminal justice system. Public confidence in juries is high and they are able to understand issues in serious fraud that are merely a question of dishonesty.

Action:
The Fraud (Trials without a Jury) Bill 2007 was proposed as an Act of Parliament with the intention to abolish trials by jury in complex fraud cases. The Bill was blocked by the House of Lords using delaying tactics. The debate has continued since 2007 with further complex, high-profile fraud cases being abandoned or failing to obtain a conviction.

PART B: Theories and explanations

B5.1. Motives

Greed is often attributed as a motive behind fraud (Nelken, 2002). Vold and Bernard (1986) state, 'the question of why white collar offenders behave the way they do can be answered in a relatively straightforward way; they want to make a profit' (p. 338). Certainly, financial strain is seen to be a principal motive for fraud as is ego/power, and these are therefore discussed below.

Financial strain is a feature of almost every type of fraudulent activity. Financial strain itself is subjective and may incorporate further sub-strands of motives. Even the affluent may feel economically deprived because of their desires, by their need perhaps to maintain appearances. Therefore, financial strain can be said to be the desire to possess something that one cannot afford. This may involve the comparison with others and attempting to maintain a certain lifestyle or the threat of losing something already owned. Furthermore, the loss of wealth may also result in a loss of power, status and pride. Lifestyle choices, such as compulsive gambling, may also result in financial stress. Relationship breakdowns and divorce settlements are further examples leading to financial strain (Duffield and Grabosky, 2001).

Ego/power

Another common motive for fraud is reported to be ego/power. This is power over both people and situations (Duffield and Grabosky, 2001).

Power over people can be a strong motivational force for fraud perpetrators in that it is an end in itself; in manipulating their victims the fraudster may take delight in the act itself and the sense of superiority they gain from it, rather than simply the outcome (Stotland, 1977). Power over a situation relates often to a sense of superiority over others. This is often the case in complex frauds where there is a certain professional pride of the fraudster (Stotland, 1977).

B5.2. Theories of fraud

Control and strain theories of fraud

It has been suggested that the reason everyone does not commit fraud at some level can be explained by control theory. This theory states that most of us are generally law-abiding and have too much to lose by not remaining legitimate and keeping within the law. As with any social control it is a mechanism that regulates behaviour through a system of punishments and rewards (Friedrichs, 2003). The majority of control theories suggest that most people are raised to adopt conventional behaviour, but something occurs during their lifetime that results in a weakening of this learned behaviour and causes them to deviate (Henry and Lanier, 2006). An opposing view of control theory is that the adoption of conventional behaviour is actually difficult to achieve and can often not be achieved, resulting in non-conformity or deviance (Henry and Lanier, 2006). It is also argued that, whichever control theory is accurate, the extent of any motivation to deviate may be too strong to prevent such deviance – known as the strain theory, the intensity resulting in the deviant freeing themselves from any guilt or allowing them to rationalise their behaviour at the time of the deviance (Downes and Rock, 1998). Strain theorists ask, 'Why do people engage in crime?' They then focus on the factors that push or entice people into committing criminal acts. Since the main objective of industrialised society is the pursuit of material success and only a proportion of people will gain this, some people will resort to illegitimate means. Merton (1938) argued that it was not deprivation that was critical, but how people react to deprivation. He came up with five modes of reacting: conformity, innovation, rebellion, ritualism and retreatism. Fraudsters are most likely to fall into the category of innovation – small but significant change in the perspective of people who have moved from conformity to innovation. People continue to seek success but now it is through innovation, and take advantage of illegal means in place of less promising conventional means in order to attain success.

Rational choice theory

Through rational choice theory, Cornish and Clarke (1986) describe crime as an event that occurs when an offender decides to risk breaking the law after considering their own need for money, and the chance of getting caught, the severity of the expected penalty, the value to be gained by committing the act. Clarke and Cornish outlined a theory of residential burglary that included the following influencing factors: whether the house was occupied, looked affluent, had bushes to hide behind, had a burglar alarm, contained a dog and was surrounded by nosy neighbours. The rational decision is always the decision that will maximise gain and minimise pain for each individual. The theory is relevant to fraud, especially due to low detection rates and the perceived leniency of punishment for those detected.

Social learning theory

Social learning theory asserts that people learn from others via observation, imitation, reinforcement and modelling (Bandura, 1973). A common statement in relation to fraud and white-collar crime at a low level is that 'everybody is doing it' and such is the relevance of the social learning theory in relation to fraud. If fraudsters are seen to be getting away with fraud then this will be copied by other people.

The fraud triangle and the fraud diamond

The fraud triangle theory (Albrecht, Wernz and Williams, 1995) posits that there are three elements to fraud: pressure, opportunity and rationalisation (Figure 5.1). Every fraud perpetrator is said to face some type of pressure and, whilst most pressures involve financial need, non-financial pressures can also motivate individuals to commit fraud (Albrecht, Wernz and Williams, 1995). Some pressures are said to be unavoidable; however, what might differentiate a person who does commit fraud from someone who does *not*, given the same pressures, is the ability to recognise impinging pressures and to manage such pressures appropriately (Davies, 2000).

The second element of the fraud triangle is *opportunity*; if a potential fraudster believes he or she can commit and conceal a fraud, they will have a perceived opportunity (Albrecht, Wernz and Williams, 1995) and they may be prompted to act upon this opportunity at some juncture (now, or in the future). Perceived opportunity is the element of the fraud triangle that is most commonly focused upon when companies seek to deter fraud; such deterrents may typically comprise security procedures and installations (Greenberg, 1997), as well as financial controls and systems.

The third element of the fraud triangle is *rationalisation*; potential fraudsters generally need to find a way to rationalise their acts, in order to make the illegal actions (and harmful outcomes) of the fraud consistent with their personal attitudes and code of conduct (Albrecht, Wernz and Williams, 1995).

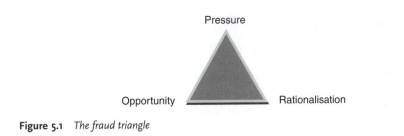

Figure 5.1 *The fraud triangle*

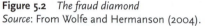

Figure 5.2 *The fraud diamond*
Source: From Wolfe and Hermanson (2004).

Attempts at rationalisation may be interpreted as a cognitive dissonance strategy (see Festinger, 1957) in which an individual will seek to reduce inconsistencies between their personal attitudes (I'm a good person) and their behaviour (but I'm not going to pay for this ticket) through the use of neutralisation strategies (it's not as if the train companies don't make lots of money anyway). Moreover, the incentives for carrying out fraudulent behaviour may themselves be viewed as discrepancies in a person's life, and a person may initially commit fraud as a means of reducing the consequent unpleasant state of tension.

Albrecht, Wernz and Williams (1995) believe that all three elements of the fraud triangle must be present for a fraud to be committed: if the perpetrator perceives a pressure and an opportunity and can rationalise their behaviour, they are said to be likely to commit fraud.

Wolfe and Hermanson (2004) went beyond the fraud triangle, hypothesising a slightly different framework to explain why people commit fraud: the fraud diamond. In this theory, the capability of an individual is a key feature in whether or not fraud will be attempted.

The four elements of the fraud diamond are reproduced below (Figure 5.2):

1. Incentive: I want to, or have a need to, commit fraud
2. Opportunity: there is a weakness in the system that the right person could exploit. Fraud is possible
3. Rationalisation: I have convinced myself that this fraudulent behaviour is worth the risks
4. Capability: I have the necessary traits and abilities to be the right person to pull it off. I have recognised this particular fraud opportunity and can turn it into reality.

PART C: Further information

C5.1. Organisations to contact for information and voluntary work

Action fraud is a service run by the National Fraud Authority – the government agency that helps to coordinate the fight against fraud in the UK. It is a facility to report fraud and for victims of fraud, and there is a network of support and information available (www.actionfraud.org.uk).

The Fraud Advisory Panel is a registered charity and membership organisation which acts as an independent voice and supporter of the counter-fraud community in the UK (www.fraudadvisorypanel.org).

C5.2. Further reading

Davies (2000) *Fraud Watch*. London: ABG Professional Information is a good general introduction to fraud, as is Doig (2006) *Fraud*. Cullompton: Willan Publishing. An interesting guide to detecting fraud is by Howard Davia (2000) *Fraud 101: Techniques and Strategies for Detection*. New York: John Wiley and Sons. Fraud specifically in relation to employee fraud is covered in detail by Hollinger and Clark (1983) *Theft by Employees*. Idaho Falls: Lexington Books; and an invaluable guide to serious fraud is Sally Ramage's (2005) *Serious Fraud and Current Issues*. New York: iUniverse, Inc.

This chapter is written by the author in a personal capacity and not as a representative of the Solicitors Regulation Authority.

chapter

6 GANGS

ELIZABETH SCOWCROFT, PHILIP BANYARD AND BELINDA
WINDER

PART A: The offence – Who, what, when, why?

A6.1. Introduction

The gang has been part of popular culture since the middle of the last century. In its original use, the term refers to a work group but it has now taken on a new and edgier meaning. A gang refers to three or more people who come together with a shared identity, most often for some shared activity. At one level, the term describes street groups of people, typically young men, and often based around a limited neighbourhood. At another level, the term can refer to organised crime where the social cohesion of the gang has a wider geographical context and a more formalised and complex set of activities. This chapter focuses on the street-level groups that are the source of moral panics in mainstream society.

A6.2. Definitions

There remains a longstanding debate within psychological and criminological literature as to what the definition of a gang should be (Sullivan, 2005; Wood and Alleyne, 2010). In part, this is due to the discussion of whether gangs from the USA, which have been studied extensively, are comparable to gangs within the UK. In response to this, the Eurogang Network propose a solution and suggest they have been able to produce a definition of gangs for use within Europe through preliminary research: 'A street gang (or troublesome youth group corresponding to a street gang elsewhere) is any durable, street-oriented youth group whose identity includes involvement in illegal activity' (Weerman et al., 2009, p. 20). This is, however, only one proposed definition that not everyone necessarily agrees with.

The definition proposed by the Eurogang Network seems feasible at a first glance; however, there are some problems with such a definition. Marshall, Webb and Tilley (2005) raise the issue that even with a well thought-out and evidence-based definition, some individuals who fit such a description may not class themselves as gang members. Gang membership is an identity that is adopted by individuals as part of a group. It has been seen within research conducted in Nottingham (Scowcroft and Winder, in prep.; see Box 6.1) that gang membership is self-selected, and even when an outsider may see an individual as fitting the stereotypical gang identity, they may not necessarily class themselves as being in a gang.

Box 6.1. Gangs in Nottingham

Interview extract:

> Cause there's certain gangs and then if you said to me am I in a gang I'd say no, but I've still got my own area . . . But my area, we're not a gang it's just an area . . .

In the above extract, the individual is aware that he may be seen by others as being a gang member, but he does not class himself as one, even though he is affiliated to a particular area, where he lives. His 'area' is not described in geographical terms but also as a name for the group he hangs around with. This area is involved in similar activities and holds similar morals to the individuals who were also interviewed, who classed themselves as gang members; but this individual makes it clear in the interview that he is not in 'a gang' (Scowcroft and Winder, in prep.).

Researchers have suggested that self-nomination is the most robust way of identifying gang membership and that academic oversimplifications of gang definitions should be abandoned, with the focus of research turning to behaviour and values (Esbensen et al., 2001; Marshall, Webb and Tilley, 2005). After all, it is the behaviour of gang members that we are interested in as researchers, since if it was not for their antisocial and criminal behaviours they would just be another group of individuals who are oriented within streets of their areas/neighbourhoods.

The US has also struggled with the issue of defining what a gang is, and researchers remain in disagreement as to the definition (Petersen, 2000; Sullivan, 2005). As with the UK gang situation, it has also been suggested that US gang research has been subjected to an academic oversimplification and that we should not focus on a definition of gangs but on the behaviour of those in gangs (as reported by themselves).

A6.3. Who?

Psychopathology

It is no surprise that as gangs appear more in the public domain, academic interest in gangs has also increased. This interest is seen as necessary, as the behaviour associated with gangs is potentially harmful to both the people involved and the rest of society. Thompson (2002 as cited in Bennett and Holloway, 2004) reported in *The Observer* that there could be as many as 30,000 gang members in the UK. Bennett and Holloway (2004) discuss the different types of gangs that might make up this number, making distinctions between the ethnicity of gangs (e.g. Asian, Turkish, Albanian), the purpose of the gangs (e.g. drug gangs or crime firms) and the gender separations (either wholly male or female 'girl' gangs). However, as some suggest the media have overstated the gang problem by exaggerating the number of people involved in gangs in the UK and hyping-up the issue (Marshall, Webb and Tilley, 2005). US gangs have also been reported to be distinguishable in similar ways with regard to ethnicity, purpose and gender (for a review, see Coughlin and Venkatesh, 2003), but not necessarily into the same groups of these distinctions.

Such differences between the types of gangs in both the UK and the US illustrate that the term 'gang' has many connotations and is a broad description for different types of groups that have something in common. The academic and social interest of such 'gangs' does not stem from the knowledge that groups are formed and they are different, but that they all involve some criminal behaviours. As Wood and Alleyne (2010) suggest, gang research would not be so compelling to those who study it, were it not for the criminal aspects associated with the group behaviours.

Even though there are differences described in these groups, the term gang is used without distinction in most research, possibly because it is assumed that the term 'gang' refers to a group involved in criminal behaviour. Certainly, in today's society, the word 'gang' is particularly associated with young men in city or urban environments who are involved in acts of social disorder and are occasionally violent. This somewhat stereotypical view seems too simplistic to describe gangs and is not a good reflection of the different types of gangs already described, such as girl gangs. This problem of classification is enhanced by some of those who are involved in gangs purposefully calling themselves a gang and describing themselves as members. It seems the label of a gang is not necessarily just a stereotype, but a real concept that is acknowledged by those involved as well as those who aren't.

Gangs have been linked to a series of antisocial and violent behaviours such as the use of knives and firearms, physical violence and drug trading (Bennett and Holloway, 2004; Bradshaw and Smith, 2005; DirectGov, 2010). In line with this, comparative studies have found that gang members are more likely to be involved in antisocial, delinquent and criminal behaviours than non-gang members in both the US and Europe (Bendixen, Endresen and Olweus, 2006; McVie, 2010; Thornberry et al., 1993).

Some researchers suggest that gang membership is connected to the psychopathology of individuals and their desire to be involved in violent behaviours. In this view, gang members are seen to be characterised by being impulsive, sociopathic and lacking morality and empathetic traits (Yablonsky, 1962). McVie (2010) also reports higher scores on impulsivity scores for self-reported gang members than non-members. Dupéré et al. (2007) investigated the individual differences of gang members and suggest they may be innately psychopathological. However, in this study psychopathic tendencies were measured using reports from parents of gang members with regard to behavioural attributes, which cannot necessarily be concluded as indications of psychopathology. As a criticism of this view Valdez, Kaplan and Codina (2000) acknowledge that gang populations have not been rigorously tested for psychopathological traits. However, it is generally agreed that the risk of becoming involved in a gang is not generated by psychopathology, but by situations in which individuals find themselves (Klein, 1995).

Drugs and alcohol

Stereotypically, gangs have been associated with drug use and drug dealing. However a US study found that drug use is not a significant predictor of gang membership (Zhang, Welte and Weiczorek, 1999), although gang membership does have a significant effect on subsequent drug use. It is suggested that, in the UK, gang membership is linked to drug use; however, this statement should be treated with much caution. The term 'drug use' can cover a range of activities and a number of different drugs could be implicated in this. Interviews with gang members in Nottingham revealed that the use of cannabis was a contributory factor to becoming a gang member. The group formed because they would be on the street smoking and therefore their social network formed around this. The interviews also revealed that drug use and dealing drugs was sometimes an activity that gang members would be involved in; however, this was not a necessity for being in a gang. In fact, some gang members said that there were boundaries to their gang membership in that they would refuse to be involved in drugs even though they were part of a gang in which drug taking or dealing took place.

In Edinburgh it has also been suggested that gang members are four times more likely than non-gang members to drink alcohol and five times more likely to have used drugs in the last year at 13 years of age (McVie, 2010).

Mental health and trauma

There is currently no empirical research that links previous trauma to gang membership. However, theories have been raised that suggest gang membership in the USA may follow from adverse family situations (Lacourse et al., 2006). Such theories suggest that when family stability is lacking, the individual utilises the gang as a 'surrogate' family and forms the relationships that are lacking at home. The interviews conducted in Nottingham support this theory to some extent; in particular, one interview with a gang member included a series of dialogues detailing feelings that his mother didn't love him, and the gang providing a sense of belonging and love that he could not get from his mother.

Non-members also speculated in these interviews that they believed that being close to their family meant they did not need to join a gang and that they saw people who had experienced some family trauma as more likely to be in a gang than those who had not. These observations suggest there is at least a perceived link between gang membership and family dysfunction. Further research will show how strong this link is and how much it is a risk factor for gang membership.

Individual differences

It has been suggested that individual differences can predict gang membership. For example, gang members have been shown to score lower on measures of IQ and self-esteem, and have a higher than average incidence of learning difficulties (for a review see Wood and Alleyne, 2010). It is thought that these individual characteristics alone are not sufficient to lead to gang membership; social and environmental factors are also necessary for individuals to join a gang. It may be the case that these differences are risk factors for delinquent behaviour, but a certain environment whereby an individual is surrounded by gangs and their values is needed for the aspiration to join a gang.

As was discussed in regard to the issues of defining gangs, the same applies when looking into individual characteristics of gang members. There seems to be no typical profile of gang members. Gang members differ in terms of their reasons for joining and their activities or roles within gangs. This means that gang members cannot be described in terms of differences from their non-member counterparts. In line with suggestions made by Esbensen et al. (2001), it is proposed that behaviours should be the focus of research for individual differences within gang members.

KEY DEBATE: Do gang members drift out of the gang as easy as they drift in?

Fifty years ago, David Matza (1964) developed the idea of delinquency and drift. At that time the moral panic about the behaviour of young people was framed around the concept of delinquency, and Matza provided a balance to the explanations that provided direct causes for the behaviour. Our positivist way of looking at the world leads us to focus on relatively simple causes for complex actions and, in so doing, we miss the wider context (see also the key debate in Chapter 8 on murder). Matza argued that young people don't fully commit to a career or delinquency but in fact drift between conventional and unconventional behaviours.

The factors that bring about this drift are clearly, in the first instance, opportunity and where you live. Matza goes on to argue that the drift into criminal behaviour is also enhanced by a sense of injustice. The drift argument suggests that many gang members will only be partially committed to the gang and gang membership will be only one of many roles and activities.

References:

Matza, D. (1964) *Delinquency and Drift*, New York: John Wiley and Sons, Inc.

A6.4. Misconceptions

Morality

One misconception that was drawn from the study completed in Nottingham revolved around the morality of gang members (see Box 6.2). The gang members that were interviewed all stated that, even though violence and crime was an aspect of their reality and an activity they associated with their membership, there were morals involved in such acts. Mainly this involved who the victims of their crimes would be; they would not be able to mug an old lady or a young child, as these would be judged unfair targets, but people outside these categories would be acceptable targets. In the same set of interviews, the non-members expressed that they felt gang members had no morals and would not have a problem intimidating, attacking or stealing from anyone, regardless of their age or ability to protect themselves. Some gang members also suggested that the violence they were involved in would only include others who were also 'on it' (i.e. also in gangs) and they would leave the non-members out of the trouble (unless they started it, of course). This was not agreed with by non-members, who believed that gang members would see both members from other gangs as targets, but also people who were not involved in any gang.

Box 6.2. Nottingham gang morality

Interview extracts:
The difference in views can be seen in the following extracts. The first is a self-reported gang member describing the way his gang had intimidated a couple as they walked past, as a way of asserting the gang's authority and showing that people should be scared of them. He seems to suggest that the couple wouldn't have been old because *that* would have been unacceptable:

> I: yeah, were they like a young couple or like?
> P1: yeah yeah yeah, like an that's like a rule we don't do none of that like (pause) anything to like, towards the old people or the young people
> I: yeah
> P1: like we wouldn't go out and barge or make a granny or a granddad feel intimidated. Its, its not one of them that's (inaudible) I will respect and …

The next extract shows how a non-member has the opposite view to this, and it is thought that anyone could be the victim of gangs, regardless of their age or status.

> Erm, I think it's just anyone, as I said er, if they see someone that's like, someone that's hopeless er they see 'em and they think they can't stick up for them self.

The following extract is also from a non-member. This individual would fit a common stereotype of a gang member, and most definitions proposed, but he just has an 'area' and not a gang. He also seems to hold the same morals as the gang members who were interviewed. He suggests that he has more morals as he

---

wouldn't beat someone up just because they are from a different area though this is what he thinks gang members will do – a seemingly common misconception.

> But I ant took it on where I've beat a guy up just cos they're not from where I'm from, if they came round my area causing trouble then I would, but I wouldn't just beat someone up just cos they're not from where I'm from.

Source: Scowcroft and Winder, in prep.

These misconceptions described above are between people of the same age, living in the same areas and being around gangs, the difference being that some are self-reported gang members and some are not. This demonstrates that even with such close demographics misconceptions are present, and these misconceptions may be even marked for the rest of the general public.

The use of morality in such situations to rationalise acts of violence has been termed *moral disengagement* (Bandura, 1999). This is the process whereby the acts committed by gang members would be morally bound and justifications for their actions sought from their pre-existing beliefs regarding what is moral and what is not (Bandura et al., 1996). In this example, victims are selected (or not) depending on whether the gang can morally disengage from them. Hyde, Shaw and Moilanen (2010) suggest that moral reasoning for violent actions is a product of the environment in which gang members find themselves.

Similar accounts of morality are also described as being present within terrorism research, and gang structure, behaviour and reasoning has been suggested to be comparable to terrorism in some respects (Wilson and Sullivan, 2007). This could identify a common theme in this type of violent crime, as the use of violence is seen as being necessary given the environment in which the offenders find themselves.

A6.5. Facts and figures

Incidence

It is difficult to estimate the criminal activity level of gangs in the UK. Each year the Home Office release the national statistics for crime rates, however, because being in a gang is not a crime this is not recorded in such reports. It is acknowledged that gang behaviour is associated with certain types of crimes, for example, knife and gun crimes, and the statistics produced by the Home Office do include these. Recent statistics show that there were 33,274 instances of crimes involving knives or sharp objects and 7966 firearm offences in the 12 months prior to June 2010 in England and Wales; however it cannot be estimated what proportion of such crimes can be attributable to gang membership (Home Office, 2010).

A consultation on the British Crime Survey by the Home Office has revealed that the survey should include the topics such as perceptions of, and involvement in, street gangs and carrying knives (Home Office, 2008), although to date such information is not available in the releases of information about crimes within the UK. If gang-related crimes were to be recorded as such in future, problems may still arise in the accuracy of recording as definitional problems would no doubt still exist and it may be difficult to ascertain whether a crime is gang related or not.

In the USA in 2008, it was reported that street gangs accounted for the largest proportion of all types of gangs active in the country and that gang crime accounted for around 80% of crime in the community (National Gang Intelligence Centre, 2009). This level of focus on gangs and gang crime is presumably because of the length of time gangs have been operating in the USA compared with that in the UK. Some may say that UK gangs are mimicking what they have learnt from larger-scale US gangs, although the level of crime may not be as significant or severe.

If you were to track the media reports of incidence of gangs over the last decade, it may seem that the UK is in trouble, as the occurrence of gang crimes, murders and risk to the public increases. This type of reporting has been suggested to be the source of a 'moral panic' situation, and some have criticised the media for sensationalising gang culture (Centre for Social Justice, 2009). The incidence rate of youth homicide has been said to be decreasing whilst the reporting of such crimes has suggested an increased incidence, which has possibly given a misleading impression of the gang problem within the UK.

Prevalence

It is difficult to estimate the prevalence of gangs in the UK due to some of the issues already discussed in this chapter. Estimates have been made about how many gangs operate and the number of gang members; for example, a report by the Metropolitan Police estimated that there were 169 separate gangs operating in London (BBC News, 2007) and that the crime committed by such gangs accounted for one-fifth of the crime in London.

Findings from a longitudinal study conducted with over 4000 young people in Edinburgh suggest that, at 13 years of age, 18% of young people self-report that they had been in a gang in the last year; this figure reduced to 12% by age 16 and reduced even further by age 18. Over these three age groups, the proportion of respondents who reported being involved with a gang that involved a strong identity, gang name and/or gang signs remained constant at approximately 5% (McVie, 2010). It has also been estimated that up to 6% of 10–19-year-olds self-report to belonging to a gang in the UK (Sharp, Aldridge and Medina, 2006).

A6.6. How are offenders caught?

Investigation

Offenders of gang-related crimes are not caught and convicted just because they are in gangs, as being a gang member is not an offence in itself. Police are aware of gangs in the UK and gang activities are investigated when an offence is committed and it seems a gang may be involved. However, such investigations would not arise from a need to catch gang members, but to catch those who may have committed an offence and who also happen to be in a gang.

The information about gang status in investigating such crimes would not be entirely useless, though; knowledge of gang status when investigating crimes such as stabbings would be important in assessing possible motives and rival gangs could be the most obvious suspects. Conviction may be aided in this way, as gang membership may serve as a good source of information, but conviction would not be for gang membership per se.

A6.7. What happens to offenders?

Sentencing

There are no official sentencing guidelines for offenders who commit gang-related offences, since being in a gang is not an illegal activity. The sentencing of offenders will depend upon the illegal activity that they have committed, whether it is part of a gang activity or committed alone. Robbery offences will be treated as such, as will drug, knife and firearm offences.

Laws exist that attempt to prevent gang activities such that in court, if an offender is known to be in a gang, it *could* lead to longer sentencing (Directgov, 2010). Knife crime is one of the crimes most highly associated with gang activities and there are strict laws surrounding knife possession; it is illegal for anyone to carry a knife in a public place without a reasonable explanation, which would not include carrying it for someone else having no intention of using it or carrying it for protection (Directgov, 2010).

Unlike those crimes that have been discussed so far in other chapters, gang membership is seen as one of the aggravating factors to sentencing of various crimes; being part of a gang is a factor of greater culpability of possession of a bladed weapon or firearm, threatening behaviour offences, theft, assault and attempted murder (Sentencing Guidelines Council, 2008a, 2008b, 2009). This list is not exhaustive, however, and the guidelines for overall seriousness of offences state that the culpability of crimes in general will be aggravated by gang membership (Sentencing Guidelines Council, 2004).

Treatments typically offered

As with the difficulty of punishment for gang membership, 'treatment' for gang membership does not exist. To be a gang member is not a disorder that should be cured, but an identity that is associated with undesirable behaviours. Klein (1995) acknowledges the normality of a population who classify themselves as gang members, and suggests that rather than therapy and treatment for those involved, educational intervention and employability training for at-risk populations would be much more effective.

There have been cases of more direct treatment of gang members in the USA and the use of clinical therapies to reduce recidivism. One example of this is the use of cognitive-behavioural therapy with adolescent gang members, and it has been suggested that such clinical approaches should be utilised in management and rehabilitation of gang members after incarceration (Di Placido et al., 2006).

In the UK, attention is more focused on the programmes developed to intervene before joining or during membership, rather than treatments offered after conviction. This cross-cultural difference could be the result of the way gangs are viewed by authorities in the two countries and the greater experience of the USA in dealing with the issue of gangs. Even though UK gangs are not necessarily a brand new phenomenon, the UK has not had as much focused attention on the issue in the past.

Relative efficacy of interventions

Evaluation studies (e.g. Di Placido et al., 2006) suggests that clinical treatments using cognitive therapies are successful in reducing the chances of reoffending and the seriousness of future crimes committed. Other studies and reviews of correctional treatments of gang members in this vein have also been shown to be effective and are reviewed in Di Placido et al.'s reporting of their findings.

Recidivism

There has been some research into recidivism of gang members, and findings suggest that there is a relationship between gang membership and criminal recidivism (Chu et al., 2010). Such a relationship was also observed during interviews in Nottingham whereby, post-conviction, individuals were respected more and were expected to rejoin their gangs (Scowcroft and Winder, in prep.) (see Box 6.3). Pitts (2007) also discusses a similar process after gang members had been imprisoned in a study of gangs in Walthamstow Forest, London. Pitts acknowledges that the conviction and incarceration of gang members could lead to greater future violence as they seek vengeance after leaving prison and have a point to prove about their status.

Co-occurrence or progression to other crimes

Zhang et al. (1999) have suggested that there are interactional effects between being in a gang and previous and subsequent criminal behaviour. For example, it is suggested that drug use is not a precursor to gang membership, whereas gang membership is found to be a precursor to subsequent delinquent behaviour and drug use. McVie (2010) also reports that, within Edinburgh, various criminal activities were found to be significant predictors of gang membership, such as violent offences, the use of weapons and theft.

Box 6.3. Cycle of crime

During the interviews with young men in Nottingham, it was observed that there was a progression of crimes during the course of being in a gang. This was described as a cycle by both members and non-members, almost as a realisation of the negative side of being part of gangs. The cycle would start as the individual would see others making money from crimes committed as part of the gang and the individual would aspire to this; the individual would join a gang and do similar things to make money; they would gain a criminal record and struggle to be legitimately employed (gang membership is also described as a job by some members); more money is desired, and therefore more crimes are committed and the severity of these crimes increases. This is a crude example of the type of cycle that was described in more elaborative dialogue during interviews, but the principles remain the same – being in a gang can very well lead to a cycle of crime and making money from it. Similarly as seen with regard to power and respect, criminal behaviour means increase in these and/or more money; a common phrase used by those in gangs when asked about the motivations during the interviews was 'Money, Power, Respect', and this was even the name of one gang described, shortened to MPR.

Prognosis

There is little research that looks at the life course of gang members. However, recent interviews with gang members and ex-members in Nottingham suggest there is a normative pattern in terms of the progression of gang membership. A common theme within the interviews was that the young men found it odd to be involved in a gang past a certain point, and that by the time they 'grow up' they should be able to settle down and not be part of the gang any more. However in the same interviews some also stated that there were gang members who had not outgrown gang membership and were still in gangs until they were middle-aged. It was suggested that this was not through choice but through necessity, as it would be too dangerous to leave because of the repercussions from other rival gangs. Gang membership had become normality and not something to do when young. This was thought of as being an extraordinary situation by other members though, and it became apparent that the normal lifespan of a gang member only took the young men through to their twenties, for example, when they recognised that they must get out of the gang and do something 'normal' with their lives.

This pattern of gang membership during youth is also supported by findings from Edinburgh, in which self-reported gang members were suggested to be mainly between the ages of 15 and 18 years, but with some as young as 10 and under and some over 21 years (McVie, 2010).

One class of street gang that does not follow this pattern and is not covered in this chapter are the sports-related groups. In particular, there has been much social concern about football gangs since the 1970s and there have been specialised police units created to monitor and disrupt the behaviour of these gangs (see Stott, 2009). These groups engage in organised, international events that often involve large-scale violence. The membership of these groups does not match the demographics of the neighbourhood street gang, in particular with regard to age.

A6.8. And the damage done . . .

Who are the victims?

From the reporting of gangs in the public domain, it might be easy to think that the general public are at risk of being victims of gangs and their associated crimes. This is true to an extent – since robbery is one of the crimes associated with gangs, the public will be at risk. However, it is in fact the gang members themselves who are more likely to be the victims of this culture and the crimes surrounding it than the rest of the general public.

The Metropolitan Police state that gang members are more likely to be the victims of crime than non-gang members (Metropolitan Police, 2010). Much of the gang violence that is described from the UK revolves around the protection of territories or 'endz'. This violence begins because of associations with rival gangs from rival areas, and the opposing gang members are likely to be the victims of violence stemming from this. Such a view can be based on anecdotal evidence of seeing the way gangs talk about their lifestyle, but this has also been found to be true in psychological research into the victims of street gangs in Europe (Klein, Weerman and Thornberry, 2006).

Kein, Weerman and Thornberry state in their 2006 article, 'Where there is violence, there are victims' (p. 428); this seems to be the key to gang violence. There are areas where gangs operate, and areas where they don't. The areas that are not associated with gangs are very unlikely to be the scene of gang violence; gang violence is focused on 'home' areas , since this is the source of the feuds and historically the reason for the emergence of the gang. This would suggest that the victims are more likely to be those who are geographically associated with gangs; that the public living in the areas associated with gangs are most at risk. Such an explanation would seem sensible, and possibly the reason new members join, adopting the 'if you can't beat 'em, join 'em' attitude or for protection against becoming the victim. And so the cycle of victims continues . . .

Cost of crime

Christensen et al. (2008) make reference to the possible economic harm of gangs in the UK through the violence with which they have been associated. It has been reported that the cost of penetrating injuries (i.e. of stabbings and shootings) to the National Health Service (NHS) is around £8000 per injury, equating to around £30 million per year. Gangs cannot be held responsible for the full extent of these costs; however, if indeed their activities and behaviours centre around this type of violence, the potential cost of such crimes should be addressed. It remains difficult to establish what proportion of these costs gangs are accountable for as victims who are associated with gangs are not likely to disclose such information when being treated, for fear of repercussions from their involvement. Some gang members also report that one of the 'rules' of being in a gang is that they keep their activities between themselves and do not disclose anything to the authorities (Centre for Social Justice, 2009); this theme of silence was also observed in the interviews conducted in Nottingham.

Fear of crime

Some research in the USA has been carried out into the fear and perceptions the public have of gangs (Lane, 2002). In the UK, no such research has been carried out to date. If media reports are taken as an indication of this, then it would appear that the fear of crime from gangs is great in the UK. Headlines and phrases such as 'Gangland Britain' (*The Observer*, 2002), or reports of numerous stabbings and their relationship to gangs, are common. However, this does not necessarily reflect the public view of gangs in general. The fear of crime from gangs could indeed be a lot less than papers and news reports suggest and may be quite localised.

Changes in attitudes and behaviours

Gangs in the UK are commonly associated with certain types of dress, language and attitudes. This association has created a fear in the general public that could be described as 'hoodie fear', named after the garment popular with young people. Again, media reports seem to have created some of the moral panic surrounding the hoodie culture as newspapers and reports focus on hoodies being banned for others' safety in public areas due to the association of this garment with crimes and a gang attitude of those who wear it. Previous garments that have been the focus for public concern include the shoes known as brothel-creepers (worn by Teddy Boys in the 1950s) and leather jackets (worn by Rockers in the 1960s).

It has been suggested that this image promoted in the media, and subsequently by the public, has led to the criminalisation and demonisation of young men, and turned the hoodie culture into something more feared than it should be (Millie, 2010). This criminalisation has spread to associations with music, and the attitudes of the general public have now moved to fear of 'chavs', 'hoodies' and 'yardies'.

However, it should be noted that this association is not necessarily discouraged by the youths it affects. Many of those who are in gangs actively dress in a certain way so that people know that they are in a gang, they listen to music that talks about (and some might say glamorises) gangs, they wear colours to associate with their gangs, have gang names, gang talk and are seemingly proud of it. So, it seems unfair to blame media hype on the change in public opinion of such youths, when it appears that the change in behaviour and attitude is the desired effect of adopting that lifestyle.

PART B: Theories and explanations

B6.1. Introduction

The difficulty in developing theories for gang membership and gang behaviour stems from the difficulties in defining them. To propose a theory of gang membership would be to assume gang membership is a definable activity, whereas this is not so easily determined. There are, however, theories that have been put forward as to why and how gangs form and what risk factors may contribute to individuals deciding to join gangs and engaging in the criminal behaviours associated with gangs.

Social identity theory

One theory that is widely accepted throughout social psychology that has been applied to gang membership is social identity theory (Garot, 2007; Wang, 1994). In relation to gang membership, this theory suggests that individuals gain a sense of group identity through being part of a group and that individuals use self-categorisation in order to form an identity (Tajfel, 1972) such that gang members give themselves a gang identity. Wang (1994) suggests that this happens as individuals utilise this social categorisation as a means of giving themselves an identity to produce the best possible outcome for their life situation. This was reflected in the interviews conducted with young men in Nottingham (Scowcroft and Winder, in prep.). One of the subordinate themes of the analysis performed on these interviews focused on the formation of a gang identity by members. This was an identity that was socially formed through a reality of a gang world situation that had become ordinary to their everyday lives.

Attachment/family

Theories such as those which assume that attachment problems may lead to risk factors of gang membership are in line with others that link attachment issues and delinquency in adolescence, whereby problematic childhoods and unsecure family situations are deemed as risk factors for gang membership and criminal behaviour associated with gangs. This is supported by findings from a longitudinal study conducted among young people in Edinburgh, as it was reported that gang members scored significantly lower on measures of parental supervision measures and were more likely to be from deprived family backgrounds than non-gang members (McVie, 2010).

Wood and Alleyne (2010) discuss family theories with regard to gang membership and argue that research suggests that, rather than attachment problems being responsible for subsequent gang membership, disorganisation of the family unit may be a more feasible explanation, although it is acknowledged that this relationship is only moderate. The concept of the disorganised family unit is a subjective one and could also be heightened by the environment in which the family finds itself (being around gangs in certain areas).

Self-esteem

Research has also focused on the self-esteem of individuals who join gangs. This approach suggests that low self-esteem is a risk factor for becoming a gang member and that young people use aggressive and violent social identities to overcome issues with self-esteem in that negative attitudes towards the self will result in delinquent behaviour (Kaplan, 1975). Wang (1994) reported research findings that, compared with non-members, gang members have a reduced sense of self-esteem. This finding has also been found to be true where self-reported gang members in Edinburgh were found to have lower self-esteem scores on personality measures than those who did not report to be gang members (McVie, 2010). The interviews with gang members in Nottingham also supported this theory, with most gang members describing their desire to appear 'big' and linking this with gang membership. Garot's (2007) ethnographic study also supported such findings, suggesting that the gang identity forms a 'tough performance' in a situation where self-esteem was previously lacking.

B6.2. Conclusion

The above theories have been shown to be good indicators of potential gang membership. It is proposed, however, that they do not function in isolation to one another and that to produce the greatest risk of delinquent behaviour typified by gang members, such theories should be taken as a whole. Attachment and social identity theory are suggested to be linked in such cases, whereby a history of poor attachment with family and friends will increase risk of gang involvement in order to gain an identity that was previously lacking (Hayslett-Mccall and Bernard, 2002). For example, in the case of a young boy, if his role as a son or brother in his family life is not claimed as an identity, he may gain identity as a gang member instead.

The social identity that is constructed in the reality of gang members can also be linked to the self-esteem theory of gang membership discussed above. In this case, the lack of self-esteem causes the individual to construct an identity that will act as a protection from the reality they face as individuals surrounded by gang members. The adoption of a 'big' identity overcomes the issues that may be present with regards to self-esteem, as they are no longer seen as weak by other people.

These contributory factors, even when combined, are not sufficient to create gang members. The social reality in which the individuals find themselves will determine how these aspects of identity formation and empowerment will interact. It was also found from the interviews with young men in Nottingham that a specific kind of reality was described by all participants who had been in or around gangs. This reality was defined in war-like terms, by militant roles that the gangs took on and matter-of-fact descriptions of ordinary (but extraordinary to others not involved in gangs) situations (see Box 6.4). This theory is also supported by research suggesting that gangs in other parts of the UK also describe their activities, roles and lives as militant (Bullock and Tilley, 2002).

Box 6.4. Nottingham's reality

Say like you're at war, for instance Meadows and St Ann's, like the WFG and Badbreed, if one of the WFG lads left WFG, all the Badbreed be down on 'em. So that's why there's a, always gonna be that war going off, all the friction and all that.

...obviously it makes me nervous but its just life innit really ya ya you're born to die really so ya jus ya gonna die some day (pause) obviously ya don't wanna go out like that but its just its just how it happens innit

Have wars, area wars, area code wars or city wars or (pause) just if you're living in the wrong street ya get battered or owt like that.

The behaviour and roles that are adopted are done so because this environment is frequently encountered by the individuals involved, rather than a different type of reality. If the reality was different, the behaviour would subsequently be different, as they do not aspire to 'appear big' in a 'war' with other areas or gangs; this is not to say their behaviour would not be delinquent, however, but it may manifest in a different way. This could be the difference between 'normal' delinquent behaviour and gang membership.

PART C: Further information

C6.1. Organisations to contact for information and voluntary work

Nacro, the national crime reduction charity, works with disadvantaged people, deprived communities and ex-offenders to give them a positive stake in society. It has unrivalled expertise in developing practical responses to crime and stimulating fresh thinking on how best to reduce it through policy, research (and indeed facilitated the research into the Nottingham gangs documented in this chapter) and campaign work.

Nacro runs preventive projects to steer young people away from crime, provides housing, education and employment programmes for ex-offenders and people at risk of offending, resettles prisoners into the community and works with families and communities to prevent crime. Visit www.nacro.org.uk.

C6.2. Further reading

Dying to Belong (Centre for Social Justice, 2009) – This report gives a good overview of how we understand gangs at present, as well as giving details about the different cities associated with gangs in the UK.

Street gang theory and research: Where are we now and where do we go from here? (Wood and Alleyne, 2010) – A great starting point to gang research, the problems, the theories and how psychology can play a part in understanding gang violence.

Hoods: The Gangs of Nottingham – A Study in Organised Crime (Carl Fellstrom, 2008) – A book that give details of the truths behind the gangs in the 'Gun crime capital of the UK'.

Reluctant Gangsters: Youth Gangs in Waltham Forest (Pitts, 2007) – A good example of a qualitative and quantitative balance in gang research. Gives detailed breakdowns of gangs in the area, and could be used as a template for other UK cities to follow.

chapter

7

INTERNET SEX OFFENCES

KERRY SHELDON

PART A: The offence – Who, what, when, why?

A7.1. Introduction

The sexual abuse of children involving the Internet is a serious and growing societal concern (Quayle and Taylor, 2003). Since the early 1990s, the Internet has become an increasingly significant factor in child sexual exploitation, facilitating a new means to commit child sexual abuse. In particular, the Internet has become the principal medium for downloading, collecting and circulating 'child pornography' (e.g. the depiction of children in sexual poses or acts with other children or adults) for personal and/or commercial reasons (Laulik et al., 2007). This offending has sparked off high-profile police operations, substantial increases in arrests and convictions and prolific legislative activity (both in the UK and elsewhere). This chapter will mainly focus on men who access, download and circulate child pornography across the Internet as the most frequently occurring type of Internet sex offender. It will outline some of the key areas in this field and raise some pertinent questions about the management and risk of individuals engaged in this activity. For instance are they child molesters or are they a new type of sex offender? And if an individual views child pornography on the Internet, is s/he likely to progress to a contact sex offence?

A7.2. Definitions

What is child pornography?

Whether an image is pornographic is a complex and difficult issue, as legal definitions differ across jurisdictions and national boundaries (Healy, 1997). Definitions also differ between those used in legal and academic contexts (Beech et al., 2008), and the issue is further confused by the lack of a clear definition of what constitutes a child, as this depends upon social, cultural, temporal, psychological, moral, sexual and religious norms (Healy, 1997). Plus, the legal age of sexual consent in many countries varies (Gillespie, 2005).

Generally, professionals within the field do not like to use the term 'child pornography'. This is because it invites comparisons to adult pornography, lending credence and legitimacy to the material and arguably minimising the material's inherently abusive nature (Taylor and Quayle, 2003), and thus the term 'child abuse images' is frequently employed. Tate (1990) suggests that images of an abusive nature are 'not pornography in any real sense, simply evidence of serious sexual assaults on young children' (p. 203). Taylor and Quayle (2003) note that the term child pornography carries international meaning and is readily recognisable; for example, UNICEF (1990) describes the 'use of children in pornographic performances and materials'.

Academic definitions try to emphasise the fact that the production of each image requires the exploitation of a child or children and therefore it is evidence of a sexual offence (Taylor and Quayle, 2003). For instance, Edwards (2000) defines child pornography as 'a record of the systematic rape, abuse and torture of children on film and photography and other electronic means' (p. 1). Of course the existence of pseudo-pornography[1] means that it is no longer possible to argue that, in every case, pornography is the record of abuse or exploitation of an actual child (Lanning, 2001).

Psychological definitions of child pornography focus on the *value* and *meaning* of the images. For instance, Svedin and Back (1996) describe child pornography as 'text, image (photo, slide, film, video or computer programme) that is intended to evoke a sexual feeling, fantasy or response in adults' (p. 9). This definition reflects the person's 'experience' with the material. With such a definition the range of materials that could evoke sexual fantasies varies widely – from photographs in a magazine to a picture of the rape of a child (Howitt, 1995).

What is the nature of contemporary child pornography?

Child pornography images available on the Internet range from everyday images of children naked to depictions of gross acts of indecency, such as penetrative sexual intercourse. Victims range from babies to teenagers. Current police seizures of child pornography collections regularly include material from the 1960s and 1970s from Western European countries and the USA (Taylor and Quayle, 2003). Such material is easily turned into digital images on the Internet and can still be identified from the file name it is given (Taylor and Quayle, 2003). For instance, 'Lolita'[2] material is referred to as 'LL'. As such, 'LL27-13' downloaded from the Internet refers to the thirteenth picture scanned from Lolita video number 27. The Color Climax Corporation in Denmark in the 1970s produced around 36 ten-minute cine films marketed under the title 'Lolita' (see Tate, 1990 for a detailed history of child pornography production). These involved young girls mainly aged between 7 and 11 being sexually abused, mainly by men. Their titles say much about their content – *Incest Family*, *Pre-Teen Sex*, *Sucking Daddy* and *Child Love*. Similarly, the widely traded child pornography magazine entitled *Lolita*, like the series of cine films, became a brand name for child pornography pictures.

Taylor, Holland and Quayle (2001a) note that Internet images are regularly part of a series and they highlight the difference between *thematic* and *narrative* series. *Thematic* series are those grouped by a similar theme relating to particular scenes or acts, for example oral sex, whereas *narrative* series are sequences of pictures relating to a single scene and depict a specific child, children or act, for example a child undressing. It is thought that the producer does not always post the series on the Internet in sequential order (Taylor and Quayle, 2003), and Taylor et al. (2001a) found that filling in gaps in a narrative series of images is of great importance in terms of helping the individual to personalise and engage with the victim, in sustaining and generating fantasy, and in terms of the structure of the collection itself.

A7.3. Who are the offenders?

In general, Internet sex offenders are male, aged 25–50 years. In comparison with child molesters they have fewer substance misuse problems but greater contacts with mental health services as an adult. Internet sex offenders are better educated, of higher intelligence and more likely to be employed than those who commit contact sex offences against children (see Burke et al., 2001; Sheldon and Howitt, 2007; Webb et al., 2007).

Psychopathology and personality characteristics

Table 7.1 presents the results of some of the few available studies that have explored the psychopathology, personality and socio-affective characteristics of Internet sex offenders. Typically, the studies made comparisons with other non-offender and sex offender samples. The table highlights which group has significantly different scores compared with the other samples, or which group has the highest percentage scoring above the normal range. As in the case of Webb et al. (2007), both samples reported abnormally high levels on a variety of characteristics.

It is difficult to draw any firm conclusions concerning the typical profile of an Internet sex offender from the findings above, for a number of reasons:

- Some studies employed what they termed 'Internet sex offenders', yet a small number of the sample had a history of prior sexual contacts against children, therefore decreasing the validity of the results (e.g. Laulik et al., 2007).
- The relatively small samples used means that it is unknown whether the findings are representative of Internet sex offenders in general.
- Participation in many studies was voluntary. Participants who self-select to participate may represent a distinct subgroup of Internet offenders.
- Many of the participants had completed a sex offender treatment programme; therefore it remains unknown whether non-treated Internet sex offenders represent a more deviant group.

Table 7.1   *Characteristics of Internet sex offenders compared with normative data, child molesters and rapists*

Study	Characteristic	Samples employed		
		Internet $n = 30$ (UK)	Normative data provided by the measures	
Laulik et al. (2007)	Schizophrenia	✓		
	Borderline personality features	✓		
	Antisocial personality features	✓		
	Depression	✓		
	Suicidal ideation	✓		
	Stress	✓		
	Low aggression	✓		
	Low dominance	✓		
	Low warmth	✓		
		Internet $n = 39$ (UK)		Child molesters and rapists $n = 39$
Bates and Metcalf (2007)	Self-esteem			✓
	Emotional congruence			✓
	Cognitive distortions			✓
	Locus of control			✓
	Empathy			✓
		Internet $n = 48$ (USA)		Child molesters and rapists $n = 104$
Tomak et al. (2009)	Psychopathic deviate			✓
	Schizophrenia			✓
		Internet $n = 90$ (UK)		Child molesters $n = 120$
Webb et al. (2007)	Psychopathy			✓
	Anxiety	✓		✓
	Problems with sexual self-regulation	✓		
	Problems co-operating with supervision, e.g. dropping out of treatment			✓
	Schizoid personality traits	✓		✓
	Avoidant personality traits	✓		✓
	Dependent personality traits	✓		✓

With these limitations in mind, Internet sex offenders appear less deviant, psychopathic and aggressive than other types of child sex offenders. Undoubtedly, however, it is the Internet offender's ability to manage their sexual interest that underlines their difference. For example, child molesters are more likely to 'act out' and break social rules through the commission of contact offences. This presents the question – are Internet offenders vulnerable to contact sex offences but have strong inhibitions, or are they a different type of offender?

A7.4. Misconceptions

Child abuse images pop up accidentally, don't they?

It seems relatively easy to 'accidentally' access adult pornography, but this seems rarely the case in relation to abusive images of children (see Sheldon and Howitt, 2007 for a discussion of this). Despite protestations from offenders, individuals do 'create the opportunity' to offend. It takes considerable time, effort and the acquisition of computer and Internet skills to locate images and it is invariably a purposeful activity (Quayle, 2004).

Adult pornography sites can be the initial starting point in the search for child pornography images (Sheldon and Howitt, 2007), with users trawling a variety of 'hyperlinks' some of which contain names indicative of child pornography, such as 'real teen sex – click here'. Some sites are flagged as illegal. Other individuals will type obvious words such as 'pre-teen', or more specialised terms such as 'boy-love',[3] into well-known search engines such as Google (see Box 7.1). Consequently the arrival of child pornography on the computer is not wholly unexpected and may indicate a pre-existing interest in paedophilic images. Offenders can employ online 'nicknames' or pseudonyms, maybe to avoid detection, but also to signal their sexual preferences to others online, e.g. 'daddy4uk' (Sheldon and Howitt, 2007).

Box 7.1. Some of the most popular methods for accessing child abuse images on the Internet

- Within Internet bulletin board systems images can be uploaded to servers under a specific newsgroup heading. This makes them available to other users of that newsgroup.
- Images can be made available to users globally though peer-to-peer (P2P) file-sharing software programmes such as *Limewire* or *Kazaa*, where they are uploaded to a dedicated server and made available via web links on a website.
- A user can share files on their computer using a file transfer protocol (FTP) server that allows other users direct access to specified areas of a user's computer.
- Images can be exchanged directly and privately between individuals using Microsoft's MSN Messenger.
- Individuals can communicate with children in chat rooms or social networking sites such as *MySpace* and *Facebook*.

Source: Beech et al., 2008; Internet Watch Foundation, 2008; Sheldon and Howitt, 2007.

Interestingly only a few offenders were found to use sophisticated methods to hide their images (20%), those that employ passwords (17%), encryption (6%), file servers (4%), evidence eliminating software (3%), remote storage systems (2%) and partitioned drives (2%) (Wolak et al., 2005).

There are also several factors unique to the Internet that make it an attractive venue for accessing child pornography images (as well as pornography and online sexual behaviour generally), including *accessibility*, *affordability* and (perceived) *anonymity* (called the 'Triple A Engine') (Cooper, 1989). In other words, images can be accessed by anyone, thousands of images can be viewed on screen, printed, stored (e.g. hard drives, memory sticks, CD-ROMS) and re-created endlessly; many images are free, and they are often accessed in the isolation of one's own home (Carr, 2004; Sheldon and Howitt, 2007).

Individuals simply 'view' these images, so where's the harm?

The term 'viewing' implies that the individuals are 'passive' in the process and that relatively little, if any harm, is done. But, users actively engage with child abuse images. For instance, some collect, catalogue and index the images they accrue (Sheldon and Howitt, 2007; Tate, 1990; Taylor and Quayle, 2003). Some distribute, trade, or swap, images between a few individuals or as part of a larger paedophile network (e.g. 'wonderland club[4]') (Middleton, Beech and Mandeville-Norden, 2005). In terms of harm, the images commonly portray the child as smiling, giving the impression that the child is enjoying their victimisation and is maybe even complicit in the abuse, but videos have been found where the producer of the video can be heard forcing a child to look at the camera and to smile (Taylor and Quayle, 2003).

Commonly, users of the material sexually fantasise and masturbate to the images to climax (Quayle, 2004; Sheldon and Howitt, 2007; Taylor and Quayle, 2003), perhaps imagining the child is performing the sexual acts they see upon them. If users confine themselves to masturbating and fantasising about the images, some might ask (as do some offenders) why society needs to control such activities. After all, many people have inappropriate fantasies (Leitenberg and Henning, 1995), and our fantasies are not legislated against. But Sheldon and Howitt (2007) argue that society should be concerned about the use of child pornography images for several reasons. First, users fuel the market by creating a demand. Second, deviant sexual fantasies based on Internet images may fuel a need to sexually abuse other children directly by users of such material. And third, child pornography may be used to groom children into sexual abuse, e.g. using the image to initiate a child into how to perform the sexual acts 'correctly'. Also, the material may 'normalise' the behaviour because other people are doing it (Jones and Wilson, 2009).

The term 'viewing' also fails to adequately describe all the activities of child pornography users. Some write paedophilic stories and 'post' them online, while others engage in 'role-playing' – talking through their fantasies with another person, perhaps another adult, whilst masturbating to their thoughts (Sheldon and Howitt, 2007). Some individuals masquerade as children (e.g. in social networking sites) to gain the confidence and trust of their victims over a period of time (from minutes to months) before introducing a sexual element into the online conversation or drawing them into intimate actions online and/or physical contact offline (Muir, 2005). Finally, the use of webcams now enables the sharing of 'live abuse' between perpetrator and victim(s). It might include the ordering or instruction of sex acts by one offender to another as well as the demonstration of offences (Sullivan and Beech, 2003).

A7.5. Facts and figures

Reliably assessing the extent of child pornography currently available and the number of users accessing it is extremely difficult, since researchers have no immunity from the legislation and independent checks are not generally available. The Internet is too large and changes too quickly to sample reliably (Calder, 2004), and research is mainly restricted to those individuals who have been caught. The international policing agency Interpol's Child Abuse Image Database (ICAID) – a global database for the forensic analysis of digital images of child abuse – currently contains over 520,000 images and has been used to identify 680 victims worldwide (Interpol, 2008). Of course this is not necessarily an exhaustive collection as many more images may be held in private collections, the sizes of which remain unknown. A UK-based Internet watchdog organisation, the Internet Watch Foundation (IWF), recently reported that they had positively identified 2755 worldwide Internet domains containing images of child sexual abuse – 80% of which were found to be commercial in nature, an increase of 33% from 2006 (IWF, 2008).

It is also difficult to quantify the number of children who are the subjects of abusive images, partly because child victims rarely disclose what is happening to them (Finkelhor, Mitchell and Wolak, 2000). In 1999 the Combating Pedophile Information Networks in Europe (COPINE) research team at University College Cork identified that four new children per month, on average, were appearing in child sex newsgroups. In August 2002, over a 6-week period 20 new children were identified and 140,000 images were posted to newsgroups of which 35,000 were images of new children, most posing erotically (Taylor and Quayle, 2003). We also have to remember that one 'still' picture can be disseminated many times on the Internet, thereby making estimates of how many children are involved in child pornography even more difficult.

A7.6. How are offenders caught?

Investigation

There are three main triggers that can initiate an investigation into child sexual abuse (Holland, 2005):

1. Disclosure by a child to their parents, or others in authority.
2. Information or 'tips' coming from a member of the public or the industry (e.g. Internet service providers), to the police or to 'hotline' providers (Jewkes and Andrews, 2005; Robbins and Darlington, 2003). For instance, both the Child Exploitation and Online Protection (CEOP) Centre (part of UK law enforcement) and the IWF have a 'report abuse' button.

3. Law enforcement agencies acting on information they are gathering whilst proactively monitoring the Internet, or as a result of information acquired in the course of other investigations. One example of proactive monitoring is the police investigation 'Operation Ore' (see Box 7.2).

Box 7.2. 'Operation Ore'

'Operation Ore' was a UK police operation, the result of the US Postal Inspection Service mounting 'Operation Avalanche'.

A Texan website belonging to Landslide Incorporation sold 'adult keys', which provided a gateway to many legal and illegal websites. It was claimed that the site had a special button for child pornography. Details of 75,000 repeat users of the site were found on the computer and these people used their credit cards to purchase access to the site for a fee of $29.95. The Federal Bureau of Investigation (FBI) passed details of over 7500 names to the UK police of people suspected of purchasing child abuse images (Howlett, 2003; McCulloch, 2005; Renold et al., 2003). Those on a list of Landslide US subscribers were contacted in a sting operation and offered the opportunity to purchase child pornography through the postal service. Many did not respond, but those that did were further investigated. As of April 2005, 4283 searches had been made leading to the arrest of 3744 men; 1848 were charged, 1451 convicted, plus an additional 500 received cautions (Akdeniz, 2006).

Detection

Law enforcement agencies face a number of difficulties when attempting to regulate online material, and there are a number of reasons why Internet sexual offenders are not always caught:

- Definitional issues such as the age of a child, which varies internationally.
- Individuals use methods (e.g. passwords) to 'hide' the images from law enforcement agencies.
- It takes considerable time to forensically examine computer hardware containing large amounts of data, and there may be trauma associated with professionals being exposed to images.
- The internal culture of the police is regarded as resistant to technological innovation, and there are subsequent problems associated with training officers.
- Few children are ever identified from pictures.
- Sometimes there are no obvious pointers in the images to suggest where the abuse is taking place (e.g. which country), and consequently national law enforcement agencies are reluctant to conduct an investigation without proof of jurisdiction.
- Producers of websites that provide access to images regularly change servers, thus making detection and removal problematic (Holland, 2005; Internet Watch Foundation, 2008; Jewkes and Andrews, 2005; Sheldon and Howitt, 2007).

There are, however, a number of strategies aimed at improving the effectiveness of policing – for instance, facial recognition software that can scan the faces of Internet victims. This minimises the duplication of work, eliminates the need for police officers to view distressing pictures and identifies new victims for prioritisation (Jewkes and Andrews, 2005). The police exploit the anonymous nature of the Internet by entering Internet chat rooms and pretending to be children. In addition, parents and children are constantly reminded of the safety message of not giving out personal information whilst online. Operation Ore also illustrates the importance of international cooperation in the regulation of online content. Of course, the Internet continues to evolve from fixed personal computer-based access to third-generation (3G) mobile phone technology, offering high-speed Internet access, video conferencing and digital audio-visual recoding technology, in the form of mobile hand-held devices (O'Connell, 2004). This presents new challenges for traditional policing and legislative systems.

A7.7. Conviction rates

UK conviction rates involving child pornography

Convictions for child pornography-related offences give some idea of the growth over the last few years. Table 7.2 shows that convictions have increased substantially over the 15-year period between 1988 and 2003 (Home Office, 2003; Renold et al., 2003). Unfortunately, the statistics do not differentiate between child pornography distributed via postal mail and that via the Internet.

The most substantial increase related to 2002–3. There are a number of reasons for this, including the introduction of new legislation and new sexual offences concerning child pornography, and the rapid increase in the use of the Internet for all purposes since the mid-1990s and thus increased police activity (Jones, 2003).

International conviction rates involving child pornography

There is no internationally agreed basis for recording crimes where the Internet plays a significant part (Sheldon and Howitt, 2007). Indeed, many individual countries do not even record whether a computer was involved in the commission of a crime. Akdeniz (2006) reported statistics from the International Records Access Clearing House provided by the FBI. From 1995 to 2003, 4439 prosecutions relating to child pornography offences lead to 3294 convictions.

Table 7.2 *Defendants found guilty at all courts for offences relating to indecent photographs of children in England and Wales, 1990–2003 (average per year)*

Type of offence	1990–4	1995–9	2000–3
Taking or making indecent photographs of children	36.4	87.4	497.3
Possession of indecent photographs of children	35.2	80.2	140.8

Of those 2849 resulted in imprisonment. The average imprisonment between 1995 and 2002 was 45 months, increasing to an average of 53 months in 2003.

Rates of other Internet sex offences

In the UK, in 2005–6 there were 238 recorded 'grooming' offences (Home Office, 2005). That is where an adult has met or communicated with a child on at least two earlier occasions, intentionally wants to meet them and engage in a sexual act (see Chapter 10 for more information on grooming). The National Children's Home (Carr, 2003) quotes 27 (mainly female) children or young people who have met an adult in real life following contact via the Internet (often in a chat room) and have been sexually assaulted by them. But this figure is based on only media monitoring, and it is unclear to what extent this presents the real level of such offending.

The USA conducted the first national study of online victimisation of minors. Finkelhor, Mitchell and Wolak (2000) conducted interviews with a sample of 1501 youths aged 10–17 years who use the Internet regularly (at least once a month for the previous six months). The sample consisted of 53% males and 47% females, with 73% non-Hispanic white. They reported that 19% of their sample had received an unwanted sexual solicitation or approach over the Internet in the previous year. The definition was extremely broad and included someone trying to get them to (unwillingly) talk about sex; someone asking unwanted intimate questions; someone asking them to do sexual things they did not want to do; and invitations to run away. In addition, 3% (one in seven of all the solicitations) included an attempt to contact the youth via telephone/postal mail and/or in person. Overall, the survey found few sexually orientated relationships between young people and adults.

A7.8. What happens to offenders?

Sentencing

In the UK, the main laws governing abusive images are the Protection of Children Act 1978 and the Sexual Offences Act 2003. Section 1 of the Protection of Children Act (amended) makes it an offence to make, take, distribute, show or be in possession with the intent to distribute or show an indecent image of a child (Gillespie, 2005). The maximum penalty for any of these offences is ten years' imprisonment. In the Sexual Offences Act 2003 there are three new offences punishable by up to 14 years' imprisonment:

1. Causing or inciting a child to become involved in pornography;
2. Controlling a child involved in pornography and/or;
3. Arranging or facilitating child pornography.

Showing a child an obscene image (not necessarily in photographic form) is also a criminal offence.

Furthermore, the Criminal Justice Act 1988 (section 160(1)) states that it is an offence for a person to have an indecent photograph or pseudo-photograph of a child in their possession. The maximum penalty for this offence is five years' imprisonment.

The Sentencing Advisory Panel (SAP) (2002) published guidance on what primary factors should be taken into account when deciding upon the correct level of sentence for those who collect, view and distribute child pornography. These include the following:

1. The extent of the offender's involvement with the material – wide-scale commercial distribution of material would attract a longer sentence than possession of material for personal use.
2. The nature of the indecent material (rather than the quantity). SAP published a five-level grading system of child pornography (see Box 7.3) – the higher the level of material, the higher the sentence.

As with other sex offenders, additional social and legal consequences of conviction can include:

- Sex offender registration. This requires a person to notify the police of their address and any subsequent changes to it (Sexual Offences Act, 2003).
- Being disqualified from working with children (Criminal Justice and Court Services Act, 2000, sections 28 and 29a).
- Laws that circumscribe one's activities, e.g. being banned from travelling abroad (Sexual Offences Act, 2003, sections 114–22).

Box 7.3. Sentencing Guidelines Council

Level 1	Images depicting erotic pictures with no sexual activity
Level 2	Non-penetrative sexual activity between children or solo masturbation by a child
Level 3	Non-penetrative sexual activity between adults(s) and children.
Level 4	Penetrative sexual activity involving a child or children, or both adults(s) and children.
Level 5	Sadism or bestiality involving a child or children

Treatment

The most frequently implemented form of treatment for sex offenders is relapse prevention (Pithers, 1990) using the risk–need responsivity (RNR) model (Andrews and Bonta, 2007). This approach has three core principles:

1. Risk: The level of treatment should be linked to risk of reoffending;
2. Need: Treatment should be aimed at the offender's criminogenic needs; and

3. Responsivity: Intervention should be based on cognitive-behavioural therapy (CBT) and tailored to the offender's abilities, motivation and learning style (Andrews and Bonta, 2007).

Since there is evidence to suggest that some Internet offenders display criminogenic needs, the use of sex offender treatment programmes (SOTP) for some would appear appropriate. In the majority of countries, Internet offenders are required to complete a generic SOTP provided by their prison or regional probation service, potentially alongside child molesters and rapists (Elliot and Beech, 2009).

Internet offenders also have specific problems related to their use of online technologies (Middleton et al., 2006). The UK Probation Service introduced a specific 'internet Sex Offender Treatment Program' (i-SOTP) that, in addition to criminogenic needs, also targets compulsivity, community engagement and online relationships, and collecting behaviours (UK National Probation Service, 2005). Similarly, the Lucy Faithfull Foundation (LFF) a UK child protection charity, provides an educational programme called 'Inform+', for self-referred individuals who have been arrested for a child pornography-related offence but are yet to receive a sentence, or who have not been provided with access to a sex offender treatment programme (LFF, 2008). Inform+ targets Internet-specific factors, such as compulsive behaviour, collecting and online fantasy.

Criminal histories, recidivism and progression to other crimes

Research has shown Internet sex offenders to be a heterogeneous group in terms of criminal histories – some with no prior criminal background (Burke et al., 2001), others with a criminal history of sexual and non-sexual convictions (Galbreath et al., 2002; Seto and Eke, 2005; Sheldon and Howitt, 2007).

KEY DEBATE: Do Internet offenders graduate to contact offences?

A key question is whether downloading Internet child pornography is associated with risk of future offending and, if so, is it a stepping stone to committing 'contact' sexual offences (Sullivan and Beech, 2003)? Internet pornography use could escalate to the commission of a contact sex offence through the process of pairing images with fantasy, masturbation and cognitive distortions (Quayle and Taylor, 2002; Sullivan and Beech, 2003) and accessing pornography implies a desire to be in sexual contact with children (Calder, 2004). But Internet offenders are not automatically at high risk of progressing to contact sex offending. Follow-up research has revealed that Internet sex offenders are significantly less likely to miss or drop out of treatment, reoffend or engage in sexually risky behaviour in the community than child molesters (Webb et al., 2007), although the numbers of Internet participants in this study was low and the follow-up period brief. Seto and Eke (2005) explored recidivism among child pornography offenders drawn from a Canadian sex offender registry database. A quarter of their sample had prior contact sexual offences and 15% prior child pornography offences. After an average time at risk of 29.7 months, 17% of the sample had re-offended. However, if this figure is broken down into sexual reoffending for those with contact sex offence convictions, other non-sexual offending and child pornography only, then 9% of the contact sexual offenders committed a further contact sexual offence and 5% committed a further pornography offence. In contrast, 1% of the child pornography-only offenders escalated to a contact sexual reoffence, although 4% of these committed a further pornography offence. The key will be to identify those men who escalate to contact sex offences. One potential difficulty is that risk assessments used to predict recidivism among sex offenders were developed with contact sex offenders in mind. Therefore, the appropriateness of these measures to predict the risk of recidivism for Internet sex offenders needs to be researched.

A7.9. And the damage done . . .

Who are the victims?

Seized collections of images are often examined with the aim of identifying the offender and proving possession of illegal material rather than identifying the victim(s) (Holland, 2005). According to the Internet Watch Foundation (2008), the ages of children in the material they assessed in 2007 were very young: 80% of the images recovered were of children under 10 years of age, 10% under 2 years of age, 33% between 3 and 6 years and 37% between 6 and 10 years. The images predominantly depicted more female (79%) than male victims (7%), with 14% of images depicting both genders. In terms of the severity depicted, over half of the images would be classified as level 4 or 5 according to the SAP guidelines shown in Box 7.3.

The impact on victims

Very little has been written regarding the impact of photographing a child in an abusive image (Palmer, 2005). Some argue that Internet crimes against children make them victims twice – first when they are abused and secondly when that abuse is seen by thousands of people on screen (Calder, 2004). Even after arrest it is difficult to eradicate all abusive images of a particular victim, and consequently it may be difficult for the victim to gain a sense of closure as the images are available as a permanent record of the abuse (Holland, 2005).

Svedin and Beck (1996) published an account of the impact of photographing children in sexual acts, among a group of Swedish children. They noted how difficult it was for the children to talk about or even admit what had happened to them. A similar phenomenon was observed in England during Operation Ore, when some children who were interviewed categorically denied they had been abused and even continued to do so when the police explained that they had seen the photographs or videos (Palmer, 2005). This denial would seem to be for a number of reasons, including the following:

- They may have been encouraged to be proactive in their own abuse or that of other children and therefore feel responsible for letting it happen.
- They are typically smiling in the images and therefore appear to be enjoying what is happening (even though they are being forced).
- The pictures may be shown to the child with threats by the perpetrator that they will show others (their parents, teachers, etc.) what they have done.
- Fear that the images could surface at any time.
- Feel humiliated regarding who may have seen the images and fearful of being recognised (Calder, 2004; Palmer, 2005).

PART B: Theories and explanations

B7.1. Introduction

Knowledge relating to why men sexually abuse children has accumulated over the last decade, and informed both the risk assessment and treatment of this population. As discussed in Chapter 10, there are a number of theories put forward to explain why men sexually molest children. But few, if any cases of Internet sex offenders would have been known to clinicians at the time that most of the major theories were developed. Little is known about why some individuals' virtual interaction with children go beyond simply sexual stimulation (Taylor and Quayle, 2006), or to what extent traditional theories of sexual abuse can be applied to Internet sex offending (Elliot and Beech, 2009). Of course the relevance of child abuse theories to Internet offenders is dependent on the extent to which Internet offenders can be seen as truly 'paedophilic'.

It is hypothesised that people can become addicted to online sexual activity such as collecting child images, and (like other forms of addiction) the activity is inherently pleasurable but develops to a point at which control is lost resulting in negative consequences. Nonetheless the behaviour continues. Technological addiction has also been described, suggesting that the Internet is merely a tool through which addictive behaviours are carried out rather than the focus for the addiction (Griffiths, 2000). Yet it is not clear why these people should become involved with online sexual activity. It is unlikely that technological addiction per se is sufficient to explain collecting child abuse images.

The following section examines the extent to which Internet offenders display some of the criminogenic factors thought to be associated with sexual offending, e.g. intimacy deficits. These factors are contained within Ward and Siegert's (2002) pathways model. Models that incorporate a number of theoretical perspectives and also address the limitations of Marshall and Barbaree's (1990) description of developmental adversities are Hall and Hirschman's (1991) typology discussion and Finkelhor's (1984) multifactorial pathways model (see Chapter 10 for a discussion of these theories).

B7.2. Attachment, intimacy and social skills deficits

Early sexualisation (e.g. childhood sexual abuse) is associated with later sexually abusive behaviour. One consequence of being sexually abused as a child is that an individual may develop distortions in their sexual 'script' that include inappropriate partners, inappropriate contexts and inappropriate behaviours (Ward and Siegert, 2002). Of course childhood sexual abuse is, in itself, insufficient to explain all sexual offending as some sexual offenders are not sexually abused. Sheldon and Howitt (2007) found that Internet-only sex offenders did not tend to be sexually abused as children – or at a rate similar to that of the general population – whereas contact sex offenders were and at a young age (on average around seven years). The abuse was also of a more extreme nature (e.g. multiple abusers, penetrative and repetitive). Contact sex offenders were also more likely to engage in sex play (e.g. fondling, masturbation) with other boys of a similar age compared with Internet offenders. Nevertheless, Internet-only offenders had other early childhood contacts conducive to the development of a sexual preference for young people. For instance they engaged in sex-play with girls of a similar age, particularly when the offender was younger than 12 years of age. Those sexual offenders who engaged in sexual play with peers when they were younger than 12 reported having more paedophilic sexual fantasies and endorsed the view that children are willing and able to engage in sexual acts with adults.

Child molesters experience intimacy and social skills deficits (Ward and Beech, 2006), and these difficulties may also be relevant for Internet sex offenders. For instance, individuals who have trouble obtaining face-to-face sexual contact and intimacy may be prone to developing online sexual habits (Putnam, 2000). Coupled with either a curious or established interest in sexual images of children, some of these individuals may be led to access child pornography online (Elliot and Beech, 2009). Middleton et al. (2006) suggest that the images represent less of a threat than initiating and/or maintaining age-appropriate relationships, and therefore a form of pseudo-intimacy can develop between the offender and particular images of children. Empirically, Internet sex offenders seem to demonstrate poor social skills including a lack of assertiveness, low self-esteem and self-efficacy, and emotional loneliness (Laulik et al., 2007; Middleton et al., 2006). Internet sex offenders are also found to score abnormally low on scales measuring 'warmth' (Laulik et al., 2007) which may, perhaps, enable this population to objectify children. This is similar to the notion that many contact child sexual abusers show little victim empathy (Fisher et al., 1999).

The Internet may also provide a social outlet for individuals who have difficulties initiating and maintaining relationships with other adults (Elliot and Beech, 2009). Quayle and Taylor (2002) found that online chat with others became more important for some offenders than the sexual arousal provided by the images, and offenders could gain popularity and status when they provided new, rare or complete sets of images. Sheldon and Howitt (2007) found that adult relationship problems are frequent precursors to offending behaviour for Internet-only offenders, contact-only child sexual abusers and mixed contact/Internet offenders. In addition, around 40–50% of their three samples reported engaging in impersonal sex, e.g. using prostitutes (although comparative data on normal populations do not appear to be available). Although the researchers found that having adult attachment deficits was more pertinent to the contact offenders they studied, those Internet offenders most at risk from going on to contact offend were those with adult attachment difficulties. They argued that this may make attachment deficits an issue pertinent to the understanding of at least some Internet offenders.

B7.3. Emotional dysregulation

Early research suggested that prolonged use of the Internet can elicit a change in mood (Kennedy-Souza, 1998) and those who misuse the Internet do so in order to help deal with difficult emotional states, such as depression (Morahan-Martin and Schumacher, 2000; Quayle et al., 2006). Certainly, contact offenders use sexual behaviours, such as masturbation, as a coping strategy to deal with negative moods far more frequently than non-sexual offenders (Cortoni and Marshall, 2001). For some Internet offenders, accessing pornography on the Internet may function in a similar way (Elliot and Beech, 2009). We know very little concerning impulsivity in Internet offenders (Elliot and Beech, 2009); however, Middleton et al. (2006) found that a sizeable number of their Internet offenders scored highly on psychological measures of impulsivity.

B7.4. Antisocial cognitions

This field describes dysfunctional belief systems that support sexual contact between adults and children (Abel, Becker and Cunningham-Rathner, 1984), and are typically called 'cognitive distortions' in child sexual abusers. The term is also used to describe justifications that sex offenders use to rationalise or excuse their offending when they are called to account by professionals and others. Hence, there is confusion about the nature of the term in that it is used to explain both (1) motivations for offending and (2) post-offence justifications for offending at the same time (see Howitt and Sheldon, 2007 for a debate around this issue).

Ward (2000) argues that there is a core set of five implicit theories in child sexual abusers. These implicit theories, or schemas, develop early in the offender's life placing them in the context of motivation rather than post-offence rationalisations (Elliot and Beech, 2009). They are used by offenders to explain and predict their own, and others', behaviour. The five implicit theories are (see Ward and Keenan, 1999):

1. Children as sexual objects;
2. Entitlement;

3. The nature of harm;
4. The world is a dangerous place; and,
5. The world is uncontrollable.

Howitt and Sheldon (2007) investigated the applicability of the implicit theory to Internet sex offenders. They compared three groups of convicted offenders on a cognitive questionnaire initially scored according to the five implicit theories: Internet-only sex offenders, contact-only sexual offenders against children and those who had both types of offences in their history. Little support was also found for the existence of the five implicit theories or 'schemas' approach to sexual offending, as the analysis yielded only two main types of distortions that they termed *children are sexual beings* and *justifications for offending*.

They also found that their Internet-only offenders could not be differentiated from contact-only offenders on the overall level of their cognitive distortions. However, some cognitive distortions were associated *more* with Internet offending than with contact offending. Specifically, Internet-only offenders were significantly more likely than contact offenders to endorse items relating to the willingness and ability of children to consent to sexual activity with adults, such as 'a child can make its own decision as to whether to have sexual activities with an adult or not'. The fact that Internet offenders reported more thoughts of this kind is difficult to reconcile with the view that cognitive distortions lead directly to (motivate) offending against children. If this view is correct, one would expect offenders with direct physical assaults against children to have the highest levels of endorsement towards items describing children as willing and able participants in sexual activities with adults, compared with those who have no such offences, i.e. Internet offenders. Yet, the authors found this not to be the case.

One explanation for such a finding is on the basis of experience of contact abuse with children (Howitt and Sheldon, 2007). Internet-only offenders may have few opportunities for their cognitions regarding children and sex to be tested against reality since they do not involve themselves sexually with minors, other than through viewing images. And we know that children are typically depicted as smiling, seemingly enjoying themselves and therefore the behaviour is perceived as 'harmless'. Plus Internet offenders are interested in children sexually but more in terms of fantasy for masturbation. In contrast, contact offenders do engage with children in sexual situations and some may realise that children do not enjoy such activities and that a certain amount of effort is required to force a child to comply sexually. In addition, contact offenders were more likely to have been abused themselves, which they may have experienced as traumatic whereas Internet offenders reported more sex-play experiences as a child than sexual abuse. These experiences are more likely to be positive and perceived as 'normal' and hence they now perceive children as enjoying sex (Howitt, 1995). This latter explanation relies on the assumption that cognitive distortions are amenable to change through experience.

B7.5. Deviant sexual scripts

There are a number of views concerning the role that sexual fantasy plays in sexual offending (Howitt, 2004):

- As a blueprint for offending – fantasy is played out through the offence.
- As a rehearsal for offending – the offender plans the offence in imagination and fantasises the stages of the offence.
- To stimulate sexual arousal – the offender fantasises on sexual themes to generate sexual arousal, perhaps in preparation for an offence.
- Fantasy and offending are not in a causal relationship but have shared origins such as through sexually abusive childhood experiences.
- Offending provides material for sexual fantasies which the offender uses in, for example, masturbation at a later stage.

These different approaches to fantasy are not mutually exclusive and it is feasible that each has a role to play in sexual offending along with others (Sheldon and Howitt, 2008).

Quayle and Taylor (2002), in their sample of Internet offenders, found that men selected images that fitted their pre-existing fantasies, and this was typically related to an increase in masturbation. Webb et al. (2007) compared Internet and contact sexual offenders and found that Internet offenders reported more problems relating to sexual preoccupation, sex as coping and deviant sexual interests. Sheldon and Howitt (2008) found that their contact sex offenders reported fewer sexual fantasies involving female children than Internet-only or mixed (those with both Internet and contact offences) sex offenders. Internet and mixed sex offenders shared similar levels of female child fantasies. In terms of sexual fantasies involving young boys, there were no significant differences between the Internet offenders and the contact offenders. These findings question any simple, direct model linking sexual fantasy to contact offending. In other words, if fantasy drives behaviour, Internet offenders should report the lowest levels of paedophilic fantasy as they have no reported acts against children, yet the reverse was true. One possible explanation for why contact sexual offenders have lower paedophilic fantasies is that they have difficulty generating fantasies about children. In this context, contact-only offenders did endorse more confrontational non-contact fantasies than Internet perpetrators, such as exposing one's genitals to an unsuspecting girl(s). Confrontational non-contact fantasies involve the response of another person and suggest that an important part of the fantasy of the offender is the reaction of another person. It suggests that the offender needs the response of the victim – perhaps to be incorporated into fantasy. It is possible that such victim responses facilitate the production of fantasy.

C7.1. Organisations to contact for information

Information, annual reviews and research reports are freely available to the public from the following organisations:

- Child Exploitation and Online Protection (CEOP) Centre; visit www.ceop. police.uk. This unit can apply full policing powers in tackling the sexual abuse of children both on- and off-line.
- Internet Watch Foundation; visit www.iwf.org.uk. A UK Internet Hotline for the public and IT professionals to report potentially illegal online content, specifically images of child sexual abuse hosted anywhere in the world and criminally obscene content and incitement to racial hatred content hosted in the UK.

C7.2. Further reading

- Sheldon, K. and Howitt, D. (2007) *Sex Offenders and the Internet*. Chichester: John Wiley and Sons, Ltd. This in-depth book examines the research base on Internet sex offenders and includes numerous case studies.
- Quayle, E. and Taylor, M. (Eds.) (2005) *Viewing Child Pornography on the Internet: Understanding the Offence, Managing the Offender, Helping the Victims*. Lyme Regis: Russell House Publishing. This book covers victim issues, as well as the management and assessment of offenders.
- Elliot, I.A. and Beech, A.R. (2009). Understanding online child pornography use: Applying sexual offense theory to Internet offenders. *Aggression and Violent Behaviour*, 14, 180–93. This review outlines the links between contemporary theories of child sexual abuse and our current knowledge of individuals who commit offences related to online child pornography.

Notes

1. Pseudo-pornography includes (1) an image of a child inappropriately sexualised, e.g. clothes removed; (2) an adult given child-like qualities, e.g. pubic hair removed; (3) an image of a child superimposed onto a sexualised picture of an adult or child; or (4) a montage of abusive images (Taylor et al., 2001b).
2. There is a film entitled *Lolita*. It was directed by Stanley Kubrick, released in 1963 and is based on Nabokov's book and is a name synonymous with child pornography and adult–child sex.

3. A term frequently used by paedophiles to justify and normalise their behaviour (De Young, 1988).
4. The Wonderland club was a 300-member organisation where an individual had to provide 10,000 sexually abusive images of children to become a 'member'. See Taylor and Quayle (2003) for a discussion of this paedophile network.

chapter

8 MURDER

DAVID WILSON

PART A: The offence – Who, what, when, why?

A8.1. Introduction

There has been surprisingly little rigorous academic attention paid to murder, to the extent that Fiona Brookman (2005, p. 1) has gone as far as to claim that the broader subject of homicide has suffered from 'academic neglect'. As a consequence, questions related to explaining what motivates one human being to kill another human being are rarely considered in criminology or psychology, despite the widespread fascination that this type of question generates more popularly. Even defining 'murder' is fraught with difficulties (see below). And what would an attempt to answer the question of motivation look like? Should we consider the wider social structure in which the murder has taken place, and into which the murderer has been socialised? In other words, is there a relationship between murder and, for example, poverty, gender or race? Or, do these 'macro' issues become less important in answering this question of motivation when we consider the 'micro' level of the dynamics of the crime itself? Are murderers 'pathological' – different, in some way, to you and me, as Eric Cullen and Tim Newell (see Box 8.1), who worked in prison with a number of murderers would have us believe – or are the roots of violence and murder far more widespread and common than we care to acknowledge?

> **Box 8.1. The mind of a murderer**
>
> When you enter the mind of a murderer, you approach with caution. There is an understandable concern about what you'll find there. (Cullen and Newell, 1999, p. 32)

This chapter seeks to answer these and other questions, and throughout presents a number of recent murder case studies to illuminate its argument. Above all, it is suggested that there can be no single, 'grand' theory of murder. So while the focus of the chapter is, in this instance, firmly rooted in individual positivism – seeking to explain the crime of murder as primarily generated by forces within the individual murderer as a result of a psychological predisposition to kill – the complex interplay between the 'faulty individual' and the 'faulty social circumstances' that permits murder is also considered by examining the incidence of serial murder in the UK since 1960 (and see Box 8.2). The complexity of this interplay is an important point to bear in mind, for murder is a diverse phenomenon – which again makes the idea of one grand, explanatory theory illogical. For example, murder is not just committed by people, but also by large, multinational corporations and even governments, to the extent that taking a life is not always universally condemned, or even classified as unlawful. To illuminate this point further we need to consider what we mean when we define and label an act as 'murder', and also consider who has the power to avoid this label being applied to their behaviour.

Box 8.2. Social marker

Murder is a social marker. The murder rate tells us far more about society and how it is changing than each individual murder tells us about the individuals involved. (Dorling, 2006, p. 9)

A8.2. Definitions

The classic definition of murder has been attributed to Sir Edward Coke and is embedded in the Crime Against the Persons Act, 1861. This stated that:

> Murder is when a man of sound memory, and of the age of discretion, unlawfully killest within any county of the realm any creature in rerum natura under the King's peace, with malice aforethought, either expressed by the party or implied by law, so as the party wounded or hurt etc. die of the wound or hurt etc. within a year and a day after the same. (quoted in D'Cruze et al., 2006, p. 3)

The only substantive change to this definition in England and Wales has been to remove the 'year and a day' rule in 1996, and the idea of 'malice aforethought' – or *mens rea* (the guilty mind) – remains central within the legal definition of murder.

Murder is thus the intentional killing of one human being by another or other human beings and is therefore different from what is called 'homicide'. In very general terms, in England and Wales, homicide is used generically to describe the killing of a human being by another regardless of motive, or whether the act was lawful or unlawful. Examples of lawful deaths, for example, might include deaths caused as a result of acts of war; when a prisoner is executed by a state that retains the death penalty; or when a boxer kills his opponent. Killings that are unlawful are described as murder, manslaughter or infanticide (terms which suggest that there are different levels of culpability), and it is the first of these unlawful killings which is the focus of this chapter. So, it should be noted that we are not discussing, for example, causing death by dangerous driving, those killed as a result of terrorist activities or, as Brookman observes:

> ... the slow and painful deaths of thousands of individuals exposed to pernicious dusts, such as asbestos, despite ample evidence, known to employers, of the potentially fatal health risks, or the negligent and fraudulent safety testing of drugs by the pharmaceutical industry, or environmental crimes that cause death due to the dumping of toxic waste and illegal toxic emissions. (Brookman, 2005, p. 3)

In short, throughout the chapter we are dealing with interpersonal murders – those routine, all too often domestic and commonplace murders that generate local newspaper headlines or, if the victim is especially newsworthy and there was some form of sexual element to the murder, national attention. Thus, the specific type of murder that we are considering does not reflect the overall extent of murder in any given year. The chapter considers only statistics from England and Wales, given that there are different criminal justice jurisdictions in Scotland and in Northern Ireland.

A8.3. How much murder?

According to the Home Office's Homicide Index – which covers the offences of murder, manslaughter and infanticide – there were 651 such deaths in 2008–9, which represented a decrease in the number of homicides of 14% over the previous recording period (Smith et al., 2010). Indeed, this was the lowest number of homicides recorded since 1998–9, when 642 such offences were recorded. Unsurprisingly, this led to a number of favourable newspaper headlines with, for example, Alan Travis in the *Guardian* noting that 'Murders drop to lowest level for 20 years in England and Wales' (*Guardian*, 21 January 2010). Here, however, we should note our previous observation that this will be an underestimate of the overall level of murder.

Even so, interrogating these figures more closely allows us to build up a picture of the type of interpersonal murder that is the focus of this chapter. More than two-thirds of murder victims were male (71%) and the most common method of killing both men and women was by a sharp instrument. In short, they were stabbed by a knife, or by a broken bottle. Indeed, despite the widespread publicity that gun crime attracts, there were only 39 shooting victims in 2008–9, which again compared favourably with the previous reporting period when there had been 53 victims. The second most common method used to murder men was by hitting or kicking (28%), and for women strangulation or asphyxiation (18%).

Female victims were more likely to have been killed by someone that they knew, such as their partner, ex-partner or lover, with around three-quarters (76%)

knowing the main suspect. Only half of male victims knew the main suspect in the murder enquiry. Overall the risk of being a victim of homicide was 12 murders per year per million of the general population – in line with the homicide rate of most Western European countries – but children under one year old were the most at-risk group of being murdered at 27 murders per year per million of the general population, and children more generally are extremely vulnerable – see Box 8.3.

Box 8.3. *Mens rea*

The majority of crimes require the perpetrator to have a *mens rea* or 'guilty mind'. This can be further differentiated into three levels of guilt or culpability: *intention* (actively knowing what you are doing is wrong), *recklessness* (closing your eyes to an obvious risk that your actions may lead to a crime being committed) and *negligence* (where a person fails to act and this omission constitutes a criminal act in itself). The only crimes (in most countries) in which *mens rea* does not need to be proved are those of 'strict liability', an example of which is selling alcohol to young people under 18 years old).

There were 50 victims under 16 years of age in 2008–9, and over half were killed by their parents (56%), such as in the cases of Ellie and Isobel Cass. A further 14% of victims under the age of 16 knew the main suspect. Again, despite the widespread publicity that cases of this kind generate, there were only two offences during this reporting period where someone under the age of 16 was killed by a stranger.

The Homicide Index also attempts to collect information about the circumstances in which these murders took place, although as of 24 November 2009 these circumstances were not known in 26% of the cases that had been recorded (a figure that will inevitably reduce as the police continue with their investigations). Over half (53%) of the murders recorded were the result of a quarrel, a revenge attack or a loss of temper, with just 7% – or 45 offences – occurring during the commission of other crimes, such as robberies or burglaries.

KEY DEBATE: Do we get the murderers we deserve?

This racy question summarises the position developed in this chapter. When we consider murder – and in particular who are the victims of murder – we can see that they are not a random cross-section of the community. Far from it, they are most commonly the elderly (see the section on Harold Shipman) or vulnerable young women or people who find it difficult to fit into mainstream society.

The uncomfortable thought arises that murderers are responding to the general attitudes in our society. They eliminate people who are not regarded as important and can be seen as acting out the wishes of the wider community. This is obviously not to say that the general public want to see old people or sex workers dead, but we are not so shocked or concerned when they go missing or are mistreated. So, do we fashion the murderers that we want?

We can put these most recent figures into an historical context by considering research conducted by Danny Dorling. Dorling looked at the 13,140 people who were murdered in the UK (note his figures include Scotland) between January 1981 and December 2000. He concludes that the overall average UK murder rate is 12.6 murders per year per million people, with the rate for men at 17 per million per year roughly double that for women at nine per million per year. As with our most recent figures, the age group with the highest murder rate are boys under the age of one, with a rate of 40 murders per million per year. During this period 50% of female homicide victims were killed by their current or former partners, and 'it is almost always parents but occasionally other family or acquaintances who kill infants' (Dorling, 2006, p. 4). Again, like our most recent figures, the most common way that people were murdered over this period is through being cut with knife or a broken glass or bottle. However, in trying to understand 'why are they murdered?', Dorling did not conclude, as our Home Office researchers did, that people were killed as a result of a quarrel or so forth, but rather:

> The summer of 1981 was the first summer for over 40 years that a young man living in a poor area would find work or training very scarce, and it got worse in the years that followed. When the recession of the 1980s hit, mass unemployment was concentrated on the young, they were simply not recruited. Over time the harm caused in the summer of 1981 was spread a little more evenly, life became more difficult for slightly older men, most of the younger men were, eventually, employed. However, the seeds that were sown then, that date at which something changed to lead to the rise in murders in the rest of the 1980s and 1990s, can still be seen through the pattern of murder by age and year … (Dorling, 2006, p. 9)

In other words, for Dorling the causes of murder are inextricably linked to macroeconomic and social factors, such as unemployment and poverty, as opposed to the micro-factors within the specific context of the murder itself that were emphasised by the researchers from the Home Office.

A8.4. How are murderers caught?

Given the essentially domestic nature of what has been described above, with most victims being in some form of relationship with, or at least knowing, their assailant, the clear-up rate for murder is high. On average in England and Wales around 90% of murders get 'cleared up', and many of these are what is known as 'self-solvers'. In other words, it is very obvious who the perpetrator is without the need to conduct very extensive enquiries, appeal to the media for witnesses to come forward or use forensic evidence and a range of specialist experts who now advise the police. Even so, there are regional variations between this national average clear-up rate for murder, and so, for example, between 1989 and 1998 the Metropolitan Police Service had a clear-up rate of 84% when nationally the figure was 92% (HMIC, 2000, p. 105). No suspect was charged – or they were acquitted at trial – in 700 offences of homicide between 1987 and 1997 (Gaylor, 2002, p. ii), and the police have a particularly poor record when it comes to dealing with the victims of homicide who have suffered from social and economic exclusion. For example, Paul Harrison and David Wilson reveal that 'as many as sixty prostitutes were murdered between 1994 and 2004, although there were only convictions in sixteen cases … the figures suggest that if you kill a prostitute you are less likely to be caught by the police than if you murder almost anyone else' (Harrison and Wilson, 2008, p. 78).

Despite the popularity of the 'police procedural' as a form of entertainment, very little has been written about how the police actually do conduct their murder enquiries. However, the Murder Investigation Manual (ACPO, 1999) – which is not in the public domain – suggests that there is a basic division between the 'initial response' of an investigation and 'secondary enquiries'. This division is of course not perfect – there can often be overlaps between these two stages of an investigation – and Brookman notes that murder investigations can often be 'chaotic and can involve a great deal of inference' (Brookman, 2005, p. 239). So too, homicides will be graded into Category A, B or C, where, for example, Category A would represent a major crime of grave public concern, such as when the victim is a child or where multiple murder or the murder of a police officer has occurred. On the other hand a Category B homicide is a major crime where the offender is not known and a Category C homicide would be a major crime, but where the identity of the offender(s) is obvious (ACPO, 1999, p. 84). This classification system seems to confirm the observation made earlier in the chapter that some murders will be viewed as more heinous than others, and which in turn might have an impact in how they are investigated or presented and viewed more broadly.

Murder investigations will be led by a Senior Investigating Officer (SIO) – who will have the rank of at least Detective Inspector – and he or she will utilise a Major Incident Room, which acts as the administrative core of the investigation and is staffed accordingly. There will also be an Outside Enquiry Team of detectives to conduct investigations – interviews and searches and so forth – that are viewed as essential by the SIO and, finally Forensic Support, who will collect, identify and analyse evidence related to the investigation.

During the 'immediate response' phase the police are attempting to preserve life (in other words, they should not presume that the victim is actually dead); preserve the crime scene; secure evidence; identify victim(s); and, finally, identify suspect(s). During the 'secondary enquiries' stage, the police develop information that has been gathered initially through a range of activities such as interviewing suspects; analysing the results of any post-mortem examinations; and considering the results of any forensic evidence that has been generated. In all of this the police are assisted by a range of national offender behavioural databases – most of which have rather catchy acronyms such as Home Office Large Major Enquiry System (HOLMES), Centralised Analytical Team Collating Homicide Expertise and Management (CATCHEM), Behavioural Analysis Data Management Auto Indexing Networking (BADMAN) and Serious Crime

Analysis Section (SCAS). Of note, HOLMES, which is essentially an information storage and retrieval system, was introduced in 1987 in the wake of Sir Lawrence Byford's report into the botched police investigation of the series of attacks and murders committed by Peter Sutcliffe, who is better known as 'The Yorkshire Ripper' (see Wilson, 2009, pp. 180–90).

Finally, it should be noted that England and Wales has the oldest and largest national DNA database in the world and that DNA profiling, first used to convict a killer in 1988, is now one of the various ways that the police attempt to bring murderers to justice. The national DNA database, established in 1995, has some five million people registered on it, and while some of the techniques associated with DNA profiling – such as low copy number – remain controversial, and there are different approaches to DNA storage in Scotland from those adopted in England and Wales, the DNA database provides some 3500 matches to crime scenes every month. Between 2007 and 2008 DNA profiles were used to solve 83 murder cases, 184 rapes and a further 15,000 crimes (see Wilson, 2010).

A8.5. What happens to offenders?

Anyone over the age of 21 who is convicted of murder is given a mandatory life sentence, and is usually described as being a 'lifer'. If someone is convicted of murder between the ages of 10 and 17, they are sentenced to detention during Her Majesty's Pleasure, or custody for life if aged over 18 but under 21 at the time of the offence. There is a also a discretionary life sentence for those over 21 who have been convicted of a serious offence, such as manslaughter, attempted murder, rape, buggery, armed robbery or arson.

All life sentences are indeterminate and thus those who commit murder will only be released when it is considered that the risk of harm that they pose to others is judged to be minimal. A small number of lifers – usually serial murderers – are considered so dangerous, or the crimes that they committed so heinous that they will die in prison. The main factors that determine when a lifer is released are the length of what is known as his 'tariff'; what courses he may have undertaken whilst in prison to change his behaviour; and whether he is still considered a danger to the public. A tariff is that part of a life sentence that must be served as a punishment for the murder that was committed, and which is also expected to act as a deterrent to others.

There are some 80 prisons in England and Wales that hold lifers, and if the lifer is male and over the age of 21 he would initially be held in a local prison until he could be sent to a 'first stage' lifer prison. Such prisons include Brixton, Frankland, Full Sutton, Gartree, Long Lartin, Liverpool, Swaleside, Wakefield, Whitemoor and Wormwood Scrubs. Each lifer has – or is supposed to have – a life sentence plan (LSP), which would include details about his offence and issues or behaviours that he would be expected to address during his sentence, such as sexual problems, temper control or drug and/or alcohol addiction. These issues are seen as being central to reducing or eliminating the risk that the lifer poses should he be released and may well have been seen as motivating factors in the murder itself (see below). The LSP is supposed to be reviewed every year, but the steady increase in the numbers of prisoners serving indeterminate sentences means that in practice this might not happen, making it difficult for some lifers to progress to the 'second stage' or 'third stage' of their life sentence. During the 'second stage' a prisoner would be sent to a prison with a lower security classification, or perhaps to HMP Grendon – the only prison in Europe to operate as a therapeutic community (Genders and Player, 1995) – before moving on to the 'third stage' of their sentence which would be spent in an open prison, where the lifer would be prepared for release.

The average time spent in prison on a life sentence is between 14 and 15 years (Prison Reform Trust, 2001, p. 3). However, it is important to remember that even though a lifer may be released from prison, the life licence remains in force for the rest of the offender's life and that the licensee remains liable to recall to prison at any time during the currency of the licence. The responsibility for the management, release and recall of lifers lies collectively with the Lifer Review and Recall Section, the National Offender Management Service, HM Prison Service, the National Probation Service and the independent Parole Board.

PART B: Theories and explanations

B8.1. Introduction

We have already indicated that there can be no single, or 'grand theory' of murder but, rather, that there is a complex interplay between the 'faulty individual' and the 'faulty social circumstances' that permits murder. However, given the focus of this book, we can pursue further the question of what it is that might be 'faulty' about the individual by considering the contributions of how to explain murder from three different branches of psychology: psychoanalytical psychology, evolutionary psychology and, finally, social learning and cognitive psychology. No attempt is made to consider purely sociological or biological explanations for murder – such as the discredited XYY theory (which suggested that murderers had an extra Y chromosome and were thus 'super males'); the part played by the male hormone testosterone, or low levels of serotonin; or the link between violent crime and the brain or the central nervous system. However, within the chapter, where it helps to explain aspects of what is being discussed, sociological and biological explanations are alluded to. To test the various psychological explanations that are presented, the chapter also considers whether they can help to explain the murders committed by the UK's most prolific serial killer – Harold Shipman.

Throughout the chapter it is helpful to bear in mind suggestions that there is a difference between 'instrumental' and 'expressive' violence (see Chapter 14 on violent crime for further reading). Put simply, instrumental violence would be used to achieve a specific, recognised objective, such as, for example, facilitating a robbery. In other words, that this form of violence is rational because it allows the perpetrator to make some type of gain. On the other hand, the objective of expressive violence is to inflict harm and is 'a less rational expression of personality or identity' (D'Cruze et al., 2006, p. 125). Expressive violence is about anger, often in response to an insult (see Box 8.5 below for an example of expressive violence). However, as with our discussion about the division of a murder investigation into an 'immediate response' and 'secondary enquiries', so too we should not presume that there is always (or perhaps ever) a clear distinction between these two different forms of violence. Often, the boundaries are blurred and fluid (and see Box 8.4).

Box 8.4. The doting father

'It sounds ridiculous, but he was a doting father', says John Mayhew of his former employee David Cass. This weekend, Cass smothered to death his children, three-year-old Ellie and one-year-old Isobel, before killing himself ... Cass, whose children's bodies were found in a caravan in Southampton on Sunday, parked in the garage where Cass had worked for four years. He had separated from the children's mother, Kerry Hughes, four months earlier and appears to have smothered the girls, before telephoning Hughes to tell her what he had done. (*Guardian*, 24 September 2008)

Box 8.5. 'Trivial incident over absolutely nothing'

A teenager who killed school-leaver Jimmy Mizen during a frenzied scuffle in a south London bakery was given a life sentence and ordered to serve a minimum of 14 years yesterday after an Old Bailey jury found him guilty of murder. Jake Fahri, 19, was said to have gone beserk after challenging Mizen and his brother in the shop and throwing a heavy glass dish of sausages at him. The dish shattered after hitting Mizen on the chin and a shard of glass cut vital blood vessels in his neck.

Mizen, who had celebrated his 16th birthday the day before, died within minutes in the arms of his brother in the bakery's storeroom, in a welter of blood, while Fahri sauntered smiling from the shop. The case is believed to be the first in which a glass dish has been classed as a murder weapon. Fahri, who pleaded not guilty, had claimed that he had been acting in self-defence.

Mr Justice Calvert-Smith told him: 'A trivial incident over absolutely nothing in a high street bakery ended three minutes later with the death of a blameless young man'.

The court was told that Fahri, who had a history of difficulties controlling his temper, had not wanted to lose face after picking a row with the two brothers as they stood in front of him in the queue at the shop, where they had gone to buy sausage rolls. Fahri demanded that they should get out of his way and became angry when Mizen's older brother Harry suggested he should say 'please'.

He promised to wait for them outside the shop and stormed back in after seeing the Mizens telephoning their older brother for help. The brothers bundled him out of the shop and he then returned a third time, wielding a metal-framed advertising sign and kicking through the shop's glass door. As 6ft 2ins tall, 14-stone Jimmy Mizen wrested the sign away, Fahri, 5ft 7ins, picked up the dish from the counter and hurled it at him.

Crispin Aylett QC, prosecuting, said: 'A trivial incident, brought about by the defendant's rudeness, escalated into something horrific. The defendant reached for any and every available weapon with which to attack the Mizen brothers. The whole incident lasted no more than three minutes – three minutes of absolute madness on the part of this defendant.'

Fahri, who lived close to the Mizen family and had attacked Harry Mizen twice previously, showed no emotion as he was sentenced, but as he was taken to the cells he called out: 'I will be all right, mum, I'll be all right' to his weeping mother in the public gallery.

Detective Chief Inspector Cliff Lyons said: 'Jake Fahri is an aggressive young man who throughout his life continually demonstrated an inability to control his emotions and restrain his temper. As we have all come to know Jimmy was the exact opposite of Fahri; a peaceful, courteous person with only the best intentions'. (*Guardian*, 27 March 2009)

There are a number of issues to consider in this report about the murder of Jimmy Mizen (see Box 8.5), especially as it touches on several of the themes that have already been discussed and others that will be discussed below. For example, we know that Fahri was convicted of murder and therefore had to be given a life sentence by Mr Justice Calvert-Smith. We know that his 'tariff' has been set at 14 years, and we can infer that work will need to be done with him in prison about his temper control before he would be considered safe to release back into the community. It is also clear that Jimmy and Harry Mizen knew Fahri previously – we are informed that Fahri had attacked Harry on two earlier occasions, and that this murder was cleared up very quickly by the police. Finally, we know that while the weapon that Fahri used was unusual – a glass dish, it fits into the general pattern of how murders are committed in that most male victims are stabbed. However, should we see Fahri's violence as instrumental or as expressive? Was his attack on Jimmy and his brother rational and done so as to achieve a specific objective, or should it instead be seen as expressing aspects of Fahri's personality and identity? Perhaps there are elements of both instrumental and expressive violence in Fahri's attack? We shall return to the murder of Jimmy Mizen and also to the murders of Ellie and Isobel Cass below.

B8.2. Psychoanalytical psychology

The foundation of psychoanalytical and clinical psychology is the work of Sigmund Freud (1859–1939), and his suggestion that the workings of the mind affect personality and behaviour – including criminal behaviour. Criminal behaviour is viewed as the product of some mental conflict, which can often be traced back to problems in childhood. Freud suggested that there were three core aspects of the human psyche: the id, the ego and the superego. The id contains the unconscious, primitive biological drives for survival, such as aggression and sex and is said to work on a 'pleasure principle'. In other words, it seeks to avoid pain but both satisfy and enjoy these primitive drives, without regard to how others might suffer, or the negative consequences that might flow from following these primitive urges. The id is also the site of the 'death instinct' – a willingness to self-destruct. The ego is the real 'self' that also controls the drives of the id by responding to the needs of others, and conforming to what is expected of an individual as a result of social convention. The superego, which like the ego develops throughout childhood, is that part of the personality which has internalised the moral and ethical rules of society, largely by the child being socialised by his parents or carers. Freud – who had quite a bit to say about violence – suggested that criminal behaviour was either the result of mental disturbance or the product of the offender's weak conscience.

A modern application of Freud's psychoanalytical approach can be found in James Gilligan's (2000) *Violence: Reflections on Our Deadliest Epidemic*, based on his interviews with violent men in his capacity as a prison psychiatrist. Indeed, in this respect he resembles Cullen and Newell, whom we encountered earlier in the chapter (see Box 8.2). For Gilligan, the internal mental conflict that is the key to understanding why some men use lethal violence is shame and loss of self-esteem. He suggests that violent men have often themselves been the objects of violence in the past – especially in their childhood – and that, as a consequence, they experience feelings of embarrassment, powerlessness and worthlessness. So, in a situation where they feel that their self-worth is being challenged, and in which they also reason that there is no other way to diminish that sense of shame – Gilligan also suggests that violent men lack the emotional infrastructure that serves to inhibit violent impulses through, for example, guilt or empathy – they will use violence to rebuild their wounded self-esteem.

This takes us back to instrumental and expressive violence and also to the murder of Jimmy Mizen. The 'trivial incident over absolutely nothing', as it was described by Mr Justice Calvert-Smith, was perhaps for Fahri something much more symbolic. From the newspaper report it would seem that the Mizen brothers had stood in front of Fahri in the queue in the baker's shop and that, when he had complained that the brothers should get out of his way, he was told that he should say 'please'. Did this trigger feelings of shame to the extent that the physically smaller Fahri believed that the only way that he could re-establish his own sense of self-worth was to use violence? He certainly seems to have wanted to continue with the incident – returning to the shop on two occasions – and thus does not seem to have been able to rebuild that sense of self-worth in any other way, and which perhaps also indicates that he lacked empathy, guilt or indeed fear for his own safety. It also suggests that while this murder may not have been premeditated, that there were also a number of opportunities for Fahri to have walked away from the baker's shop and which would have allowed the conflict to have come to a more peaceable conclusion. Here too we might remember the importance of 'micro' rather 'macro' explanations of murder. What seems to have mattered were not great sociological or cultural questions of age, gender, race or poverty, but rather the dynamics of the incident in the shop itself. None of what has been described is meant to excuse Fahri's behaviour and nor should we ignore the fact that this analysis is difficult to test in any empirical way.

Indeed, one of the major criticisms of psychoanalytical approaches is that they are difficult to prove. We cannot directly observe the id, the ego or superego and nor can we actually prove (or disprove) that they exist – despite attempts to do so through, for example, psychoanalysis, ink blot tests or dream analysis. How then can we be certain that they play any role at all in shaping an individual's behaviour? We might also criticise psychoanalytic psychology for being overly deterministic. In other words, everything is explained by internal conflicts and tensions within the individual's psyche, and thus, for example, environmental factors are overlooked. However, especially with Gilligan's work, there are inter-esting ideas that work well with attempts to understand how social situations can influence human behaviour. This is a theme that is taken up within our dis-cussion of social and cognitive psychology below and, in particular, where we discuss the work of the criminologist Jack Katz. So too we should not ignore the fact that HMP Grendon, which uniquely operates on psychotherapeutic princi-ples within a series of therapeutic communities housing very violent offenders, is the only prison in the country that is able to demonstrate a treatment effect. In other words, their psychodynamic approach to working with violent offenders reduces the incidence of their future reoffending (Marshall, 1997; Taylor, 2000).

B8.3. Evolutionary psychology

The basic premise of evolutionary psychology is bound up with biological assumptions that human existence is primarily determined by genetic adaptation and inheritance – in other words, that human behaviour has ancient biological origins and that the behaviour of humans has thus undergone a process of natu-ral selection to ensure that the adaptive 'selfish genes' which ensure reproductive success are passed on from one generation to the next. 'Proximate' accounts within evolutionary psychology suggest immediate causes or factors as to why an individual might respond to a given situation, while 'ultimate' accounts look much more historically into our evolutionary past for an explanation. So, would murder be an adaptive or a maladaptive strategy to ensure that one's genes are passed on from one generation to another? Would killing parents or one's children make sense from an evolutionary psychological perspective?

David Buss (2005) in *The Murderer Next Door* uses an evolutionary psycho-logical approach to explain that murder is evolutionarily functional and, as such, a normal trait in human beings that is inherently logical, especially as it is a behaviour that it advantageous to reproduction. At the most obvious level, for example, the killer survives and is thus still able to reproduce, while his victim perishes, effectively ending this genetic line. So too the killer – should he wish – would be able to have sex with his victim's mate, and will also through the murder have scared other would-be killers by his behaviour. In turn, Buss suggests, this will make him more attractive to even more potential mates, given that he will be able to provide protection from other predatory men. Indeed, so great are the advantages of murder that Buss questions why there are so few.

A less enthusiastic, but still evolutionary, approach can be found in Martin Daly and Margo Wilson's (1988) *Homicide*. They suggest that murders are usually the result of young men trying to gain dominance over other young men – and here we could also reconsider the murder of Jimmy Mizen from this perspective – or women trying to gain independence from proprietary partners. As such, murder is not pathological but rather a strategy to survive in situations where resources or breeding opportunities are scarce. In keeping with the idea that murder is a strategy for ensuring the survival and continuance of the killer's genes, Daly and Wilson suggest that homicide will occur less often between individuals who are genetically related and point out that, whilst most murders take place within families, such killings occur between spouses, who are of course not genetically related. They also theorise that children are more likely to be killed by step-parents rather than biological parents, who do not have a genetic relationship to these dependent children but who may be seen by the step-parent as a drain on resources in the household.

Unfortunately for Daly and Wilson, evidence from this country does not support this theory. For example, just over 90% of children who are murdered are killed by a biological parent and only 8% by a step-parent (Brookman, 2005, p. 81). Here too we should remember the murders of Ellie and Isobel Cass (see Box 8.2) and not only question why they were killed by their biological father, but also why he then chose to commit suicide. This hardly makes sense from an evolutionary perspective, whether considered from a proximate or ultimate account. David Cass – the 'doting father' – effectively ended his own genetic inheritance, and it is difficult to explain this act either from the 'here and now' of the murder itself, or through attempting to decipher his behaviour as an evolutionary adaptation more historically. So too Buss's theory that murder makes genetic sense is rather undermined by his own observation that there should be more rather than fewer murders. If murder was an adaptive, as opposed to a maladaptive, evolutionary strategy, then it would be much more common than it is, which further suggests that if humans have progressed biologically without resorting to murder in great numbers, then we should view murder as a pathological and not a normal trait in human behaviour.

B8.4. Social learning and cognitive psychology

Social and cognitive psychology is concerned with how behaviour is affected by social situations and focuses on the immediate, interpersonal dynamics of those situations that produce violence. As such the focus is not so much on the individual and his personality but rather on how external factors affect human behaviour. Particular attention is paid to how people process information and why they might perceive some situations as ones in which they will have to use violence. Beck (1999), for example, suggests that in fact aggressors – through a process of 'cognitive distortion' – perceive themselves to be the victims in a violent situation and so have to fight to re-establish their sense of worth and self-esteem. Of course not all individuals would react to the same situation in the same way, and so it is also necessary to differentiate between situational instigators that may motivate aggressive behaviour and the more lasting structural components of a child's background that mould and socialise a child to respond in a violent way. In relation to this latter issue, social learning theory suggests that the acquisition of any particular behaviour by a child – in this case violent behaviour – occurs through learning by direct experience (the child has been the object of violence), or through observation (that is to say, through watching violence being used on siblings or parents, or on television).

Social learning theory is most closely associated with Albert Bandura (1973) and his work on aggression. Bandura suggested that we have to think about three crucial aspects to understanding aggression: the acquisition of aggressive behaviour; the process of instigation of the aggression; and, finally, the conditions that maintain the aggression. We have already discussed the first of these aspects – how aggressive behaviour is acquired – but have not yet discussed how aggressive behaviour might be instigated or maintained. By 'instigated' Bandura means to suggest that an aggressive encounter was often the product of certain environmental conditions that had previously produced violence. So too violence might be 'maintained' because this type of behaviour has been positively reinforced in the past and the aggressor has gained some sense of pride or achievement from behaving in this way.

Like Bandura, Jack Katz (1988) in *The Seductions of Crime: The Moral and Sensual Attractions of Doing Evil* has been concerned with analysing the situational and 'foreground' factors of violence, and he pays particular attention to the emotional or psychological state of the murderer at the time of the murder – in other words, what it feels and means to kill and what is achieved as a consequence. Katz describes different emotional levels that are involved in the 'typical murder', such that the killer commits an 'impassioned attack' or a 'righteously enraged slaughter' of a victim who has humiliated the attacker. Thus, through this slaughter the killer can defend his sense of 'good' against 'evil' by transforming his humiliation into a rage that will prove fatal. In this way, what Katz argues has links to the work of Gilligan and Beck, in that all three emphasise that instead of violence being senseless it has meaning and value for the attacker. Once again we might want to reinterpret the murder of Jimmy Mizen through the lens of these hypotheses. Did Fahri see himself as the victim in this social encounter with Jimmy and Harry Mizen? Did he transform his humiliation into rage? What was it that Fahri hoped to achieve through his use of violence?

B8.5. Serial murder – Dr Harold Shipman

In the same way that Brookman bemoaned the lack of serious academic attention to murder, so too we could make the same complaint that the phenomenon of serial murder has suffered from a similar absence of academic scrutiny (for an overview see Wilson, 2007). Serial murder is a form of multiple murder, and to be labelled as a 'serial killer' the perpetrator has to have killed three or more victims over a period of greater than 30 days. Thus, there is a numeric threshold to the number of people who are victimised and an element of time over which these victims are killed, before this label can be applied. Using this definition allows us to differentiate serial murderers from 'spree' or 'mass killers' – who might kill the required (or indeed more) number of victims, but in a shorter space of time. And, in the same way that we described that there can be no single, or 'grand' theory of murder, there are also at least two ways in which to consider serial murder. The first is the 'medical–psychological' tradition which looks for the roots of the phenomenon within the personality of the individual serial killer, and the second is a 'structural' perspective which seeks to understand what types of societies facilitate serial killing.

The medical–psychological tradition suggests that, in early theorising about the subject, there are four distinct types of serial killers (see Box 8.6). However, as far as the UK is concerned, Wilson (2007, 2009) has been at the forefront of attempts to apply a structural approach to understand why the UK has had greater or lesser numbers of serial killers at some points in our history than at others, and whether underlying social and economic factors create the circumstances that lead to some people falling victim to this type of killer. However, for the purposes of this chapter we consider Britain's most prolific serial killer – Dr Harold Shipman – and attempt to see whether it is possible to understand his behaviour within the various psychological theories that have been outlined, or from within the 'medical–psychological' tradition of theorising about serial killers.

Box 8.6. Types of serial killers (male)

Visionary	Killer is impelled to murder because he has heard voices or seen visions demanding that he kill a particular person, or category of people. The voice or vision may be for some a demon, but for others may be perceived as coming from God.
Mission	Killer has a conscious goal in his life to eliminate a certain identifiable group of people. He does not hear voices, or have visions. The mission is self-imposed.
Hedonistic	Killer kills simply for the thrill of it – because he enjoys it. The thrill becomes an end in itself.
Power/Control	Killer receives gratification from the complete control of the victim. This type of murderer experiences pleasure and excitement not from sexual acts carried out on the victim, but from his belief that he has the power to do whatever he wishes to another human being who is completely helpless to stop him.

Source: Adapted from Holmes and De Burger (1988).

Shipman was convicted at Preston Crown Court on 31 January 2000 of the murder of 15 of his patients, whilst he was working as a general practitioner (GP) from a singleton practice in Market Street, Hyde, near Manchester and with one count of forging a will (for a general introduction to the background of the Shipman case, see Peters, 2005). Shipman was sentenced to life imprisonment, but ultimately took his own life whilst serving his sentence at HMP Wakefield, in January 2004.

In Hyde, Shipman originally worked at the Donneybrook Practice, before setting up his solo practice in Market Street in 1992. During his time in the town he rapidly gained a reputation as being a particularly good, 'old-fashioned' doctor – especially with elderly people, whom he was prepared to visit in their own homes. A measure of his esteem in the Hyde community can be gleaned from the fact that there was a 'Shipman's Patient Fund', which raised money to buy medical equipment for his practice and that when allegations about the murders that he had committed started to circulate, a group of incredulous patients formed a support group for their erstwhile GP (Peters, 2005, pp. 12–15). At the time of his arrest over 3000 patients were registered with his practice, a not inconsiderable number for a sole practitioner.

It would seem that Shipman was caught largely through a bungled attempt to forge the will of his last victim – Kathleen Grundy, whom he murdered on 24 June 1998, which raised the suspicions of Mrs Grundy's lawyer daughter, Angela Woodruff. So poorly was the will forged that some suggest that Shipman may have wanted to have been caught, although others have suggested that this raises the issue that there may have been a financial motive for Shipman's killings. When he was arrested for the murder of Mrs Grundy it would seem that Shipman was killing at the rate of once every ten days and Dame Janet Smith – who chaired an enquiry into the murders that he committed – concludes that by that time Shipman was 'no longer in touch with reality' (www.the-shipman-inquiry.org). His first victim would appear to have been Eva Lyons, who was killed on the day before her 71st birthday in March 1975, and over the next two decades until the murder of Mrs Grundy it is believed that Shipman killed 215 people – mostly elderly women (171 women and 44 men), and Dame Janet has suspicions about the deaths of another 45 of his former patients, making a total of some 260 people whom he may have killed.

How should we explain Shipman's behaviour? Most obviously he would seem to fit the typology of the 'power-control' serial killer. However, do any of the other theories that we have used help to explain his behaviour and how he was able to escape justice for so long? In other words, does psychoanalytical and clinical, evolutionary or social and cognitive psychology help us to understand why Shipman became the UK's most prolific serial killer?

The murders that Shipman committed do not seem to be able to be explained by evolutionary psychological theories. Taking the lives of his elderly victims did not, for example, enable his genetic line to survive more than it would have had they lived and nor is it possible to see these deaths as contributing to making him more desirable to other potential mates. And while social and cognitive psychology may help to explain what Shipman did through using the idea of 'cognitive distortion' – he may have perceived that he was in fact helping (as he saw it) his sick and elderly patients to achieve a more peaceful end, it is not realistic to imagine that these murders were committed as a result of a 'righteously enraged slaughter', or that Shipman saw himself as a victim in this process. After all, he also initiated the circumstances which led to these deaths. Perhaps he felt powerlessness, worthlessness or embarrassment – feelings that were overcome by the act of taking the lives of others? In doing so – like the power-control serial killer – through the deaths of his victims he was able to achieve a sense of control in his life that he felt was ordinarily denied to him. This is an interesting theory from within the tradition of psychoanalytical and clinical psychology, but one which cannot be readily tested now, or indeed at the time, as Shipman refused to speak about what it was that motivated him to kill. In short, at the end of the day, we cannot really understand what it was that motivated Shipman to kill. However, does this prevent us from drawing other conclusions about his activities?

Perhaps we should note that Shipman's victims were largely elderly women and while others may speculate about the psychological mechanisms that enabled Shipman to commit his crimes, it might be argued that we need also to embrace a more structural approach that brings us closer to understanding the meaning of serial killing at a societal rather than an individual level. In brief, the actions of serial killers, sadly but usefully, identify social breakdowns. In this respect, the warning is dire. Serial killers prey on the vulnerable. Within the UK the vulnerable are those who cannot compete within the structural conditions of patriarchal capitalism – those people who, for various reasons, do not feel able to 'answer back' to those whom this structure adorns with power – often the power of life and death. Thus Shipman's murders escaped attention for so long because ultimately there was inadequate social protection for the group on which he preyed. Shipman's murders should have contributed to a debate about the place of the elderly in late modernity and the professional organisation of general practice, although it is questionable whether this has been achieved. Instead, the desire to pathologise Shipman – to blame him alone for his crimes – has allowed us all to escape some hard conclusions about why the elderly were and remain so vulnerable to attack by those who want to harm their fellow human beings.

So, in the same way that we have to remember the complex nature of the phenomenon of murder – a phenomenon that cannot be explained by a single or grand theory – so too the incidence of serial murder would seem to be best explained by combining individual and structural accounts.

PART C: Further information

C8.1. Organisations to contact for information and voluntary work

There are a number of organisations that work with the families of the victims of murder. These would include Victim Support (www.victimsupport.org.uk) – the national charity for victims and witnesses of crime in England and Wales and, at a regional level, Support after Murder and Manslaughter – SAMM (www.samm.org.uk) – a registered charity founded in 1990 that works in conjunction with the West Midlands Police in Birmingham. The charity New Bridge (www.newbridgefoundation.org.uk), founded in 1956 to create links between prisoners and the community, recruits, trains and pays the expenses of a national network of volunteers to write to and visit people in prison – including those who have committed murder.

C8.2. Further reading

For those new to the subject, Fiona Brookman's (2005) *Understanding Homicide*, London: Sage is an invaluable guide and has been liberally used throughout the chapter. So too Shani D'Cruze, Sandra Walklate and Samantha Pegg (2006) *Murder*, Cullompton: Willan and Peter Morrall (2006), *Murder and Society*, Chichester: John Wiley and Sons are both very accessible. For those interested in serial murder, David Wilson (2007) *Serial Killers: Hunting Britons and Their Victims, 1960–2006*, Winchester: Waterside Press is a good starting point, and the Shipman case was considered more fully in Keith Soothill and David Wilson (2005), 'Theorising the puzzle that is Harold Shipman', *Journal of Forensic Psychiatry and Psychology*, Vol. 16, No. 4, pp. 658–98.

chapter

9

PAEDOPHILIA AND SEXUAL CHILD CONTACT OFFENCES

BELINDA WINDER AND KAREN THORNE

PART A: The offence – Who, what, when, why?

A9.1. Introduction

There are a broad range of individuals with different preferences who sexually offend against children: such individuals can be categorised, for the most part, as *infantophiles* (who offend against children under five years of age), *paedophiles* (who offend against pre-pubescent children) and *hebophiles* (who offend against post-pubescent children who are nevertheless under the age of consent). Some researchers make the distinction between those attracted to female post-pubescent children (*hebophiles*) and those attracted to male post-pubescent children (*ephebophiles*), but *hebophilia* is typically used as the generic term for both. This chapter will focus mainly on paedophiles as the most frequently occurring type of child sexual offender; however, many individuals offend against children but would not qualify for the clinical diagnosis of paedophilia (see Section A9.2).

The activities of paedophiles include a wide range of behaviours and may or may not involve the use of force. Some paedophiles limit their behaviours to downloading pictures of children to masturbate to (see Chapter 7 – internet sex offences); others expose themselves (exhibitionism – see Chapter 14) or masturbate in front of their victim, fondle their victim or get the child to touch their genitals. Other paedophiles will coerce or force their victim to participate in oral, genital or anal intercourse, or other acts such as bestiality.

A9.2. Definitions

What is paedophilia?

Paedophilia is a disorder in which individuals have a sexual attraction to pre-pubescent children. This attraction to children is not illegal, but any sexual activities in which individuals engage with children *are*.

In legal terms, the offences relating to paedophilia include sexual assault, penetration and rape, causing or inciting a child to engage in sexual activity, engaging in sexual activity in the presence of a child, causing a child to watch a sexual act, arranging or facilitating the commission of a child sexual offence, abduction (i.e. kidnapping a child for a sexual purpose) and meeting a child following grooming (see Box 9.1 and Box 9.2). However, typically, paedophiles touch their victims, manipulate the child's genitals, and encourage the child to do the same to them rather than seeking to penetrate or rape the child. Exceptions to this include, in particular, incest or intra-familial offenders, and paedophiles with a preference for older children or those who are aroused by the physical coercion of their victims (Hall and Hall, 2007).

Often the terms paedophile and child sex offender are used interchangeably. However, some paedophiles are not known to have offended against children; similarly, many sex offenders with child victims are not paedophiles. Paedophilia refers specifically to a sexual *preference* for children. Many sex offenders with child victims have the capacity to be sexually aroused by children but do not have a preference for them.

Box 9.1. What is grooming?

Grooming is where an adult tries to make friends with a child (and potentially their parents too), thereby setting the basis for engaging in sexual acts with that child at some later date. While the paedophile is engaged in grooming a child, they are likely to show the child special attention, give them presents, spend money on them and spend time listening to them – a powerful lure for many children. Since many parents are so terrified about stranger danger, the kindly next-door neighbour (who gets on so well with their child) offering to babysit is almost too good to be true. And indeed it may be.

Box 9.2. Grooming case study

Grant, a man 50+ years old with a record of offences for touching young girls, put it this way: 'I think it's quite misunderstood, see, my grooming...I'd very rarely buy presents and stuff like that...it was mostly just in what I did or helped or listened to them or reading to them, spending time or giving attention or that type of thing, which probably is what a child would want more than a present anyway' (Winder and Grayson, in prep.).

In medical terms, paedophilia has been defined as a psychosexual disorder in which individuals have recurring, sexually arousing fantasies about pre-pubescent children (generally meaning under the age of 13 years) over a period of at least six months, where the person has acted on these sexual urges and/or fantasies, or the urges/fantasies have caused them significant distress or inter-personal difficulty (APA, 2000). It is a paraphilia (see Chapter 14 for more information on other paraphilias). Moreover, it is important to remember that because of the egosyntonic nature of paedophilia (see Box 9.3), many individuals with paedophilic fantasies, urges or behaviours may not experience significant distress per se at their arousal (APA, 2000), but their concerns may be based on the difficulties (such as spending time in prison) it may cause them in their lives.

Box 9.3. Definition: Egosyntonic

When something is described as egosyntonic, it means that the attitude, drive or behaviour is consistent with one's ideal self-image – that is, if I am rather a stubborn person, I might think that this is a good thing – and call myself a strong, determined person. Most personality disorders are egosyntonic and consequently are difficult to treat as people do not feel that they have a problem or need to change.

Individuals with paedophilia typically are attracted to children of a particular age range. Specific types of children may be targeted based on personal characteristics (hair colour, personality type, e.g. affectionate and extrovert). Children who are vulnerable in some way may be targeted (e.g. those with learning disabilities, who appear neglected or unloved, or who are deaf); such children may be more accessible to paedophiles, and also calculated (by the offenders) as less likely to report abuse. Barbaree and Marshall (1989) reported that approximately one-third of men who sexually offended against children had a preference for male victims (with the homosexual offenders preferring pubescent boys with a mean age of 12.5 and heterosexual offenders preferring pre-pubescent boys, with a mean age of 7.5). Thus, the majority of paedophiles have a preference for female children, typically 8–10-year-olds (APA, 2000). Another distinction that has been made about child sex offenders is as fixated or regressed (Groth and Birnbaum, 1978). Fixated individuals are described as having been arrested in their psychosexual development and, from adolescence, having been primarily or exclusively sexually attracted to significantly younger individuals. Regressed individuals are defined as individuals who have not shown any predominant sexual attraction to younger individuals but whose sexual interests have focused on peers or adults.

A9.3. Who?

For an individual to be a paedophile, they must be 16 years or over and at least five years older than the child or children they are targeting (APA, 2000).

Paedophiles may be male or female, although the majority (90%) of sexual offences against children are carried out by males (Finkelhor, 1994). However, female sex offenders are more likely to escape detection as their offences may not be deemed as serious (Vandiver and Kercher, 2004) or the offences may be disguised in the process of care-giving activities, such as bathing (Groth and Birnbaum, 1979).

There is some dissent as to whether paedophiles are likely to be involved in other types of crime. Simon (1997) reported that, unlike rapists and violent offenders, paedophiles may not be involved in any other type of crime; however, Soothill et al. (2000) found in their follow-up of 7442 sex offenders after 32 years that 58% of them had been convicted of another (non-sexual) offence, and thus it is unclear whether sex offenders are 'specialists' (confine their illegal activity to sex offending) or 'generalists' (commit a range of crimes, including sex offences). Paedophiles typically report that they notice their attraction to pre-pubescent children around the time of their own puberty (Freund and Kuban, 1993); this is perhaps not surprising as it is the time that we all begin to notice our sexual preferences. However, some paedophiles report their interest in pre-pubescent children as developing later in life (APA, 2000; Hall and Hall, 2007).

Contact with children will invariably be a feature of their life, whether in their home circumstances (i.e. children or stepchildren) or they may actively seek opportunities to interact with children (teaching, coaching, voluntary work, care homes, theatre groups, religious groups, etc.).

Psychopathology

Whilst a considerable amount of research has been conducted in order to understand how paedophiles might differ from non-paedophiles, the evidence is inconclusive, and when set against the baseline of offenders generally it is unconvincing. The inclusion of paedophilia in the *Diagnostic and Statistical Manual of Mental Disorders* (DSM-IV) identifies it as a mental disorder, yet it is probably more correct to explain its inclusion as a psychosexual disorder; moreover, its inclusion as a mental disorder should not be used as a justification for individuals – that they 'cannot help' what they are doing.

Drugs and alcohol

Paedophiles are not generally associated with drug or alcohol abuse; however, alcohol may be used in the commission of offences (e.g. in the giving of alcohol to children or taken by the offender prior to the commission of the offence and potentially acting as a disinhibitor to offending).

Mental health and trauma

Paedophilia does seem to be associated with a history of childhood trauma in the form of sexual abuse, in that many paedophiles report being sexually abused as a child. However, most children who are abused do not go on to offend against children in a sexual way. Paedophiles have been found to report more negative early experiences (such as emotional neglect) and difficulties controlling or regulating their emotions (e.g. in dealing with stress) than non-offenders (see Lee et al., 2002).

Individual differences

Theories of paedophilia typically associate paedophilia with low self-esteem, shyness, awkwardness in social situations and problems with forming intimate relationships. However, this only appears to be true of a subgroup of paedophiles (see Okami and Goldberg, 1992). Research has not shown a clear picture of personality differences in paedophiles.

A9.4. Misconceptions

Stranger danger

A common misconception is that children are most at risk from strangers, and that sex offenders are 'dirty old men in raincoats'. In fact, approximately three-quarters of victims are said to know their abuser well (Snyder, 2000), but child victims are also less likely to report their abuse, or delay reporting the abuse where the perpetrator is well known to them. Where the perpetrator is a relative or step-parent, Arata (1998) showed that 73% of children did not report the abuse, and thus there are huge biases in reporting rates.

My child likes them so they can't be doing anything wrong

Probably the best way of refuting this statement is from the words of a convicted serial paedophile, who puts it thus: "because I think that some people think that because their child wants to be with a person then there's no chance that they're doing something that they wouldn't like, but the child has a different outlook to that. You know, they can overlook or don't even take much notice of certain things because their priorities are different ... if they are getting attention and affection from somebody, they don't think much of it at the time if somebody's doing something amiss. I think some parents – a lot of people – seem to think that a child would immediately try to stay away from a person who did that ... but it's not the case" (Winder and Grayson, in prep.). In fact, many individuals with paedophilia interact very easily with children, and children feel comfortable in their presence.

Paedophiles will not have sex with other adults

Some individuals are sexually attracted only to children (*exclusive type*), whereas others may also be attracted to adults (*non-exclusive type*). Research by Abel and Harlow (2001) suggested that only approximately 7% of paedophiles are of the exclusive type. Paedophiles have been known to target single women with very young children through 'lonely hearts' advertisements specifically to spend years grooming them so that they can abuse the children once they reach an age that is attractive to the paedophile. Howitt (2002) reports that approximately one in eight of exclusive (fixated) paedophiles have been married but that about three-quarters of non-exclusive (regressed) paedophiles have been married.

Women are not paedophiles

Although the figures for child molestation by females are typically low (e.g. Abel and Harlow reported this as being 1%), one of the reasons for this may be that females may find it easier to molest children while undertaking 'care-giving' or 'nurturing' activities (Groth and Birnbaum, 1979). In cases of hebophilia, a typical public reaction has been to see the sexual activities between teenage boys and adult women not as abuse but as a 'fortunate rite of passage' (Vandiver and Kercher, 2004).

He's not dangerous, just a sad old man flashing at me

In fact, non-contact offences, such as voyeurism and exhibitionism are a predictor of later serious sexual offences (see Chapter 14). Therefore, people are encouraged to report any incidents to the police as they may lead to someone having access to treatment before such behaviours become more serious.

A9.5. Facts and figures

Incidence

One of the problems with calculating the number of instances of sexual abuse is that there is substantial under-reporting of sexual offences. The reasons for this are numerous: people may feel uncomfortable answering questions about sexual abuse, they may not recall incidents or, because they do not feel they have been affected by an act, they may not label it as abuse. However, official police statistics show that more than 20,000 acts of sexual abuse were committed against children in England and Wales in 2009, with almost a quarter of those offences with victims of ten years or younger. Over 800 of these offences were against children aged 4 and under, with 163 of them against children aged 1–2 (NSPCC, 2009).

Prevalence

It is difficult to ascertain the prevalence of paedophilia – few paedophiles seek treatment unless they have entered the legal system following conviction for an offence. Hall (1995) reported the findings of a study in which one-quarter of men (sampled from a 'normal' population of US adult males, recruited through newspaper advertisements) showed greater physiological arousal to erotic stimuli of children than to adult women. In this same study, approximately one-fifth of the participants reported some level of 'paedophilic' interest although only 4% said they had committed child sex offences.

In a European study, 3–36% of girls and 1–15% of boys reported having experienced sexual abuse before 16 years of age (Lampe, 2002). In a meta-analysis carried out by researchers in the USA, the overall prevalence of sexual abuse in childhood was 13% of all male children and 30–40% of female children (Bolen and Scannapieco, 1999). It is clear even from these figures that there are huge variations in the data, with the 'true' rate of incidence believed to be masked by extreme under-reporting. Cawson et al.'s (2000) study of 2869 young people (aged 18–24) in the UK, conducted using computer-assisted surveying so that the participants could type their answers directly into a laptop computer to optimise the accuracy of the self-report data, found that 1% of children aged under 16 experienced sexual abuse by a parent or carer and a further 3% by other relatives. Eleven percent of participants said they had been sexually abused by people known but unrelated to them, whilst 4% had experienced sexual abuse by an adult stranger or someone they had just met.

A9.6. How are offenders caught?

Investigation

Sexual offences are under-reported and child sex offences are the least reported of all sexual offences. Of course, the problem of child sexual abuse has become increasingly well publicised, and this may encourage more victims to come forward at the time of their abuse. Investigation may follow deliberate or accidental disclosure; the latter is more common in pre-school-aged children whilst deliberate disclosure is more common in adolescents (DeVoe and Coulborn-Faller, 1999). Suspected or actual child abuse may be brought to the attention of the police from a range of sources, including the victims, witnesses of an offence, health or social services, teachers or counsellors/psychologists, anonymous calls, offender managers or by police officers themselves who have developed concerns during their routine contact with the public (see NCPE, 2005).

Detection

Paedophilia is seriously under-reported as a crime, for a number of reasons: children may be too young to understand what is happening to them, or not be capable of relating that to someone else; victims may not realise they have been abused (e.g. with inappropriate touching); victims may not realise until many years later that the behaviours they have been subjected to were 'not normal', and even where victims may understand that they have been abused, they may not report this to anyone. Cawson et al. (2000) reported that almost three-quarters (72%) of sexually abused children did not tell anyone about the abuse at the time, 27% told someone later and around a third (31%) still had not told anyone about their experience(s) by early adulthood.

In fact, paedophilia is one crime in which offenders may find themselves being arrested and convicted decades after the offence (see previous section on the *investigation* of child contact sexual offences).

Conviction

Convictions for child sex abuse offences may rely solely upon the testimonies of the alleged perpetrator and the victim, who may be either a child or an adult testifying in a historical case (Benneworth, 2009). Consequently, convictions may be both difficult to secure and involve additional trauma for the victim, who will need to testify and potentially relive their abuse experiences in doing so. Plea-bargaining, in which the perpetrator admits to a lesser charge (e.g. pleads guilty to sexual assault rather than rape), spares the victim further anguish but will result in a shorter prison sentence for the perpetrator. Anecdotal evidence suggests that plea-bargaining is reasonably common.

A9.7. What happens to offenders?

In the UK, the Criminal Justice Act (2003) introduced new sentences to protect the public from dangerous sexual offenders, including extended sentences, whereby offenders served their given prison sentence but were also subject to an extended licence period of up to eight years (see Box 9.4). The court can also impose a disqualification order to prevent offenders from working with children in the future.

Sentence length will vary depending on the age of the victim and the seriousness of the offence, with different starting points set for different offences. The starting points for sentences where the victim is under the age of 13 years are higher than for those where the victim is over 13. In the UK, children under 13 are not deemed able to give consent to sexual activity; after this age, children may give consent but the activity is still illegal. Sentences for offenders will be varied from these starting points depending on the presence of aggravating factors (e.g. victim vulnerability, presence of others, additional degradation of the victim) or mitigating factors (mental illness, remorse, admissions to the police, plea, etc.). Offences are considered more serious if the act is penetrative or where the victim's ability to give consent is impaired, either due to mental capacity issues or administration of alcohol or drugs.

Box 9.4. Licensing of convicted sex offenders

Sexual Offences Prevention Orders (SOPOs) were introduced as part of the Sexual Offences Act in 2003; SOPOs impose restrictions on convicted sex offenders who are considered still to pose a risk of serious sexual harm. Thus, a SOPO might forbid an offender from being alone with children under 16. If the offender breaches these prohibitions, they may receive up to five years' imprisonment. The 2003 Act also introduced Risk of Sexual Harm Orders, which are the SOPO equivalent for those who have not committed sex offences but who are considered at risk of doing so; and Foreign Travel Orders, which ban convicted paedophiles from travelling abroad where it is believed they might seek to go to another country to commit child sexual abuse.

Also introduced in the UK was a new type of sentence, the *indeterminate public protection* sentence (IPP), which dictated that offenders could not be released until their level of risk was manageable within the community. Once released, offenders would still be subject to terms of their licence for a minimum of ten years and must apply again to a Parole Board for their licence to be removed.

Sexual offenders are automatically required to register with police after conviction. They are required to notify the police of their names, date of birth, home address and national insurance number and of any subsequent changes to these. This requirement lasts for periods of time that vary according to the seriousness of the offence, but it is a lifetime requirement for anyone imprisoned for 30 months or more. This enables police to monitor the whereabouts and activities of anyone required to register.

Treatments typically offered

Treatment interventions for paedophilia typically fall into two categories – those seeking to modify the deviant paedophilic arousal and those aiming to target *criminogenic* need (factors that are associated with reoffending but which can be changed, such as alcohol dependency or beliefs that children are not hurt by sexual abuse) and reduce sexual recidivism.

Treatments that seek to modify deviant sexual arousal can use behaviour modification techniques (based on conditioning theory) or pharmacological interventions such as anti-libidinal or selective serotonin reuptake inhibitor (SSRI) medication. In some particularly serious cases, chemical or surgical castration of offenders has been used. The aim of such interventions is to inhibit pathological sexual interest and, in many cases, treatment providers will seek to increase healthy sexual interest at the same time as decreasing deviant interest.

A broader range of interventions have tried to target criminogenic need and reduce the risk of sexual recidivism. Psychodynamic, cognitive-behavioural, multisystem therapy and relapse prevention models have all been used to try to treat paedophiles in custodial and community settings. Currently the most favoured treatment options are cognitive-behavioural interventions, which are usually delivered on a group basis. These programmes often incorporate techniques that draw from other models (e.g. relapse prevention models). HM Prison Service provides six Sex Offender Treatment Programmes (SOTPs) targeting different levels of risk rather than offender type: Core SOTP (medium and high risk), Becoming New Me (core programme for offenders with Intellectual Difficulties), Extended SOTP (high and very high risk), Rolling SOTP (low risk), Healthy Sexual Functioning (high-risk men with offence-related sexual interests) and Better Lives Booster. The aim of such programmes is to improve offenders' understanding of their risk factors and how to manage these, and to improve victim empathy and an offender's ability to take responsibility for offending. Programmes incorporate relapse prevention techniques and, in some instances (The Healthy Sexual Functioning Programme), can also include behaviour modification techniques.

Recently, organisations such as Circles of Support and Accountability (UK) have been developed in response to the growing recognition that sexual offenders require ongoing support and assistance with their risk management in the community. Whilst not a treatment programme per se, Circles of Support provide a social support network to offenders who might otherwise be at risk of reoffending, aiming to reduce the emotional loneliness and social isolation that may have contributed to offending in the first place.

Relative efficacy of programmes

Paedophilia has proven a challenging area in which to achieve long-term treatment change and overall treatment efficacy has been low. Treatments aimed at changing sexual preference (e.g. behavioural modification) have demonstrated some success in changing offenders' sexual arousal patterns whilst in treatment and when followed up over the short term. However, there is limited evidence of this having a long-term impact on sexual preference or behaviour after treatment. Pharmacological treatments have proved effective with some offenders for whom change can be demonstrated for the duration of the treatment, but long-term compliance with treatment can be low. It is also unclear how such treatments actually work and it is likely that these interventions work by reducing arousal levels rather than changing the underlying sexual preference for children.

Studies of the long-term effectiveness of cognitive-behavioural interventions have produced some positive results. Contemporary treatment programmes have been found to result in up to 40% reduction in recidivism in the general sex offender population (Hanson et al., 2002; Losel and Schmucker, 2005). However, what is not clear is how effective these interventions are specifically for men with paedophilic interests. The HM Prison Service Core SOTP was examined by Friendship et al. (2003), who found that its impact differed according to the level of risk presented by the offender. The Core SOTP was most effective with medium-risk men; however, there was little impact on high-risk men. Given the highly pathological nature of paedophilia this is perhaps not surprising. Paedophiles are likely to require high levels, or 'dosage', of treatment.

Psychodynamic treatment programmes are not well documented, and their apparent unstructured approach has meant that there are very few well-controlled outcome evaluations of such interventions. Those studies that do exist do not indicate a reduction in recidivism as a result of treatment; indeed, some suggest an increase in risk following treatment (Furby et al., 1989; Romero and Williams, 1983).

Paedophilic offenders who have good support networks in the community can manage their risks more effectively once they have undertaken treatment and have ongoing support. Offenders who have been involved in Circles of Support and Accountability have reoffended at a lower rate than a matched comparison group (Wilson et al., 2002).

KEY DEBATE: How effective is treatment for paedophiles?

There has been considerable research into the efficacy of treatment for individuals who have committed sexual offences against children. After more than 30 years, researchers still seek more robust knowledge about what treatment works, how much it reduces reoffending and what factors contribute to its effectiveness.

It has been suggested that treatment reduces reoffending from approximately 25% (i.e. without treatment, one-quarter of sexual offenders reoffend) to 10–15% (Sex Offender Treatment Review Working Group, 1990); however, this figure has been challenged, and this disagreement is typical amongst researchers in the area. One of the key problems is the quality of the treatment outcome studies – how well did they systematically capture all the data required to conduct an analysis of the effectiveness of treatment? At its most extreme the debate can be framed around the question of whether treatment has any measurable benefit at all. If the answer is negative then this will challenge how we deal with convicted paedophiles.

The Collaborative Outcome Data Committee was set up in 1997 to help with this and to promote high-quality treatment evaluation studies. Both papers cited below report findings from the Committee.

References:
Hanson, R.K., Gordon, A., Harris, A.J.R., Marques, J.K., Murphy, W., Quinsey, V.L. and Seto, M.C. (2002). First report of the Collaborative Outcome Data Project on the effectiveness of psychological treatment of sex offenders. *Sexual Abuse: A Journal of Research and Treatment*, 14, 169–94.

Lösel, F. and Schmucker, M. (2005). The effectiveness of treatment for sexual offenders: A comprehensive meta-analysis. *Journal of Experimental Criminology*, 1, 117–46.

Recidivism

One problem in assessing recidivism is that the number of convictions for sexual offences in the UK is falling – it has halved since 1981. This means that the base rate of offending (i.e. the rate of untreated sexual offender recidivism) is too low to show much statistical difference when compared with treated sex offenders. However, Soothill et al. (2000) carried out an extensive follow-up study of 7442 sex offenders in England and Wales. These offenders had all been convicted of a sexual offence in 1973, and the authors looked at the criminal records of these individuals after 32 years; they found that 58% of them had been convicted of another (non-sexual) offence, whereas only one-quarter of them had been convicted of another sexual offence. Where the offenders were convicted of another sexual offence, individuals were typically convicted of the same sexual offence as previously. This was true for all groups except those convicted of indecent assault against boys – these offenders were reconvicted of a range of 'second' offences.

Co-occurrence or progression onto other crimes

The paraphilias as a group have a high rate of co-morbidity with one another and an equally high rate of co-morbidity with major depression, anxiety disorders and substance abuse disorders. A person diagnosed with paedophilia may also meet the criteria for exhibitionism or for a substance abuse or mood disorder. Paedophiles are more likely to engage in other paraphilic behaviours than men selected from the general population. A substantial proportion of paedophiles have engaged in at least one other type of sexual offence, such as exhibitionism or voyeurism. The co-occurrence of paraphilias and different offence types suggests that the factors that increase the likelihood of one paraphilia also increase the likelihood of others.

Particularly worrying are those offenders who are diagnosed with paedophilic and sadistic interests, as they are the group most likely to cause physical injury to a child during a sexual offence than those without a sadistic interest.

Prognosis (life course information)

There is no clear understanding of the life course of paedophilia. It has long been inferred that paedophilia is stable across an individual's lifespan, as older paedophiles often report their interest in children being present from a young age themselves. Approximately 50% of offenders against unrelated males report the age of onset of their paedophilic interest as before 18, while 40% of offenders against unrelated females and 25% of incest offenders report their age of onset as being before 18.

Some have suggested that paedophilic interests may be more changeable, waning over time. This is because many children and adolescents with sexual behaviour problems, which may include offending against other children, do not go on to commit further offences. However, it is likely that other factors such as sexual precocity, normative play or sexual experimentation are motivating such behaviours rather than true paedophilic interests. Juveniles who persist in offending against children into adulthood are more likely to have paedophilic interests.

As paedophiles age there does appear to be a general decrease in their risk of offending, but this is likely to be as a result of decreases in arousability and sexual drive rather than paedophilic interest. So overall, the prognosis for paedophilia is poor (APA, 2000); however, individuals can be helped to manage their risks and develop adult attachments.

A9.8. And the damage done...

Who are the victims?

The number of offences recorded against girls was six times higher than the number against boys (NSPCC, 2009). However, sex offenders who have a paedophilic interest are more likely to have multiple victims, male victims and unrelated child victims than non-paedophilic offenders (Seto and Lalumiere, 2001). Females and younger children are more likely to be abused in their own homes, whilst males and older children are more likely to be abused outside their own homes in locations such as fields, railways and so on (Hall and Hall, 2007).

Research has shown that children from lower-income families are slightly more at risk of becoming victims, as well as children who are victims of other forms of crime, violence and abuse. In addition, those children who had 'parental inadequacy' (such as parents not being around or supervising their children appropriately, where there is conflict in the home, where parents use harsh punishments on their children and/or emotionally deprive them) were more vulnerable to being the victim of child sex offenders (Finkelhor, 1994).

Costs of crime

The physical and psychological costs of child sexual offences are high and can be lifelong. Physical effects on victims can include injury, pregnancy and sexually transmitted infections. Psychological effects can include, fear, shame, embarrassment, humiliation, inability to trust, inability to form intimate relationships in adulthood, self-harm and suicide.

There are also considerable economic costs to society as a whole as a result of such offences. The cost of imprisoning an offender alone is approximately £29,000 per year (the cost of prosecuting them is substantially higher than this).

In cases where a custodial sentence is considered necessary, prisons with sex offender treatment programmes saved the taxpayer £35,213 per offender (in terms of the costs of responding to and investigating crime, of bringing to trial and punishing offenders and of treating injuries) through reduced reoffending rates and, if victim costs (i.e. the tangible and intangible costs to the victims of crime such as the cost of property damaged or stolen, and the cost of pain and suffering) are included in the calculation, that figure jumps to £130,578 (Matrix Knowledge Group, 2007).

Fear of crime

High-profile media coverage of cases of child abduction, sexual assault and murder has led to the fear of this type of crime being heightened. The general perception is that this type of offence is commonplace and, as a result, there is frequent hostility to the resettlement of paedophiles in the community. In fact, this type of crime is thankfully extremely rare and more children are murdered every year by parents and carers than by paedophiles (see NSPCC, 2010).

Parents are also fearful of the danger that strangers present to their children more generally and are often reluctant to let them roam too freely for fear of being victimised by paedophiles. In fact, most child sex offence victims are known to the perpetrator, and the perpetrator is known to the victim and their family or may actually be part of the family (Waterhouse and Carnie, 1992).

Changes in attitudes and behaviours

The activities of paedophiles have resulted in a change in attitudes and behaviours of parents. Increasingly, parents are fearful of their children being victimised and this has led to greater reluctance to let children play as freely as they used to.

Concern about paedophiles living in communities has led to calls for greater public disclosure of offenders' status and whereabouts, commonly referred to as Sarah's Law in the UK. Those public disclosure pilots that have taken place have received relatively low numbers of enquiries given public attitudes and behaviour towards paedophiles. Those who have applied to the scheme for disclosure tend to view them positively and they have contributed positively to the protection of children and general levels of understanding about the risks posed. Where disclosures take place, applicants often find it difficult to keep this information to themselves, even though they are aware of the restrictions that had been placed on them by the police. Concern that such pilots would drive offenders 'underground', and cause them to change their behaviour, appear not to have materialised and, although paedophiles report anxiety about negative community reaction, this anxiety had decreased as pilots progressed. However, the offenders questioned about this had not personally had any information about them disclosed and that may have impacted on how they viewed the process (Kemshall et al., 2010).

PART B: Theories and explanations

B9.1. Introduction

Early theories explaining paedophilia were unifactorial (e.g. there was one driving explanation, albeit biological, psychoanalytical or evolutionary). However, most researchers now accept that paedophilia results from a number of factors and 'theory knitting' (see Ward and Hudson, 1998), in which researchers seek to integrate the most useful and empirically based ideas in a field such as sexual offending to create a comprehensive framework to explain a behaviour, and has been welcomed by researchers in this area. In order to 'theory knit', researchers identify both the shared and unique features of existing theories. You will see as you read through the various theories that explanations of sexual offending have become increasingly more sophisticated, but our starting place is one of the most widely known theories of sexual offending, by David Finkelhor.

B9.2. Finkelhor's precondition model

In 1984, David Finkelhor wrote about the pressing need for a comprehensive theory of child molestation in order to promote and guide the development of empirical research in this area. He outlined the disparate and partially developed ideas that existed at that time on child contact offences, together with the family-systems model of father–daughter incest, and pointed out that the available information and theories did not link what was known about offenders with what was known about victims and their families. Moreover, the available theories had a number of shortcomings: they were not comprehensive, focusing on rather narrow offence domains (father–daughter incest and male offender with multiple child victims external to their family). Furthermore, Finkelhor believed they neglected sociological factors. Consequently, Finkelhor produced the *Four Pre-conditions Model of Sexual Abuse* to address these shortcomings.

Finkelhor's (1984) model (see Box 9.5) stated that all factors relevant to sexual offences against children could be incorporated into one of four preconditions that needed to be met before a sexual offence against a child would occur. The model was later refined by Araji and Finkelhor in 1985 and 1986.

Box 9.5. Four preconditions model of sexual abuse

Precondition 1: A potential offender needed to have *some motivation to abuse a child sexually*.

Precondition 2: The potential offender had to overcome *internal inhibitions* against acting on that motivation.

Precondition 3: The potential offender had to overcome *external impediments* to committing sexual abuse.

Precondition 4: The potential offender or some other factor had to undermine or *overcome a child's possible resistance* to the sexual abuse.

Source: Finkelhor, 1984, p. 54.

Araji and Finkelhor (1985, 1986) later refined Finkelhor's earlier theory, categorising explanations of paedophilia into four basic types.

1. *Individuals who are emotionally congruent towards children.* These individuals have an emotional need to relate to children and typically some difficulties in relating to adults. Lack of self-esteem or lack of psychological or social maturity or sexual abuse in childhood are seen as some of the factors that might lead to emotional congruence with children.
2. *Sexual arousal to children.* Some individuals are sexually aroused by children; this is suggested as potentially being due to factors such as socialisation by child pornography or advertising to regard children as sexual objects, hormone abnormalities or deviant sexual behaviour patterns following sexual abuse in childhood.
3. *Blockage.* This is where individuals turn to children as a sexual outlet as adult sexual and emotional gratification is unavailable.
4. *Disinhibition.* This looks at why some adults are not deterred by societal prohibitions against sex with children. Individuals may use alcohol or other substances to remove inhibitions or they may be under stress in their lives, which acts as a disinhibitor.

B9.3. Sexualisation theory and the cycle of abuse

Howells (1981) considered the possible link between sexual arousal to pre-pubescent children and paedophilia in terms of classical conditioning, stating 'large numbers of "normal" pre-pubescent children will have experienced arousal and orgasm with "immature" partners (although the partners will be of a similar age to themselves). A series of such experiences would be expected to classically condition arousal to the physical cues provided by such immature partners (e.g. the absence of pubic hair, "young" body builds, etc.)' (p. 67). This explanation suggests that repeated peer to peer sexual activity may leave some children with a learned pattern of sexual arousal to pre-pubescent children.

Furthermore, this statement sets up a broader discussion that incorporates a more uncomfortable area in sexual offending research, that of the cycle of sexual abuse (see Johnson and Knight, 2000), in which repeated sexual contact between a child and abuser leads via classical conditioning to patterns of arousal between a child and adult. The sexually abused child may then, as an adult, go on to commit acts of sexual abuse against pre-pubescent children, recreating the circumstances of arousal to which they were previously subjected.

Research provides some evidence that male children who have been abused by a female may be at a higher risk of going on to abuse children themselves. For instance, Glasser et al.'s (2001) analysis of 843 individuals attending a specialist forensic psychotherapy centre found that for males (but not females) the risk of being a perpetrator of sexual abuse against children was positively correlated with childhood sexual abuse experiences, with the overall rate for perpetrators being 35% and the rate for non-perpetrators being 11%. Significant factors were being abused by a female relative (sister or mother), and having suffered parental loss (death, divorce, separation) in childhood. The authors clearly state that their research, with its various limitations, do not provide strong support for the cycle of abuse; however, they state that prior victimisation could be a mediating factor that increases the probability of the individual subsequently going on to abuse other children.

Moreover, the problems of compulsive sexual behaviour have been high-lighted by Coleman (1992) as being strongly linked to early childhood trauma or abuse, and/or being brought up in an environment which is highly restricted in terms of being able to express one's sexuality. Compulsive sexual behaviour and obsessive thoughts may be driven by anxiety reduction mechanisms rather than by sexual desire; whilst sexual activity may provide temporary relief, it will also prompt further anxiety and distress, leading again to obsessive thoughts and compulsive behaviours in a self-perpetuating cycle of sexual offending and distress.

B9.4. Marshall and Barbaree's integrated theory of sexual offending

Marshall and Barbaree's (1990) integrated theory of sexual offending was designed to explain both child and adult offences, as well as sexual deviance, and its focus appears to be exclusively on explaining sexual offending by males (although we must remember that in 1990, when this theory was first published, female sexual offending was almost unheard of in terms of public knowledge or convictions of females for sexual offending other than as the partner in crime for a male sex offender). The authors emphasise the role of learning experiences, sociocultural factors, biological processes and developmental experiences. They argue that 'the task for human males is to acquire inhibitory controls over a biologically endowed propensity for self-interest associated with a tendency to fuse sex and aggression' (p. 257).

Thus it is suggested that we have a genetic basis for both aggression and engaging in sexual behaviour, and that for both these processes puberty is a critical period in terms of their development. Marshall and Barbaree weave in the importance of developmental influences thus, stating 'the early developmental influences of boys who are later to become sex offenders inadequately prepares them for the dramatic changes in bodily functioning which occur at puberty and which initiate a strong desire to engage in sex and aggression' (p. 261). So, boys who have not been properly 'socialised' into containing their aggression (perhaps by parental displays of domestic violence) or who have not been taught or had modelled appropriate ways of interacting socially in sexual or quasi-sexual situations (i.e. what do you do when a girl turns down a date or sexual intercourse?), will not have learnt how to cope with the emerging sexual and aggressive desires of adolescence, and Marshall and Barbaree note that two of the most important outcomes of parenting are to provide young males with self-confidence and the strong emotional attachments to others.

In addition to these early developmental influences, Marshall and Barbaree highlight the importance of the sociocultural context in which young boys grow up, namely factors such as how the media portray sex and violence against women, and exposure to pornography are all thought to have an effect on men's behavioural inhibitions over their sexual and aggressive impulses (i.e. they may 'normalise' rape-supportive beliefs or 'rape myths'; see Box 11.2).

Finally, transitory situational influences, such as being drunk or feeling angry or stressed, may also catalyse sexual offending in an individual who has been subject to poor parenting and negative sociocultural attitudes, but who has inherited an easily roused capacity to act in a sexually aggressive way.

B9.5. Hall and Hirschman's quadripartite model of sexual aggression

The quadripartite model of sexual aggression was initially (1991) formulated as a theoretical explanation of sexually aggressive behaviour (e.g. rape) by males against females and was later reworked to explain child sexual abuse (1992). Hall and Hirschman conducted a thorough literature review examining the characteristics of sex offenders, and proposed that there were four (hence 'quad') factors ('parts') that were important motivating factors that increased the probability that an individual would sexually offend against children, namely: sexual (physiological) arousal to children; thoughts that justify sexual offending against children; a negative emotional state; and personality problems or disorders. One or more of these factors may have a greater or lesser impact on different sub-types of sexual offenders, and this will have relevance for the assessment and treatment of these different types of offender. Each of these four factors, which all have empirical backing, will be examined below.

Factor 1: *Sexual (physiological) arousal to children*

This motivation is simply the physiological arousal to children. This sexual arousal to children can be measured using equipment such as the penile plethysmograph (PPG) (see Box 9.6 for more information about the PPG). Tests with the PPG have demonstrated that child sex offenders show significantly greater arousal to child stimuli than non-child sex offenders and non-sex offenders (Freund and Blanchard, 1989). Hall and Hirschman (1992) reported that individuals who were primarily characterised by this factor tended to have multiple victims, but rarely used physical violence against their victims while offending, and were unlikely to show aggression in their life generally.

Box 9.6. Penile plethysmograph

The set-up of this apparatus comprises a small room where the participant sits and listens to the soundtrack of a sexually suggestive scenario in which, for example, a young girl is described playing and potentially being involved in sexual acts. The apparatus involves the participant putting an inflatable sleeve over their penis (the latter will have first been measured in its flaccid state) whilst sitting on an inflatable cushion so the technician can recognise whether the male participant is trying to clench his buttocks in order to prevent an erection. If/when the participant becomes aroused at listening to the scene, the extent to which their penis becomes erect (i.e. the extent to which they are aroused) is measured. The technician sits in a small room next door to the participant, working the apparatus and recording the results electronically. The technician will be responsible for protecting the validity and reliability of the results and will also be able to stop the test if the participant becomes distressed. Appropriate clinical uses for the PPG are to show patterns of sexual arousal (e.g. for particular victims types); to help encourage offenders to accept their arousal to, for example, children; to assist in identifying treatment needs and to indicate where progress has been made in, for example, changes in sexual interest from children to adults. However, it should be stated that the PPG cannot be used to establish an individual's guilt or innocence in respect of a particular offence (BPS, 2008).

Factor 2: *Thoughts that justify sexual offending against children*

This motivating factor is concerned with the cognitive/mental processes used in justifying one's emotions and behaviour (and the consequences of the offending behaviour). This will include the use of cognitive distortions (see Box 9.7 for an explanation of cognitive distortions) and rape myths (see Chapter 10, Boxes 10.2 and 10.3 for more information on rape myths) to minimise the harm the offender is causing to the victim, or even to justify the action itself: 'Well, she looked 16 dressed like that.' It is concerned with the attitudes, beliefs and rationalisations used in explaining away the offending behaviour. Offenders for whom this factor was highly relevant were typified by date-rapists where considerable planning had taken place (but there was less deviant sexual arousal to children).

> **Box 9.7. What are cognitive distortions?**
>
> CDs are well-established and generalised offence-related beliefs that facilitate (in this case) sexual offenses against children. They are generally recognised as faulty thinking patterns that may exist for a range of reasons, but which inevitably serve a purpose for the individual, such as facilitating denial of responsibility or of the negative consequences; minimisation of the damage caused to others; or helping an individual avoid facing painful emotions such as shame or guilt.

Factor 3: *A negative emotional state*

Affective dyscontrol – or poor emotional self-regulation – is the third factor presented in the quadripartite model. In particular, poor emotional self-regulation, coupled with a negative emotional state (e.g. anger or depression) is recognised as an antecedent of sex offending. The problem is perceived as being with inhibitory control, such that negative emotions affect the individuals to such an extent that they are unable to overcome their inappropriate urges. Different negative emotional states are identified as being coupled with particular offences: for rapists, this is anger, and for paedophiles, this is depression.

Factor 4: *Personality problems or disorders*

The final factor in the quadripartite model is personality problems or disorders that might make individuals vulnerable to committing sexual offences against children. Hence negative childhood experiences (harsh punishment, being abused or neglected as a child) are seen as contributing to the development of personality traits (e.g. selfishness, narcissism) associated with personality disorders.

Thus, in Hall and Hirschman's quadripartite model, these four factors reviewed above are seen as leading to vulnerability, which may then be triggered by situational variables, such as opportunity, leading to sexual offending against children. Only one motivational factor is sufficient catalyst to cause offending to occur, assuming it is potent enough to exceed the barrier that usually inhibits the act of offending (Hall and Hirschman, 1992).

B9.6. Ward and Siegert's pathways model

Ward and Siegert integrated previous theories into one comprehensive theory, producing a multifactorial model – i.e. a number of determinants to be considered individually and/or in combination to explain sexual offending against children. They proposed five pathways, or psychological mechanisms, that make the offender vulnerable to offending against children. Each pathway represents different aetiological factors – individuals are postulated as exhibiting one main pathway, with the other four also demonstrated with varying intensities. Each pathway represents a distal factor (causal factors captured by predisposition of offender, the origins of which may be genetic, biological and/or developmental). Distal factors are consequently 'activated' by proximal factors (e.g. stress, feeling down or angry) that culminate or trigger the predisposition to sexually offend against children.

Pathway 1: *Intimacy and social skill deficits*

As a consequence of abuse or neglect during childhood, there may be difficulties with emotional relationships and an insecure attachment style. Ward and Siegert hypothesise that offenders following this pathway offend only when adult partners are not available, so the child is used as an 'adult substitute'. Thus, faced with rejection or emotional loneliness, the offender may turn to children to fulfil their emotional needs.

Pathway 2: *Deviant sexual scripts*

Sexual scripts guide our behaviour in sexual/social situations. According to Ward and Siegert, 'a sexual script spells out when sex is to take place, with whom, what to do, and how to interpret the cues or signals associated with different phases in a sexual encounter. These cues can be internal to the individual, interpersonal, or broadly cultural in nature' (p. 332). Early experiences again said to lead to deviant and distorted sexual scripts (e.g. involving age of partner, inappropriate behaviours). Sexual cues may be intertwined with feelings of affection or closeness.

Pathway 3: *Emotional dysregulation*

Self-regulation is important if we are to function effectively as human beings – enabling us to achieve our goals by changing ourselves or our behaviours. Part of self-regulation is the regulation of our emotions – sometimes we try to cheer ourselves up, or indulge in an emotional state, but other times we need to reduce our emotional levels (e.g. anger, fear, guilt). Sex offenders may show emotional dysregulation and offend against children to cope with feelings of stress or depression.

Pathway 4: *Cognitive distortions (also called antisocial cognitions)*

Ward and Siegert's Pathways Model identifies five cognitive distortions: (1) children as sexual objects; (2) the offender is entitled to have their sexual needs met; (3) the world is a dangerous and untrustworthy place – children are not a threat and give comfort that other adults do not; (4) the offender is not in control of their actions – which are blamed on external factors, such as stress or drugs, etc.; and (5) not all sexual activity is harmful, and children may benefit in a number of ways from sex with adults.

Pathway 5: *Multiple dysfunctional mechanism*

This is where offenders have a combination of the other four pathways, but will generally have deviant sexual scripts (pathway 2) as part of this combination.

Box 9.8. Case study 2

Grant, a convicted paedophile, tried to explain his behaviour thus: 'I've tried to identify that in, in my own thinking at the time and all I could identify was the fact that I wanted company and I found the children more comforting to be with than anybody else and I found them, that they liked being with me and I found that rewarding, and that I was finding some sort of usefulness, and to be liked and needed, you know . . . and that was all I was after, but then the situation that followed was the fact that I'd be liked and trusted and um in situations where I was taking them out on my own, and then if they showed any interest in any type of, that type of thing (sexual contact) . . . then I would go, that would be it, I wouldn't – there were no barriers . . . (to offending)' (Winder and Grayson, in prep.).

See Chapter 14 for more information on Ward and Siegert's Pathways Model, including a discussion of its strengths and weaknesses.

PART C: Further information

C9.1. Organisations to contact for information and voluntary work

The websites below are two organisations for the treatment of all types of sexual abusers. Both websites offer information on research, employment and training. These are good websites for accessing up-to-date research and information and for anyone wishing to work in this field.

Association for the Treatment of Sexual Abusers: http://www.atsa.com.
National Organisation for the Treatment of Abusers: http://www.nota.co.uk.

There are also a number of charitable organisations aiming to reduce sexual offending through research and also by helping offenders to manage their risk.

Circles of Support: http://www.circles-uk.org.uk.

Circles of Support and Accountability is a UK-based charity committed to reducing sexual offending by supporting sexual offenders. Volunteers are specially trained to work with sexual offenders and support them in their reintegration back into the community. Their website provides information about how to become involved as a volunteer.

The Lucy Faithfull Foundation: http://lucyfaithfull.org.

The Lucy Faithfull Foundation is a UK Charity that is committed to reducing the risk of children being sexually abused, through research and treatment of abusers. Their website has information on research and training opportunities, as well as information on victim support.

NSPCC: https://www.nspcc.org.uk.

The National Society for Prevention of Child Cruelty is also dedicated to tackling child sexual abuse. They have services to protect children and young people and to help them overcome this abuse (such as ChildLine, below) and conduct research, deliver training and provide other resources to help improve the lives of children.

ChildLine is the UK's free, 24-hour, confidential helpline; it is run by trained volunteers and is available to all children and young people who wish to report or talk about their abuse, or even to talk through their own problematic behaviour.

The National Association for People Abused in Childhood: http://www.napac.org.uk/.

NAPAC is a UK charity that provides help and support for adults who were abused in childhood. Their freephone helpline is 0800 085 3330; they have opportunities for volunteers and also have advice and information for people supporting others coming to terms with their childhood sexual abuse.

C9.2. Further reading

Salter, A.C. (2003) *Predators: Pedophiles, Rapists, and Other Sex Offenders*. New York: Basic Books.

This is a really readable book written by Anna Salter, a therapist with a PhD in Psychology, who studied both sex offenders and victims – it contains a lot of rich material from interviews.

Stinson, J.D., Sales, B.D. and Becker, J.V. (2008) *Sex Offending: Casual Theories to Inform Research, Prevention and Treatment*. Washington, DC: APA.

This is a really comprehensive book detailing theories and explanations of sexual offending, from single-factor theories to the more complex (and more recent) integrated theories of sexual offending.

chapter

10 RAPE OF ADULTS

NICHOLAS BLAGDEN, SARAH PEMBERTON AND CLARE BREED

PART A: The offence – Who, what, when, why?

A10.1. Introduction

Rape remains one of the most under-reported and least prosecuted of all violent crimes (Walby and Allen, 2004); every 34 minutes a rape is reported to the police in the UK, yet only 1 out of 20 of those rapes reported leads to a conviction (Fawcett Society, 2008). These figures do little to encourage women to report rape, and also demonstrate failings with the criminal justice system (CJS) at responding to rape.

This chapter will highlight the multifaceted nature of rape, in terms of aetiology, motivation, decision making and treatment. The aim is to provide an overview of definitions, concepts, theory and treatment in order to better understand why some individuals commit rape. While there are differences and debates with regard to concepts and theory, what will become clear is that there is no archetypal 'rapist'. What they do have in common is gender; however, rapists differ in their motivations, economic and class background, race and ethnicity and modus operandi (method of operation). The authors of this chapter acknowledge male rape as a significant reality. Home Office (2010) statistics have recorded that 1174 men were raped in 2009/10; however, this chapter specifically focuses upon male sexual violence towards women, as the majority of adult rape victims are female and the perpetrators are male.

A10.2. Definitions of rape

In criminal justice settings, the term 'adult rapist' is usually applied to those who have been convicted of the offence of rape contrary to sections 75 and 76 of the Sexual Offences Act 2003 (see Box 10.1) and the victim is an adult.

Rapists are generally subdivided into two categories – 'stranger' (those rapists *not* known to the victim) and 'acquaintance' (those rapists who are known to the victim). Salter (2001) also splits rapists into two further categories – 'opportunistic' and 'compulsive'. The 'opportunistic' rapists are those who take sex because the opportunity arises, for instance while committing the burglary of someone's home. The compulsive rapists are those who create opportunities to rape and are generally motivated by anger and erotic motivation (Salter, 2001).

Box 10.1. The definition of rape as defined by the Sexual Offences Act 2003

(1) A person (A) commits an offence if:
  (a) he intentionally penetrates the vagina, anus or mouth of another person (B) with his penis;
  (b) B does not consent to the penetration; and
  (c) A does not reasonably believe that B consents.
(2) Whether a belief is reasonable is to be determined having regard to all the circumstances, including any steps A has taken to ascertain whether B consents.
(3) Sections 75 and 76 apply to an offence under this section.[1]
(4) A person guilty of an offence under this section is liable, on conviction on indictment, to imprisonment for life.

Source: Sexual Offences Act 2003, p. 7.

The Sexual Offences Act 2003 provides a complete overhaul of the law to date. Some of the main changes to the act include the incorporation of oral penetration to the definition of rape and the inclusion of 'consent' as a legal definition. Other important legislative developments prior to the Sexual Offences Act 2003 included 'male rape' being recognised as a criminal act in the Criminal Justice and Public Order Act 1994 alongside the recognition of marital rape in the Criminal Justice Act of 1991 (marital rape was first recognised as a criminal activity by the House of Lords in 1991 but it was not until 1994 that this became part of statute).

A10.3. Who?

This section will consider the impact that drugs and alcohol, as well as individual differences, have upon the perpetrators of rape.

Drugs and alcohol

There is still limited research about the use and misuse of substances either in the commission of the act of rape (such as to overcome internal inhibitions in performing the rape) (Finkelhor, 1984) or in its facilitation (such as the use of drugs in date rape). Furthermore, evidence regarding specific drugs (e.g. Rohypnol) and their role in rape is still unclear, with Horvath and Brown

(2007) finding that in rape offences where drugs and alcohol are implicated, the victim had typically been drinking of their own volition (self-intoxicated). While the true incidence of drug-facilitated rape is not clear, it is likely to be higher than statistics suggest as victims are often unaware they have been targeted (Webber, 2010). A study by Muehlenhard and Melaney (1989) found that 77.6% of women respondents had been involved in some form of sexual assault while 7.1% of men had been involved in unwanted sexual intercourse. Elsewhere it has been reported that around 90% of sexual assaults on female students involve alcohol (Weir, 2001). The use of any substance to lower inhibition and enhance the potential for unwanted sexual intercourse could be considered a date rape drug (ibid.).

However there are interesting findings related to attributions and blame when alcohol is used in the offence of rape, and these attributions vary considerably (Adams-Curtis and Forbes, 2004; Girard and Senn, 2008). Rapists have been seen to use drug-use/addiction as an excuse for their offending behaviour and as a way of externalising blame (Scully and Marolla, 1984). However, while the use of alcohol and/or drugs in the facilitation of rape may increase blame on the perpetrator, this is not always the case. Instead, the inverse may occur – that is, the woman may be blamed because 'she put herself in that position'. Rape myth acceptance, for instance, may play a role in victim blaming and facilitate the view that the woman played some part in the rape (see Box 10.2 for an explanation of rape myths).

Box 10.2. What are rape myths?

Rape myths provide people with stereotypical or false beliefs about the prevalence of sexual violence. This is often accomplished by victim blaming that shifts the blame away from the offender and onto the victim.

Girard and Senn's (2008) study on undergraduate students' perceptions on the effect of voluntary and involuntary drug use on attributions about sexual assault found that women were seen as playing a role if they had voluntarily consumed drugs prior to the offence. While participants assigned blame to the perpetrator in sexual assaults facilitated by alcohol or drugs, women's voluntary consumption of drugs prior to a sexual assault increased victim blame (Girard and Senn, 2008). Worryingly, the same use of attributions and rape myths has been found to influence jurors' decision making in cases of rape. Finch and Munro (2005) found that jurors frequently held views about the attribution of blame and responsibility that were inconsistent with the application of the law. Jurors were found to consider many extra-legal factors when reaching a decision. These included rape myths and stereotypical conceptions about intoxication, sexual assault and drug-facilitated rape. They also found a surprising level of condemnation for victims, with victims generally blamed unless there was clear evidence that the perpetrator had committed wrongdoing. This has been demonstrated further by the reduction in compensation for those victims of rape who had consumed alcohol at the time of the offence, as it was judged to be a contributing factor to the offence occurring (Williams, 2008).

Individual differences

While research tends to label sexual offenders into categories (rapist, child molester) in order to examine the differences between groups, this largely ignores the individual differences within groups. Research has shown that rapists differ in terms of sexual preference, psychopathy and level of empathy shown towards the victim (some rapists are empathetic, others are not, while some are ambivalent) (Langton and Marshall, 2001). There is also variability in the levels of abuse rapists use in their offending. Some rapists use threats or force to facilitate coercive sexual acts, while others are more aggressive and some sadistic, taking pleasure in the pain and fear they are inducing in the victim (Hudson and Ward, 1997; Langton and Marshall, 2001).

As highlighted in the Section 'introduction', there are rapists who are opportunistic and some who are compulsive, some who will seek out strangers and others will rape women known to them (Salter, 2001). The heterogeneity in rapists has led some authors to create typologies of rapists. Table 10.1 is presented below, based on Knight and Prentky's (1990) typology as detailed by Langton and Marshall (2001).

Other types of rapist that have been identified, but the consistent finding is that there do appear to be differences in the use of force, motivation, socialisation, victim empathy and deviant sexual interest. For instance, two 'power-type' rapists have been identified – power-assertive and power reassurance. A power-assertive rapist believes that men should dominate women and that he is entitled to sex whenever he wants. Links here can be made with the feminist explanations of rape that will be explored later in this chapter. The male perpetrator will be a selfish individual, and during the offence will be concerned with sexual gratification (Carney, 2004). The power-reassurance rapist will suffer from feelings of inadequacy; his offending will be a way of reassuring himself of his own masculinity and his dominance over women. This type of rapist will use the minimal

Table 10.1 *Typology of rapists*

Rapist type	Description
Opportunistic	Offences are unplanned, impulsive, with the goal being immediate sexual gratification.
Pervasively angry	The offence is an instance of poor behavioural control. The degree of force and violence used is excessive and brutal. Resistance from the victim is likely to exacerbate violence.
Sexual	The sexual type can be subdivided into two categories – sadistic and non-sadistic. The sexual aggression of the sadistic rapist is manifest in the humiliation of the victim and the infliction of physical harm. Non-sadistic rapists are characterised by having an enduring sexual preoccupation with the offence occurring through the manifestation of deviant sexual interests.
Vindictive	This type of rapist shares the characteristics of aggression and force of the pervasively angry, but anger is not part of a general disposition; instead it is specifically targeted at women. There is a 'sexual component in the assault behaviour but the aggression is not eroticised [*sic*], suggesting that paraphilic fantasies are not involved' (Langton and Marshall, 2001, p. 505).

amount of force in the offence because he wants the victim to desire them. He will fantasise that the victim will enjoy the offence and that she will want to do it again voluntarily (ibid.). However, it could be argued that this simply forms part of the excuse-making that the perpetrators of such rapes uphold.

Rapists differ both within and between offences, which supports the argument that there is no one type of rapist. Rapists rape for different reasons and for different motivations. While they differ in terms of level of intimacy deficits, attachment and deviant arousal when compared with other sexual offenders, rapists also differ from each other as to why they rape.

A10.4. Misconceptions

When we think of rape, the perpetrator is often thought of as someone the victim does *not* know, that is a man hiding in a bush waiting for his victim. The perpetrator will also be represented as someone who is suffering from some kind of perversion and who is not clinically 'well' or 'normal'. These are, however, misconceptions and the reality is somewhat different. For instance, the British Crime Survey (BCS) (2004) found that only 17% of rapes were committed by a stranger, with most being committed by partners/former partners or acquaintances. These common stereotypes (or rape myths) affect how both men and women view rape. This is evidenced not only through the practices of professionals within the CJS but also by the way in which a woman who has been raped rationalises her situation by comparing herself to every rape case she has ever heard of (Mackinnon, 1987). To what extent does her experience match stereotypical representations and popular assumption: was it rape or 'something else'? (Berrington and Jones, 2002, p. 315). So whilst stranger rape cases are rare, they capture the public imagination more avidly than acquaintance rape and cause a great deal of misdirected fear (Pakes and Winestone, 2007). However, statistically speaking, women are less safe in their homes, with friends or acquaintances than with strangers (Salter, 2001).

KEY DEBATE: Is rape considered a serious offence in the UK?

For:
Due to an increased recognition of the seriousness of rape from organisations like Rape Crisis and the Fawcett Society, there have been numerous changes to legislation and policy that have reaffirmed the seriousness of rape. It could be argued that the Sexual Offences Act 2003 went some way to clarifying issues regarding consent. There is now greater reporting of rape by victims, which the British Crime Survey (2001) highlighted as a problem. Indeed rape reporting has increased since then: 2001/2, 9734; 2005/6, 13, 712; 2008/9, 12,165 (Kelly, Lovett and Regan, 2005; Fawcett Society, 2007).

Recognition of the seriousness of rape has led to the implementation of Sexual Assault Referral Centres (SARCS), which are victim-centred and provide support for the victims of rape, including the forensic examination, crisis intervention and emotional support and information/advice. Early indications are that SARCS make a difference for rape victims and are an excellent example of voluntary and public sector collaborative working (Robinson and Hudson, 2009). There are also now dedicated rape investigation units that provide a single point of contact for victims and improve rape victim care. These include Operation Topaz (West Yorkshire) and Operation Sapphire (London/Lambeth Borough).

Against:

The conviction rate for rape still remains low and it remains one of the most under-reported and least prosecuted of all violent crimes (Walby and Allen, 2004). While the reporting of rape has increased (up to around 40% from 2001), the conviction rate continues to decline and is now around 5.3% (Kelly, Lovett and Regan, 2005). Stereotypically there is a tendency to see forcible stranger rape as 'serious and proper' rape while acquaintance rapes are, by implication, seen not so serious or as 'something else' (Berrington and Jones, 2002, p. 315). This is exemplified in the recent comments by Justice Secretary, Kenneth Clarke who appeared to intimate that there were serious 'proper' rapes and less serious ones (before later backtracking to stating that all rape is serious). While legislation has made some attempt to clarify issues of consent and to some extent improve the experience of the criminal justice system (CJS) for rape victims, sentencing is still inadequate. According to the sentencing guidelines the starting point for a single offence of rape by a single offender is five years (if the victim is over 16 years of age) (CPS, 2011). However, they are eligible for a one-third reduction in tariff if they enter a guilty plea, which means some rapists will serve only 18 months.

When we consider that rape myths and stereotypical thinking affect jurors' decision making (see Finch and Munro, 2005) and that a third of the public view rape victims as somewhat responsible for their attack, coupled with current sentencing guidelines, it is difficult to argue that rape is taken seriously.

Action:

In order to think critically about the debate, students should follow the link: http://www.bbc.co.uk/news/uk-politics-13444770 and read the transcript from a recent interview with Kenneth Clarke where he is questioned about his views on rape. Does this interview add support in favour or against rape being viewed a serious crime?

Myths surrounding rape have become deeply entrenched within UK society. Amnesty International (2005) reported that more than a quarter[2] of those asked said that they thought a woman was partially or totally to blame for being raped if she was wearing provocative clothing. In addition, more than one-fifth held the same view if the woman had multiple sexual partners in the past. More than a quarter of those asked said that a woman was partially or totally responsible for being raped if she was drunk, and more than a third held the same view if the woman had failed clearly to articulate a verbal 'no' to the man (Amnesty International, 2005).

Myths allow us to 'disguise a social reality or rather, to describe the world in terms favourable to the position of a particular group' (Sachs, 1978, p. 31). Rape myths disguise the existence of rape and describe the world in terms favourable to the position of men who rape. Rape myths obscure the true nature of rape (Brownmiller, 1975) and shift blame away from the offender and onto the victim (Gray, 2006), often discouraging women from reporting a sexual assault. The subscription to rape myths is commonplace within the CJS; rape myths have found their way into the police force and courts, influencing policemen, police-women, juries and judges alike. Highly publicised cases such as that of Kirk Reid and John Worboys have done very little to alleviate the concerns over the CJS and the subscription to rape myths. Individually, Worboys (black-cab driver) and Reid sexually assaulted and raped hundreds of women before they were caught. In both cases, police ignored evidence and intelligence that could have led them to the rapists years earlier. In the Worboys case, victims said they were simply not believed when they said they had been attacked by a black-cab driver (Laville, 2009).

Box 10.3. Common rape myths

- Do not go out alone at any time; women are most likely to be raped outside, in dark alleyways late at night; this is the best way for a woman to protect herself.
- Women who are sexually assaulted 'ask for it' by the way they dress or act; rape only happens to young women.
- Everyone knows when a woman says no, she often means yes; women secretly want to be raped.
- The woman was drunk/took drugs/had a bad reputation/wore tight clothes/seduced him/probably got what she was asking for.
- Women can't be raped by their partner.
- Women eventually relax and enjoy it; they secretly want to be raped.
- If the woman did not get hurt or fight back it could not have been rape.
- Men who rape or sexually assault are mentally ill.
- The man was drunk/on drugs/depressed/under stress/wasn't himself.

Source: From Rape Crisis, 2007.

This next section will now examine two of these myths in greater detail, dispelling them and presenting the reality rather than the myths that surround rape.

The myth: Rape is committed by men who are psychopathic individuals whom the victim does not know.

The facts: There is a widely held assumption that men who commit sexual offences against women differ from the rest of the male population; they must be sick or mentally ill (Epps, Haworth and Swaffer, 1993). This depiction of the psychopathic individual who is unlike 'normal' men is simply not the reality of rape and results in 'normal' men being disassociated from crimes of sexual violence carried out against women (Berrington and Jones, 2002). Studies have indicated that as few as 5% of men are psychotic at the time of their crimes (Scully and Marolla, 1985); very few convicted rapists are referred for psychiatric treatment. Furthermore, this myth is centred on the premise that the victim does not know her attacker. In 85% of cases the rapist is known to the woman; he may be a friend, colleague, relative, husband or ex-partner and approximately 50% of rapes occur in the home of the woman or the attacker (Rape Crisis, 2007). So for women who walk alone at night, this is the least of their worries.

The myth: Women cry rape

The facts: In part this myth functions to deny the widespread prevalence of sexual victimisation. This 'myth' is further exacerbated by the isolated examples the media print about false allegations of rape (N-Dubz 2009 false allegation claim – see Michaels, 2009) rather than representing the true extent of sexual assault. Research from the Fawcett Society has established that the levels of false reports of rape are 'no higher than false reports of any other crime'. Only 3% of rape accusations are considered to be 'probably or possibly false' according to police categorisation, which is no higher than in any other type of crime (Fawcett Society, 2008).

A10.5. Facts and figures

Incidence: Since 2004, the official measuring of sexual offences altered as a result of the Sexual Offences Act 2003, which came into force in 2004. Sexual offences are split into two parts: most serious sexual crimes and other sexual offences. Most serious sexual crimes include rape, sexual assault and sexual activity with children. Other sexual offences include buggery and incest (Home Office, 2007). Home Office figures suggest that in 2008/9, 12,165 females (all ages) reported an offence of rape (Home Office, 2009). In total, 40,787 offences were recorded within the most serious sexual crime category, accounting for less than 1% of all recorded crime (Home Office, 2009). Official figures for male rape stood at 968 offences in 2008/9.

Official statistics do not measure the true extent of crime within society, but instead present us with statistics upon crimes that have been reported and recorded. Recently (September 2009) the BBC found that some UK police forces have been failing to record more than 40% of rape cases. Victim surveys such as the BCS make attempts to fill the void of official statistics, but these too have limitations, including an unwillingness of 'victims' to discuss/complete questionnaires about the sexual violence they have experienced. Therefore, it is possible to say that the true extent of rape within the UK is much greater that the official statistics suggest.

Prevalence: Amnesty International state that on average 167 women are raped every day in the UK; the BCS (2001) have reported that 1 in 20 women (aged between 16 and 59) in England and Wales have been the victim of rape. These are disturbing figures that dramatically exceed the presence in official statistics.

A10.6. How are offenders caught?

Investigation

The investigation of rape, in most cases, begins with the victim's decision to report it. Although there is no time limit set on investigating incidents of sexual violence, the sooner a rape is reported to the police, the greater the chances of the police recovering evidence and the pursuance of a successful prosecution. The advice to victims is: *do not* wash, eat or drink, smoke or go to the toilet. The forensic medical examination will enable DNA to be collected, physical injuries to be photographed and documented and the doctor will also be able to ascertain whether the perpetrator gave the victim a substance, such as drugs or alcohol, which enabled him to commit the offence (Rights of Women, 2008).

Depending on geographical location, both medical treatment and the forensic medical examination for rape victims can be arranged to take place in a Sexual Assault Referral Centre (SARC)[3] rather than at a police station. SARCs are available 24 hours a day and are usually run through local partnerships between the police, national health services and voluntary organisations (http://www.homeoffice.gov.uk/crime-victims/reducing-crime/sexual-offences/sexual-assault-referral-centres/), but are sadly few and far between.

The police are responsible for investigating the alleged offence by gathering evidence. Evidence will be collected through witness statements, forensic medical examination, taking photographs of the scene of the assault, seizure of CCTV, mobile phones and computers where appropriate and by arresting and interviewing the alleged perpetrator. If the perpetrator is a stranger to the victim, the victim will be required to look through photographs of known sex offenders. If this is not successful, then an artist's impression may be created based on the victim's description and, if a suspect is arrested, then the victim may be required to take part in an identity parade. All of the evidence collected will be put together and then passed over to the Crown Prosecution Service (CPS) who will make the decision as to whether to prosecute and, if this is successful, the case will then be prepared for court (Rights of Women, 2008).

It has been argued that rape victims' experiences of the CJS can be harmful to the victims and lead to secondary victimisation – that is victimisation which stems from reliving the experiences through the adversarial criminal justice process (e.g. through questioning from police (Orth, 2002; Goodey, 2005)). Indeed, Goodey (2005) has found that the anticipation of questioning in the court is a significant contributor to withdrawal of rape charges. Kelly, Lovett and Regan (2005) found that there are high attrition rates in rape cases. In 2002 11,678 rape offences reached court and 655 led to conviction; however, of those 258 entered a guilty plea meaning that only 3.4 % of rape cases (where a not guilty plea was entered) secured conviction. It is unsurprising then that criminal proceedings have been found to cause psychological harm to victims (Orth, 2002).

There are, however, some inherent difficulties in securing conviction in rape cases, particularly those where the offender is known to the victim. Cases often rely heavily on the evidence given by the victim, which in many cases becomes the victim's word against the perpetrator's. Also, where both victim and perpetrator are intoxicated the problems can intensify. However, the police take allegations seriously and unlike some violent crimes each case will be investigated by a Detective Inspector. Indeed, some force areas have taken on board the criticisms from victims, victim charities and academics and have set up units dedicated to rape investigations. For instance in West Yorkshire 'Operation Topaz' has become the first rape investigation unit to lead the investigation from initial report through to conclusion at the court. This 'one-stop shop' unit ensures that victims get continuity care, and that they are given the support and advice they need and an enhanced quality of service. All members of Operation Topaz are specifically trained to work with rape victims

Detection

As discussed above, the policing of acquaintance rape is very much reactive and is reliant on victims reporting such crimes before cases can be investigated, detected and convicted. In terms of police profiling of offences, which is more applicable to serial stranger-type rape cases, public protection intelligence desks within each borough of the Metropolitan Police will link rapes together (by victim/suspect description) if a pattern of offending behaviour is identified. However, it is important to remember that the prevalence of stranger-type rape cases is much lower than those committed by perpetrators whom the victim knows.

Conviction

The term 'conviction rate' refers to the proportion of rapes reported to police that result in the alleged perpetrator being found guilty in a court of law (Fawcett Society, 2007).

As already stated, every 34 minutes a rape is reported to the police in the UK; only 1 of 20 of those rapes reported to the police leads to a conviction (Fawcett Society, 2008). It is estimated that 1 in 4 women worldwide may experience sexual violence by an intimate partner during their lifetime (WHO, 2002). Yet, rape remains one of the most under-reported and least prosecuted of all violent crimes and, as a result, the number of reported rapes is lower than the incidence and prevalence rates (Walby and Allen, 2004). In 2008, approximately 6.5% of alleged rapes led to a conviction, and the proportion of cases resulting in successful prosecution is falling (Guardian, 2009). Jones et al. (2009) found that women were unlikely to report sexual assault to the police if the assailant was known to them. Other research has found that women are often reluctant to report rape to the police, principally because they don't think that the police will take it seriously but also because women fear being blamed (Westmarland, 2004). Most rape victims who report the offence to the police will never see their case get to court, let alone a conviction. This may be as a result of individual police officers failing to investigate allegations properly or a rejection by the Crown Prosecution Service on grounds of insufficient evidence.

A10.7. What happens to offenders?

Treatments typically offered

Her Majesty's Prison Service of England and Wales offers the following cognitive behavioural treatment programmes for sexual offenders (SOTP): Rolling, Core, Extended, Becoming New Me, Booster and the Adapted Better Lives Booster Programme (all of these are group interventions). The Core SOTP is for men of medium to very high risk of sexually reoffending. Rapists of adult women will typically be assessed for the Core SOTP in the first instance. The Prison Service also offers the Healthy Sexual Functioning Programme (HSFP). This is facilitated on a one-to-one basis, and is suitable for men who are at high risk of sexually reoffending and who have current offence-related sexual fantasies. This is a secondary treatment programme, which would typically follow the Core or Extended SOTP.

Relative efficacy of programmes

Thornton (2000) summarised the impact of the early SOTP on reconviction rates. The sample consisted of 647 treated sexual offenders and 1910 untreated sexual offenders. They were all discharged from prison between 1992 and 1996 from a sentence of at least four years. Both groups were categorised according to their level of prior risk based on their past record. Rates of reconviction for sexual and other violent offences were focused upon. The results showed that the early SOTP seemed to have been effective in producing a substantial reduction in serious reoffending for medium-risk offenders (medium–low-prior risk offenders showed a reduction of 79% of serious reoffending, and medium–high-prior risk offenders showed a reduction of 59% of serious reoffending). The high-risk offenders showed little impact of treatment. The psychological factors underlying their offending are wide ranging, and it seems likely that only a more intensive and comprehensive programme would impact on their offending. The 2000 revision of the SOTP Core Programme combined with the SOTP Extended Programme was developed to address the needs of such high-risk sexual offenders.

Recently there has been debate as to whether the treatment for rapists should be undertaken separately instead of being mixed with that for other offenders, as is currently the norm. Eccleston and Owen (2007) have suggested that by mixing rapists with other sexual offenders therapists may not be addressing their treatment needs effectively. Rapists need greater time on managing their impulsivity, problem solving and antisocial attitudes, while more attention must be paid to rapists' implicit theories (i.e. 'women are sexual objects') (Eccleston and Owen, 2007).

Recidivism

Research has found that rapists with psychopathic characteristics and deviant sexual preferences recidivate more frequently than other groups of rapists (Hildebrand, De Ruiter and De Vogel, 2004). However, the evidence base for treatability in rapists is limited. Alexander (1999) found little difference in sexual recidivism for treated and untreated rapists (20.1 and 23.7%, respectively). While Maletzky (1991) found that 13.8% of rapists were arrested by the police in the follow-up period after treatment, as compared with 1.3% of child offenders.

In a meta-analysis, Hanson and Bussiere (1998) found that 18.9% of 1839 rapists sexually reoffended over an average follow-up period of 4–5 years, while 22.1% violently reoffended.

Prognosis (life course information)

Craissati, Webb and Keen (2005) argue that the combination of a risk measure (e.g. RM2000) with a rating for childhood abuse/trauma, and consideration of personality disorder in adulthood, may significantly improve the ability to identify those rapists at highest risk of community failure. This identifies concerns relating to anti-authoritarian attitudes, involvement with criminal peers, resumption of substance misuse, chaotic lifestyle and refusal to comply with treatment conditions. Interventions include the need to manage boundaries without confrontation, whilst adhering to statutory expectations, and creative use of available resources to match the individual needs of the offender (Craissati, 2005).

PART B: Theories and explanations

B10.1. Introduction

The current dominant psychological explanations and theoretical positions regarding rape centre around social cognition. Indeed since the mid-1980s there has been a large body of research that has demonstrated a clear link between rape-related cognition, the act of rape and sexually aggressive behaviour towards women (Langton, 2007). However, this dominant psychological position is not without critique and contestation. In particular, feminist writers and discursive psychologists have been critical of such a focus. Feminist writers have argued that rape is something men do to women in societies characterised by a patriarchal order (i.e. where men are dominant). They would argue that in order to understand rape we have to go beyond cognition and personality traits and instead focus on the 'practical ideologies' that govern acts of rape (Lea and Auburn, 2001). In such a way we must focus on the ideological context, power and gender in the construction of rape. One such example may be the use of 'rape myths' (see Burt, 1980) to legitimise and account for rape. Similarly, feminist victimologists have been critical of 'positivist' victimology for their engaging in 'victim-blaming' based on gender stereotypes and assumptions on what behaviour is 'appropriate' for women (Wolhuter, Olley and Denham, 2009).

This next section will focus on dominant explanations of rape within psychology, alongside the more contested feminist perspectives regarding rape. By doing this we are attempting to present a holistic view of the theoretical frameworks of rape and the social context within which the act occurs.

Rape and cognition

Cognition is an important area of research for forensic psychology and is now of central importance to understanding the motivations and aetiology of sexual offending. Research on cognition in sexual offenders has helped shape both the assessment and treatment of offenders, with sex offender treatment programmes based on cognitive-behavioural therapy. Until recently much of the research has focused on 'surface' cognitions, though currently there is a recognition that 'deep' cognitions provide a more complex and comprehensive explanation of sexual offender cognitions.

'Surface' cognitions are the offender's articulated thoughts, desires, beliefs and attitudes which seem to sustain and maintain their offending behaviour and are often referred to as 'cognitive distortions' (Fisher and Beech, 2007). Marshall and Barbaree (1990) argue that cognitive distortions are 'beliefs, attitudes and perceptions which are non-consensual and distorted, and which appear to maintain the deviant behaviour of the sex offender' (Marshall and Barbaree, 1990, p. 369). Similarly, Murphy (1990) argues that cognitive distortions are 'self-statements made by offenders that allow them to deny, minimise, justify and rationalise their behaviour' (Marshall, 1990, p. 332). Thus the rapist's claims that the women 'wanted it', 'led them on', were 'asking for it' or that 'all women want sex' all serve to minimise the offender's behaviour and justify his position. Often, such articulations serve to present the offender in a more favourable light. Scully and Marolla (1986) examined the accounts of denying and admitting convicted rapists. They found that both types of rapist used excuses and justifications in their accounts. Relatedly, admitting rapists attempted to negate a 'rapist identity' by presenting themselves as 'nice guys' and 'decent' people.

Below is an extract from an offence account (see Box 10.4) from a research interview that focused on participants' reasons for maintenance and overcoming denial of their offence (see Blagden, Winder, Thorne and Gregson, 2011). Harvey is a 30-year-old man who is currently serving 6 years for the aggravated rape of his sister-in-law.

Box 10.4. Case study: Harvey

Offence: Aggravated rape
Sentence: 6 years

We had a close relationship [him and victim] anyway, a friendship relationship, but she was a very attractive girl ... I think I had thoughts, illicit thoughts about her and I think I dwelt on those thoughts erm through watching the pornography

---

and getting a more depraved thought of what sex is, more and more thoughts built up about her . . . So it's a build up of the thoughts that made me cross over from fantasy over reality. I had a stressful kind of job; I was just sacked from my job a week before the offence . . . So that was a contributing factor, I don't know how much, in terms of pushing me from fantasy to reality.

[I said] I'd slept with her but I didn't rape her it's consensual. There'd been bits in the past where she'd flirted with me and stuff, so I knew there was a bit of grounds to say she was a player and come onto me before . . .

. . . the reason I denied it was because I couldn't believe I'd done it, it was totally out of character – no way. Number two, I don't think anybody else could believe I'd done it

There are elements of his offence account, although he is admitting the offence, which would be classed as containing cognitive distortions. It can be noted that he externalises blame for the offence by claiming that his loss of employment contributed to his offending behaviour. He also attempts to excuse and rationalise his behaviour by contending that the offence occurred because of his thoughts at the time, which had become preoccupied with a more 'depraved' view of sex. Through accounting for his behaviour in such a way he is able to divorce himself from the act and not see his behaviour as part of him. This can be noted when retrospectively accounting for why he denied and minimised because he could not believe he had done it and that it was 'out of character'. When Harvey accounts for what he pleaded to the police and in court he again externalises blame by propounding that the rape was in actuality a consensual act. He rationalises this by suggesting she had flirted with him in the past and brings her character into question when he comments that there was 'grounds to say she was a player'. It is also noteworthy that at the beginning of the extract he comments that 'she was very attractive', almost implying that her attractiveness was a contributor to the offence. Some of Harvey's accounting would also suggest subscription to rape myths (see Burt, 1980).

However, the use of cognitive distortions (CDs) in explaining sexual offending has been criticised, with their usefulness questioned. There is much disagreement about the term and the function that this serves. For instance, are CDs beliefs and attitudes that facilitate offending, or are they post hoc rationalisations that minimise shame and guilt? Indeed, accepting the universality of CDs doesn't tell us much about what CDs are, what functions they serve and how they affect offending behaviour (Howitt and Sheldon, 2007). It has subsequently been argued that CDs are 'founded on a simplistic view of human cognition . . . its longevity is explained by the absence of any significant additional theory development in this area' (Ward, Polaschek and Beech, 2006, p. 122). There has thus been a shift in the literature away from surface cognitions to the underlying cognitive schemata that drive the behaviour.

Implicit theories/schemas in adult rapists

The practical difference between an implicit theory and a schema is yet to be fully clarified, though it would appear that their meanings and implications are essentially the same (Mann and Shingler, 2006). Ward (2000a) and Ward and Keenan (1999) propose that cognitive distortions arise from our underlying causal or implicit theories. As such, implicit theories can be thought of as an individual's personal theory of the world. The term implicit theory, then, has its roots in the developmental literature of children's cognitive development. According to this position children act like scientists who develop theories in order to explain or predict the world around them, and these theories are used to process information and experience and enable individuals to make sense of their world (Thakker, Ward and Navathe, 2007).

Implicit theories (IT)/schemas are the organising framework for processing new information and making sense of that information. Since sexual offences occur within interpersonal contexts, the schemas/implicit theories most relevant will be concerned with the processing of social and interpersonal information (Mann and Schingler, 2006). Implicit theories then enable 'individuals to explain and understand aspects of their social environment, and, therefore, to make predictions about future events . . . such theories are called implicit because they are rarely articulated in a formal sense and may not be easily expressed by an individual' (Ward, 2000b, p. 495). An IT or schema-based theory of cognition in sexual offenders centres on the notion that dysfunctional cognitive schemas bias information processing 'in such a way as to make sexual assault a likely behavioural response' (Mann and Schingler, 2006, p. 175).

Ward and Keenan (1999) found that child abusers generally conformed to five implicit theories, and these were later supported in the research by Marziano et al. (2006). The identified implicit theories were entitlement (offender entitled to sex); dangerous world (real-world rejecting, children non-threatening); children as sexual objects (children have sexual needs and desires); uncontrollable (no control over sexual preference for children); and nature of harm (no harm to child). The approach by Ward and Keenan (1999) has been adopted by other researchers and applied to adult rapists (Polaschek and Ward, 2002; Fisher and Beech, 2007). Similarly, five implicit theories were found for adult rapists and are detailed in Box 10.5 (Polaschek and Ward, 2002; Polaschek and Gannon, 2004; Fisher and Beech, 2007).

Box 10.5. Implicit theories

Entitlement: This was found to be broadly similar to the IT held by child abusers. For rapists this IT proposes that men require their needs, including sexual needs, to be met on demand. Mann and Shingler (2006) argue that sexual entitlement can be considered an IT/schema because it is specifically concerned with the relationships between self and others.

Dangerous world: This again was similar to the child abusers – the world is seen as a dangerous place with other people rejecting and abusive. Thus, if women are perceived as threatening they may become victims of sexual abuse. It is important to note within this theory that, although the world is seen as dangerous, the offender perceives himself as being able to retaliate and assert his dominance.

Women as sex objects: Within this IT women are perceived as being in a state of constant sexual reception. Women are perceived as overly sexualised and whose purpose is to meet the sexual needs of men. As such women are seen as constantly desiring sex, whether consensual or coerced.

Women are unknowable: This IT proposes that, due to either socialisation or biology, women are inherently different to men and so cannot be understood by men. Through believing women are inherently different this facilitates harm towards women and can promote adversarial views towards women. This IT is self-serving insofar as it allows the offender to pursue his own needs while providing justification for ignoring women's beliefs, desires or values.

Male sex drive is uncontrollable: Within this IT men's sexual drive is believed to be uncontrollable. The rape-supportive version of this IT stems from the rapist's belief that men's sexual energy is difficult to control, with women perceived as having a key role in its loss of control.

It must be noted that, as with all types of sexual offenders, both between and within offence types there is no one profile, dominant image or typology of a rapist. In short rapists will differ with regards to their goals, motivations and reasons for offending. Some rapists may use rape to punish, degrade, humiliate or for sadistic motivations (Knight and Prentky, 1990; Malamuth and Brown, 1994), while some may rape to attain positive effects for themselves such as sexual desire or intimacy. As such, rapists' use of aggression or violence will differ from one offence to the next. Polaschek et al. (2001) proposed a preliminary model of rapists' offence processes that attempted to describe the cognitive, behavioural, motivational and contextual factors associated with rape. They found that the goal of committing a sexual offence was rarely explicit early in the offence process. Indeed, there have been many different goals seen to be implicated in sexual aggression including sex, antisocial opportunism, intimacy, dominance and harm. Thus Polaschek et al. (2001) propose an offence model which notes that rape occurs from a disparate range of distal goals and that there are numerous pathways in the offence of rape.

However, these dominant cognitive explanations are not without critique. From an epistemological position such approaches privilege 'in-head' constructions and take offenders' verbalisations as reflecting their mental state. However, there is often a discrepancy between what people think and what people say (Auburn, 2005; Maruna and Mann, 2006). Discursive psychologists are critical of the application of cognitive theory in explaining people's behaviour. For instance, they argue that cognitive distortions should not be seen as mental entities, but rather as something people 'do' (Auburn, 2005). From a discursive position cognitive distortions become a way for offenders to manage their accountability (i.e. make themselves look better. Auburn (2005) argues that cognitive distortions are a form of 'narrative repair' that offenders use to police their accounts and construct more desirable ones. Furthermore, the above theories fail to consider the issues of gender, power and patriarchy when trying to understand why men rape women. Feminists maintain that rape is an expression of male power, not lust or desire, and this explanation of rape will be considered next.

Rational choice

It has been contended that, although there may be differences in motivation within rapists for offending (see Fisher and Beech, 2007), there will be some elements of planning in most offences. Some may rigidly plan, others may wait for the right opportunity, while others will act impulsively. This thinking broadly conforms to a rational choice perspective in which the decision-making process of offenders and subsequent criminality occur because crime is perceived as the most adequate way of achieving the desired benefits (e.g. sexual gratification (Beauregard and LeClerc, 2007)). The decision to offend is seldom based on one decision and will often depend on situational cues – for example, the victim may be alone in a park (desired location for offence), but their interaction with a bystander will mean that the offender will have to reassess the situation and perhaps not commit an offence on this occasion. As such, Beauregard and LeClerc (2007) argue that sexual offending is based on 'premeditated opportunism', where the offending scenario gives way to situational cues that trigger the offence.

However, such explanations of offending behaviour tell us little about offenders' motivations for offending (whereas the cognitive theories discussed do give us insights into aetiology). Ward and Hudson (2000) attempt to address this by arguing that offence planning can be explicit, systematic and analytical (this conforms more to rational choice), but can also be implicit and initiative (from offender's schemata). For Ward and Hudson (2000), the commission of an offence comes from internal processes called 'automatic goal-dependent action plans', which can be understood as autonomous decision-making processes based on underlying beliefs, attitudes and values. So it is the rapist's beliefs and attitudes that lead to offending.

B10.2. Feminist explanations of rape

Due to the highly gendered nature of rape, some of the most important contributions to the understanding of sexual offending have come from feminist thinking. One important contribution is the seminal work *Against Our Will*, by Susan Brownmiller (1975), who sought to expose the myths surrounding rape by providing an insightful analysis of male power that placed rape and other forms of male violence against women at the heart of the said analysis.

Although feminist perspectives were and still are very diverse, they share a common commitment to eradicate gender inequalities. Feminist literature challenged the view that rape was simply another form of heterosexual sex and made explicit the conceptualisation of rape – i.e. that it was not about sex, but instead about notions of male power and violence. Feminism accounts for rape as a result of patriarchal dominance, and Corrin (1996) argues that 'men's use of power within patriarchal societies to privilege themselves over women is at the core of male sexual violence' (p. 3). Rape therefore needs to be considered in terms of the wider social context of the power of men and the consequential subordination of women (Segal, 1990), and not by simply pathologising the individual or accounting for rape as a result of biology. Scully (1990) argued that 'only profound social change at both the micro and macro levels of society is capable of eroding the rape-supportive elements of our culture' (p. 166). So the eradication of sexual violence will only occur if it is addressed as a societal problem rather than as an individual one.

Feminist literature has provided a diverse range of explanations for rape and sexual offending more generally. These account for the gendered nature of rape and wider social forces and critically consider the relationships between power, gender and hegemonic masculinity. One criticism often directed towards a particular branch of feminist explanations concerns relativism (i.e. feminist relativist approaches). This stems from the argument that there are multiple realities and truths and so it is not possible to reach an understanding of how the world really works (Ward, Polaschek and Beech, 2006). This approach is therefore critiqued for denying the 'realness' of rape by suggesting that it is merely an interpretation (please refer to Edwards, Ashmore and Potter, 1995; Gill, 1995; Hepburn, 2000 for a fuller discussion on/retort to this critique). Ward, Polaschek and Beech (2006) further argue that while it is correct to account for and understand cultural and other social factors, they constitute only one piece of the aetiological puzzle. Therefore, a comprehensive explanation of sexual offending requires an integrated approach that accounts for psychological properties, e.g. intimacy deficits, attachment, deviant sexual preferences and impulsivity, as well as the biological processes involved in creating offence-related vulnerabilities alongside consideration of the wider social context of the power of men and the subordination of women (Ward, Polaschek and Beech, 2006).

PART C: Further information

C10.1. Organisations to contact for information and voluntary work

Rape Crisis (England and Wales) is a registered charity that supports the work of Rape Crisis Centres in England and Wales. It is a feminist organisation that exists to promote the needs of women and girls who have experienced sexual violence, to improve services provided for them and to work towards the elimination of sexual violence.

http://www.rapecrisis.org.uk

The website provides students with an abundance of useful information on sexual violence including access to latest reports and publications detailing sexual violence, but also information on volunteering opportunities with Rape Crisis.

Rape Crisis (England and Wales) also provide support for those who have experienced sexual violence via their national freephone helpline: 0808 802 9999. This line runs twice a day, 365 days of the year between 12.00 and 14.30 and 19.00 and 21.30. It is based at the Rape and Sexual Abuse Support Centre (RASASC) in Croydon, south London and will be answered by fully trained and experienced women who take calls nationally from female and male survivors as well as from non-abusing families, partners, friends and other agencies. The helpline number is completely free of charge from landlines and public phones, and calls will not appear on the caller's bill; calls are also free from the six main UK mobile networks: 3, Orange, Virgin, Vodafone, T-Mobile and O2.

Surviving Trauma After Rape   http://www.starproject.co.uk/

The Surviving Trauma After Rape (STAR) Project is a free support service for females and males aged 14 and over who have been raped or sexually assaulted. STAR offers counselling, emotional and practical support throughout West Yorkshire. STAR helpline: 01924 298954

The Fawcett Society is a UK campaign for equality between women and men, campaigning about range of issues including rape.

http://www.fawcettsociety.org.uk

The website contains a wealth of useful resources, including information on internship and volunteer roles, which are not only a great way to contribute to Fawcett's leading work on gender equality but also a fantastic opportunity to gain valuable experience of working in the voluntary sector.

C10.2. Further reading

Brownmiller, S. (1975). *Against Our Will: Men, Women and Rape*, New York: Simon and Schuster.

Burt, M.R. (1980). Cultural myths and supports for rape. *Journal of Personality and Social Psychology*, 38, 217–30.

Notes

1. If the prosecution can prove at the time of the alleged rape that the victim did not or could not consent, then the defendant must respond to these allegations. Section 75 of the act outlines these evidential presumptions, which include the use of violence, threats of violence, if the victim was asleep, unconscious or drugged. Section 76 of the act is where the attacker deceives the victim to the nature/purpose of the act and where the attacker intentionally induces the victim to consent by impersonating someone she knows.

2. ICM interviewed a random sample of 1095 adults aged 18+ by telephone on 7–9 October 2005. Interviews were conducted across the country and the results have been weighted to the profile of adults. ICM is a member of the British Polling Council.

3. In 2008, there were 20 SARCs in the UK, with a promise by the government that a further 18 would be opened.

chapter

11

SHOPLIFTING AND KLEPTOMANIA

ANTHONY MCNALLY AND LAURA HAMILTON

PART A: The offence – Who, what, when, why?

A11.1. Introduction

Kleptomania in itself is not a crime; rather, it is a mental disorder that involves compulsive stealing. The compulsive element of this disorder relates to an inability to resist the urge or impulse to steal, even if it is against the person's will. Stealing, in relation to kleptomania, most typically involves theft from shops (i.e. shoplifting) even though the individual has money to pay for the stolen items or does not need the stolen goods. Although it may appear that shoplifting and kleptomania are closely connected, there are important differences regarding the motivation for offending. Many people believe that shoplifting may be due to personal material need superseding the personal availability of money to purchase. For some, material gain motivates their shoplifting offences; however, for others, repetitive shoplifting may reflect an irresistible impulse associated with an underlying mental disorder, labelled kleptomania. Regardless of the motive, shoplifting is associated with considerable economic and social costs. For instance, the Centre for Retail Research (2005) estimated shoplifting cost a massive £3.4 billion per year, which is equivalent to £115.91 for every UK taxpayer.

A11.2. Definitions

Fullerton and Punj (2004, p. 201) write, in their brief history of kleptomania, that the Swiss Physician Mathey in 1816 noted 'a unique madness characterized by the tendency to steal without motive and without necessity'. Mathey termed this madness 'klopemania' or stealing insanity. In 1838, French Physicians Esquirol and Marc coined the term kleptomania to account for the stealing insanity noted amongst women often of high social and economic status. These seminal writers on kleptomania characterised this stealing insanity in terms of:

- Irresistible impulses to steal objects of trivial value and which made no economic sense for the thief; and
- A sense of exhilaration and relief of tension triggered by the acts of theft.

Kleptomania has generated considerable scepticism since its inception in the nineteenth century, primarily around the idea that it pathologises criminal behaviour and potentially gives those who break the law a way of avoiding criminal responsibility. In 1980, kleptomania was officially classified in the *Diagnostic Statistical Manual* (*DSM-III* – American Psychiatric Association) as an impulse control disorder, and remains unchanged in *DSM-IV* (2000) and in the new version of *DSM-V* due for publication in 2012.

DSM-IV (2000) diagnostic criteria for kleptomania characterised the mental disorder as involving a recurrent failure to resist impulses to steal objects that are not needed either for personal use or for their monetary value (Criterion A). Kleptomaniacs will experience an increasing sense of tension immediately before committing the theft (Criterion B), with pleasure, gratification or relief occurring at the time of the theft (Criterion C). *DSM-IV* distinguishes the type of stealing associated with kleptomania, specifying that the stealing is not motivated by anger, revenge, delusion or hallucination (Criterion D) and the stealing behaviour should be no better accounted for by conduct disorders, manic episodes or antisocial personality disorder (Criterion E). The diagnostic criterion for kleptomania has not changed significantly since Mathey, Esquirol and Marc's original description of the phenomenon. However, it is important to note that although kleptomaniacs may gain pleasure or gratification through relief of tension at the time of theft, this may not be sustained, as gratification turns to guilt and emotional distress about having committed the offence (Aboujaoude, Gamel and Koran, 2004).

The Theft Act (1968) defines theft as 'the illegal taking of another person's property without their permission with the intent to permanently deprive the owner', and 'it is immaterial whether the appropriation is made with a view to gain, or is made for the thief's own benefit'. Accordingly, under UK Law, kleptomaniacs who are caught stealing are guilty of theft in the same way as non-kleptomaniac offenders, that is unless the kleptomaniac offender can prove the act of theft was an involuntarily action caused by a complete lack of control over an irresistible impulse at the time of the offence.

A11.3. Who?

Schlueter et al. (1989) distinguish between kleptomaniacs and shoplifters, arguing that kleptomaniacs are non-rational as they steal to meet a desire, whereas non-kleptomaniac shoplifters are rational and shoplift to meet certain goals, such as financial gain or to raise social standing by owning desired objects. Blanco et al. (2008) acknowledge that shoplifting can be due to kleptomania, but state that theft can also simply be criminal behaviour motivated by thoughts of financial gain, thrill seeking or an act of defiance against society.

DSM-IV (2000, p. 668) states that the actual onset of kleptomania is variable, and it can begin in childhood, adulthood and, more rarely, in late adulthood. There is little systematic information on the course of kleptomania, but *DSM-IV* describes three potential courses:

1. Sporadic with brief episodes and long periods of remission;
2. Episodic with protracted periods of stealing and periods of remission; and
3. Chronic with some degree of fluctuation.

At this time little is known about who suffers from kleptomania, with much of the research being carried out under the presumption that kleptomania is only exhibited in those who can afford but steal items, namely middle- or upper-class white women (Kohn, 2006). This presumption stems from the origins of kleptomania in nineteenth and early twentieth centuries, where it was considered a disorder that afflicted middle- and upper-class females who were frequently caught shoplifting in the newly developing department stores. There have also been many contemporary sensationalised news reports of wealthy high-profile women shoplifting, such as the Hollywood actress Winona Ryder and Champion tennis player Jennifer Capriati. These accounts project the idea that shoplifting may be a 'women's disorder', with repetitive shoplifting underpinned by kleptomania being conceptualised as a disorder found only within more affluent social groups.

Grant and Odlaug (2007) proffer that there are few epidemiological data regarding kleptomania, and therefore no firm conclusions can be drawn about who suffers from the disorder. Some argue that the preconception that kleptomania is associated with more affluent women may have impeded research, and currently little is known about the prevalence of kleptomania in males, ethnic minorities and those of lower economic status. The few empirical studies conducted suggest that the majority of kleptomaniac patients are females (McElroy et al., 1991; Sarasalo, Bergman and Toth, 1996); however, drawing conclusions from these empirical studies is problematic as they are likely to be biased by gender differences around assigned diagnosis and accessing treatments. For instance, men are more likely to be diagnosed with antisocial personality disorder and sent to jail for repetitive stealing rather than being provided the opportunity to engage in psychological treatments. Additionally kleptomania is also likely to be diagnosed alongside other psychiatric disorders, in particular depression, bipolar disorder, substance dependency and histrionic, paranoid, schizoid or borderline personality disorder (Baylé et al., 2003; Grant, 2004).

KEY DEBATE: Is kleptomania a mental disorder or an excuse to steal?

Mental disorder

Kleptomania is classified as a mental disorder in *DSM-IV*, and the sufferer is thought to be driven by uncontrollable urges to repeatedly steal items they may not need or could afford to buy. These urges stem from chemical imbalances, neurological damage and/or reflect an entrenched maladaptive learning process for coping with childhood traumas. Given the biological and/or psychological dysfunction underpinning kleptomaniacs' urge to engage in criminal behaviour, it is argued that legal sanctions and deterrence strategies are unlikely to reduce the offending behaviour. Rather, it is suggested that kleptomaniacs require psychiatric treatment to reduce their desire to steal, such as cognitive-behavioural therapy and pharmacological interventions such as selective serotonin reuptake inhibitors (SSRIs).

Excuse to steal

Inherent in *DSM-IV*'s conceptualisation of kleptomania is the notion that stealing is a mental disorder if the sufferer repeatedly steals items for the thrill rather than for personal use or instrumental gain. Sceptics suggest that kleptomania can be used as an excuse by wealthy shoplifters to avoid taking responsibility for their criminal acts, whereas less affluent individuals who repeatedly steal to survive are not deemed suitable for a diagnosis of kleptomania – they are 'bad not mad'. This disorder suggests that you are a thief if you steal to survive but may not be a thief if you steal for a thrill and can afford to pay for the stolen item.

References:

Abelson, E.S. (1989). The invention of kleptomania. *Signs. Journal of Women in Culture and Society*, 15 (1), 123–43.

Grant, J.E. (2006). Understanding and treating kleptomania: new models and new treatments. *Journal of Psychiatry Science*, 43 (2), 81–7.

A11.4. Misconceptions

Common misconceptions regarding kleptomania and shoplifting are as follows:

- *Shoplifting is only committed by those of low social economic status as a way of obtaining item(s) they want/need but cannot afford.* Research exploring the motives of kleptomaniacs indicates that there are some individuals who steal items they can afford and/or steal items that are of no monetary or intrinsic value to them (Aboujaoude, Gamel and Koran, 2004; Fullerton and Punj, 2004). For others, theft from shops is a way of gaining thrills by getting away with crime and duping others; it can also be a way that children and teenagers elevate their status within groups, i.e. by showing daring to peers (Blanco et al., 2008; Wong, 2005).
- *Shoplifting is only committed by teenagers.* Research indicates there is no age limit for committing theft from shops; however, onset of this type

of offending behaviour most frequently occurs in late childhood and adolescence. The onset and course of kleptomania remain uncertain.

- *Shoplifting does not hurt anyone, and businesses are covered by insurance.* The Commerical Victimisation Survey (Shury et al., 2005) investigated experiences of victimisation in the retail and manufacturing sector. It found that 'nearly one in ten businesses was not covered at all by insurance against crime' and approximately a third were only partly covered against theft offences. The Centre for Retail Research (2005) estimates the total cost of shoplifting at £3.4 billion, with the public paying a further £1.7 billion to support the police, courts, and the criminal justice system (CJS) in dealing with thieves. Additional costs include business disruption, retail security costs and losses of taxes from stolen goods. The Centre for Retail Research (2005) suggest the annual costs of shoplifting in the UK 'could entirely fund a combination of 11,700 more beat constables, 9230 nurses, 5500 more classroom teachers, and 64 million new books in school libraries'.

A11.5. Facts and figures

Little is known about the prevalence of kleptomania in the UK, and even less is known about its potential causal role in theft. Prevalence estimates from the USA suggest that less than 1% of the US population would meet diagnostic criteria for kleptomania.

In the UK there are two main complementary approaches to gathering facts and figures about crime:

1. *Police-recorded crime data* provide a good measure of trends in well-reported crimes and can be used for local crime pattern analysis.
2. *The British Crime Survey* (BCS) results are based on interviews and with the public provide a better reflection of the true extent of household and personal crime, because this includes crimes that are not reported to the police.

Police recorded crime data between 2002 and 2010 suggest that, on average, 300,000 shoplifting offences are recorded each year in England and Wales, with minor year-on-year variations being noted. Unfortunately the BCS provides no insight into the incidence and prevalence of shoplifting, as it covers only the victimisation of the adult population resident in households, whereas shoplifting is considered a crime against commercial or public sector bodies.

The Home Office attempted to capture the extent and costs of crime to the retail and manufacturing sector in England and Wales with the Commercial Victimisation Survey (CVS; Shury et al., 2005). During the CVS survey some 4000 retailing premises and 2500 manufacturing premises were interviewed by telephone about any crime they had suffered over the previous year, the cost of crime, their concerns about problems and crime in the local area, the action they had taken to respond to criminal incidents and their crime prevention precautions. The CVS survey found that commercial servicers were more likely to report theft by outsiders (64% for manufacturers, 55% for retailers) and less likely to involve the police in relation to offences by employees. The most common reasons for not reporting the crime to the police were the following:

- It was seen as too trivial.
- Lack of faith or confidence in the police to do anything about it (or had not done anything in the past about similar incidents).
- In cases of theft and fraud by employees it was frequently felt that it would be inappropriate to involve the police.

The CVS (2005) also found that theft by employees, by outsiders and by persons unknown was most likely to be experienced by larger retailers located on the high street and indoor shopping centres. Customer theft from local corner stores was also problematic, and employee theft was more prevalent in shops selling food and groceries.

A crime survey by the British Retail Consortium (2010) has found that there were almost half a million thefts from shops between 2008 and 2009, which equates to nearly one a minute, costing the industry £1.1 billion. The figure could even be double the reported rate, as many such crimes go unidentified and reported. A rise in middle-class shoplifters between 2008 and 2009 was noted, with the motive being maintenance of their standard of living rather than stealing to sell items on. Some of the most frequently stolen items include cosmetics, perfume, alcohol, fresh meat, mobile phones, DVDs and small electrical goods and gadgets.

A11.6. How are offenders caught?

In 2009–10, 307,845 shoplifting offences were recorded by the police with 189,046 (detection rate 61.4%) resulting in some sort of sanction. The specific conviction rate for shoplifting in the UK could not be identified from National Statistics, as the data are subsumed within a broad category entitled theft and handling stolen goods. In 2008, the conviction rate for theft and handing stolen goods was 90%, and if this could be extrapolated to shoplifting it would mean that the majority of individuals identified as potentially committing a shoplifting offence will go on to be convicted (Ministry of Justice, 2010).

Relying solely on police-recorded crime data is problematic, as these statistics are likely to underestimate massively the true incidence and prevalence of shoplifting in the UK since they rely on crimes being reported, retailers successfully apprehending suspects and the acquisition of sufficient evidence to permit prosecution.

A11.7. What happens to offenders?

The Theft Act (1968) considers theft to be the illegal taking of another person's property without their permission with the intent to permanently deprive the owner, and is punishable by fines and jail terms. The UK Sentencing Guidelines Council (2008) make the following suggestions for sentencing of those who steal from shops:

- A fine should be the starting point for the first-time opportunist thief who steals from a shop on impulse.
- Where thieves target small independent retailers this will be an aggravating feature and will be likely to attract a higher sentence.
- Previous convictions generally make an offence more serious. Persistent shoplifters will face a community or custodial sentence, even if the other characteristics of the specific offence would otherwise warrant a lesser penalty.
- The starting point for members of organised shoplifting gangs who intimidate their victims or use or threaten force is 12 months' custody.

In the UK, shoplifting accounts for the largest single group of adult offenders sentenced each year. In 2004, more than 60,000 offenders were sentenced for theft from a shop in the UK, with the majority (97%) being tried and sentenced in a magistrates' court. Sentences meted out for theft from shops were absolute or conditional discharge (27%), fines (22%), community penalties (27%) and about a fifth (21%) of shoplifters received a custodial sentence. Offenders that were given a custodial sentence for shoplifting receive on average three months or less (Dennis, 2006). Statistics from the Ministry of Justice (2010) suggest that there was a 30% increase in the number of theft reoffences in the UK between 2007 ($n = 19,661$) and 2008 ($n = 25,490$). This increase was due to rising shoplifting reoffences, as they accounted for 87% of all theft reoffences between 2007 and 2008.

Kleptomania is unlikely to be accepted as a legal defence for theft in the UK, unless the defendant can prove a lack of control or lack of freewill over their choices and behaviour. When caught stealing, kleptomaniacs are therefore likely to face the same legal difficulties as non-kleptomaniacs, although the potentially repetitive nature of kleptomaniac stealing could increase the chances of a custodial sentence. Clinical studies carried out by Sarasalo, Bergman and Toth (1996) and McElroy et al. (1991) have reported that 64–87% of kleptomaniac patients have a history of being apprehended and report a lifetime mean of three apprehensions. Grant and Kim (2002) report that 15–23% of kleptomaniac patients have been jailed for shoplifting. To date there has been no research investigating the level of recidivism amongst kleptomaniacs.

Models of intervention for kleptomaniacs and shoplifting

Interventions for shoplifters and kleptomaniacs can be categorised in terms of the philosophy of punishment underpinning them:

1. Deterrence: Punishing a person or seeing another person punished will deter re-engagement in the criminal behaviour.

2. Retribution: Offender made other(s) suffer so they deserve to suffer – eye for an eye (revenge) – redress the imbalance of justice (e.g. prison sentence).
3. Restitution: Offender does something to compensate the victim or society (e.g. through paying money for the stolen goods or community work).
4. Rehabilitation: This helps a convicted offender minimise their risk or remove their risk of re-offending (e.g. treatment programmes).

Punitive, restitution and rehabilitation strategies are often used in combination for shoplifters, with sanctions for crimes including paying for goods stolen, community service, undertaking victim reconciliation programmes and psychological treatment programmes (Krasnovsky and Lane, 1998).

Treatment for kleptomaniacs typically relates to the provision of psychological and medical treatment once the disorder has been diagnosed. The criminal behaviour associated with kleptomania and shoplifting is typically dealt with using situation control strategies that reduce the opportunities for theft, such as CCTV.

Shoplifting preventative strategies

Shoplifting generates enormous annual costs, and many businesses have adopted crime prevention interventions to combat it. The Centre for Problem-Oriented Policing (2010) notes that many businesses have hired store detectives, trained staff in shoplifting detection and banned known shoplifters. Some businesses have also established early warning systems whereby they inform each other of the presence of shoplifters. Other deterrence strategies include the use of CCTV and electronic article surveillance, such as electronic tags and ink tags. Attempts to design out crime are reflected in changing store layout to reduce the opportunities for theft and keeping 'hot' items in view of employees. To date there has been little systematic evaluation of these crime prevention initiatives. The effectiveness of deterrence strategies with kleptomaniac offenders is particularly questionable, as supposedly the disorder is underpinned by an irresistible urge to steal that is unlikely to be inhibited by the increased risk of being apprehended.

Treatment and relative effectiveness of treatment

Kleptomania is classified as an impulse control disorder in *DSM-IV*, and it has also been considered as part of the obsessive compulsive spectrum disorder (Grant and Kim, 2002; Rossi, 2006). Pharmacological approaches for kleptomania have attempted to balance the neurochemistry, in particular serotonin.

Selective serotonin reuptake inhibitors (SSRIs), such as fluoxetine and paroxitine, have been prescribed to kleptomaniacs with little to no effect on the reported symptoms of kleptomania (Grant and Polenza, 2004; Phelan, 2002). Other studies suggest that mood disorders, such as depression, can spur kleptomaniac behaviour (Lamontagne et al., 2000). Mood stabilisers, such as lithium and sodium valproate, have been prescribed to good effect to kleptomaniacs with co-occurring mood disorders; however, no controlled studies of treating kleptomania with mood stabilisers have been published (Grant, 2006). These psychopharmacological interventions have not been used solely to treat the antisocial act of shoplifting.

Kleptomania and shoplifting have been treated using psychosocial and psychodynamic psychotherapies. The effectiveness of this form of psychotherapy is difficult to ascertain, and to date there have been no tightly controlled studies assessing the efficacy of psychological interventions for kleptomania and shoplifting. Preliminary research suggests that psychological treatments used in conjunction with pharmacological approaches may be helpful in reducing symptoms of kleptomania. More recently, cognitive-behavioural therapy (CBT) has been utilised to treat kleptomania, with patients showing some short-term benefits. To date, there have been no large-scale control studies investigating CBT interventions and the follow-up period after treatment has been short (Grant, 2006).

A11.8. And the damage done...

The Centre for Retail Research (2005) estimated the social and economic costs of shoplifting, stating that the amount stolen by thieves from retail shops and stores was approximately £1.7 billion, which is equivalent to six new fully equipped hospitals, 11,740 extra police constables on beat patrol and Customs and Excise tax losses of almost £170 million. Costs for retail security staff and anti-theft equipment were estimated at £960 million per year. Overall it was estimated that shoplifting cost the UK economy £3.4 billion, which represents an average of £115.91 for every UK taxpayer or £58.14 per head of the population each year.

To date there has been no large-scale epidemiological study investigating kleptomania in the UK, and therefore the damage done by kleptomaniacs is impossible to estimate. The cost to the US economy of shoplifting alone is estimated at about 10 billion dollars per year (Hollinger and Davis, 2003), with kleptomania being implicated in about 5% of the 2 million shoplifters charged annually in the USA (Aboujaoude, Gamel and Koran, 2004; McElroy et al., 1991). Based on the overall shoplifting costs of $10 billion, this 5% translates into a $500 million annual loss to the economy attributable to kleptomania, and this cost excludes stealing from friends and acquaintances, and costs incurred by the legal system managing the estimated 100,000 arrests (Hollinger and Davis, 2003). Additionally, the illegal behaviour of kleptomaniacs can also impact negatively on their family, causing personal shame and social embarrassment, whereupon family therapy may be the only course of action to negate negative family outcomes.

PART B: Theories and explanations

B11.1. Theoretical explanations of kleptomania

Psychoanalytic explanations

Early psychoanalytic explanations of kleptomania and compulsive stealing have been proposed. These explanations mostly deal with women and argue that kleptomania and repetitive stealing are caused by impaired psychosexual development. The founder of psychoanalysis, Sigmund Freud, saw kleptomania as a result of the sufferer being trapped in the anal stage of childhood development, where they were deprived of the pleasure of the maternal comforts of breast milk and had to give up faeces when being toilet trained. Freud believed that kleptomaniacs never get over this deprivation, consequently developing intrapsychic conflict and deep urges to steal, with the theft symbolically representing the reacquiring of pleasures from childhood (Fullerton, 2007). Psychoanalysts such as Wilhem Stekel, Franz Alexander and Sandor Rado proffered that female kleptomania was driven by penis envy, with stealing representing the female's repressed urges to 'take hold of something forbidden' – usually an object that could be symbolic or phallic in nature. Female castration complex was also suggested, where young girls develop fantasies about having a penis and fear losing it. Initiation of menstrual cycles causes feelings of loss of the penis through bloody castration, and this leaves the girl feeling weak and vulnerable, which was suggested as being combated through compulsive shoplifting by Fullerton and Punj (2004).

Biological explanations

More recently, biological explanations suggest that kleptomania is the result of acquired brain injury and neurochemical imbalances in the brain. Rossi (2006) states that 'for Kleptomania biological traits are consistent with the classification as an obsessive compulsive spectrum disorder in which serotonin is the primary mediator of aggression and uninhibited urges' (p. 157). Other studies report that kleptomania can occur after traumatic brain injury and carbon monoxide poisoning (Aizer, Lowengrub and Dannon, 2004; Yüksel et al., 2007).

Social explanations

Abelson (1989), in her paper entitled 'The Invention of Kleptomania', argues that the disorder 'is linked to rigid gender roles which assigned consumption activities to women, and, under the rubric 'kleptomania' it was used to define gender – as well as classed based notions of theft' (p. 123). In other words, kleptomania was incepted as a psychiatric disorder to maintain social inequality, promoting gender stereotypes and protecting the affluent from being labelled criminal. Indeed, Abelson goes as far as suggesting that kleptomania is another name for 'middle class shoplifting' (p. 135). Various social theories have been offered as explanations of shoplifting, in particular strain theory (Merton, 1938) and general strain theory (Agnew, 1992). These emphasise that shoplifting is caused by an uneven distribution of wealth and restricted access to opportunities for social advancement. To meet these unmet needs the less affluent are thought to engage in deviant behaviour, such as stealing for economic and material gain (Ray and Briar, 1988). Others suggest that some people shoplift due to thrill seeking and peer pressure, especially children and juveniles (Lo, 1994).

Cognitive-behavioural explanations

Behavioural and cognitive-behavioural models conceptualise kleptomania as unwanted behaviours that are the result of operant and respondent conditioning, shaping, behavioural chaining, distorted cognitions and impoverished coping skills (Kohn, 2006). Some behavioural explanations assume that stealing behaviour is perpetuated by positive reinforcement, which stems from the positive release of emotions, economic gain and acquisition of desired objects through stealing. Negative reinforcement is also thought to play a role, in that stealing may provide relief from negative thoughts and feelings, such as tension and anxiety. Persistent engagement in the behaviour is thought to intensify the pairing (e.g. between anxiety reduction and shoplifting) and may result in other antecedents or cues becoming contingently linked with shoplifting, creating a powerful behavioural chain. Over time, shoplifting may become an entrenched maladaptive coping strategy for managing internal and external stressors, with over-reliance hindering the development of alternative pro-social coping methods.

Kohn (2006) writes that if an individual derives pleasure or release from a behaviour, and they experience minimal or no negative consequences or punishment, then this increases the likelihood of the behaviour re-occurring and habituation may result in more audacious offences being committed over time. Tonglet (2002) noted that shoplifting is often considered to be a low-tariff crime with a low risk of apprehension. Other cognitions and perceptions, such as 'I'm smarter than others and can get away with it'; 'they deserve it'; 'I want to prove to myself that I can do it'; and 'my family deserves to have better things', are all types of cognitions that may maintain engagement in shoplifting (Kohn and Antonuccio, 2002). Kleptomaniacs report feelings of guilt and remorse after committing the crime, although behavioural explanation would suggest that these potentially inhibiting emotions come too late in the behaviour chain to prevent the crime.

C11.1. Organisations to contact for information and voluntary work

Kleptomaniacs and Shoplifters Anonymous is an online self-help group established in 1992. The site offers a safe, confidential and non-judgemental place for compassion, understanding and recovery from 'addictive–compulsive' dishonest behaviour, primarily shoplifting, fraud, kleptomania and embezzlement. They offer counselling with experts on shoplifting addictions over the phone or Skype as well as programmes to combat addictions, such as the Shulman programme. The site also offers information on shoplifting statistics and information on kleptomania: http://www.kleptomaniacsanonymous.com/.

National Association of Shoplifting Prevention (NASP) is an online resource that offers self-help to shoplifters, support and shoplifter education programmes, shoplifting statistics and offers guidance to businesses on the prevention of shoplifting: http://www.shopliftingprevention.org/main.asp.

C11.2. Further reading

Abelson, E.S. (1989). The invention of kleptomania. Signs. *Journal of Women in Culture and Society*, 15 (1), 123–43. Abelson explores kleptomania in relation to class and gender and how the rise of the consumer society gave rise to kleptomania as an illness of middle- and upper-middle-class women. Abelson suggests that kleptomania is really a term used to mediate the seriousness of the crime of theft and was put in place to protect women of higher social standing from being connected with shoplifters from the lower classes.

Aboujaoude, E., Gamel, N. and Koran, L.M. (2004). Overveiw of kleptomania and phenomenological description of 40 patients. Primary care companion, *Journal of Clinical Psychiatry*, 6c (6), 244–7. This article reports on the preponderance, negative personal and social impact of kleptomania, co-morbidity and treatment needs. The authors suggest that more awareness of kleptomania, empathy towards those afflicted and rigorous research into treatment options are needed to mitigate kleptomania's personal and societal costs.

Grant, J.E. (2006). Understanding and treating kleptomania: New models and new treatments. *Journal of Psychiatry Science*, 43 (2), 81–7. This account goes a long way to elucidating the kleptomania phenomenon, which the author suggests has been neglected. Grant points to not only the positive treatment effects but also the problems surrounding the efficacy of treatment for kleptomania and contemplates that future research is required in order to gain fuller understanding of the phenomenon and its treatment.

chapter

12 STALKING

MÉLODIE FOELLMI, JOANNA CAHALL AND BARRY ROSENFELD

PART A: The offence – Who, what, when, why?

A12.1. Introduction

With over two decades of research on stalking, the legal and mental health understanding of this topic has gone from viewing stalking as a rare act of victimisation that concerns only celebrities and public figures to a much broader and more complex conceptualisation that encompasses a wide range of behaviours, settings and perpetrators. This chapter provides an overview of what is currently known about stalking offenders and their victims, follows theories and research of stalking behaviour as they have evolved over time, and explores some of the opportunities for future research in this burgeoning area of forensic psychology.

A12.2. Definitions

Legal and mental health professionals have not yet achieved consensus on a definition of stalking. Rather, a variety of behaviours can be captured under the umbrella of stalking and many of their common features are subjective in nature (Dennison and Thomson, 2005). The critical elements of stalking that are common to most legislative and research definitions are that stalking is the wilful, malicious and repeated following or harassing of another person. In order to qualify as stalking, the pursuer's behaviour must be intentional and must involve what a *reasonable person* would interpret to be a credible threat to the victim's safety and/or must instil fear in the victim (Dennison and Thomson, 2005; Meloy, 2007).

However, many of the concepts central to the above definition of stalking, such as intent, credible threat and reasonable fear, are difficult to define and operationalise. First, how can we determine what constitutes intent in stalking?

If stalking behaviour is, in part, attributable to interpersonal deficiencies, as will later be discussed, can one truly make the case that stalkers usually intend to provoke the type of reaction that they elicit from their victims? Second, the question of what constitutes a threat is complex, as many perfectly legal actions can be interpreted as threatening in the context of previous communication. For example, sending flowers or an affectionate Facebook message could instil fear in a stalking victim if it represents the continuation of a pattern of harassment. Criminal charges resulting from behaviours that are typically legal are often contentious, as they arguably infringe on basic constitutional freedoms. Likewise, the subjectivity of what constitutes a credible threat is often debated, as legal factfinders typically judge threat by a 'reasonable person' standard (i.e. whether a typical person would perceive actions as threatening). These definitional issues are of paramount importance to the advancement of stalking research, because they influence who is studied by researchers and how the law responds to perpetrators.

A12.3. Who are the perpetrators?

Individuals who engage in stalking are a heterogeneous group, who vary with respect to their motivations, victims and the types of behaviours in which they engage. However, they are typically older and better educated than the general offending population and often exhibit mental health symptoms in conjunction with troubled interpersonal relationships (Kropp, Hart and Lyon, 2002).

A12.4. Types of stalking offenders

Several researchers have proposed typologies to help distinguish different types of stalking offenders, on the basis of presumed motivation or observed behaviours. Mullen et al. (1999) put forward the most widely accepted typology of stalking, based on their analysis of offenders referred for treatment at a forensic mental health centre. They identified five types of stalking offenders who differed in their relationship to the victim, the type of targeted individual and their motivation for stalking. They described *rejected stalkers*, the most common type, as those who stalk an ex-intimate partner after a break-up, typically because they are unable to let go of the relationship or perhaps want some type of revenge. *Intimacy-seeking stalkers* use stalking behaviour in an attempt to initiate a relationship with a person with whom they have no prior relationship, and are most likely to suffer from erotomania, a delusional disorder in which the individual falsely believes that the object of their affection is in love with them. *Incompetent stalkers* use stalking as a strategy for initiating a relationship because they do not possess the necessary cognitive or social skills to understand and engage in acceptable courting behaviour. In contrast to the first three types, the primary intent of *resentful stalkers* is to instil fear in their victims, and they do so to obtain revenge for a perceived wrongdoing or unfairness on the part of the victim. Finally, *predatory stalkers* are the rarest group, and stalk their desired victim in anticipation of a sexual assault. Although other empirically based typologies of stalking have been proposed, these share a number of similarities to the above description from Mullen et al. (2000) (e.g. Kropp, Hart and Lyon, 2002; Zona, Palarea and Lane, 1998).

Prevalence studies estimate that approximately 80–90% of known stalking cases involve male perpetrators (AuCoin, 2005; Dressing, Gass and Kuehner, 2007; Purcell, Pathé and Mullen, 2002). However, this discrepancy may also reflect cultural biases and current criminal justice practices, as women are less likely to be charged with a stalking offence or instil fear into their victims compared with men who stalk women. For example, researchers have found that while women engage in many behaviours that fit the legal definition of stalking (Meloy and Boyd, 2003; Purcell, Pathé and Mullen, 2001), these behaviours are less likely to be *perceived* as stalking than when the same behaviours are engaged in by men (Wigman, 2009).

Psychopathology

Stalking behaviour is largely, but not exclusively fuelled by psychopathology (Mullen et al., 2006; Rosenfeld, 2003). Early stalking research focused on the paranoia and delusional beliefs that characterise erotomanic stalkers (Mullen et al., 1999; Whyte et al., 1999). However, empirical studies of stalking offenders have shown that erotomania and other psychotic disorders are present in only a small minority cases (Rosenfeld, 2003). Stalking offenders do, however, suffer from a wide range of Axis I mental disorders (McEwan, Mullen and Purcell, 2007). In particular, many offenders have a history of substance abuse that is linked with their stalking behaviour, and substance abuse increases the risk that offenders will be violent in the context of stalking (Mullen et al., 1999; Rosenfeld and Harmon, 2002). Although Axis I mental disorders may contribute to the severity or duration of stalking, the presence of a disorder rarely *explains* the stalking behaviour (Kropp, Hart and Lyon, 2002; Mullen et al., 1999).

In addition to major mental disorders, a relationship between stalking and personality disorders has been frequently observed, particularly because stalking is often a long-standing pattern of behaviour. The average duration of stalking victimisation is roughly two years, but can last for decades in some cases (Spitzberg and Cupach, 2007). Estimates of the prevalence of personality disorders (and Cluster B disorders in particular) among stalking perpetrators vary, but may exceed 50% (Rosenfeld, 2003). Psychopathic symptoms are more rarely reported, but when present are associated with an elevated risk of physical violence (Storey et al., 2009). However, Cluster B personality disorders (e.g. borderline, narcissistic, antisocial) in general are associated with elevated rates of both violence and renewed stalking behaviour (e.g. after an initial arrest) (Rosenfeld, 2003; Rosenfeld and Lewis, 2005). It should be noted, however, that studies of psychopathology in stalking offenders derive largely from individuals who have been convicted of a stalking-related crime, and often only those referred for mental health evaluation or treatment. Thus, published research findings may not apply to the large proportion of perpetrators who are not brought to the attention of the criminal justice system (CJS), such as those who engage in brief or non-threatening types of stalking behaviours.

KEY DEBATE: Is stalking a legal or mental health issue?

Compare legal responses to stalking with mental health responses to the behaviour. How do the two disciplines' goals conflict with regard to stalking offenders? What are the consequences for the offender, victims and society of approaching stalking from a legal perspective or a mental health perspective? How might we best combine the two approaches?

Points to consider

The legal perspective emphasises punishment, and protecting society by keeping the offender away from the public through orders of protection or imprisonment. This approach does not emphasise treatment for mental health problems that may underlie the behaviour. The mental health perspective emphasises treatment, which should produce long-lasting change if effective. However there is little research in the area of treatment effectiveness for stalking offenders, and stalking offenders who receive potentially ineffective mental health treatment may continue to victimise individuals in society.

References:

Dennison, S.M. and Thomson, D.M. (2005). Criticisms or plaudits for stalking laws? What psycholegal research tells us about proscribing stalking. *Psychology, Public Policy, and Law*, 11 (3), 384–406. doi: 10.1037/1076-8971.11.3.384.

Rosenfeld, B., Fava, J. and Galietta, M. (2009). Working with the stalking offender: Considerations for risk assessment and intervention. In: J. Werth, E. Welfel and A. Benjamin (Eds.), *The Duty to Protect: Ethical, Legal, and Professional Considerations for Mental Health Professionals* (pp. 95–109). Washington, DC: American Psychological Association. doi: 10.1037/11866-007.

Mental health and interpersonal functioning

A common theme in stalking is social inadequacy. Individuals who engage in stalking may not know how to properly initiate a relationship, may not pick up on clues that a person is not interested in them, may not know how to communicate their frustration effectively or may have poor conflict resolution skills. These characteristics are central to Mullen et al.'s (1999) *incompetent* stalker category, but they are common in virtually all stalking offenders. Although no researchers have systematically studied social competence in stalking offenders, interpersonal relationships are clearly problematic for these individuals. Stalking offenders are significantly more likely to be insecurely attached than other offenders or community samples (Dutton and Winstead, 2006; Tonin, 2004) and tend to experience a high degree of negative emotions (such as shame) when faced with interpersonal rejection (Dennison and Stewart, 2006). Kamphuis, Emmelkamp and de Vries (2004) described the individuals in their sample of ex-intimate stalkers as 'relatively functional people with strong sensitivities to rejection, abandonment, and loss' (p. 169).

A12.5. Misconceptions

Members of the public often acquire their knowledge of stalking behaviour from media reports of psychotic individuals stalking celebrities or public figures. However, the portrayal of stalking in the media does not represent the vast majority of offenders, who are not delusional and generally harass an ex-intimate partner rather than a public figure. Similarly, stalking need not involve actually following or contacting the individual – cyberstalking is an increasingly common and recognised problem (see Box 12.1). Advances in legislation reflect this broader conceptualisation of stalking as encompassing a wide range of behaviours and occurring in a variety of contexts and relationships. While public awareness lags behind social science research and legislation, the general public is gradually beginning to understand the broader implications of the term *stalking*.

Box 12.1. Cyberstalking

Key debate on cyber-harassment (by Catherine Millman)

A key debate surrounding cyber-harassment centres on whether cyber-harassment is a new phenomenon or an extension of offline harassment (Bocij, 2004). Bocij and McFarlane (2003) view cyber-harassment as distinct from offline harassment, as they argue that the press and governments distinguish between the two, perpetrators of cyber-harassment use online methods only and cyber-harassment can only have existed (by definition) since the evolution of the Internet. Furthermore, they argue that despite the Internet being available since the 1980s, perpetrators of cyber-harassment were not utilising the Internet in their campaigns against their victims. Bocij and McFarlane may give too much credence to the media distinguishing between offline and online harassment, as the media sensationalise stories to sell their product. However, within England and Wales, offline and online harassment are prosecuted using the same piece of legislation that does not define harassment (Basu and Jones, 2007). Instead, harassment is defined by the impact the perpetrator's behaviour has on the victim (Petch, 2002). Contradicting Bocij and McFarlane's claims, Sheridan and Grant (2007) found that instances of 'pure' cyber-harassment (i.e. solely online) are rare and that, more often, perpetrators use both online and offline methods to pursue their victims. Furthermore, they reported that cyber-harassment has the same impact on victims as offline harassment. Finally, the way in which individuals are using the Internet has evolved with technological advances, which may account for increases in the prevalence of cyber-harassment. Increasing accessibility to the Internet (Dutton, Helsper and Gerber, 2009) and high levels of online self-disclosure (Joinson, 2006) provides perpetrators with unprecedented access to, and information about, potential victims and/or their social networks. Arguably, as more knowledge is gained about cyber-harassment, it appears that cyber-harassment is not different from offline harassment (by Catherine Millman).

References

Basu, S. and Jones, R.P. (2007). Regulating cyberstalking. In F. Schmalleger and M. Pittaro (Eds.). *Crimes of the Internet*. UK: Prentice Hall.

Bocij, P. (2004). *Cyberstalking: Harassment in the Internet Age and How to Protect Your Family*. Westport, CT: Praeger.

Bocij, P. and McFarlane, L. (2003). 7 fallacies about cyberstalking. *Prison Service Journal*, 149, 27–42.

Dutton, W.H., Helsper, E.J. and Gerber, M.M. (2009). Oxford Internet Survey 2009 Report: The Internet in Britain. Oxford, UK: Oxford Internet Institute, University of Oxford.

Joinson, A.N. (2006). Internet behaviour and the design of virtual methods. In C. Hine (Ed.). *Virtual Methods: Issues in Social Research on the Internet*. Oxford, UK: Berg.

Sheridan, L.P. and Grant, T. (2007). Is cyberstalking different? *Psychology, Crime and Law*, 13, 627–40.

Cultural norms are also critically important when differentiating stalking from appropriate courtship behaviour. Pursuit in the face of initial rejection can be considered normal courting behaviour, and it may sometimes be difficult to distinguish normal persistence from criminal behaviour, particularly given variations in cultural practices and contexts (Coker et al., 2008). Of course, determining whether courtship behaviours are normatively appropriate depends on the cultural norms in which the behaviour occurs, but little research has directly compared stalking behaviours or perceptions across cultures (Jagessar and Sheridan, 2004).

A12.6. Facts and figures

Lifetime prevalence estimates for stalking in North America, Europe and Australia vary widely, typically ranging from 7 to 32% for women and from 2 to 17% for men; yearly prevalence estimates range from 0.5 to 1% for women and from 0.2 to 0.4% for men (Basile et al., 2006; Budd and Mattinson, 2000; Dressing, Gass and Kuehner, 2007; Mullen et al., 1999; Purcell, Pathé and Mullen, 2002; Tjaden and Thoennes, 1998). These estimates depend heavily on the definition of stalking used, with lower prevalence estimates in those studies with more rigorous definitions (e.g. Basile et al., 2006). Despite these high prevalence rates, a small proportion of stalking cases are reported to law enforcement, either because victims fail to recognise that the perpetrator's actions constitute stalking or they are not sufficiently concerned about the behaviours (e.g. when a female perpetrator stalks a male victim; Wigman, 2009). Nevertheless, risk of violence is an important element of stalking, influencing both definitions as well as legal responses.

Stalking and physical violence

Nearly 40% of stalking cases involve some sort of violent victimisation (Rosenfeld, 2004). Ex-intimate stalkers are most likely to physically assault their victims, which is not surprising considering that many ex-intimate stalkers were physically abusive to their partners before the end of the relationship (Morisson,

2008; Rosenfeld, 2004). Stalking offenders are at particular risk of engaging in physical violence towards the victim if they have previously made threats towards the victim, have a history of drug or alcohol abuse, experience high levels of anger and humiliation, tend to project blame and are insecurely attached (Morisson, 2008; Rosenfeld, 2004). In rare cases stalking may culminate in homicide, though the exact rate of stalking-related homicide, while unknown, is very low (Rosenfeld, 2004). Risk factors for stalking-related violence are addressed in more detail below.

A12.7. How are offenders caught?

As previously noted, a major obstacle to prosecution of stalking cases is that many cases of stalking are not interpreted as such by victims, or constitute behaviours that are not typically recognised as criminal acts (e.g. non-threatening telephone calls). Stalking behaviours may only be perceived as illegal when the perpetrator shows clear and repeated intent to arouse fear in the victim (Dennison, 2007). Perhaps because stalking has only recently been introduced as a legal term, public perceptions of stalking do not necessarily align with legal definitions (Dennison and Thomson, 2005). Because most stalking behaviours are not illegal in isolation, it is difficult for outside observers and law enforcement to determine whether a crime has occurred.

Justice responses to stalking may follow a similar pattern as responses to interpersonal conflicts or domestic abuse, in that law enforcement is often reticent to intervene in situations where the perpetrator and victim know each other, particularly if they have a prior relationship. To the extent that the perpetrator's actions are not inherently illegal (e.g. sending flowers or leaving telephone messages) and do not involve an explicit threat to the victim, legal decision makers may be reticent to convict offenders when they cannot show proof of intent. In a survey report of stalking in the USA, victims reported that in 71% of cases when they contacted police about being stalked, the perpetrator was not prosecuted (Baum et al., 2009). Baum and colleagues (2009) also found that of those stalking perpetrators who were charged, only 12% were convicted and an additional 28.5% had a restraining order or order of protection filed against them (based on victim reports). Further compounding problems in prosecution is the possibility that individuals may claim they are being stalked in order to seek revenge from their partners, or genuinely (but wrongly) believe they are stalking victims when in fact they are not (Dennison, 2007; Sheridan et al., 2003).

A12.8. What happens to offenders?

As noted above, a common course of action for legal decision makers is to issue an order of protection or restraining order against stalking offenders (Baum et al., 2009). Although restraining orders may provide a sense of relief and safety for victims, empirical data show that these restrictions are often ineffective (Logan and Walker, 2008). Between 35 and 45% of stalking offenders violate an existing order of protection in the course of their stalking (Häkkänen, Hagelstam and Santtila, 2003; Logan and Cole, 2007). In addition to having a restraining order filed against them, stalking offenders are sometimes sentenced to prison terms or probation, are referred to treatment programmes or are ordered to pay a fine (Baum et al., 2009). However, the effectiveness of these various criminal justice responses to stalking is questionable. Recidivism is a common problem, as stalking is by nature persistent. Based on a survey of 28 studies on stalking, Spitzberg and Cupach (2007) determined that the average length of stalking for a victim is 22 months, and Rosenfeld (2003) found that 50% of stalking offenders reoffended, typically within the first year after their arrest. This topic is described in more detail below.

Treatment for stalking offenders

Despite the overlap between stalking, social adjustment and psychopathology, few mental health interventions have specifically targeted stalking offenders (and are described in more detail below). Individuals who are prosecuted for stalking offences may receive whatever type of mental health treatment is most readily available, but typically this constitutes anger management or substance-abuse treatment, neither of which addresses the cognitions or behaviours that perpetuate stalking. Stalking offenders who suffer from a psychotic disorder may also receive treatment for their psychotic symptoms, although many of these offenders refuse available treatments (e.g. psychotropic medications). Moreover, because resources in the criminal justice system (CJS) are scarce, many offenders receive no treatment while incarcerated or have insufficient monitoring after their release, which may in part account for the high recidivism rate found among stalking offenders. Paradoxically, there is a growing belief among legal decision makers that stalking is an irremediable behaviour, and sentences for stalking have been increasing in length partly due to this erroneous perception (Dennison and Thomson, 2005).

Prognosis

Given the chronic and persistent nature of stalking, as well as the absence of effective treatments specifically developed for stalking offenders, the prognosis for cessation of stalking is relatively poor. As noted above, recidivism rates are high (roughly 50%) – a fact that is troubling since stalking can have lasting negative effects on the victim (as described below), as well as a destructive impact on the perpetrator's functioning. Stalking often consumes the perpetrator's attention and tends to perpetuate distressing cognitive and emotional patterns such as rumination (Dennison and Stewart, 2006). Even if stalking perpetrators are not prosecuted, the obsessive and persistent nature of stalking often prevents offenders from more productive work and social relationships.

A12.9. And the damage done...

Victims of stalking

Individuals who identify themselves as victims of stalking are predominantly lower-income Caucasian females who are unmarried (Baum, Catalano and Rand, 2009; Tjaden and Thoennes, 1998). Reports of stalking are particularly common in college settings, and for women who have terminated a relationship characterised by domestic violence (Melton, 2007; Mustaine and Tewksbury, 1999). Stalking can result in both physical and psychological harm to victims. Kuehner, Gass and Dressing (2007) found that victims of stalking had elevated rates of depression, anxiety and post-traumatic stress disorder (PTSD – see Box 12.2) compared with a gender- and age-matched sample.

Box 12.2. Post-traumatic stress disorder

Post-traumatic stress disorder (PTSD) is a type of anxiety disorder that can develop amongst people who have witnessed or experienced a traumatic event, such as injury (self or others), death or threat/fear of death, or even natural disasters. Symptoms typically fall into three main categories: 'reliving' the event through nightmares or flashbacks, avoidance (e.g. feeling detached, not being able to remember parts of what happened or avoiding things or places that remind you of the event), and arousal (hyper-vigilance, having an exaggerated response to things that startle you, having trouble sleeping).

Pathé and Mullen (1997) also found that stalking victims experienced sleep and appetite disturbances and often reported suicidal thoughts. Longer duration of stalking (in excess of two weeks) was associated with significant increases in psychological and lifestyle disturbances (Purcell, Pathé and Mullen, 2004). Stalking victims often make significant changes to their daily lives such as changing their schedules, reducing social outings, missing or quitting jobs, changing their phone numbers, changing their appearance, relocating or even going into hiding (Abrams and Robinson, 2002; Purcell, Pathé and Mullen, 2004).

In addition to coping with the psychological consequences of stalking, many victims suffer physical harm in the course of stalking. Victims who are younger, are being harassed by ex-intimates or who receive direct threats are at highest risk of physical assault (Thomas et al., 2008). Given the potentially serious ramifications of stalking, many victim service agencies provide specialised services for stalking victims and governmental agencies in the UK, USA and Australia have funded numerous initiatives focused on decreasing the frequency and impact of stalking (Miller, 2001; http://www.stalkingawarenessmonth.org/; http://www.ncjrs.gov/stalkingawareness/). A number of resources for victims of stalking are provided at the end of this chapter.

PART B: Theories and explanations

B12.1. Introduction

A growing area of research has focused on understanding and explaining stalking behaviours and offenders. As noted above, much of this research has focused on empirically or theoretically derived typologies of stalking offenders and identifying variables that differentiate offenders who engage in stalking from other types of criminal behaviour. However, much of this research has focused on demographic and clinical characteristics of these offenders, with far less enquiry into psychological characteristics (e.g. personality traits) or theoretical models that might help explain stalking. The limitations of this literature may be due to the fact that motivations for stalking and types of stalking offenders vary considerably and may not fit into a single, unified theory.

B12.2. Theories of stalking

Historical studies and the evolution of thinking

While individuals have engaged in stalking behaviours for centuries, the increase in public attention paid to stalking over the last 20 years is largely due to intense media coverage of a few stalking cases involving celebrities that resulted in homicide. Individuals who stalk celebrities often suffer from a delusional disorder (erotomania), in which they believe they have a relationship with the celebrity. However, as this research literature has evolved, it has become clear that delusional disorders account for a small proportion of stalking offenders. Instead, researchers began to realise that stalking perpetrators could not be described as a homogeneous group, but are rather comprised of many different types of offenders varying in regard to several factors such the motivation for stalking, the relationship to the victim and the psychological symptoms exhibited by the offender. Although these typologies have helped advance stalking research, they have fallen short, to date, of helping clinicians identify the causes of stalking or identify individuals who may be at risk for engaging in this behaviour. More recently, research has shifted towards identifying such risk factors, in the hope of developing assessment strategies and decreasing victimisation.

Fear of rejection

Reid Meloy, one of the first psychologists to focus attention on stalking offenders and behaviours, hypothesised that stalking is a maladaptive response to rejection or the fear of rejection (Meloy, 1996, 1998). According to Meloy, individuals who exhibit excessive narcissistic personality traits need intimate romantic relationships to validate their inflated self-image. He suggests that their aversive personality traits make them more likely to experience rejection, and they have difficulty tolerating this rejection when it does occur. The narcissistic individual may turn to stalking, unable to accept the fact that their affection is not reciprocated. Zona et al. (1998) also found that those who view rejection as an attack on self-image are more likely to persevere with efforts to maintain the relationship through stalking behaviours.

Maladaptive reaction to negative emotions

Other theorists have proposed that stalking is a maladaptive reaction to the experience of negative emotions (Dennison and Stewart, 2006; McCann, 2001; Meloy, 1998). McCann (2001) suggested that jealousy and envy are the key factors in relationship violence, which is frequently linked to stalking behaviours. Dennison and Stewart (2006) suggested an alternative theory of stalking focusing on different negative emotions: guilt and shame. According to their theory, individuals who engage in stalking experience shame in response to rejection due to a belief that others are negatively evaluating him or her. This feeling of shame predisposes an individual to anger, angry outbursts and less empathy towards the victim. Their lack of empathy impedes the ability to take another's perspective and understand the problematic nature of their stalking behaviour, and therefore they experience little guilt about their harassment (Dennison and Stewart, 2006).

Attachment theory applied to stalking

More recently, researchers have begun to explore the utility of attachment theory (Ainsworth, 1989; Bowlby, 1969) for understanding stalking behaviour (MacKenzie et al., 2008; Wilson, Ermshar and Welsch, 2006). This theory of stalking suggests that disturbances in attachment formation in childhood result in stalking behaviours in adults due to an impaired ability to manage relationships. Theorists have varied in their views of the types of attachment disturbances (e.g. neglect, overprotective parents and/or abuse) and the resulting pathological attachments (e.g. paranoid, insecure or disorganised) in adulthood, but the link between early attachment disturbances and stalking has received some empirical support (Fein and Vossekuil, l998; Kienlen et al., 1997; MacKenzie et al., 2008). For example, Wilson, Ermshar and Welsch (2006) conceptualised stalking as a self-defeating behavioural manifestation of extreme insecure attachment they termed 'paranoid attachment'. McCann (2001) theorised that a disorganised attachment pattern in infancy (i.e. a disorganised, inconsistent pattern of parent–child interactions) leads to coercive behaviours, such as stalking, among adults as an attempt to aggressively control one's environment. Although the theories described above provide a starting point for developing a theoretical framework for understanding stalking, none of these models comprehensively address the causes of stalking. In addition, most of these theoretical models have received limited, if any, empirical support.

Psychological research on stalking began a mere 20 years ago, and despite impressive advances in the field thus far, many important questions remain unanswered. The following areas are in particular need of further investigation.

B12.3. Future directions

The causes of stalking

In order to treat stalking offenders, it is essential that we better understand how stalking behaviour emerges and is maintained over time. Stalking behaviour appears to be determined by a multitude of factors that interact in complex ways. Therefore, future research into the causes of stalking will need to consider how intrapersonal, interpersonal and contextual factors interact to increase or decrease risk for stalking. This research should also incorporate victim characteristics and behaviours, rather than focusing exclusively on perpetrators, in order to better understand the myriad of influences that lead to stalking.

Theories addressing the cognitive mechanisms involved in stalking are also noticeably lacking. One starting point for researchers might be the extant research on behavioural and cognitive processes common in narcissistic, borderline and antisocial personality disorders (i.e. Cluster B disorders), as these personality disorders are often found in stalking offenders (Rosenfeld et al., 2007). Cognitive mechanisms commonly found in insecurely attached individuals and individuals who ruminate, have obsessive thoughts or exhibit disinhibited behaviour are also important to examine. Hopefully, such research will provide insight into the cognitive and behavioural processes that increase or decrease stalking behaviour.

It is also important to better understand affective patterns in stalking offenders. A key determinant of stalking behaviour seems to be the individual's reliance on others for affective well-being and a tendency to experience vivid and persistent negative emotions when faced with interpersonal rejection (Dennison and Stewart, 2006). Further research on the affective components of stalking will help professionals understand how negative emotionality interacts with cognitive patterns, such as rumination, interpersonal relationship factors and contextual factors that lead to stalking behaviours.

Despite a growing trend towards integrating contextual variables into psychological approaches towards violence risk assessment and management, research on the contextual determinants of stalking is virtually inexistent. The contribution of everyday circumstances, opportunities and resources to stalking behaviour is not well understood, and warrants further investigation. An interesting staring point suggested by some authors is to apply routine activities theory (Cohen and Felson, 1979) to stalking, based on the hypothesis that stalking behaviour may vary as contextual factors make it easier or more difficult to engage in (Mustaine and Tewksbury, 1999; White et al., 2000).

Recidivism

Research investigating recidivism in stalking offenders is quite limited, with only one published study to date investigating this topic. Rosenfeld (2003) found that about 50% of stalking offenders were known to have reoffended, and the majority of those did so during the first year after their index arrest. This study identified a number of variables that were associated with higher risk of continued offending. For example, offenders who were previously involved in an intimate relationship with the target of their harassment were the subgroup most likely to continue their harassment despite arrest and/or intervention. Another risk factor for recidivism was the presence of a 'Cluster B' personality disorder (i.e. antisocial, borderline and/or narcissistic), and the presence of a personality disorder in combination with a history of substance abuse was a particularly strong predictor of reoffence, explaining more reoffence behaviour than either variable considered alone. Interestingly, individuals with a delusional disorder such as erotomania had a lower risk of reoffending than non-psychotic offenders (Rosenfeld, 2003), perhaps because of a greater likelihood of court-ordered treatment. Although these findings help understand the trajectory of stalking behaviours, no other researchers have focused on this important topic and further investigation is clearly warranted.

Risk factors for violence

Another important topic in stalking research, which has received far more attention than recidivism, is identifying risk factors for stalking-related violence. Research has consistently identified several risk factors that, when present, increase the chances that an individual will engage in physical violence in the context of their stalking behaviours. Rosenfeld and Harmon (2002) published one of the largest studies of stalking-related violence, identifying several risk factors. They reviewed the case files of 204 individuals referred for a forensic evaluation who were charged with stalking or harassment in New York City. They found that violence was significantly more likely in cases where the victim was a former spouse or intimate partner, where the primary motivation to stalk was anger or revenge, where the perpetrator had previously threatened the victim and when the perpetrator had a history of drug or alcohol abuse. However, other variables often associated with violence, such as prior criminal history or previous violent behaviour, were not associated with violence in stalking cases.

In a review of the literature on stalking-related violence, Resnick (2007) distinguished between risk factors associated with ordinary violence and risk factors for severe violence and homicide. In that review, risk factors for ordinary violence included substance abuse, prior criminal offences, making threats, suicidal ideation and a prior intimate relationship with the victim. However, the risk factors for severe violence included appearing at the victim's home, a history of prior violence, severe depression, threats to harm the victim's children and placing threatening messages on the victim's car (Resnick, 2007). This literature, while enhancing our ability to assess the risk of violence in stalking cases, also needs further investigation.

Treatment implications

The absence of a clear theoretical framework for understanding stalking behaviours may explain why effective treatment options for stalking offenders have not been identified. However, as the psychological factors that are associated with stalking and harassment have become increasingly recognised, the need for clinical interventions designed to target these issues has also emerged. In response to this need, Rosenfeld et al. (2007) adapted dialectical behaviour therapy (DBT; Linehan, 1993) to specifically target stalking behaviours and offenders. DBT has both empirical and broad clinical support as the preferred treatment modality for borderline personality disorder, and is increasingly used with multi-diagnostic difficult-to-manage patients, criminal offenders and individuals with antisocial personality characteristics (e.g. Berzins and Trestman, 2004; Fruzzetti and Levensky, 2000; McCann, Ball and Ivanoff, 2000). Furthermore, DBT lends itself well to adaptation for stalking offenders given the emphasis on behaviour change and improving interpersonal effectiveness. Rosenfeld et al. (2007) provided preliminary support for this treatment approach (described in more detail below), but more systematic evaluations of DBT for stalking have not yet been published.

Violence risk assessment

In order to best reduce the occurrence of violence in stalking cases, it is crucial for mental health professionals to possess reliable and valid risk assessment tools. The Guidelines for Stalking Assessment and Management (SAM; Kropp, Hart and Lyon, 2008) represent the most promising tool designed to assess risk for future stalking or violent offences. Although little research to date has utilised this new measure, the foundations and approach behind this structured professional judgement (SPJ) technique are well established and support its potential utility. Future research is needed to address SAM's reliability and validity for evaluating and managing violence risk due to stalking across the range of settings in which it occurs, in order to permit professionals to use the tool with confidence.

Research studies comparing high-risk and low-risk offenders (with regard to violence and/or renewed stalking) will also help mental health and legal professionals to prioritise stalking cases. If high-risk stalking offenders can be accurately identified early in their offending trajectory, mental health professionals may be able to achieve more favourable outcomes for these individuals by intervening early with appropriate services. Few researchers have formally assessed the rate with which stalking offenders reoffend, or the characteristics that correspond to a higher or lower risk of recidivism (Rosenfeld, 2003). Future research is needed to better understand the characteristics of offenders who recidivate, whether with the same or different victims, in order to identify intrapersonal, interpersonal and contextual factors that increase or decrease the risk of recidivism.

Risk management and treatment studies

Perhaps the most urgent need in stalking research is for intervention approaches with stalking offenders. To date, only a handful of researchers have addressed this important issue and empirically supported treatments have not yet been established. As noted above, Rosenfeld et al. (2007) described a pilot study supporting the use of DBT in a group of stalking offenders who were court mandated to mental health treatment. Their data, while preliminary, were encouraging, demonstrating a reduced risk of recidivism among treatment programme completers compared with treatment drop-outs, and among all treatment programme participants relative to published recidivism rates. An alternative approach to the treatment of stalking offenders, using an intervention they termed the problem behaviour model, was described by Warren and colleagues (2005); however, this brief report provided no data regarding the feasibility or effectiveness of this intervention. Certainly, any intervention developed specifically for the treatment of stalking offenders will need to address the specific behaviours, cognitions and emotions that characterise stalking offences. Further, researchers should recognise the many challenges to conducting treatment research with stalking offenders, as recruiting large samples into a randomised study is extremely difficult due to the forensic setting (Purcell, Flower and Mullen, 2009).

Future research

Future research should also focus the helping to identify individuals at high risk of engaging in stalking. Identifying 'at-risk' individuals, whether through the use of formal screening tools or simply by identifying pertinent risk factors, might lead to preventative interventions targeting the risk factors for stalking. Although challenging, some successes have emerged in related research areas, such as the identification of youth at risk for antisocial behaviours (e.g. Olweus, 2005).

Finally, a number of researchers have offered typologies of stalking offenders in order to describe the differences in their behaviours and motivations. Future research should critically evaluate these typologies to determine whether they help professionals better to manage and intervene with stalking offenders and reduce the risk of harm to victims. Continued research examining stalking typologies may also help identify different aetiologies and characteristics of this heterogeneous group of offenders.

PART C: Further information

C12.1. Organisations to contact for information and voluntary work

Over the past two decades, a number of organisations have emerged that provide resources for stalking victims and the legal and mental health professionals who work with these offenders. Although always changing, the following organisations were available at the time of writing: in the UK, the National Association for the Support of Victims of Stalking and Harassment (NASH) provides telephone support to victims in crisis and general information. Residents of the UK can also contact the London-based Suzy Lamplugh Trust (www.suzylamplugh.org/advice/stalking.htm) for information and advice on dealing with stalking victimisation.

Residents of the USA can contact the National Center for Victims of Crime's Stalking Resource Center (SRC), funded by the Department of Justice. Information on services provided by this initiative is available at the SRC's website: www. ncvc.org/src/index.html. Victims can access help through the NCVC's victim helpline. The UK-based Suzy Lamplugh Trust also provides additional resources in the United States at http://www.menstuff.org/resources/resourcefiles/stalking.html#us. In Canada, the Canadian Resource Center for Victims of Crime in Ottawa, Ontario, and Victims for Justice in Windsor, Ontario are two organisations that provide services for victims of stalking.

Australia has a variety of stalking victims' associations, including the Victims Referral and Assistance Service in Melbourne and the Victims of Crime Bureau, both of which help victims and professionals who deal with stalking victimisation. A more complete list of Australian stalking resources is featured on the Suzy Lamplugh Trust website: http://www.menstuff.org/resources/resourcefiles/stalking.html#us.

C12.2. Further reading

Baum, K., Catalano, S., Rand, M. and Rose, K. (2009). Stalking victimization in the United States. Bureau of Justice Statistics Special Report, http://bjs.ojp.usdoj.gov/ index.cfm?ty=pbdetailandiid=1211.

Meloy, J.R. (1998). *The Psychology of Stalking*. San Diego, CA: Academic Press.

Mullen, P., Pathe, M. and Purcell, R. (2000). *Stalkers and Their Victims*. Cambridge, UK: Cambridge University Press.

Pathe, M. (2002). *Surviving Stalking*. Cambridge, UK: Cambridge University Press.

Pinels, D. (2007). *Stalking: Psychiatric Perspectives and Practical Approaches*. New York, NY: Oxford University Press.

chapter
13

VIOLENT CRIME: ROBBERY AND ASSAULT

MELANIE K. T. TAKARANGI AND HEATHER D. FLOWE

PART A: The offence – Who, what, when, why?

A13.1. Introduction

A crime of violence is an act in which an offender uses illegitimate force against a victim. Violence may be the offender's sole objective or used as a means to accomplish a goal, such as theft. This chapter focuses on assault and robbery, two types of violent crime. These are serious crimes that can lead to grave physical and psychological injury. Studying the characteristics and patterns of violent crime inform both crime prevention strategies and offender treatment programmes.

There are also theoretical reasons to study violent crime. Psychologists are interested in applying social, developmental, behavioural and cognitive theories to describe and predict real-world behaviour. Legal psychologists, in particular, may study a given behaviour such as aggression because it is likely to manifest within a criminal context.

Criminal assault and robbery are both forms of aggression. Aggression is the intent to inflict harm, which includes physical injury and psychological harm (Blackburn, 1993). Researchers typically distinguish between types of aggression. At one extreme, aggression may be instrumental because it is used to achieve an objective. At the other extreme, aggression may be hostile, stemming from anger. As we shall see, an act of aggression can at times be both instrumental and hostile in its intent (Anderson and Huesmann, 2003). See Box 13.1. This chapter will provide information about characteristics of these crimes, and present the key theoretical explanations in psychology that have been posed to account for them.

> **Box 13.1. Black Friday shopping mobs**
>
> The biggest shopping day of the year in the USA is *Black Friday*, which falls on the day after Thanksgiving. In recent years, shoppers and retail workers have incurred significant physical injury on Black Friday. For instance, in 2008, a Walmart store employee was stampeded to death inside the store by a mob of shoppers. More than 2000 people had queued outside for the chance to obtain Black Friday bargains, which were limited in supply. As the opening hour drew near, shoppers pushed and banged against the glass door entrance, causing it to bow and crash open. The mob of shoppers raced through the broken glass, trampling to death the employee who stood in their path. In other cases, shoppers have pushed and hit one another in confrontations over highly coveted sale items.
>
> After reading this chapter, ask yourself the following questions: How would you characterise the type of aggression that the shoppers seem to be displaying? How could retail establishments prevent this kind of aggression from occurring?

A13.2. Definitions

The term 'assault' is regularly used in everyday language and in law to cover both assault and battery. Criminal assault is any act in which a person intentionally or recklessly causes another person to expect immediate and unlawful personal violence to be carried out against them. Battery is the actual infliction of unlawful force upon another person, however slight the touching may be (Offences Against the Person Act, Sections 42 and 47). The police in the UK distinguish between assault with no injury, assault with minor injury and wounding (with the latter clearly being the most serious). Acts of domestic assault are included within these offence categories.

An offence of robbery is committed when a person steals by using force or by seeking to instil fear of being subjected to force (Theft Act 1968, Section 8(1)). In determining criminal penalties for robbery in the UK, five types of robbery are distinguished: street robbery or 'mugging', robberies of small businesses, relatively less sophisticated commercial robberies, violent personal robberies in the home and professionally planned commercial robberies.

A13.3. Who are the offenders?

Violent offending is reliably associated with a range of demographic variables according to the Home Office (2010). The majority of offenders are young (16–24 years of age). School-age children (15 years of age or less) committed 8% of violent crimes in 2008/9 (Home Office, 2009). Violent crime is usually committed by a lone assailant. Robbery, however, is more likely to be perpetrated by multiple assailants compared with assault.

The vast majority of violent offenders in the UK and abroad are male. This finding is consistent with a large body of psychological research. Data obtained from self-reports and objective sources show that men are more aggressive than women (Archer, 2004; Archer and Haigh, 1997; Buss and Perry, 1992; Campbell, 2006; Eagly and Steffen, 1986; Smith, Waterman and Ward, 2006). Furthermore, men's aggression is qualitatively – not just quantitatively – different from women's aggression. Men tend to score higher on measures of physical, direct, instrumental aggression, while women seem to favour less direct, reactive forms of aggression (Archer and Haigh, 1997; Campbell and Muncer, 1987; Campbell, Sapochnik and Muncer, 1997).

According to the British Crime Survey (BCS) (Home Office, 2010), 50% of violent offenders were under the influence of alcohol, while 20% were under the influence of drugs at the time of their offence. These figures fit with a large body of existing research on the relationship between alcohol consumption and violent behaviour. For example, people convicted of committing violent offences such as assault often have a history of heavy drinking, and many report being intoxicated at the time they committed their offence (Greenfeld and Henneberg, 2001; Roizen, 1997; Singleton, Farrell and Meltzer, 1999; see also Boles and Miotto, 2003). Moreover, higher levels of alcohol abuse are associated with a greater likelihood of committing violent crime (Collins and Messerschmidt, 1993; Fergusson and Horwood, 2000).

When thinking about the relationship between alcohol and violence, several other explanations should also be kept in mind. Both alcohol consumption and violence often occur in social settings, so it could be that sometimes they just co-occur, rather than that one causes the other. It is also difficult to assess whether the violent behaviour would have occurred even in the absence of alcohol, and it may be that intoxicated people are more likely to be caught. In addition, alcohol outlets such as bars are likely to attract people – such as young males – who are already more likely to perpetrate violence (Gruenewald et al., 2006).

A13.4. Misconceptions

You cannot be found guilty of assault unless you have actually injured someone

This is not true. The crime of assault simply means that the perpetrator, by their behaviour, has made (e.g. by picking something up to throw at the potential victim, or by uttering a verbal threat) another person expect to be injured. The law states that there must be four conditions for assault to occur:

1. *Awareness*: the victim must be aware that they are about to be injured (if, for example, they were asleep, then the offender would be charged with wounding the victim rather than assault per se).
2. *Immediacy*: the threat of violence must be in the here and now rather than the next day or week. However, simply not knowing what the perpetrator is going to do next and being aware or fearful that they might commit a violent act against the victim is sufficient for assault to be proven (see *R v. Constanza*

[1997] Crim LR 576 and/or *Smith v. Chief Constable of Woking* (1983) 76 Cr App R 234).

3. *Unlawful*: the threat is not lawful; for example, it is not part of legal military action.

4. *Personal violence*: the victim must be expecting some contact. This may be considerable (a broken nose, fractured ribs, etc.) or may simply be touching.

The threat must be physical or verbal

Case law in 1997 (R v. Ireland [1997] 3 WLR 534 House of Lords) decided that *silence* could also constitute a threat in certain circumstances. In the case of R v. Ireland, the defendant had made a number of telephone calls to three women over a period of time in which he did not say anything, but stayed on the line, scaring the women. The judge in this case upheld his conviction, creating case law by deciding both that silence could amount to an assault and that psychiatric injury (the stress and fear caused to the women victims) did amount to bodily harm.

It is only legal to hurt someone in self-defence when you have already been injured by the perpetrator

This is not true. In some countries such as the UK the act of self-defence may be pre-emptive; in other words, you may hit out in self-defence before you have suffered any injury at all providing you do so with a reasonable level of force (i.e. you do not over-react to the perceived threat) and in good faith (i.e. you really believe you are about to be attacked).

KEY DEBATE: Should parents limit children's and adolescents' exposure to violent media?

For:
A recent policy statement issued by the American Academy of Pediatrics states that violent media is a health risk. Exposure to violence in the media, including music, television and video games, has been found to increase aggressive thoughts, behaviours and emotions. The association between aggressive behaviour and media violence exposure is nearly as strong as the association between smoking and lung cancer.

Against:
Children and adolescents should be allowed to see violent media as long as a responsible adult explains the content to them. Parents and guardians can explain to children the difference between reality and fantasy. Additionally, recent research has found that action-packed video games can increase perceptual and attention skills. One reason this could be true is because action video games may be more engaging than other types of video games.

References:
Anderson, C.A., Gentile, D.A. and Buckley, K.E. (2007). *Violent Video Game Effects on Children and Adolescents: Theory, Research, and Public Policy*. Oxford: Oxford University Press.
Dye, M.G.W., Green, C.S. and Bavelier, D. (2009). The development of attention skills in action video game players. *Neuropsychologia*, 47(8–9), 1780–9.

A13.5. Facts and figures

There were an estimated 2,087,000 violent criminal incidents in England and Wales in 2009/2010 according to the BCS (Home Office, 2010). Assault without injury accounted for the largest percentage (39%) of all violent incidents, followed by assault with minor injury (25%), wounding (21%) and robbery (16%).

Of the violent incidents reported to the BCS, 38% were incidents of stranger violence, 33% were acquaintance violence, 14% domestic violence and 19% were muggings (robbery and snatch theft). (Note that these percentages do not add up to 100 due to rounding up and also because of the inclusion of snatch theft in mugging.) A weapon was used in 19% of these violent incidents, with knives being the most frequent type of weapon used (5% of cases). The use of firearms is rare (firearms are counted as being involved in an incident if they are fired, used as a blunt instrument against a person or used as a threat); in the UK they account for approximately 2% of the incidents reported (Home Office, 2010). See Box 13.2 for a case that illustrates the relationship between weapons and psychological threat.

The majority (89%) of robberies reported to the police in 2009/10 were of personal property; the remainder were robberies of business property (such as robberies in a shop). Crime is geographically concentrated to a larger extent in robbery compared with other crimes. In 2009/10, more than 60% of robberies reported to the police in England and Wales were recorded in just 3 out of 44 police forces: the Metropolitan Police, Greater Manchester and the West Midlands.

Box 13.2. The Granny Bandit

Seventy-nine-year-old Melvena Cooke may be the oldest person in Chicago history to be charged with attempted bank robbery. Wearing a black trench coat, sunglasses and a sun visor emblazoned with the word 'Princess', Cooke brandished a gun and demanded $30,000 from a teller. She left the bank empty-handed and was apprehended within minutes. The gun turned out to be a toy.

Can a person be convicted of armed robbery with a toy gun? According to the US Supreme Court, guns are characteristically dangerous, their display instils fear in the average citizen and they can be used as a bludgeon (McLaughlin v. United States). Therefore, even when a gun is a toy, unloaded or inoperable, robbery defendants may receive enhanced penalties for using a dangerous weapon.

The Supreme Court's stance that the victim's perception of threat is an important legal consideration is interesting from a psychological point of view. Psychologists are interested in the concept of *construal*, which refers to process by which people perceive, comprehend and interpret the world around them. Psychological research has shown that our construal of situations affects our judgements and actions. Therefore, a toy gun that is construed as threatening can potentially induce fear and even escalate aggression between the victim and the perpetrator.

A13.6. How are offenders caught?

Analyses of Home Office data indicate that few violent incidents result in a prosecution. Less than 15% of robbery and assault incidents reported on victim surveys end in a criminal conviction. What accounts for the low conviction rates? There are numerous factors that underlie this so-called 'dark figure' of crime. The foremost explanation is that the victim often does not report the incident to the police.

Victims are more likely to contact the police when the perpetrator is a stranger rather than a family member, spouse or acquaintance (Home Office, 2009). However, even serious assaults committed by strangers are often not reported. An Australian study of emergency room visits found that 57% of persons who were alleged assault victims had not reported the incident to the police, and only 6% of the remaining victims intended to report to the police after leaving the hospital (Cuthber, 1991). The vast majority (77%) of the incidents were alleged assaults that had been committed by strangers.

Victims may not report to the police because they are afraid of offender retaliation. Moreover, in some communities people who report crime to the police are stigmatised (see Box 13.3). Victims may also consider the incident too minor to report or view the situation as a personal matter. Another reason why victims may not report is because they are involved in crimes themselves. Robbers often select victims who are involved in criminal activities, such as drug dealing (Wright and Decker, 1997).

Box 13.3. Stop snitching culture and violent crime reporting

The controversial *Stop Snitchin'* campaign gained notoriety in the USA in 2004 with the launch of an underground video that urged people not to cooperate with the police. The video featured purported criminals from the city of Baltimore's drug trade as well as Carmelo Anthony, an NBA basketball player. The *Stop Snitchin'* motto has since appeared in other hip-hop lyrics and on caps and t-shirts.

Legal officials have long contended with the problem of reluctant and uncooperative witnesses. However, law enforcement experts say the problem has reached epidemic status, due in large part to the *Stop Snitchin'* campaign. Arrest and conviction rates for violent crime have dramatically fallen. The proportion

---

of violent crimes cleared by an arrest has dropped by about 10% since the late 1990s according to Federal Bureau of Investigation (FBI) statistics. The clearance rate for murder is about 60% on average across cities in the USA. In some cities, however, the murder clearance rate has fallen to single digits.

For crimes that are reported to the police, the sanction detection rate for robbery is only 20%, and 49% for crimes of violence against the person (Home Office, 2008). 'Sanction detections' include offences that are cleared through a formal sanction, such as a person being charged or cautioned. There are several factors that contribute to the low sanction detection rate in violent offences. For example, forensic approaches are limited when the duration of the offence was only seconds long. In such cases, it will be difficult for the victim to describe or identify the assailant. Moreover, many offences occur in public places, such as a street, footpath or alleyway. As a result, the crime scene is contaminated and it is difficult to collect evidence relating solely to the case in hand.

Among cases that are prosecuted, the conviction rate in the Crown Court is 69% for crimes of violence against the person and 75% for robbery (Home Office, 2007). Among adults sentenced, 29% were given a custodial sentence in violence against the person cases, and 54% were given custodial sentences in robbery cases. On average, those convicted were sentenced to 17 months in custody for assault and 31 months for robbery. In both robbery and assault, the criminal sanctions administered depend on the severity of the offence, degree of harm (physical and psychological) caused to the victim, extent of premeditation and characteristics of the defendant, such as remorse and cooperation with investigators.

A13.7. What happens to offenders?

In the USA, violent offenders tend to be dealt with by punishment or incapacitation (i.e. removed from society and placed in prison). However, in other jurisdictions (such as the UK, Canada, Australia and New Zealand) the focus has been much more on rehabilitation through treatment programmes. Although there are specialist progammes designed for perpetrators of domestic violence, other available programmes to address violent crime are not offence-specific (Gilbert and Daffern, 2010). Thus, this section will concentrate on treatment for generally violent offenders, a group that includes people who have committed assault or robbery.

Violent offender programmes underpinned by the principles of cognitive behaviour therapy (CBT) began in the 1980s (Polaschek, 2010b). Originally these programmes focused on the management of anger, an approach that was based on the idea that violent crime results from a tendency among some people to experience more anger, and to express it more often and more violently (Polaschek, 2006). However, the potential efficacy of anger management programmes appears to be limited. To be effective, treatment programmes need to address multiple aspects of an offender that are known to predict criminal behaviour – known as criminogenic needs (Polaschek, 2010b; Watts and Howells, 1999). Successful violent offender treatment programmes should also match the intensity of the programme to offenders' risk (most programmes target medium- and high-risk offenders) and consider offender responsivity issues such as intellectual and social difficulties, and programme responsivity issues such as treatment readiness and psychopathic traits. Recent treatment programmes for violent offenders, based on these principles, tend to be multi-modal. Box 13.4 gives one example.

Box 13.4. The Rimutaka Violence Prevention Unit

The treatment programme at Rimutaka prison in Wellington, New Zealand was established in 1998 to address the needs of serious violent offenders. This medium-secure unit is a completely separate unit within the prison and receives three cohorts (groups of ten men) per year. Criteria for transfer to the programme include a current violent offence or history of violence, an appropriate security level, willingness to transfer and the absence of any major mental disorders, neurological problems or inadequate literacy skills. Over seven months, the men take part in a series of group-based modules, facilitated by two therapists; sessions fill approximately 8–12 hours per week. In addition to a four-week assessment and a two-week induction, men on the programme complete modules dealing with offence chains, the restructuring of offence supportive thinking, mood management, victim empathy, moral reasoning, problem solving, communication and relationship skills, and relapse prevention planning. Community reintegration issues are also addressed, along with the cultural needs of Maori and Pacific Nations men who are a majority in the programme. The completion rate of the programme is up to 75%, and evidence of programme efficacy is encouraging.

Source: Polaschek, 2010b; Polaschek et al., 2005.

The relative efficacy of treatment

In terms of predicting future violence after treatment, researchers typically examine treated offenders' reconviction rate over a certain period of time after release from prison, if offenders are not already based in the community (Polaschek, 2010b; see Polaschek and Dixon, 2001 and Wilson, 2002, for discussion and evaluation of a community-based treatment programme). To assess whether treatment has been effective, treated offenders are compared with other groups of untreated offenders to give an idea of what might have happened in the absence of treatment. The available evidence on multi-model CBT programmes shows a reduction in violent recidivism after treatment (Cortoni, Nunes and Latendresse, 2006; Di Placido et al., 2006; Hatcher et al., 2008; Polaschek, 2010a; Polaschek et al., 2005; Wilson, 2002). Despite this success, future considerations for this area include developing a clear theoretical basis for treatment design and addressing the diversity of needs among violent offenders (Polaschek, 2006).

Although violent crime is an umbrella term for a diverse range of offences – including assault and robbery – it nonetheless implies an offending specialisation in violence. Although there may be some variation in results depending on whether offending behaviour is measured by official statistics or self-report, and whether or not specialisation is confined to specific offence types (Lynam, Piquero and Moffit, 2004), violent offenders are generally not specialists (Polaschek, 2010b). For example, serious violent offenders tend to have a long history of diverse criminal behaviour, and may be categorised as 'life-course persistent' general offenders (Moffit, 1993; Polaschek, Collie and Walkey, 2004).

A13.8. And the damage done . . .

Who are the victims?

There are factors that can systematically increase the risk that someone becomes a violent crime victim. Many theories of criminal behaviour and victimisation are based on this premise. For example, routine activities theory, a major theory in criminology, states that predatory crime is contingent on there being a suitable target (person, object or place), a willing perpetrator and the lack of a suitable guardian (e.g. police patrols, friends, CCTV).

The overall risk of violent victimisation is 3% according to the 2009/10 BCS. Men are more than twice as likely than women (4.2% versus 1.8%, respectively) to be subject to a violent crime. Women, however, have a higher risk than men for some types of violent crime, such as domestic assault (64% of domestic assault victims are women). For both men and women, the ages of 16–24 are associated with the highest rate of victimisation. Thereafter, violent crime risk decreases with increasing age. Additionally, as noted earlier, people who frequent pubs or wine bars more than once a week have a higher risk of suffering violent crime (12%) than those who visit pubs or wine bars less than once a week on average (8%) or not at all (2.2%). Persons who are unemployed have a higher risk of violence compared with those who are employed (7.7% versus 3.3%). However, full-time students have a particularly high risk of violence (8.2%) compared with the rest of the population. These victimisation risk factors have also been found in the USA and Australia.

As mentioned earlier, a significant proportion of violent crime victims are acquainted with the perpetrator. There are several reasons why offenders may deliberately select acquaintances or family members. Robbery is more lucrative when the victim is a family member, as compared with a stranger (Felson, Baumer and Messner, 2000). Some acquaintance crimes are dispute-related. Robbery may be committed to collect on a debt (Black, 1983; Feeney, 1986). Violent crime may also stem from seeking revenge or retribution against an acquaintance or family member. Acquaintance robberies compared with stranger robberies are more likely to involve injury to the victim, which suggests punishment as a possible motive (Felson, Baumer and Messner, 2000).

According to the BCS (2009/10), victims were injured in about half of all violent crimes. The most frequent injuries reported were minor bruising or a black eye (31%), followed by cuts (15%) and severe bruising (14%). Victims required medical attention in 17% of violent incidents. About 3% of all violent incidents resulted in an overnight hospital stay. Victim injury costs have been estimated (in 1989, US dollars) at $2093 for assault and $2245 for robbery (Miller, Cohen and Rossman, 1993). Victims are less likely to be injured in robbery compared with assault.

Cash and mobile phones are the most frequently stolen items (Smith, 2003). For robbery or assault victims in the USA in 2006, the median economic loss was $100 (U.S. Department of Justice, 2006). In the UK, commercial armed robbery nets about £500 on average (Matthews, 1996). The amount stolen in attacks on security vehicles ranged from £10,000 to £2.3 million and the amount stolen from betting shops ranged from £160 to £5000.

Given the economic losses and physical dangers associated with violent crime victimisation, it is perhaps not surprising that many people fear being victimised. *Fear of crime* refers to the negative emotional state felt by individuals when they consider the threat of victimisation (Rader, 2004). Gender is reliably associated with fear of crime (Woolnough, 2009). Women are more likely than men to fear robbery victimisation, despite the fact that the risk of robbery is lower for women than for men (Reid and Konrad, 2004). Media reports of violence also may heighten fear of crime, especially if the audience is similar demographically to the crime victim portrayed (Chiricos, Eschholz and Gertz, 1997).

PART B: Theories and explanations

B13.1. Introduction

In explaining violent crime within this chapter, we rely on the assumption that aggression is a key ingredient and will focus on the causes of aggressive and violent behaviour underlying violent offences, such as robbery and assault. Read Box 13.5 and reflect upon how each theory we present would 'explain' what happened.

Box 13.5. Child torturers

In January 2010, two young brothers were given an indeterminate sentence for a 'sadistic' assault on two children in Edlington, UK. The brothers allegedly attacked and tortured two children with knives, sticks, bricks and burning cigarettes, leaving one for dead. The children were also forced to engage in sexual acts with each other. The brothers, aged 9 and 11 at the time of the attack, faced a minimum of five years in detention. They may never be released because of the brutality of their crimes and the significant danger they may pose to the public. Previous to the attack, they allegedly assaulted another child in the neighbourhood. The brothers have not shown remorse to date.

The brothers had been expelled from school three years previously. More recently, the boys had been placed in the care of social services. Their parents

---

were reportedly addicted to drugs and alcohol, and they allowed the brothers to smoke cannabis, drink alcohol and view pornography. There was also evidence that domestic violence had occurred in the home.

How would each of the theoretical accounts presented in this chapter account for the behaviour? Which theoretical explanation seems to best account for the behaviour, and why?

B13.2. Theoretical perspectives

Rational choice perspective

The study of criminal decision making originated from rational choice models of criminal behaviour. Rational choice models are based on the assumption that an offender responds to incentives and evaluates the costs and benefits of committing a particular offence. Robbery seems to lend itself well to the study of criminal decision making. First, would-be offenders have to consider robbery as an acceptable form of behaviour. Thereafter, a potential offender has to determine which type of target (victim) to select in order to achieve their objective. Other types of decisions are also made, including whether to recruit accomplices, how complex the robbery scheme should be and whether a weapon ought to be used.

In determining whether to commit a robbery, costs could include the risk of being physically harmed and the risk of getting caught and having to serve a lengthy prison sentence. Benefits could include the probability of achieving a large financial payout and gaining status in the eyes of one's peers. If the benefits are perceived to outweigh the costs, then the crime will be committed. Rational choice models have figured in crime prevention strategies (Cook, 1980). For example, retail stores have implemented frequent cash drops to reduce the financial rewards of robbery and CCTV to increase the odds that the offender will be caught.

There is evidence to suggest that some robbers take actions to minimise the risk of being caught while trying to maximise their financial gains. Conklin (1972) found that robbers selected locations in which they assumed (sometimes incorrectly) that the financial pay-off would be relatively high and the risk of detection would be low. Other research, however, indicates that most street robbers rarely weigh the costs and benefits of committing a crime (Shover and Honaker, 1992). Rather, the majority of robberies are 'opportunistic' and impulsive. Empirical research with convicted robbers finds that advance planning is usually not evident (Silberman, 1978). Feeney (1986) concluded from his research that street robbery and muggings are usually accomplished without any preparation. A substantial proportion of perpetrators report that they did not intend to commit robbery (it happened 'just like that') and that they became involved in robbery 'accidentally'. The majority of the offenders reported that they had not given any thought at all to the possibility of being arrested. Taken together, research with actual offenders seems to suggest that rational choice models apply only to some types of robbers, such as those who are not acting under the influence of alcohol or drugs. However, whether offender self-reports can be used as a method to test rational choice models depends on the extent to which offenders can monitor, remember and report their thought processes to researchers – and this is assuming they do so truthfully!

Psychodynamic theory

The Freudian or psychodynamic perspective on aggressive behaviour comes from Freud's (1920) biologically based dual-instinct theory. According to Freud, humans are driven by both a pleasure-seeking 'life instinct' and a self-destructive 'death instinct'. People resolve conflict between the two by manifesting the destructive tendencies associated with the death instinct in negative behaviour – such as aggression – towards other people. Aggressive energy or angry emotion builds up, rather like the pressure build-up in a hydraulic system (Bartol and Bartol, 2005) or a kettle being brought to the boil. If the energy is not released in a controlled way, it is likely to manifest itself as violence. According to this theory, people who commit crime have not had the right opportunities to manage and regulate their excess energy. There may be constructive ways to discharge extra energy, or 'let off steam' appropriately, through catharsis. For example, catharsis may be achieved by playing sport or, vicariously, by watching sport. The implications for controlling violent crime are that providing people with socially appropriate opportunities for catharsis may reduce aggressive and violent behaviour.

However, there is no physiological evidence for the constant build-up on which this theory is premised. In addition, despite popular belief in the concept of catharsis, most empirical research has not supported this hypothesis (e.g. Bushman, Baumeister and Stack, 1999). Unsurprisingly, catharsis does not tend to be a component of modern treatment programmes for violent offenders.

Frustration–aggression hypotheses

In the 1930s, Dollard and colleagues (Dollard et al., 1939) proposed that aggression results from frustration. According to this perspective, frustration (including annoyance, etc.) occurs when some sort of goal-directed behaviour is externally thwarted in some way. For example, a student with the aim of achieving a first-class degree feels frustrated by the lecturer who sets a difficult examination and marks harshly, resulting in a fail. This theory posits that aggression occurs because our natural tendency is to end the frustration we are experiencing. Central to this perspective are the claims that frustration always results in aggression, and aggression is always a result of frustration.

This theory is important for raising the idea that external influences (e.g. of frustration) may react with characteristics that are internal to the individual. However, not everyone responds aggressively to frustration; we might instead respond by withdrawing from the situation, feeling negative emotion or doing other, non-aggressive behaviours to overcome goal barriers (Baron and Richardson, 1994; Krahe, 2001). For example, the failing student may become sad, doubtful about their abilities or plan to study much harder for the next exam. In addition, other factors – such as threat of punishment, or fear of consequences – may determine whether frustration leads to aggression. Alternatively, these factors may result instead in the displacement of aggression onto another target (Miller, 1948; Marcus-Newhall et al., 2000). For example, the failing student may pick a fight with his girlfriend rather than complain to the lecturer with whom he is angry.

Frustration–aggression theory was subsequently revised by Berkowitz (e.g. Berkowitz, 1962, 1965; see also below), who proposed that frustration generates anger, and it is anger that creates a 'readiness' for possible aggressive behaviour. Berkowitz also emphasised that frustration is only one of a number of factors that might set this process in motion.

Cognitive neo-association theory

Following on from his revisions to frustration–aggression theory, Berkowitz proposed that aggressive stimuli, affect and motor reactions are cognitively linked, and that certain triggers can activate these links. According to Berkowitz, the role of negative affect is particularly important; it tends to arise in response to an unpleasant event, and triggers either a fight or flight response. In the fight response, aggression-related tendencies are activated, while in the flight response, escape motives are activated. Berkowitz suggested that the likelihood of the fight – as opposed to the flight – response can depend on the intensity and severity of the negative affect (or mood). His theory is useful for thinking about relapse prevention in light of potential triggers (what activates our fight response) and in terms of using techniques to help with mood management in treatment.

Excitation transfer theory

As Berkowitz pointed out, an aggressive reaction may depend on how aversive stimuli (things we don't like) are interpreted. The excitation transfer perspective (Zillman, 1979) emphasises physiological arousal and how this arousal may be 'labelled' differently depending on the circumstances. A driver who experiences a rush of adrenaline after narrowly missing hitting another car might label their arousal as anger or relief). Moreover, sometimes arousal from one situation might be inappropriately associated with another situation, outside of a person's awareness. For example, somebody who is still 'hyped' after playing and winning an intensive rugby game may be more likely to feel aggressive in a post-game social situation. In such a case, the positive 'hyped-up' arousal from the rugby game reinforces negative arousal (perhaps teasing from another team member) in the post-match social situation.

Social learning theory

According to social learning theory, aggression and violence, like other kinds of behaviour, are acquired and maintained through observational learning and direct experiences. Thus, people may learn aggression early on if they have many chances to observe it, if they are reinforced for their own aggression ('that's right, show him who's boss') and internalise standards that support aggression. For example, someone who grows up in a violent neighbourhood, where goals are met by using violence and violence is viewed as positive, may well take these experiences and beliefs on board. According to social learning theory, aggression can be learned from the behaviour of models, who could include parents, peers or figures in the media; it is about seeing what important people around you do and what happens to them, and taking this on board yourself. Thus, the imitation of a model becomes more likely if the model is reinforced with positive consequences, and less likely if the model is punished. Positive reinforcers include tangible rewards (e.g. in the case of robbery), social reward and approval (e.g. within gangs, during war); negative reinforcers could include a decrease in some other aversive situation, such as being bullied or teased or told off.

The classic study in support of social learning theory is the Bobo doll study (Bandura, Ross and Ross, 1961), in which children who had previously seen adults behaving aggressively towards an inflatable doll were more likely then to be aggressive towards the doll. More recent research on media influences provides additional support.

Box 13.6. The onlooker

Consider the following scenarios: you are having a drink at your local pub and you catch a fellow patron staring intently at you; you are walking down the main street and a passer-by almost knocks you down as he passes. These kinds of situations are ambiguous because an onlooker would not necessarily know whether the patron was being friendly or hostile, or whether the knock was accidental or intentional. What do you think in each scenario? What would you do? Do you know someone who might act differently to you?

However, as with the other theories discussed, there are limitations to social learning as an explanation for aggressive behaviour and violence: not everybody does behave aggressively. Another limitation is how this theory accounts for the intention to harm, which is supposed to be a key component of aggression but would not always translate as part of the social learning process. It is also difficult to assess to what extent we should expect aggression-related learning to generalise (or not) from one setting to another. Finally, this theory does not explain why some people – for example, those with a history of violent criminal behaviour – choose to desist from crime even if they are still being reinforced for it. Treatment-wise, social learning suggests that direct experience of punishment for violent criminal behaviour, such as imprisonment, should reduce recidivism. Similarly, observing the negative repercussions of others' violence should act as a form of deterrence to an individual. However, research generally shows that punishment as a form of deterrence is not an effective method of crime prevention (Beyleveld, 1980).

Social cognitive theories

Recent theoretical work on understanding aggressive and violent behaviour has focused on an interplay between social and cognitive factors, particularly on how people process social information and potential biases in thinking. Socio-cognitive models of aggression have become the dominant theoretical framework for understanding aggression. These theories have an extensive empirical under-pinning, and a solid basis for treatment – although to date the theory–treatment links are limited (Gilbert and Daffern, 2010).

Social information processing

In the 1980s and 1990s, Dodge and colleagues (e.g. Crick and Dodge, 1994; Dodge and Frame, 1982) proposed a social information processing model of aggression based on their research with aggressive children and adolescents. According to this model, aggressive behaviour is the end product of a biased chain of social information processing. This chain can be divided into three steps, which include: (1) selective attention to hostile cues; (2) attributing hostile versus innocuous intentions to actors; and (3) selecting an aggressive or non-aggressive solution to the problem. Research appears to support all three steps of this model. For example, people who have a tendency to be angry or aggressive are more likely than others to attend to and process aggression-related infor-mation (Cohen, Eckhardt and Schagat, 1998; Smith and Waterman, 2004; van Honk et al., 2001). They also tend to apply aggressive meanings to ambiguous social situations, a phenomenon known in the literature as the hostile attribution bias (HAB; Dodge, 1980; see also Copello and Tata, 1990; Dill et al., 1997; Kirsh and Olczak, 2002).

Finally, research has shown that aggressive people are not good at generating pro-social solutions to aggression-related problems, and are thus more likely to select aggressive solutions to conflict situations (Bettman, 1998; Gouze, 1987; Lochman and Dodge, 1994).

Cognitive scripts

In one popular socio-cognitive account, aggressive people's knowledge structures about aggression are said to feed into cognitive scripts (or event schemas; Fiske and Taylor, 1991) about aggressive situations and events. A script is the cogni-tive representation of a particular sequence of behaviours or events relating to a familiar or typical situation (Abelson, 1981; Schank and Abelson, 1977). To use an oft-cited example, when dining out, most people expect their dining experience to unfold in a particular way, in accordance with what psychologists would call a 'restaurant script'. Thus, upon entering a restaurant we expect first to be seated, next to be offered the menu, a waiter or waitress appears and asks if we would like to order drinks, they reappear with our drinks and ask for our meal order, and so on. In other words, scripts contain expectations about how we should behave, the likely consequences of our behaviour and also beliefs about what responses are appropriate or inappropriate in a particular context (Krahé, 2001). These scripts are stored in the memory, to be retrieved and updated when necessary.

Huesmann (1988) proposed that scripts are one key mechanism by which aggressive behaviour is learned in childhood. Like regular scripts, aggressive scripts contain information about how to respond aggressively; for example, if someone threatens you, you might have a sequence of behaviours in mind for how to retaliate (Anderson and Bushman, 2002). According to Huesmann, children develop aggressive scripts as a result of both their own behaviour (enactive learning) and the observation of others. For example, children may experience positive consequences for using aggression as a means of problem solving, or see other people being rewarded for their use of aggression. Huesmann (1988) suggested that aggressive scripts are resistant to change, and tend to persist into adulthood.

The General Aggression Model

Anderson and Bushman (2002; Anderson, Anderson and Deuser, 1996; Anderson et al., 1995) have developed a comprehensive multifactorial socio-cognitive framework for explaining aggression. Importantly, their model draws together ideas from social information-processing theories, as well as from other cognitive theories.

In the General Aggression Model (GAM), Anderson and Bushman (2002) model an aggressive episode, which is assumed to occur within the context of 'an ongoing social interaction' (p. 34). They divide the episode into three stages, and describe the various factors thought to influence an individual at each of the stages. Stage 1 considers the range of inputs – both person and situational factors – that contribute to aggressive behaviour. Personal characteristics include gender, biological and genetic factors, hostile traits such as narcissism, aggressive–supportive beliefs, attitudes and values, personal goals and behavioural scripts. Situational factors include aggressive cues such as violent media, provocation, frustration, aversive conditions such as noise, pain and heat, the physiological and psychological effects of alcohol and drugs, and incentives for aggression. Stage 2 describes the routes by which the various inputs can lead to a present internal state that predisposes an individual to an aggressive act. Anderson and Bushman identify three internal mechanisms, which interact in combination with one another: cognition (e.g. hostile thoughts), affect (e.g. a bad mood) and arousal (e.g. you are provoked or 'hyped-up' about something). Stage 3 is labelled outcomes, and describes the process by which inputs, plus any effects of cognition, affect or arousal, are appraised by the individual before action is taken. Immediate appraisal is based on automatic processes such as inference, and may lead to impulsive action or, if time and other cognitive resources allow, to reappraisal of the situation. Other factors that may influence the episode include expectations and goals, socialisation, opportunities to aggress, inhibitory processes, motivational factors and anger.

In short, the GAM draws together literature on cognitive processes, structures and other factors, to explain the temporal process of an aggressive incident. The model is well grounded in scientific research, and gives a coherent multifactor account of aggression that is open to further empirical testing. One potential shortcoming of the GAM is that it could be viewed as overly inclusive. That is, this model runs the risk of encompassing so many explanations of aggression that it (1) ends up explaining none of the specific mechanisms well, and (2) becomes unfalsifiable because everything 'fits' within it. Despite this cautionary note, the GAM has made an important and timely contribution to the field of aggression, most notably for its amalgamation of the literature and creation of fertile ground for future empirical advances.

KEY DEBATE: Media violence and violent crime

One area of psychology whose findings have created great debate in the public domain is the relationship between media violence and aggressive and violent behaviour. There are well-known cases in which the two are anecdotally linked – for example, the Columbine shootings – as well as technological advances and the consequent availability of violent media in a variety of forms including television, films, video games, music videos and so on. These activities have sparked common interest in the question: Does exposure to violent media lead to harmful consequences? A series of reports and reviews conducted by both governmental and non-governmental agencies, and dating back to 1954, unanimously concluded that the answer to this question is YES. Indeed, in 2000, six major professional societies signed a statement with the following conclusion: 'at this time, well over 1,000 studies . . . point overwhelmingly to a causal connection between media violence and aggressive behavior in some children' (Joint Statement, 2000, p. 1). Moreover, in a particularly striking illustration, Anderson and Bushman (2001) compare the strength of this relationship with other known correlations from the medical literature; notably, the relationship between media violence and aggression is stronger than the relationship between – among others – condom use and sexually transmitted HIV, passive smoking and lung cancer at work, and calcium intake and bone mass.

How does exposure to media violence lead to aggression? Several of the theories discussed in this chapter can help us to understand the possible mechanisms. For example, social learning and social cognitive theories suggest that viewing violence may lead to aggression through direct imitation of aggressive models, through observational learning of various behaviours, behavioural scripts and schemas, attitudes and beliefs and expectations about the outcomes of aggression (Anderson and Gentile, 2008). Moreover, exposure may act in a similar way to other environmental triggers (such as heat, insults, etc.), potentially causing negative affect that leads to aggression. In addition, physiological arousal experienced due to exposure may cause aggression through excitation transfer. The GAM is a useful model for bringing these different factors together.

Despite the potential for reduction of aggression and violence through reduction of exposure to violent media, few studies have examined the potential for interventions or the effectiveness of these (Anderson et al., 2003). Evidence to date suggests that interventions targeting attitudes or involving parents are the most likely to reduce exposure to violent media (Anderson et al., 2003). In addition, one recent school-based intervention has shown some promising results in this respect (Rosenkoetter, Rosenkoetter and Acock, 2009).

PART C: Further information

C13.1. Organisations to contact for information and voluntary work

Citizen Advice Bureau (www.cas.org.uk).

The Citizens Advice Bureau helps people resolve their legal, money and other problems by providing free information and advice, and by influencing policy makers. Also see website for volunteer opportunities.

Crime Stoppers (www.Crimestoppers-uk.org).

Report crimes anonymously in the UK.

National Offender Management Service (www.noms.justice.gov.uk).

A Ministry of Justice service that is committed to rehabilitating offenders through programmes that address the causes of offending behaviour.

Office for Victims of Crime (http://www.ojp.usdoj.gov/ovc/help/natorg.htm).

Based in the USA, provides links to services to help victims of crime, including:

■ The Centre of Restorative Justice and Peace Making: http://www.cehd. umn.edu/ssw/rjp/.
■ Identity Theft Resource Center: http://www.idtheftcenter.org/.
■ National Association of Crime Victim Compensation Boards: http:// www.nacvcb.org/.

Victim Support (http://www.victimsupport.org.uk/).

Independent charity that serves victims and witnesses of crime across England and Wales. Every year they contact over 1.5 million people after a crime to offer help. See website for services and volunteer opportunities.

C13.2. Further reading

The following readings have been selected to provide more in-depth coverage of the psychological theories presented in this chapter. These readings also provide more extensive information regarding the methods that are used to study violent and aggressive behaviour.

Bartol, C.R. and Bartol, A.M. (2005). *Criminal Behavior: A Psychosocial Approach.* Upper Saddle River, NJ: Pearson.

Feeney, F. (1986). Robbers as decision-makers. In D.B. Cornish and R.V. Clarke (Eds.), *The Reasoning Criminal: Rational Choice Perspectives on Offending* (pp. 53–71). New York: Springer-Verlag.

Krahé, B. (2001). *The Social Psychology of Aggression.* East Sussex: Psychology Press.

chapter

14

VOYEURISM, EXHIBITIONISM AND OTHER NON-CONTACT SEXUAL OFFENCES

KERENSA HOCKEN AND KAREN THORNE

PART A: The offence – Who, what, when, why?

A14.1. Introduction

Non-contact sex offences involve a sexual offence, occurring in the absence of physical contact between perpetrator and victim. The absence of physical contact is intended by the offender. The three most common non-contact sex offences after Internet child abuse (which is covered in Chapter 7) are voyeurism, exhibitionism and telephone scatologia (making obscene telephone calls).

Compared with other sexual offences, non-contact sexual offending is under-researched and so relatively little is known or understood about these behaviours. Much of the research surrounding these behaviours is over 20 years old and has less relevance to current theory. This chapter will focus primarily on voyeurism, exhibitionism and telephone scatologia as these are some of the most commonly occurring non-contact sex offences.

A14.2. Definitions

Voyeurism involves the offender watching others, in a sexual way, without the victim's knowledge. This is sometimes referred to as 'peeping', which has its origins from Peeping Tom, who watched Lady Godiva ride naked through Coventry. Voyeurs commonly enjoy watching others who are naked, taking off clothes or sometimes while they are having sex. They may also have more subtle interests such as looking up skirts or down low-cut tops. Exhibitionism involves the offender exposing a body part, normally genitals, to victims and may also involve obscene suggestions or comments being made to the victim. This is sometimes referred to in lay terms as 'flashing'. Telephone scatologia involves the offender telephoning others and making sexually inappropriate comments, breathing heavily or making threats to the victim.

What is voyeurism?

DSM-IV-TR (2000) defines voyeurism as recurrent, intense and sexually arousing fantasies, sexual urges or behaviours involving the act of observing an unsuspecting person who is naked, disrobing or engaging in sexual activity. These urges or fantasies have to be present for a period of at least six months and the person must have acted on these urges. However, this is a narrow criterion for defining voyeurism as it states that victims should be in the process of undressing, be naked or involved in sexual activity. In reality, voyeurs may be sexually interested in watching a wide range of behaviours, such as defecating and urinating. Others enjoy looking at underwear or intimate parts of the body that the victim did not intend to show. The common themes in these behaviours are that the voyeur enjoys watching others engaging in behaviours that are private and/or not intended by the victim to be viewed by others. For the voyeur, it holds an element of secrecy, that they are viewing others when they shouldn't be.

The legal definition of voyeurism reflects the broader understanding of voyeurism: 'for the purposes of obtaining sexual gratification, and knowing that the other person does not consent to being observed, observing another person engaged in a private act' (Sexual Offences Act, 2003).

What is exhibitionism?

In medical terms, exhibitionism is defined as a paraphilic disorder in which the individual has 'recurrent intense sexually arousing fantasies, sexual urges or behaviours involving exposing one's genitals to an unsuspecting stranger' over a period of at least six months and which cause distress or impairment in functioning for the individual (APA, 2000).

However, in legal terms exhibitionism is defined as the intentional exposure of the offender's genitals, intending someone will see them and be caused alarm (SOA, 2003). This is a broader definition of the behaviour and does not require it to be a persistent problem for the individual to be considered an exhibitionist. This can mean that someone can legally be classed as an exhibitionist when they do not have a deviant pathological interest (i.e. 'true exhibitionist'). True exhibitionism is different from behaviours such as streaking (pranks) or stripping (financially motivated), which look behaviourally similar but are enacted for different reasons.

Exhibitionism can involve the perpetrator masturbating, attempting to strike up a conversation with the victim and using sexually explicit language or using sexual language generally. It may involve the practice of having sex in a public place with the intention of being seen by non-consenting victims. Exhibitionists employ a range of methods to attract their victim's attention – for example, calling a victim over to their car to ask for directions whilst they masturbate in their seat. Most incidents of exposure occur in public places, although perpetrators will tend to select more isolated areas in which to commit the offence (e.g. in quiet areas like parks or car parks). The exhibitionist derives sexual pleasure from the act of exposing, although the reaction they aim to evoke in victims can vary from shock and fear to hoping the victim will become aroused and initiate some kind of sexual contact with them.

What is telephone scatologia?

Medically this is defined as seeking sexual gratification by making obscene phone calls to unconsenting adults (APA, 2000). The caller becomes sexually aroused by exposing victims to sexually explicit material. Not all prank or nuisance calls are sexually motivated and would not therefore constitute telephone scatologia.

Unlike other non-contact offences, the legal definition of this behaviour focuses on the behaviour itself and less on the sexual arousal derived from it by the perpetrator (i.e. under the Telecommunications Act (1984), making an obscene phone call is defined as 'sending a message or other matter that is grossly offensive or of an indecent, obscene or menacing character').

Telephone scatologia can involve a range of behaviours including the perpetrator boasting about their genitals and describing themselves masturbating, or making sexual and other propositions/threats towards the victim. Perpetrators may also use some kind of ruse to manipulate the victim into revealing sexually intimate information about themselves. This discussion may then lead to offensive remarks being made. Common ruses for eliciting such information include acting as a sexual survey researcher (Schewe, 1997) and posing as another woman (Pakhomou, 2006). A small number of obscene phone callers target female staff of crisis lines on the pretext of requesting help, only to use this as a means of discussing sexually explicit material to masturbate to.

Other non-contact offences

Other non-contact sexual offences can include possession, manufacture and distribution of illegal pornography (featuring children, or violence) or theft of items such as underwear for use in sexual fantasy. There are also some sexual offences that are technically non-contact, in that they do not involve physical contact between perpetrator and victim, but which were intended by the perpetrator to be a contact offence. For example, the new charge of Grooming with Intent has no physical contact because the perpetrator was stopped before they could make contact, but the intention was to have physical contact with the child. These offenders are different from other non-contact sex offenders, such as voyeurs, exhibitionists and obscene phone callers who do not intend to have physical contact with the victim.

The activity of 'dogging' involves elements of both voyeurism and exhibitionism and is the practice of having sex (normally in a parked car) and allowing others to watch, and/or watching others have sex, in a public place (usually woodland or park areas) (Bell, 2006). This behaviour is illegal; however, it is distinct in nature from voyeurism and exhibitionism because it is committed by consenting adults. Because it involves consenting adults, it is seen as being less deviant and more socially acceptable.

KEY DEBATE: Do non-contact sex offenders graduate to contact offences?

For:
Retrospective studies of contact sex offenders suggest that a significant minority have committed non-contact sexual offences in their past. When looking at non-contact offenders' further offences, evidence suggests that 38% of further offences were 'hands-on' offences. Therefore the risk of non-contact offenders committing contact offences is well documented.

Against:
The research shows that non-contact sexual offenders are highly likely to continue to commit non-contact offences. Although there is some evidence to suggest that contact sexual offenders have committed non-contact offences, it has not been consistently evidenced that non-contact offenders are at risk of committing contact offences. Until this changes, non-contact sexual offenders should be viewed as a distinct group of sexual offenders.

A14.3. Who?

Like other sexual offences, non-contact sex offenders may be male or female, but are more commonly male. Women do commit indecent exposure, although this is perceived, according to Balsam (2008), as non-deviant, and is met with approval by some of the male audience. Certainly, women are less likely to be convicted for non-contact sex offences.

The age of the offenders varies across studies from 25 (Berah and Myers, 1983) to 35 (Bader et al., 2008), although there is a general consensus that such offences begin early in offenders' lives. Voyeurism usually begins before the age of 15 years and exhibitionism before the age of 18. The incidence of exhibitionism is lower in the 40+ age group.

All races and socio-economic groups are represented amongst those presenting with paraphilias, and therefore it is reasonable to expect that the same will be true of non-contact sexual offenders with an interest in voyeurism and exhibitionism. Many exhibitionists are married or in a relationship, although some degree of sexual dysfunction is not uncommon. Offending behaviours may increase during times of stress or when the offender has time on his hands!

More is known about the demographics of telephone scatologists. They are more commonly heterosexual males, discovered in young adulthood, possess an average or elevated sex drive, have limited social interactions, secondary level education, have menial jobs and have tried and failed to maintain long-term marital-type relationships (Pakhomou, 2006). Perpetrators of obscene phone calls are frequently acquainted with the victim, although the victim may not recognise them at the time of the call or even subsequently (Buck et al., 1995).

Given the high drive people have to engage in non-contact sex offences, individuals will often choose occupations and hobbies that increase the likelihood that they will be able to offend. For example, voyeurs may choose to work in rental properties in order to have opportunities to peep on unsuspecting people, commonly installing video recording equipment to capture their interest.

Psychopathology

The absence of research into non-contact sex offences means that relatively little is known about how non-contact sex offenders differ from contact sex offenders. The presence of many non-contact sexual offences in the *DSM-IV-TR* criteria for paraphilias indicates that such disorders are viewed as mental disorders amongst clinicians. However, medicalising such behaviours should not remove responsibility from the offender for their behaviour. It is more helpful to consider them as psychosexual disorders rather than mental disorders.

Early research on exhibitionism, largely from a psychoanalytic background, suggested an immature personality and narcissistic ego. More recent research suggests exhibitionism, like paedophilia, is characterised by the suppression of anger, which is directed inwards. It also suggests that there is no specific psychopathology unique to exhibitionists in terms of their personality (Langevin et al., 1978) and they are similar in characteristics to other sexual offenders (e.g. poor relationship skills) (Lee et al., 2001; Murphy, 1997). Miner and Dwyer (1997) note that exhibitionists are similar on measures of psychosocial development to child molesters, as both groups have problems with trusting, feelings of shame and the need for immediate gratification and lack of long-term goals. Exhibitionists did show greater feelings of isolation and despair than other sex offender groups, however. Exhibitionism has therefore been conceptualised as being a less severe paraphilic disorder compared with other paraphilic groups.

Paraphilias have been found to trigger psychological disturbances such as guilt, shame, isolation and impaired capacity for normal social and sexual relationships (Thibaut et al., 2010). There is little to indicate that there is any significant psychopathology in telephone scatologists, although Matek (1988) suggests that they have low self-esteem and may have hostility/anger towards women.

Drugs and alcohol

Långström and Seto (2006) studied rates of self-reported exhibitionism and voyeurism in the general population in Sweden. They found that both behaviours were associated with higher rates of alcohol and drug use. In Bader et al.'s (2008) exhibitionist sample, 27.4% were suspected of alcohol abuse and 34.9% of illegal drug abuse. Higher rates of drug and alcohol abuse have also been found in a sample of paraphilic men attending a treatment centre (Kafka and Hennen,

2003). These rates of drug and alcohol use in paraphilic populations may reflect the underlying characteristic of risk taking found to be present in sexual offender populations.

Interestingly, there is less evidence of substance misuse in telephone scatologists. Matek (1988) reported that intoxication was not commonly associated with telephone scatologia. There is no clear explanation of why this is so.

Mental health and trauma

In forensic and clinical samples of men with paraphilias, research suggests that there is an association with mental health problems. Kafka and Prentky (1994) and Kafka and Hennen (2003) found higher rates of mood disorders (e.g. depression) and anxiety disorders (e.g. social phobia). Of course forensic and clinical samples are subject to certain bias that might overinflate the association between mental illness and paraphilias. However, Långström and Seto (2006) found that self-reported exhibitionism and voyeurism in the Swedish general population were associated with higher rates of psychological problems, suggesting that the association is not a result of sampling bias. In an exhibitionist sample, Bader et al. (2008) found that 24.4% had suspected mental illness symptoms and 3.8% had developmental disabilities. Less is known about the relationship between mental health and voyeurism and telephone scatologia.

Trauma in childhood, such as emotional abuse or neglect, can have a significant impact on neurological development, and impaired neurological development has been associated with sexual offending behaviour. Exhibitionists are more likely to have experienced trauma in the form of emotional abuse and family dysfunction than non-sex offender groups, but a similar rate to other paraphilic groups such as voyeurs. The rates of sexual abuse amongst exhibitionist appear to be consistent with those observed in the general population (Murphy and Page, 2008).

Evidence suggests that telephone scatologia is not commonly associated with learning disabilities, brain damage or psychosis.

A14.4. Misconceptions

Flashers are a nuisance and nothing more

In fact, non-contact sex offences have one of the highest reconviction rates of any sexual offending behaviour. Research by Abel et al. (1988) suggests that exhibitionism is amongst the most common of sexual offences. Exhibitionists also report more fantasies about offending before their first offence than do child molesters; and following their first offence have more fantasies about the offence than do child molesters (Dandescu and Wolfe, 2003). Because of the strength of the sexual urge to expose, it tends to be repeated frequently and even in the same location at the same time of day (which is very useful in terms of detection).

Women don't flash

There is a common misconception that women do not engage in exhibition-ist, voyeuristic or obscene telephoning unless these behaviours are motivated by something other than sexual arousal, i.e. finance. Whilst it is true that the major-ity of offender samples are men, Långström and Seto (2006) found that 2.1% of female respondents had exposed themselves and 3.9% reported a lifetime inci-dence of voyeurism. It is possible that women exposing themselves have some level of social acceptance, which means the behaviour is reported less frequently.

There is no harm in peeping

Interestingly, voyeurism has been a criminal offence in England and Wales only since May 2004. However, research suggests that contact offenders have typically commenced their 'career' in sexual offending with non-contact offences such as voyeurism, and these may be individuals with high levels of deviant sexual arousal who are on a slippery slope to committing contact offences.

They are just nuisance calls

Telecommunications companies often refer to obscene phone calls as 'nuisance calls', supporting the idea that this offence is trivial. However, this is a highly repetitive behaviour. The caller often derives their sexual gratification not from the act of calling, or from the obscenities they say to the victim, but from the sex-ually explicit response from the victim (Alford et al., 1980; Almansi, 1979; Dalby, 1988). The resulting interaction can leave victims fearful and likely to receive further calls if the caller receives the reaction they are looking for.

If you are ex-directory you won't receive nuisance calls

Public access to a women's telephone number does not make them any more or less likely to receive obscene phone calls than those who are ex-directory (Tseloni and Pease, 1998).

A14.5. Facts and figures

Incidence

As with all sexual offences, a key problem in calculating the number of non-contact sexual offences is that they are substantially under-reported and can be difficult to detect. If a victim of voyeurism is unaware they are being watched, who is likely to report the offence? Some have argued that if the victim of voyeurism is not aware they are being watched, they may not be vic-tims at all (Doyle, 2009). Official police statistics indicate that 7528 offences of exhibitionism or voyeurism were reported to police in England and Wales in 2008/9. International surveys of women indicate that exhibitionism occurs more frequently than police and crime statistics suggest. These surveys suggest that between 32 and 39% of college women and 40–48% of women in the general population have been exposed to (Murphy and Page, 2008). It has been well established that exhibitionism impacts on a large number of people but that most victims of exhibitionism do not report the offence to the police. As few as 28.6% of victims actually report offences (Riordan, 1999). There is little information about the incidence of voyeurism.

In 1989 in the Washington, DC area, 22,000 complaints were received about obscene phone calls, indicating this is a common behaviour. Smith and Morra's (1994) findings, that only 7–20% of sexually provocative phone calls are actually reported to telephone companies, suggest that the incidence of obscene phone calling is significantly higher. However, it is difficult to know how many calls one individual might make or how many of these callers would satisfy the criteria for telephone scatologia.

Prevalence

There has been limited research into the prevalence of non-contact sex offences despite being the most common law-breaking sexual behaviours in the general population. Långström and Seto (2006) reported that 3.1% of their sample of the Swedish general population had exposed themselves on at least one occasion and 7.7% had become sexually aroused by spying on others having sex on at least one occasion.

Abel and Rouleau (1990) interviewed 142 exhibitionists who revealed that between them they had exposed themselves to 72,974 victims, suggesting that exhibitionist acts occur up to 150 times more often than police statistics document. Hucker (2009) suggests that approximately 30% of offenders have exhibitionist tendencies.

A14.6. How are offenders caught?

Investigation

Non-contact sexual offences are investigated in much the same way as all other sex offences. However, because of their very nature, non-contact sexual offences often present particular difficulties for investigators. For police the key problem is establishing the identity of the offender. With exhibitionists the offence tends to be brief, and at a distance, and with the victim's attention normally being drawn to the genitals, this reduces the chance of getting a good description of the recognisable characteristics of the offender! However, most do not make serious attempts to hide their identity and taking such risks may contribute to their sexual arousal. Because exhibitionism tends to be a high-frequency behaviour and is likely to be repeated by the offender, police have more of an opportunity to build up evidence in order to identify a perpetrator and the likelihood of arrest is higher.

Voyeurism is rather more difficult for police to detect. Usually, the victim is not even aware an offence has taken place so formal reporting rates are likely to vastly underestimate actual offending. This is especially true in cases where the offender has used recording equipment to capture the private behaviour. In such circumstances the presence of such recordings may, however, assist in convicting offenders.

Obscene phone callers also present a challenge to identify. Unless the victim recognises the voice of the caller there is little opportunity to trace the perpetrator. The caller can sometimes be traced using caller identification processes utilised by the telephone company. However, with the increasing use of caller 'withheld' numbers this can become very difficult.

Detection

Of the 7258 offences of exhibitionism or voyeurism reported to the police in England and Wales between 2008 and 2009, 28% of cases saw the offender identified and punished for their offence (National Crime Statistics, 2010). This rate of detection is similar to that for offences such as burglary, theft from/of motor vehicles and fraud, and reflects the difficulty in identifying the perpetrators of such offences.

Very few obscene callers are actually apprehended, probably because of the difficulties in identifying them. Telephone companies are able to prevent further calls reaching the victim by excluding all non-identifiable numbers. As such, many offences are prevented from occurring as opposed to being 'detected'. In the most extreme criminal cases, line traces are used to detect perpetrators; however, this tends to be reserved for particularly serious crimes and offences threatening national security.

Conviction

Clear and careful identification of offenders is a key principle of the Police and Criminal Evidence Act (PACE) 1984. Where identification of offenders is particularly difficult, as in non-contact sexual offences, securing a conviction can be more problematic. Therefore conviction rates can be particularly low for these types of offences. In such cases, conviction is reliant on good identification of the perpetrator, on offenders admitting offences to police or on other evidence linking offenders to the offence (e.g. possession of video recordings taken during the offence).

Because most offences of obscene phone calling are dealt with by preventative measures (i.e. blocking calls) and because of the difficulties in identifying perpetrators, conviction rates for this offence are particularly low.

A14.7. What happens to offenders?

Perhaps reflecting society's view of non-contact sexual offences as a nuisance and not a danger, non-contact sex offenders are more likely to be sentenced to probation orders and community sentences than they are to a custodial sentence.

An offender convicted of a basic offence of exposure with no aggravating or mitigating factors can expect to be sentenced to a community order for the offence. If, however, they are a repeat offender the sentencing judge's starting point will be a 12-week custodial sentence and this will be varied up or down depending on mitigating or aggravating factors to the case, with a maximum penalty of two years' imprisonment.

Similarly, an offender convicted of a basic offence of voyeurism, with no aggravating or mitigating factors, can expect to be sentenced to a community order. An offence with aggravating factors can expect to receive a custodial sentence of up to 18 months and an offence with serious aggravating factors (such as recording sexual activity and placing it on the Internet or circulating it for financial gain) can expect to be sentenced to custody for up to two years.

A finding of guilt for an offence of making obscene phone calls can lead to a term of imprisonment of up to six months, but more often leads to a non-custodial (suspended) sentence.

Treatments typically offered

During the last ten years, very little has been published on the treatment of non-contact sex offences. The work that has been available regarding the treatment of exhibitionism and voyeurism has largely been drawn from the general approaches to treating sex offenders, including non-contact sex offenders.

The most common treatment approach used with sex offenders, including non-contact sexual offenders, is cognitive-behavioural treatment (CBT) programmes such as those run by HM Prison Service and the National Probation Service. Offenders are filtered into treatment programmes according to risk level rather than offence type. As such, non-contact sexual offenders are typically offered a range of CBT-based courses, which are aimed at improving their understanding of risk factors, victim empathy and ability to take responsibility for offending. Empathy development is a crucial part of these courses for non-contact sex offenders, particularly exhibitionists, as they are less likely than other offenders to recognise the harm their offences cause (Morin and Levenson, 2008).

A range of behavioural conditioning techniques have been developed for use with sexual offenders, and their use with non-contact sex offenders has been specifically evaluated. These techniques can be based on the principles of either operant or classical conditioning. Techniques such as aversion therapy (with ammonia), covert sensitisation and masturbatory reconditioning are usually combined together with the aim of reducing unhealthy sexual arousal and increasing healthy sexual arousal in offenders (e.g. Marshall, 2006). Most methods have been applied with non-contact sex offenders.

Another common pathway for the treatment of non-contact sexual offenders is based on a biological or medical approach. Offenders can be treated for high levels of testosterone using hormonal treatments, commonly called anti-libidinal medication. These work by reducing testosterone levels and therefore sexual drive. Alternatively, offenders may be prescribed selective serotonin reuptake inhibitors (SSRIs). These are more commonly known for their use as antidepressants; however, they have proved effective in reducing deviant fantasy, urges and sexual impulsivity (Greenberg et al., 1997) with non-contact sex offenders and mixed sex offender samples.

All three treatment approaches can be combined together to work with non-contact sexual offenders. There seems to be a general agreement amongst clinicians that CBT should commence with all offenders and pharmacological treatments should be offered alongside. Which pharmacological treatment will be offered will depend on presenting issues and risk.

Relative efficacy of treatment programmes

Contemporary treatment programmes based on cognitive-behavioural techniques have been found to result in up to 40% reduction in recidivism in the general sex offender population (Hanson et al., 2002; Losel and Schmucker, 2005). However, Langevin (1983) noted that assertiveness training with exhibitionists and voyeurs was not successful, with all the sample reoffending. Given the deficits non-contact sexual offenders have in victim empathy, it is likely that those programmes that directly target this need are going to provide better treatment outcomes.

Behavioural approaches to treating exhibitionists have reported some success, although there are notable gaps in follow-up research. Maletzky (1991, 1997) reports a failure rate of only 13% when using assisted covert sensitisation with exhibitionists. Follow-up of cases using ammonia aversion therapy suggests that, at least in single-case studies, offenders have remained offence free at 12 month follow-up (Marshall, 2006). Similarly the limited evidence available indicates that the voyeurs respond positively to the use of behavioural treatment approaches (see Mann et al., 2008).

Medical/biological approaches to treatment of sexual offenders generally have proved very effective in reducing reoffending (Meyer et al., 1992). Whilst there is some debate over what SSRIs are directly impacting on with voyeurs and exhibitionists (i.e. underlying co-morbid features such as anxiety or mood disorders, or diminution of libido), it is clear that they do have a positive treatment effect with this group (Abouesh and Clayton, 1999; Guay, 2009; Kafka, 1991, 1994). The effectiveness of hormonal treatment (i.e. anti-libidinal medications) with exhibitionists is not well researched, but those who have used it have reported poor outcomes (Langevin et al., 1979). However, it is important to remember that those offenders who come into contact with clinical services and are prescribed medication are often those who are most in need of intervention and have more deviant arousal to be managed. Treatment using pharmacological approaches is less common for those offenders who present lower levels of risk and deviant sexual interests.

Overall, using a combined approach to treatment by psychotherapy and pharmacology is associated with better treatment outcomes than either treatment on their own (Guay, 2009; Thibaut, 2010).

Recidivism

Rates at which offenders reoffend are difficult to assess accurately. Most available information reports the rate at which offenders are convicted of further offences rather than the rate at which they reoffend, because of the difficulty in detecting such behaviour.

When exhibitionists were subject to long-term follow-up, 23.6% were found to have been reconvicted for a further sexual offence (Firestone et al., 2006). Some research has found sexual rearrest rates to be 20.5% (Romero and Williams, 1985). However, most studies have reported reoffence rates for exhibitionism being in excess of 40%, suggesting that this group may exhibit particularly high rates of recidivism. Little is known about recidivism rates for voyeurism or telephone scatologia.

Recidivism rates are generally considered to be lower among treated sexual offenders than those who have not been through treatment. However, given the different rates of recidivism and treatment effectiveness reported in the literature, it is not possible to determine what works for whom (i.e. whether certain types of offender recidivate at higher rates than others following treatment or whether certain types of treatment are more effective for certain types of sex offender).

Co-occurrence or progression on to other crimes

Scant research on co-morbidity with telephone scatologia and other paraphilias indicates that it has some association with voyeurism, compulsive masturbation and phone sex dependence (Price et al., 2002). Other researchers such as Freund et al. (1988) have suggested that it is more strongly associated with exhibitionism. Longo and Groth (1983) found a childhood history of exhibitionism (24%) and voyeurism (54%) in a sample of adult male sexual offenders. Voyeurism was more common in the history of adult rapists, while exhibitionism was more common in the histories of child molesters.

In the general population, exhibitionism has a high rate of co-occurrence with voyeurism (Långström and Seto, 2006). It has also been found to co-occur with other paraphilia-related disorders such as compulsive masturbation and phone sex dependence.

So whilst research has found variable results regarding co-occurrence of non-contact sexual offences, researchers generally agree that exhibitionism, voyeurism and telephone scatologia are seldom observed as solitary disorders in clinical samples (Abel et al., 1988; Price et al., 2002). Therefore those assessing offenders presenting with one or other disorder should not neglect the possibility that others co-exist. Assessors should also be mindful that co-occurrence may reflect a common underlying interest (i.e. those who consistently expose to young children may also have paedophilic interests).

Of key concern to clinicians is the progression of non-contact offenders to contact sexual offences and other offences in general. Overall, retrospective studies that focus on progression to contact offences provide variable outcomes. The trend in findings is that a significant minority of child offenders and rapists have a history of non-contact sex offences, and many non-contact offenders report histories of hands-on sex offences. The few prospective studies that exist, such as that by Firestone et al. (2006), suggest sexual re-offence rates of 23.6%, with 19 of the 49 exhibitionists studied being convicted of further sexual offences progressing to hands-on offences.

Exhibitionists who also have a rape or child molestation charge are more likely to have committed higher numbers of indecent exposures and have a history of physical assault charges (Bader et al., 2008). Whilst this suggests a link between exhibitionism and progression to more serious offences (sexual and physical assault), the nature of this link is unclear. It is likely that for some offenders there is a high level of general antisociality and exhibitionism, and this may be just one way in which this is manifested rather than exhibitionists being at increased risk of progressing to physical assault.

Prognosis: Life course

Sex offenders who have paraphilias are likely to start offending at an earlier age than those who do not have a paraphilia (Dunseith et al., 2004). However, most will not come into contact with the criminal justice system (CJS) until they are in their mid-20s (Berah et al., 1983).

DSM-IV-TR suggests that paraphilic voyeurism and exhibitionism are lifelong phenomena. However, others have argued that there is insufficient information known about the natural history of paraphilias such as voyeurism and exhibitionism to be confident about this. Instead it is likely that, as with other sexual desires, an interest in voyeurism and exhibitionism may wax and wane and may be a stage in an individual's sexual development – for others it may be a point of fixation.

A14.8. And the damage done . . .

Who are the victims?

Victims of non-contact sexual offences are usually female adults (Bader et al., 2008), although offences against female adolescents and children are also common. In a national probability sample, Finkelhor et al. (2005) found that in the USA approximately 1.6 million young people between the ages of 2 and 17 are exposed to each year.

There is an increase in voyeuristic/exhibitionism offences being reported during school holidays and summer months (D.C.R. Wakeling, personal communication, 29 April 2010). School holidays and warmer weather increase offenders' access to victims as children are more commonplace in public areas and victims of all age groups tend to wear less as it is warmer, thus making voyeurism, and exhibitionism, easier.

Research into obscene phone calls to women in England and Wales found that females were most vulnerable to threats and obscene phone calls. Tseloni and Pease (1998) found that young, single or divorced women who had children and who lived on their own in inner cities were prone to receiving obscene phone calls. These victims were typically educated to a higher than basic standard and had an average family income. The caller is unknown or unidentifiable to most victims (Smith and Morra, 1994), although many perpetrators know their victims in that they may have seen them or be a very distant acquaintance.

Cost of crime

The highly repetitive nature of non-contact sexual offences means that many offenders have multiple victims, thus increasing the damage done. Many victims report psychological distress and traumatising effects caused by such offences (Cox and Maletzky, 1980). Victims of the non-contact sexual offence of telephone scatologia are targeted in their own home and may be subject to threats of physical assault/violence. They have no way of knowing whether the caller intends to act out such threats or if he is just bluffing. Callers can make repeated calls to specific victims, further heightening victims' uncertainty about their own safety or that of their family or home.

Fear of crime

Victim fear, both during and after a non-contact sexual offence, is frequently underestimated. Victims typically report that they don't know whether the offender plans to rape or physically assault them, whether they are the being stalked or targeted specifically or whether the offence will somehow escalate. For example, experiencing obscene phone calls induces a fear of crime, particularly of burglary and other offences where the person is targeted (Pease, 1985; Tseloni and Pease, 1998). The more obscene the phone calls received, the higher the fear of crime reported by victims (Tseloni and Pease, 1998), and the repetitive nature of the offence can lead women to believe their home is being observed by the perpetrator of the calls.

PART B: Theories and explanations

B14.1. Introduction

Theories that attempt to understand non-contact sexual offending are few and far between, and most are not well developed. Although some theories have been proposed, there has been a distinct lack of research to empirically test and develop these theories further and a significant amount of the literature is over 20 years old. There is no good scientific reason why a theory that attempts to explain only non-contact sexual offending has not emerged. The literature on sexual offending in general does contain a number of theories that attempt to explain specific types of sexual offending (see

Chapters 7, 10 and 11); however, these tend to focus on contact sexual offenders such as adult rapists and child abusers. As discussed previously within this chapter, there are misconceptions about the seriousness of non-contact sexual offences, and this may be reflected in the general lack of research and theory development.

Recently there has been a growing recognition within the literature that non-contact offenders are probably more deviant than previously thought (Firestone et al., 2006). The absence of good theoretical models for non-contact sexual offending creates difficulties in the assessment and treatment of these groups, and there have been calls from academics and practitioners for more research in this area (Mann et al., 2008; Morin and Levenson, 2008).

There is reason to assume that the general theories of sexual offending will account for non-contact sexual offending. For example, research by Kafka and Prentky (1992) has found that hypersexuality is a characteristic found in contact and non-contact sexual offenders and could account for the high co-occurrence of paraphilias. Not all of the research into theories of sexual offending is clear about the number and type of non-contact sexual offenders in their samples. Some sample groups of sexual offenders will have also included non-contact offenders as well as contact offenders. It is also possible that research samples containing contact sexual offenders will have included those with a history of non-contact sexual offending.

B14.2. Courtship disorder

There is one theory that specifically attempts to explain three of the most common non-contact offences: voyeurism, exhibitionism and telephone scatologia. This was proposed by Kurt Freund (1990) and is known as courtship disorder. It suggests that exhibitionism, voyeurism and telephone scatologia all represent a maladaptive way of trying to form a relationship. In this theory offenders are seen as wanting relationships but unable to achieve them, and instead they get stuck in a distorted phase of the courtship process. The courtship process is conceptualised as having four stages. The first stage involves looking for a potential partner; the second involves interacting without touching a partner, such as talking and non-verbal communication; the third stage involves touching each other, such as kissing and holding hands; the final stage is sexual intercourse. These phases are seen as being cyclical, with one phase progressing to the next, although it is accepted that the time between stages varies greatly and it is possible to move back to a previous stage. Within courtship disorder, the offender has a distorted the cycle because they over-focus on one phase. Different types of sexual offences are seen as relating to problems with the different phases (see Table 14.1).

This theory only applies to men who offend against adult women, as Freund suggests that those who offend against children are more likely to be paedophilic. Research findings that are consistent with the courtship disorder theory are the lack of a relationship and/or relationship difficulties (e.g. lack of trust).

Table 14.1 *The stages of courtship disorder and corresponding sexual offences*

Phase of the courtship cycle	Sexual offence
1) Looking for a partner	Voyeurism
2) Interacting with a partner (pre-tactile)	Exhibitionism, telephone scatologia
3) Tactile interaction with a partner	Frotteurism[1], toucherism[2]
4) Sexual intercourse	Rape

Note: [1]Sexual arousal resulting from touching strangers, usually on their genitals, bottom or breasts, with various parts of the offender's body. Offences are normally committed in busy public places like public transport, because they create opportunities to be in close contact with victims. Normally, frotteurs will rub themselves on the victim.
[2]Sexual arousal from touching strangers in sexual places, using their hands, touchers are likely to grab breasts and buttocks and them run away.
Source: Freund (1990).

This theory takes account of the empirical research that has observed that this cluster of paraphilias is highly co-morbid (e.g. Lang et al., 1987) and the desired target person or victim is a stranger, whereas most other paraphilias involve individuals known to the person. It also fits nicely with the research that finds exhibitionists commonly report the desire for their victims to want to have intercourse with them (Bader et al., 2008). However, it does not explain why other paraphilias, such as sadomasochism and transvestism (Kafka and Prentky, 1992; Långström and Seto, 2006) have also been found to co-occur with these disorders. On the surface, neither of these disorders would seem to fit within the courtship process. However, Lang et al. (1987) found in their sample of cross-dressing exhibitionists that part of the motivation for cross-dressing involved a need to be admired (by either males or females), suggesting that transvestism may serve the same function as exhibitionism for some. However, they also found that a motivator for cross-dressing for the majority was due to a fetish desire (becoming aroused by the clothing). The courtship disorder model proposed by Freund does not account for this.

There are mixed results in the few empirical investigations of this model. Freund and Seto (1998) found that rapists who had also exposed were more likely to commit other offences relevant to courtship disorder than non-exposing rapists. They therefore suggest that exposing could be used as a behavioural marker to indicate 'rape proneness'. Lang et al. (1987) found a co-occurrence of the sexual behaviours identified in courtship disorder (exhibitionism, voyeurism, frotteurism and rape) only in violent exhibitionists, leading them to suggest that courtship disorder applies specifically to violent exhibitionists. This conclusion needs further testing. They instead suggest that narcissism (a personality trait where the individual desires others to admire them) is a better explanation of non-contact sexual offending, including voyeurism. However, Lang et al. (1987) conclude this on the basis that many of their sample reported to wanting the victims to be pleased and impressed by them exposing, and only just over half would actually have intercourse with the victim if she offered it. They did not attempt to measure any other traits of narcissism in their sample or further investigate the concept. There is not enough convincing evidence to support the assumption that wanting to please or impress a victim adequately reflects narcissism.

Langevin and Lang (1987) suggest that there is more evidence to suggest a difference between the courtship disorders than similarities, although they acknowledge greater similarity between exhibitionism and voyeurism.

One thing this theory doesn't really explain is *how* offenders become distorted in the courtship cycle. It does not identify the mechanisms that result in an offender being unable to form relationships pro-socially, or those that cause the offender to be become focused on a distorted aspect of the courtship process. One defining attribute of a 'good' theory is its ability to suggest the mechanisms underlying the behaviour (Ward and Seigert, 2002). Morin and Levenson (2008) have criticised this theory as being too difficult to test empirically, partly because it doesn't specify mechanisms. There is research to suggest that exhibitionists do experience problems with social sexual competence (Longo and Groth, 1983); however, these findings could equally be explained by more established and testable theories such as attachment theory (Ward et al., 1995).

B14.3. Biological theory

There are some general theories of sexual offending that aim to explain all sexually abusive behaviour and can be used to explain non-contact sexual offending. The first of these is the monoamine hypothesis. Monoamine neurotransmitters are responsible for the electrical communication in the brain and there are thought to be millions of neurotransmitters, but only a few have been identified and studied. It is widely recognised that neurotransmitters are critical in all behaviour but relativity little is known about their specific roles, although one neurotransmitter can be responsible for multiple functions. Neurotransmitters implicated in sexual and aggressive behaviour are thought to be relevant to sexual offending and, in particular, the neurotransmitter serotonin (5HT) has been implicated. Amongst other things, 5HT acts as an inhibitor on arousal and mood. Therefore when there are lower levels of 5HT, behaviours that might normally be inhibited, such as aggressive ones, are not. A number of studies have found an association between low 5HT and violent behaviour (see Raine, 1993, for a review). Kafka (1997) suggests that the same applies to sexual behaviour, and lower levels of 5HT result in an increase in sexual behaviour. This is relevant to understanding exhibitionism and voyeurism in particular, because these offenders have been observed to respond positively to SSRI medication, which increases levels of 5HT. Abouesh and Clayton (1999) propose that exhibitionism and voyeurism could be seen as being a manifestation of obsessive compulsive disorder (OCD). The compulsive urges described by many of these offenders parallel those described by individuals with OCD (see Chapter 12 for more on compulsive behaviour), and OCD is thought to occur in part due to lower levels of 5HT failing to inhibit the compulsive behaviour. While this theory has good clinical utility because it offers a clear treatment pathway (SSRIs), it currently lacks empirical evidence.

B14.4. Love map

A love map is a representation of what a person is sexually attracted to. It is like a blueprint or template for sexual attraction and behaviour, which provides an outline of ideal partner characteristics and the process involved in initiating and maintaining a relationship. The term love map was first used by John Money (1986), who developed the concept drawing on animal studies. Each individual has their own love map, which will reflect their own specific interests in a partner (physical characteristics, personality characteristics and lifestyle characteristics) as well as a set of expectations and beliefs about the course of sexual contact (such as frequency, type) and relationships. The contents of a love map will also reflect the social context of the individual, perhaps by incorporating elements of social and cultural norms. Successful relationships normally result when two people have compatible love maps. Partners who have incompatible love maps are more likely to have an unsuccessful relationship, since there will be disagreement on some aspects of sex and relationships.

Money believes that love maps can become 'vandalised'. This is normally the result of an inappropriate or unhealthy sexual experience in early life, when the developing brain is forming all blueprints about the world, including the love map. Such an experience is likely to be incorporated into the love map, resulting in development of an 'atypical' love map. Atypical love maps will include paraphilic love maps, including those relating to non-contact sexual offending. We know from modern neurobiological research (Creeden, 2009) that new neural pathways can be stimulated and formed in adults, which suggests that love maps are not rigid and can be altered. This allows for the possibility of treatment helping those with paraphilic love maps.

B14.5. Conditioning theory

Laws and Marshall (1990) draw on learning theory and the research that says that human behaviours, including our sexual interests, are learned processes. There are two types of learning (or conditioning) processes: classical and operant conditioning. These two processes can operate independently, or together.

Based on these principles, Laws and Marshall propose that sexual interests are learnt through a series of associations, which are reinforced through masturbation and tend to go unpunished in the early stages because the behaviour is secret. They give a very interesting account of how a rapist acquires a sexual interest in violence through this process (see Laws and Marshall, 1990). This theory is relevant to understanding how all types of sexually abusive interests might develop, but it is especially applicable to non-contact sexual offences. Many accounts by voyeurs say that their sexual interest began because they accidentally saw another person in the process of undressing, having sex and so forth. and that they found this arousing. This is the first stage of classical conditioning, since they are *associating* voyeuristic behaviour with a positive feeling. This is then reinforced further by masturbation to these thoughts and ejaculation, and by seeking out further opportunities to watch others and continuing to masturbate. This interest is further reinforced by negative reinforcement, because enjoyment of non-voyeuristic fantasies becomes weaker (if it even existed), therefore producing an increase in voyeuristic fantasy. The behaviour may not be subject to punishment as this tends to be secret and, as we have already seen elsewhere in this chapter, the chances of actually getting caught and convicted are low. Laws and Marshall also point out that 'normal' or non-deviant sexual behaviours may be punished by caregivers, thereby reducing the enjoyment of healthy sexual behaviour. Committing a non-contact sexual offence may not always produce a rewarding experience for the offender; for example, a voyeur may not find someone to watch or an exhibitionist may not get the desired response from a victim. However, according to learning theory, this is more reinforcing and is known as intermittent reinforcement. Intermittent reinforcement, where reinforcement does not occur every time but every now and then, is the most powerful type of reinforcer. This is why gambling is so addictive.

This theory helps to explain why many non-contact sexual offences tend to be high-frequency, as many report their offending to feel like an addiction or compulsion. The research that shows that because non-contact sexual offenders respond positively to behavioural reconditioning treatment, this would support the utility of this theory. As already noted in this chapter, techniques that try to modify sexual interests using conditioning theory have seen success, which suggests that these interests were learnt. This theory relies heavily on the belief that the offending behaviour is motivated purely on the basis of deviant interests. This would explain the research findings that some non-contact offenders don't wish for contact with their victims (e.g. they are not offending as an attempt to have a relationship).

B14.6. Pathways model

The theories discussed so far represent single-factor theories. This means that they suggest a single factor as being responsible for explaining why an individual sexually offends. For obvious reasons, their theories can be limiting, and it is evident from the research that single-factor theories cannot account for all sexual offending. Therefore a theory of sexual offending that explains the different reasons why individuals commit sexual offences is preferable. In an attempt to produce a comprehensive theory of this nature, Ward and Seigert (2002) combine aspects from other theories to produce a model of multiple pathways to offending, these pathways representing psychological vulnerabilities to sexual offending, which can be triggered by situational variables (e.g. victim access, relationship breakdown). They propose that there are five pathways, which might lead men to sexually offend (See Table 14.2).

One strength of this model is that it accepts that sexual offenders will have different underlying motivations for offending, and it recognises the varied research findings that reflect this. This theory accepts that multiple factors will influence a person to develop psychological vulnerabilities to offend. Although this

Table 14.2 *Pathways to sexual offending*

Pathway	Characteristic
1. Multiple dysfunctional mechanism	Have a combination of any of the other four problems but generally will have deviant sexual scripts
2. Deviant sexual scripts	Sexual interest in the offending behaviour
3. Intimacy deficits	Difficulties achieving and maintaining emotional intimacy with an adult
4. Emotional dysregulation	Poor emotional management
5. Antisocial cognitions	Attitudes that support offending

Source: Ward and Seigert (2002).

model was developed in order to explain child abusers (see Chapter 9), it is arguably applicable to all types of sexual offending. Research with non-contact sexual offenders shows that a range of motivations exist which could be mapped onto this model. For example, we have already discussed the different theories that suggest that deviant sexual interests (conditioning theory), intimacy problems (courtship disorder) and problems controlling impulses (monoamine hypothesis) are relevant to non-contact sexual offenders. Compared with contact sexual offences such as rape and child abuse, there is relatively little research into the role of antisocial cognitions in non-contact sexual offending, and so this is certainly an area where further research is needed.

This theory represents probably the most useful model on which to understand sexual offending. It has also helped practitioners to structure assessment and treatment approaches because, once a pathway has been identified, risk management strategies relating to that pathway can be put in place.

PART C: Further information

C14.1. Organisations to contact for information and voluntary work

There are no organisations that specialise in the treatment of paraphilias. The websites below are two organisations for the treatment of all types of sexual abusers. Both websites offer information on research, employment and training. These are good websites for accessing up-to-date research and information and for anyone wishing to work in this field.

Association for the Treatment of Sexual Abusers: http://www.atsa.com/htm.
National Organisation for the Treatment of Abusers: http://www.nota.co.uk/htm.

Circles of Support and Accountability are a UK-based charity committed to reducing sexual offending by supporting sexual offenders. Volunteers are specially trained to work with sexual offenders and support their reintegration into the community. Their website provides information about how to become involved as a volunteer.

Circles of Support: http://www.circles-uk.org.uk/htm.

The Lucy Faithfull Foundation is a UK Charity that aims to reduce the sexual abuse of children through research and treatment of abusers. Their website has information on research and training opportunities.

The Lucy Faithfull Foundation: http://lucyfaithfull.org.

C14.2. Further reading

Laws, D.R. and O'Donahue, W. (Eds.) (2008) *Sexual Deviance Theory, Assessment, and Treatment* (2nd edn) New York: Guilford.

This is a great book that provides comprehensive reviews of the paraphilias, online sex offending and sexual deviance in females. There are two chapters on each sexual behaviour, and each chapter covers psychopathology and theory, as well as assessment and treatment. This book is probably one of the best sources for understanding the range of sexual deviations.

CONCLUSION

BELINDA WINDER AND PHILIP BANYARD

So, you're thinking about becoming a forensic psychologist? It's worth thinking about what this will involve and what you have to do. In this chapter we will look at the sorts of things that forensic psychologists do, the key skills they need and ethical dilemmas they have to deal with. First, though, we will have a look at how forensic psychology is (mis)represented in the media and how the general public often have an unrealistic expectation of what psychologists can achieve.

Forensic psychology in the public imagination

I blame Sherlock Holmes. Since Arthur Conan Doyle created the great detective we have clung to the idea that a very observant person will be able to read clues in behaviour so well that they will be able to spot the murderer and second-guess their next move. This image of the super-analyst is a staple part of popular fiction and appears in crime stories and medical dramas. And then there is the popular image of Sigmund Freud (and all subsequent psychotherapists) as someone who could read into the mind and motives of his patients in a forensic way.

The most watched TV show in the world is the US medical drama *House*, in which the lead character is able, on the smallest piece of evidence, to infer from someone's behaviour what the state of their relationships are as well as the state of their body parts. Sadly, the truth is that this sort of analysis of behaviour is not possible. For a start, human behaviour is less predictable than presented in these shows, and the massive individual differences between us means that it is very difficult to observe the behaviour of a stranger and be able to read their intentions.

Fiction is one thing but professional practice is another. We all like a good story and it would be churlish to criticise authors for creating unrealistic fictional characters. Their task is write a story that we want to read or watch, not to represent the world as it is. Professional psychologists on the other hand have a duty, enshrined in their professional code, not to misrepresent their skills.

One aspect of the work of forensic psychology that has captured the public imagination is offender profiling, where there is an attempt to create a picture of the person responsible for a crime. On TV this was captured in the series *Cracker*, and if you search the Internet you will find a number of professionals prepared to refer to themselves as 'the real Cracker'. The problem here, as David Wilson points out in his chapter on murder, is that the profilers have had some spectacular failures and very few real successes. The excessive expectations of profiling as portrayed in the media are on a level with asking a clairvoyant to find a murderer or a medium to talk to the (dead) murder victim to find out 'whodunnit'. This is not to say that profiling is unable to provide any helpful information – far from it. The work of David Canter, for example, has developed techniques for plotting the behavioural patterns of serial offenders that have been used to identify possible suspects.

The reality of forensic psychology is much less racy than we are led to believe by television drama but, to our minds, much more interesting. We'll go on in the next section to look at some examples of what forensic psychologists do.

What forensic psychologists do

Forensic psychologists deal with psychological aspects of legal processes; for example, their role might be to understand psychological problems associated with offending behaviour; to plan, conduct or evaluate the treatment and rehabilitation of offenders; to apply theory to the detection and investigation of criminal conduct; or to help with crime prevention measures. They work in prisons, secure hospitals, court settings, with the police and probation services, health and social services, and at universities and as private consultants.

The work of forensic psychologists can be broken down into five main areas: *assessment, formulation, intervention, evaluation/research* and *communication*. As a forensic psychologist you may find yourself doing any or all of these, so let us consider what each entails.

1. *Assessment; analysing individuals*
    As a forensic psychologist your job may be to assess individuals in a range of forensic settings (e.g. in prison, the courts, in a secure hospital, in police stations). You may use psychometric tests, interviews and observations to try to understand what risk they present to others, why they have developed in a particular way that may bring them to the attention of the criminal justice system and what treatment needs such individuals have.

2. *Formulation; describing an individual client's problems or needs*
    Formulation is where the forensic psychologist puts together all the information they have obtained in the assessment stage (e.g. data from their interviews, observations and psychometric tests) and integrates this with any other information they have about their client, together with relevant information from psychology and psychological research generally. The forensic psychologist will collate and combine all this information to come up with a framework or individualised theory which, in their opinion, best represents that individual client's problems or needs. This corresponds to a diagnosis but is more individual than the medical diagnosis and is not looking for a label to give someone.

3. *Intervention; setting things in motion to help the client*

   Forensic psychologists intervene to produce change in their client or improve interactions with others, generally through treatment (e.g. anger treatment programmes for violent offenders). However, it may also include other interventions, such as the training of others or developing your own skills through supervision or training. In such cases, the need for these interventions will have been identified through the psychologist's assessment of self or others (e.g. 'I do not know what is expected of me as an expert witness') and formulation ('I therefore need training from the British Psychological Society in how to prepare for Court'), leading to an intervention such as going on a training course to help improve your skills as an expert witness. Many of the interventions that forensic psychologists do are concerned with the treatment of offenders, although, not all are and there are many other avenues we need to consider, such as looking at our skills as individual practitioners and improving forensic environments for others (e.g. thinking about how we can best help vulnerable witnesses in court).

4. *Evaluation and research; analysing and reflecting on what we are doing and checking to see whether it works*

   Research includes the ongoing evaluation of assessment, formulation and intervention and includes studying the validity and reliable of psychometric tests – for example, measuring the effectiveness of treatment programmes we offer to offenders, and measuring the changes in offenders by assessing how far the treatment 'worked' for this individual offender and whether they now present a reduced risk to the public?

5. *Communication*

   Forensic psychologists, not surprisingly, find that effective communication skills are an essential part of their job. As a forensic psychologist, you will be communicating with many different individuals, some of whom will have an intellectual disabilities, learning disabilities or mental illnesses. You will need to be able to communicate well with co-workers and also with members of the court; for example, you may be required to give evidence in an oral hearing (where an offender is seeking an appeal on a parole refusal) or as an expert witness in the Crown Court. Forensic psychologists need to be able to communicate effectively with individuals, and groups, across a range of both formal and informal settings and they may also need to disseminate research findings more widely to peers and perhaps to society generally via the media.

Ethical dilemmas for forensic psychologists

The British Psychological Society (BPS) has published a set of ethical principles with guidance for how psychologists should interpret these. The most recent revision of the principles was published by the BPS in 2009, and you can read them in full on their website (http://www.bps.org.uk/the-society/code-of-conduct). There are also numerous texts that explore the general ethical issues that psychologists face if you want to explore these ideas further (e.g. Banyard & Flanagan, 2011).

The BPS principles are designed not just for research psychologists but also for practising psychologists such as forensic psychologists. The *BPS Code of Ethics and Conduct* (BPS, 2009) is a relatively brief document (about 30 pages) and explains how the code was developed, as well as suggesting how ethical decisions should be taken.

The Code is based on four ethical principles: *respect, competence, responsibility* and *integrity*. Each of these principles is accompanied by details of the standards that are expected of UK psychologists. We will go through the ethical principles in turn and look at how they affect the behaviour of forensic psychologists.

1. *Respect*

   Everyone expects a little bit of respect, but it means different things to different people. The UK government has a Respect Agenda, which is concerned with encouraging people to be nice to each other and behave as good citizens. The Football Association also has a Respect Campaign as it tries to get players, coaching staff and spectators to behave well towards referees, and there is even a political party called Respect. Maybe the term 'respect' has been devalued by its overuse, but in the context of the BPS Code it has a very clear meaning.

   First, there are issues of *general respect* for a person's individuality, and it is important that psychologists do not show any prejudice on the basis or age, gender, disability, ethnicity, religion and so on. They should also respect the knowledge and expertise of others.

   Secondly, there are issues of *privacy and confidentiality*. It is important to keep records of what you do as a psychologist, but these records need to be secure so that personal information can not be disclosed to anyone else. Any disclosure needs to be agreed with the person who gave the information or data. This sounds very clear-cut, but there are some puzzles around this issue as you have to consider what you would do if someone disclosed a crime to you or suicidal thoughts. Should you tell someone?

   Thirdly, there are issues of *informed consent* and in any work with people, as a forensic psychologist it is important that the clients are aware of the procedures they are letting themselves in for and make an informed choice to proceed.

   Finally, there are issues of *self-determination*, meaning that it is important that the client stays in control of their situation, which is particularly difficult with people sent to forensic psychologists by the courts.

2. *Competence*

   There is more to ethics than just rights and wrongs – there are also issues about how well you do your work. For example, it is necessary for forensic psychologists to be *aware of professional ethics*: ignorance is not an excuse for making ethical mistakes, and in fact is a mistake in itself. *Making ethical decisions* is more difficult than it seems and it is important to be careful and thoughtful when making those decisions. This involves taking responsibility for any decisions that are made, consulting ethical codes and getting colleagues to look over your decisions and comment on them. It is also important to *recognise the limits of your competence* and acknowledge what you don't know as well as what you do. It is also important to be able to *reflect on your own competence* and make the decision to seek help and stop working if your work is being affected by changes to your physical or mental health. This is a tough call to make.

3. *Responsibility*

   Psychologists have responsibilities to clients, the general public and to their profession. The last thing you want to hear is someone saying, 'You've let your clients, down, you've let your profession down, but most of all you've let yourself down.' Balancing out the various demands is not an easy call. For example, most psychiatric medication has harmful side effects and some of these are permanent. The medications that are commonly used to reduce the symptoms of psychosis can bring on the symptoms of Parkinson's disease or the distressing condition of tardive diskinesia, where the patient develops permanent embarrassing facial movements. To protect the patient from harm you might recommend that they do not take the medication, but that might result in an increase in their symptoms and put other people at risk from their disturbed behaviour.

4. *Integrity*

   Being honest and open about things is something that many of us aspire to do but is hard to achieve. Psychologists need to *honest and accurate* about their training and expertise, and our comment about the excessive claims of profilers falls into this category. A further issue concerns avoiding exploitation and conflicts of interest. The central issue is one of power – and the psychologist will have more power than the other person in the relationship. *Maintaining personal boundaries* can be problematic, but the code of practice is very strong in stating that psychologists should 'refrain from engaging in any form of sexual or romantic relationship with persons to whom they are providing professional services, or to whom they owe a continuing duty of care, or with whom they have a relationship of trust. This might include a former patient, a student or trainee, or a junior staff member' (BPS, 2009, p. 22). See Hamilton (2010) for research in this area.

Finally, there is the issue of addressing ethical misconduct and, if confronted about ethical behaviour, it is expected that psychologists will cooperate with any enquiry in a positive way. Also, it is expected that, regardless of friendship or other constraints, a psychologists will report behaviour of colleagues they believe to be in conflict with the ethical code. This again is a tough one because it is one of the basic rules of human interaction not to snitch, but it is not acceptable simply to turn a blind eye to situations you know are wrong.

OK – so we've looked at what forensic psychologists do, and considered the code of conduct and ethics that they work to; we'll now go on to look briefly at how you can become a forensic psychologist.

How do you become a forensic psychologist?

In order to be able to use the protected title of Registered Forensic Psychologist, you will typically need to gain the following qualifications:

1. You should have Graduate Basis for Chartered Membership (GBC) with the British Psychological Society (BPS). This is obtained by either gaining an undergraduate psychology degree that is accredited by the BPS or completing a BPS accredited conversion course.

2. You will then need to undertake a BPS accredited MSc in forensic psychology, such as the one we offer here at Nottingham Trent University (this will constitute stage 1 of your training in forensic psychology on submission of application to the BPS – see the BPS website for current fees and procedures to have your qualifications recognised by the BPS).

3. You will need to complete stage 2 of the BPS' qualification in forensic psychology. This is typically carried out whilst working as a trainee psychologist in the prison service or another forensic setting, and most people should be able to access funding from their employers, whilst also receiving a salary. Completion of stage 2 takes a minimum of 2 years of supervised practice and involves four core roles where the trainee is expected to prove both their competence and their capacity for reflection (the latter by completion of a reflective practice diary that is ongoing through their stage 2 work). The four core roles are *interventions, research, communicating with other professionals* and *training*. The student is required to provide two examples of each key role, and this is submitted together with their reflective practice diary, to the BPS assessors. Some universities offer a Doctorate programme in forensic psychology instead of stage 2. After completion, this qualification should make you eligible to become a Chartered member of the Society.

4. On completion of stage 2, you will be a Chartered member of the BPS, and you will also need to register with the Health Professions Council so that you can use the special title of 'Registered Forensic Psychologist'.

What can I do now?

If you are still interested in forensic psychology, and you have made it to this final paragraph, then there is something else you should do. As a forensic psychologist you will need to become very aware of what pushes your buttons – what makes you upset or angry (or happy)? The phrase 'Know Thyself' was written above the Temple of Apollo in Delphi, in Ancient Greece, and in our opinion it captures perfectly the first step that a forensic psychologist, a reflective practitioner, should aim for. Know thyself so you can better understand and help and work objectively with others. And why not start by immersing yourself in a few good books and films and seeing which characters you sympathise with, and thinking about why you have those preferences?

Final word

We hope that you have enjoyed this book and found it helpful in your studies. We have tried to give a varied and wide-ranging account of how forensic psychology explains and responds to crime in the UK. Good luck with your studies.

REFERENCES

Abel, G. & Harlow, N. (2001). *The Stop Child Molestation Book*. Philadelphia, PA: Xlibris.

Abel, G. G. & Rouleau, J. L. (1990). The nature and extent of sexual assault. In Marshall, W. L, Laws, D. R., and Barbaree, H. E. (Eds.), *Handbook of Sexual Assault: Issues, Theories and Treatment of the Offender*. Plenum Press, New York.

Abel, G. G., Becker, J. V. & Cunningham-Rathner, J. (1984). Complications, consent, and cognitions in sex between children and adults. *International Journal of Law and Psychiatry*, 7, 89–103.

Abel, G. G., Becker, J. V., Cunningham-Rathner, J., Mittelman, M. & Rouleau, J. L. (1988). Multiple paraphilic diagnoses among sex offenders. *Bulletin of the American Academy of Psychiatry and Law*, 16, 153–168.

Abelson, E. S. (1989). The invention of kleptomania. *Signs: Journal of Women in Culture and Society*, 15 (1), 123–143.

Abelson, R. P. (1981). Psychological status of the script concept. *American Psychologist*, 36, 715–729.

Abouesh, A. & Clayton, A. (1999). Compulsive voyeurism and exhibitionism: A clinical response to paroxetine. *Archives of Sexual Behaviour*, 28 (1), 23–30.

Aboujaoude, E., Gamel, N. & Koran, L. M. (2004). Overview of kleptomania and phenomenological description of 40 patients. *Primary Care Companion, Journal of Clinical Psychiatry*, 6 (6), 244–247.

Abrams, K. M. & Robinson, G. E. (2002). Occupational effects of stalking. *Canadian Journal of Psychiatry*, 47, 468–472.

ACPO (1999). *Murder Investigation Manual*. London: ACPO (unpublished).

Adams-Curtis, L. E. & Forbes, G. B. (2004). College women's experiences of sexual coercion: A review of cultural, perpetrator, victim and situational variables. *Trauma, Violence & Neglect*, 5 (2), 91–122.

Adinkrah, M. (1999). Spousal homicides in Fiji. *Homicide Studies*, 3, 215–240.

Agnew, Robert (1992). A general strain theory of crime and delinquency. In *Criminological Theory: Past to Present (Essential Readings)* (pp. 151–160). Los Angeles: Roxbury.

Aizer, A., Lowengrub, K. & Dannon, P. N. (2004). Kleptomania after head trauma: Two case reports and the combination treatment strategies. *Clinical Neuropharmacology*, 27 (5), 211–215.

Ainsworth, M. D. (1989). Attachment beyond infancy. *American Psychologist*, 44, 709–716.

Ainsworth, P. B. (2000). *Psychology and Crime: Myths and Reality*. Harlow: Pearson.

Akdeniz, Y. (2006). Internet pornography. Paper presented at the *Forensic Psychology and Crime Conference, the Forensic Psychology Group/British Psychological Society (NW Branch)*, Manchester Metropolitan University, 4 February 2006.

Akers, R. L. (1990). Rational choice, deterrence, and social learning theory in criminology: The path not taken. *The Journal of Criminal Law and Criminology*, 81, 653–676.

Albrecht, W. S., Wernz, G. W. & Williams, T. L. (1995). *Fraud – Bringing Light to the Dark Side of Business*. New York: McGraw-Hill.

Alexander, M. (1999). Sexual offender treatment efficacy revisited. *Sexual Abuse: A Journal of Research and Treatment*, 11, 101–116.

Alford, G., Webster, J. & Sanders, S. (1980). Covert aversion of two interrelated deviant sexual practices: Obscene phone calling and exhibitionism. A single case analysis. *Behaviour Therapy*, 11, 15–25.

Allen, C. (2005). The link between heroin, crack-cocaine and crime. *British Journal of Criminology*, 45, 355–372.

Almansi, R. J. (1979). Scopophilia and object loss. *The Psychoanalytic Quarterly*, XLVIII (4) 601–609.

American Psychiatric Association (APA) (1980). *Diagnostic and Statistical Manual of Mental Disorders, Third Edition (DSM-III)*. Washington, DC: Author.

American Psychiatric Association (APA) (1994). *Diagnostic and Statistical Manual of Mental Disorders, Fourth Edition (DSM-IV)*. Washington, DC: Author.

American Psychiatric Association (APA) (2000). *Diagnostic and Statistical Manual of Mental Disorders (4th ed.)* – Text Revision. Washington, DC: Author.

Amnesty International (2005). *Sexual Assault Research: Summary Report*. Available at http://www.amnesty.org.uk/news_details.asp?NewsID=16618, accessed on 13 January, 2010.

Anderson, C. A. & Bushman, B. J. (2001). Effects of violent video games on aggressive behavior, aggressive cognition, aggressive affect, physiological arousal, and prosocial behavior: A meta-analytic review of the scientific literature. *Psychological Science*, 12, 353–359.

Anderson, C. A. & Bushman, B. J. (2002). Human aggression. *Annual Review of Psychology*, 53, 27–51.

Anderson, C. A. & Gentile, D. A. (2008). Media violence, aggression, and public policy. In E. Borgida & S. Fiske (Eds.), *Beyond Common Sense: Psychological Science in the Courtroom* (pp. 281–300). Malden, MA: Blackwell.

Anderson, C. A. & Huesmann, L. R. (2003). Human aggression: A social-cognitive view. In M. A. Hogg & J. Cooper (Eds.), *The Sage Handbook of Social Psychology* (pp. 296–323). Thousand Oaks, CA: Sage.

Anderson, C. A., Anderson, K. B. & Deuser, W. E. (1996). Examining an affective aggression framework: Weapon and temperature effects on aggressive thoughts, affect, and attitudes. *Personality and Social Psychology Bulletin*, 22, 366–376.

Anderson, C. A., Deuser, W. E. & DeNeve, K. (1995). Hot temperatures, hostile affect, hostile cognition, and arousal: Tests of a general model of affective aggression. *Personality and Social Psychology Bulletin*, 21, 434–448.

Anderson, C. A., Gentile, D. A. & Buckley, K. E. (2007). *Violent Video Game Effects on Children and Adolescents: Theory, Research, and Public Policy*. Oxford: Oxford University Press.

Anderson, C.A., Berkowitz, L., Donnerstein, E., Huesmann, R.L., Johnson, J., Linz, D., Malamuth, N. & Wartella, E. (2003). The influence of media violence on youth. *Psychological Science in the Public Interest*, 4, 81–110.

Andrews, D. A. & Bonta, J. (2007). *The Psychology of Criminal Conduct*, fourth edition. Cincinnati, OH: Anderson.

Arata, C. M. (1998). To tell or not to tell: Current functioning of child sexual abuse survivors who disclosed their victimization. *Child Maltreatment: Journal of the American Professional Society on the Abuse of Children, 3,* 63–71.

Archbold (2010). *Criminal Pleading Evidence & Practice.* London: Thompson Reuters.

Archer, J. (2002). Sex differences in physically aggressive acts between heterosexual partners: A meta-analytic review. *Aggression and Violent Behavior, 7,* 313–351.

Archer, J. (2004). Sex differences in aggression in real-world settings: A meta-analytic review. *Review of General Psychology, 8,* 291–322.

Archer, J. (2006). Cross-cultural differences in physical aggression between partners: A social-structural analysis. *Personality and Social Psychology Review, 10,* 133–153.

Archer, J. & Haigh, A. M. (1997). Do beliefs about aggressive feelings and actions predict reported levels of aggression? *British Journal of Social Psychology, 36,* 83–105.

Arson Prevention Bureau (APB) (1998). *Accommodating Arsonists in the Community: Guidance for Hostel Mangers.* London: Arson Prevention Bureau.

Arson Prevention Bureau (APB) (2003). Detecting and convicting the arsonist: Lessons from the United States. An Arson Prevention Bureau Research Paper. Available at www.arsonpreventionbureau.org.uk, accessed on 30 November 2011.

Arson Prevention Bureau (APB) (2010). Statistics – Key stats and long-term trends in arson. Available at www.arsonpreventionbureau.org.uk/view/Document.aspx?Document_ID=596, accessed on 4 November 2010.

Ashton, J., Brown, I., Senior, B. & Pease, K. (1998). Repeat victimization: Offender accounts. *International Journal of Risk, Security and Crime Prevention, 3,* 269–279.

Association of Certified Fraud Examiners [online] *Report to the Nations 2010.* Available at acfe.com, accessed on 7 September 2010.

Asthana, A. & Doward, J. (2010). Prisons minister says criminals could cut jail sentences by saying 'sorry'. *The Observer,* Sunday, 25 July. Available at http://www.guardian.co.uk/society/2010/jul/25/criminals-should-say-sorry, accessed on 30 November 2011.

Auburn, T. (2005). Narrative reflexivity as a repair device for discounting cognitive distortions in sex offender treatment. *Discourse and Society, 16,* 697–718.

AuCoin, K. (2005). Children and youth as victims of violent crime. *Juristat,* 25 (1) (Statistics Canada Catalogue no. 85-002-X). http://www.statcan.gc.ca/bsolc/olc-cel/olc-cel?catno=85-002-XIE2005001806&lang=eng, accessed 12 Feb 2012.

Australian Institute of Criminology (2004). *The Cost of Bushfires.* Bush-FIRE Arson Bulletin No. 2, Canberra.

Bader, S. M., Schoeneman-Morris, K. A., Scalora, M. & Casady, T. K. (2008). Exhibitionism: Findings from a midwestern police contact sample. *International Journal of Offender Therapy and Comparative Criminology, 52,* 270.

Balsam, R. H. (2008). Women showing off: Notes on female exhibitionism. *Journal of American Psychoanalytical Association, 56,* 99.

Bandura, A. (1973). *Aggression: A Social Learning Theory Analysis.* Englewood Cliffs, NJ: Prentice-Hall.

Bandura, A. (1983). Psychological mechanisms of aggression. In R. G. Geen and E. I. Donnerstein (Eds.), *Aggression: Theoretical and Empirical Reviews* (Vol. 1, pp. 1–40). New York: Academic Press.

Bandura, A. (1999). Moral disengagement in the perpetration of inhumanities. *Personality and Social Psychology Review* (Special Issue on Evil and Violence), 3, 193–209.

Bandura, A., Barbaranelli, C., Caprara, G.V. & Pastorelli, C. (1996). Mechanisms of moral disengagement in the exercise of moral agency. *Journal of Personality and Social Psychology*, 71, 364–374.

Bandura, A., Ross, D. & Ross, S. A. (1961). Transmission of aggressions through imitation of aggressive models. *Journal of Abnormal and Social Psychology*, 63, 575–582.

Banyard, P. & Flanagan, C. (2011) *Ethical Issues in Psychology*. London: Routledge.

Barbaree, H. E. & Marshall, W. L. (1989). Treatment of the sexual offender. In: R.M. Wettstein (Ed.), *Treatment of the Mentally Disordered Offender*. New York: Guilford Press.

Barnes, P. & Sharp, D. (1999). *The Fraud Survey – 1998*. Leicester: Association of Certified Fraud Examiners.

Baron, R. A. & Richardson, D. A. (1994). *Human Aggression*. New York: Plenum Press.

Bartol, C. R. & Bartol, A. M. (2005). *Criminal Behavior: A Psychosocial Approach*. Upper Saddle River, NJ: Pearson.

Basile, K. C., Swahn, M. H., Chen, J. & Saltzman, L. E. (2006). Stalking in the United States: Recent national prevalence estimates. *American Journal of Preventative Medicine*, 31, 173–175.

Bates, A. & Metcalf, C. (2007). A psychometric comparison of Internet and non-Internet sex offenders from a community treatment sample. *Journal of Sexual Aggression*, 13 (1), 11 –20.

Baum, K., Catalano, S., Rand, M. & Rose, K. (2009). Stalking victimization in the United States (NCJ 224527) Washington, DC: U.S. Department of Justice, Bureau of Justice Statistics. Available at from http://www.ovw.usdoj.gov/docs/stalking-victimization.pdf, accessed on 29 May 2010.

Baylé, F, J., Caci, H., Millet, B., Richa, S. & Olié, J, P. (2003). Psychopathology and comorbidity of psychiatric disorders in patients with kleptomania. *American Journal of Psychiatry*; 160, 1509–1513.

BBC (2009). *Records of Rape Crime 'distorted'*. Available at http://news.bbc.co.uk/1/hi/uk/8266014.stm, accessed on 14 January 2010.

BBC News (2007). Police identify 169 London gangs. BBC website. Available at http://news.bbc.co.uk/1/hi/england/london/6383933.stm, accessed on November 2010.

Bean, P. (2008). *Drugs and Crime*. Devon: Willan Publishing.

Bean, P. T. & Wilkinson, C. K. (1988). Drug taking, crime and the illicit supply system. *British Journal of Addiction*, 83, 533–539.

Beauregard, E. & LeClerc, B. (2007). An application of the rational choice approach to the offending process of sex offenders: A closer look at the decision-making. *Sexual Abuse: A Journal of Research and Treatment*, 19 (2), 115–133.

Beck, A. T. (1999). *Prisoners of Hate: The Cognitive Basis of Anger, Hostitlity and Violence*. New York: HarperCollins.

Beech, A. R., Elliott, I. A., Birgden, A. & Findlater, D. (2008). The Internet and child sexual offending: A criminological review. *Aggression and Violent Behavior*, 13, 216–228.

Bell, D. (2006). Bodies, Technologies, Spaces: On 'Dogging'. *Sexualities*, 9, 387.

Bendixen, M., Endresen, I. M. & Olweus, D. (2006). Joining and leaving gangs: Selection and Facilitation Effects on Self Reported Antisocial Behaviour in Early Adolescence. *European Journal of Criminology*, 3, 85–114.

Bennett, T. (1995). Identifying, explaining and targeting burglary hot spots. *European Journal of Criminal Policy and Research*, 13, 113–123.

Bennett, T. & Holloway, K. (2004). Gang membership, drugs and crime in the UK. *British Journal of Criminology*, 44, 305–323.

Bennett, T. & Holloway, K. (2005). *Understanding Drugs, Alcohol and Crime*. Berkshire: OUP.

Bennett, T. & Wright, R. (1984). *Burglars on Burglary: Prevention and the Offender*. Aldershot: Gower.

Bennett, T., Holloway, K. & Williams, T. (2001). *Findings 148 Drug Use and Offending*. London: Home Office.

Benneworth, K. (2009). Police interviews with suspected paedophiles: A discourse analysis. *Discourse & Society*, 20 (5), 555–569.

Berah, E. F. & Meyers, R.G. (1983). The Offense Records Of A Sample Of Convicted Exhibitionists. *Bulletin of the American Academy of Psychiatry and the Law*, 11, 365–369.

Berkowitz, L. (1962). *Aggression: A Social Psychological Analysis*. New York: McGraw-Hill.

Berkowitz, L. (1965). Some aspects of observed aggression. *Journal of Personality and Social Psychology*, 2, 359–369.

Berkowitz, L. (1989). Frustration-aggression hypothesis: Examination and reformulation. *Psychological Bulletin*, 106, 59–73.

Berkowitz, L. (1993). *Aggression: Its Causes, Consequences, and Control*. New York: McGraw-Hill.

Berrington, E. & Jones, H. (2002). "Reality vs. Myth: Constructions of Women's Insecurity", *Feminist Media Studies*, 2 (3), 307–323.

Berzins, L. & Trestman, R. (2004). The development and implementation of dialectical behavior therapy in forensic settings. *International Journal of Forensic Mental Health*, 3, 93–103.

Bettman, M. D. (1998). *Social Cognition, Criminal Violence, and Psychopathy*. Unpublished doctoral dissertation, Queen's University, Kingston, Canada.

Beyleveld, D. (1980). *Bibliography on General Deterrence Research*. Farnborough, UK: Saxon House.

Black, D. J. (1983). Crime as social control. *American Sociological Review*, 48, 34–45.

Blackburn, R. (1993). *The Psychology of Criminal Conduct*. Chichester: Wiley.

Blanco, C., Grant, J., Petry, N. M., Simpson, B., Alegria, A., Min Liu, S. & Hasin, D. (2008). Prevalence and Correlates of Shoplifting in the United States: Results from the National Epidemiologic Survey on Alcohol and Related Conditions (NESARC). *American Journal of Psychiatry*, 165, 905–913.

Blumstein, A. (1995). Youth violence, guns and the illicit-drug industry. In C. Block & R. Block (Eds.), *Trends, Risks, and Interventions in Lethal Violence: Proceedings of the Third Annual Spring Symposium of the Homicide Research Working Group*. Washington: U.S. Department of Justice.

Bolen, R. M. & Scannapieco, M. (1999). Prevalence of child sexual abuse: A corrective metanalysis. *The Social Service Review*, 73, 281–313.

Boles, S. M. & Miotto, K. (2003). Substance abuse and violence: A review of the literature. *Aggression and Violent Behavior*, 8, 155–174.

Boreham, R., Fuller, E., Hills, A. & Pudney, S. (2006). *The Arrestee Survey Annual Report Oct 2003 – Sept 2004*. London: Home Office.

Bowen, E.; Gilchrist, E. A. & Beech, A. R. (2005). An examination of the impact of community-based rehabilitation on the offending behaviour of male domestic violence offenders and the characteristics associated with recidivism. *Legal and Criminological Psychology*, 10, 189–209.

Bowlby, J. (1969). *Attachment and Loss. Vol. 1. Attachment*. New York: Basic Books.

Bradford, J. (1982). Arson: A clinical study. *Canadian Journal of Psychiatry*, 27, 188–192.

Bradshaw, P. & Smith, D. J. (2005). Gang Membership and Teenage Offending, Edinburgh Study of Youth Transitions and Crime. *Research Digest*. No. 8.

Brand, S. & Price, R. (2000). *The Economic and Social Costs of Crime* (Home Office Research Study 217). London: HMSO.

Brantingham, P. L. & Brantingham, P. J. (1984). *Patterns in Crime*. New York, NY: Macmillan.

Brett, A. (2004). "Kindling theory" in arson: how dangerous are fire setters? *Australian and New Zealand Journal of Psychiatry*, 8, 419–425.

British Psychological Society (BPS) (2008). *Penile Plethysmography: Guidance for Psychologists*. Leicester, UK: British Psychological Society.

British Psychological Society (BPS) (2009) *Code of Ethics and Conduct*. Leicester, UK: British Psychological Society.

British Retail Consortium (2010). RETAIL CRIME SURGES DURING RECESSION. Available at http://www.brc.org.uk/details04.asp?id=1680.

Brookman, F. (2005). Understanding Homicide, London: Sage

Brookman, F. & Maguire, M. (2003). *Reducing Homicide: A Review of the Possibilities*. RDSOnline Report 01/03. London: Home Office.

Brooks, T. (2004). The right to trial by Jury. *Journal of Applied Philosophy*, 21: 197–212.

Brownmiller, S. (1975). *Against Our Will: Men, Women and Rape*, Simon and Schuster, New York.

Buck, W., Chatterton, M. & Pease, K. (1995). *Obscene, Threatening and Other Troublesome Telephone Calls to Women in England and Wales: 1982–1992*. London. Home Office.

Budd, T. & Mattinson, J. (2000) *The Extent and Nature of Stalking: Findings from the 1998 British Crime Survey*, Home Office Research Study 210. London: HMSO.

Bullock, J. & Tilley, N. (2002). *Shootings, Gangs and Violent Incidents in Manchester: Developing a Crime Reduction Strategy*. London: Home Office.

Bullock, K. & Jones, B. (2004). *Acceptable Behaviour Contracts Addressing Antisocial Behaviour in the Borough of London* (Home Office Report 02/04). London: HMSO.

Bureau of Transport Economics (BTE) (2001) Economic Costs of Natural Disasters in Australia. Report 103, Bureau of Transport Economics, Canberra.

Burke, A., Sowerbutts, S., Blundell, B. & Sherry, M. (2001). *Child Pornography and the Internet: Policing and Treatment Issues*. Paper presented at the ANZAPPL conference, Melbourne, Australia.

Burrows, J. & Speed, M. (1996). Crime analysis: lessons from the retail sector? *Security Journal*, 7, 53–56.

Burt, M. R. (1980). Cultural myths and supports for rape. *Journal of Personality and Social Psychology*, 38, 217–230.

Bushman, B. J., Baumeister, R. F. & Stack, A. D. (1999). Catharsis, aggression, and persuasive influence: Self-fulfilling or self-defeating prophecies? *Journal of Personality and Social Psychology*, 76, 367–376.

Buss, A. H. & Perry, M. (1992). The Aggression Questionnaire. *Journal of Personality & Social Psychology*, 63, 452–459.

Buss, D. (2005). *The Murderer Next Door: Why the Mind is Designed to Kill.* New York: Penguin.

Butler, G. (1994). Commercial burglary: What burglars say. In M. L. Gill (Ed.), *Crime at Work: Studies in Security and Crime Prevention*. Leicester: Perpetuity Press.

Calder, M. (2004). The Internet: potential, problems, and pathways to hands-on sexual offending. In M. Calder (Ed.), *Child Sexual Abuse and the Internet: Tackling the New Frontier*. Lyme Regis: Russell House Publishing.

Calder, M. C. (Ed.) (1999). *Working with Young People Who Sexually Abuse: New Pieces of the Jigsaw Puzzle*. Dorset: Russell House Publishing.

Campbell, A. (2006). Sex differences in direct aggression: What are the psychological mediators? *Aggression and Violent Behavior*, 11, 237–264.

Campbell, A., Sapochnik, M. & Muncer, S. (1997). Sex differences in aggression: Does social representation mediate form of aggression? *British Journal of Psychology*, 36, 161–171.

Campbell, J. C. (2007). Prediction of homicide of and by battered women. In J.C. Campbell (Ed.), *Assessing Dangerousness: Violence by Batterers and Child Abusers* (2nd ed.). New York: Springer Publishing Company.

Campbell, J.C. (2002). Health consequences of intimate partner violence. *The Lancet*, 359, 9314, 1331–1336.

Campbell. A. & Muncer, S. (1987). Models of anger and aggression in the social talk of women and men. *Journal of the Theory for Social Behavior*, 17, 489–511.

Cannon, M. (2001). The perils of prediction. *British Journal of Psychiatry*, 179, 495–496.

Canter, D. and Fritzon, K. (1998). Differentiating arsonists: A model of firesetting actions and characteristics. *Legal and Criminological Psychology*, 3, 73–96.

Canter, D. & Almond, L. (2002). *The Burning Issue: Research and Strategies for Reducing Arson*. London: Office of the Deputy Prime Minister.

Caplan, D. (1999). Internal controls and the detection of management fraud. *Journal of Accounting Research*, 37 (1: Spring), 101–117.

Carnes, P.J. (2001). Cybersex, courtship and escalating arousal: Factors in addictive sexual desire. *Sexual Addiction and Compulsivity* 8 (1), 45–78.

Carney, M., Buttell, F. & Dutton, D.G. (2007). Women who perpetrate intimate partner violence: A review of the literature with recommendations for treatment. *Aggression and Violent Behaviour*, 12, 108–115.

Carney, T.P (2004). *The Practical Investigation of Sex Crimes: A Strategic and Operational Approach* Florida: CRC Press.

Carr, A. (2004). *Internet Traders of Child Pornography and other Censorship Offenders in New Zealand*. The Department of Internal Affairs. Te Tari Taiwhenua, New Zealand. Available at http://www.dia.govt.nz/Pubforms.nsf/URL/entirereport.pdf/$file/entirereport.pdf, accessed on 5 November 2009.

Carr, J., (2003). *Child abuse, child pornography and the Internet*. National Children's Home. Available at www.nch.org.uk, accessed on 11 April 2005.

Cattaneo, L. B. & DeLoveh, H. L. M. (2008). The role of socioeconomic status in helpseeking from hotlines, shelters, and police among a national sample of women experiencing intimate partner violence. *American Journal of Orthopsychiatry*, 78 (4), 413–422.

Cawson, P., Wattam, C., Brooker, S. & Kelly, G. (2000). *Child Maltreatment in the UK: A Study of the Prevalence of Child Abuse and Neglect*. Available at www.nspcc.org.uk/inform, accessed on 10 July 2010.

Centre for problem- oriented policing (2010). *Shoplifting Prevention*. Available at http://www.popcenter.org/problems/shoplifting/summary/, accessed on 30 November 2011.

Centre for Retail Research (2005). *What Society Pays for Crime against Shops*. Available at http://www.retailresearch.org/whatsocietypays.php.

Centre for Social Justice (2009). Dying to belong: An in-depth review of street gangs in Britain. London: Centre for Social Justice. Available at http://www.centreforsocialjustice.org.uk/client/downloads/DyingtoBelongFullReport.pdf, accessed on November 2010.

Child Exploitation and Online Protection Centre (CEOP) (2008–9). *Annual Review*. Available at http://www.ceop.gov.uk/downloads/documents/CEOP_Annual_Review_2008-09.pdf, accessed on 5 November 2009.

Chiricos, T., S. Eschholz, & M. Gertz (1997). Crime, news and fear of crime: Toward an identification of audience effects. *Social Problems*, 44, 342–357.

Christensen, M. C., Nielsen, T. G., Ridley, S., Lecky, F. E. & Morris, S. (2008). Outcomes and costs of penetrating trauma injury in England and Wales. *INGURY, International journal of the care of the injured*. Vol 39. 1013–1025.

Chu, C. M., Daffern, M., Thomas, S. & Lim, J. Y. (2010). Violence risk and gang affiliation in youth offenders: a recidivism study. *Psychology, Crime & Law*. Vol 1. 1–17.

Clare, I.C.H., Murphy, G.H., Cox, D. & Chaplin, E.H. (1992). Assessment and treatment of fire-setting: A single-case investigation using a cognitive-behavioural model. *Criminal Behaviour and Mental Health*, 2, 253–268.

Clarke, R. V. & Cornish, D. B. (1985). Modelling offenders' decisions: A framework for research and policy. In M. Tonry and M. Morris (Eds.), *Crime and Justice: An annual review of research*, Vol. 7. Chicago: Chicago University Press.

Clarke, R.V. (1983). Situational crime prevention: Its theoretical basis and practical scope. In M. Tonry and N. Morris (Eds.), *Crime and Justice: an annual review of research*, Vol. 4. Chicago: Chicago University Press.

Clarke, R.V. (1992). *Situational crime prevention: successful case studies*. Albany, NY: Harlow and Heston.

Cohen, D. J., Eckhardt, C. I. & Schagat, K. D. (1998). Attention allocation and habituation to anger-related stimuli during a visual search task. *Aggressive Behavior, 24*, 399–409.

Cohen, L.E. & Felson, M. (1979). Social change and crime rate trends: a routine activity approach. *American Sociological Review, 44*, 588–608.

Coker, A. L., Sanderson, M., Cantu, E., Huerta, D. & Fadden, M. K. (2008). Frequency and types of partner violence among Mexican American college women. *Journal of American College Health, 56*, 665–673.

Coleman, E. (1992). Is your patient suffering from compulsive sexual behaviour? *Psychiatric Annals*, 22(6), 320–325.

Coleman, K. & Osbourne, S. (2010). Homicide. In K. Smith, J. Flatley, K. Coleman, S. Osborne, P. Kaiza & S. Roe (Eds.), *Homicides, Firearm Offences and Intimate Violence 2008/09. Supplementary Volume 2 to Crime in England and Wales 2008/09 (2nd Ed)*. London: Home Office. Available at http://rds.homeoffice.gov.uk/rds/pdfs10/hosb0110.pdf, accessed on 30 November 2011.

Collins, J. J. (1993). Drinking and violence: An individual offender focus. In S. E. Martin (Ed.), *Alcohol and Interpersonal Violence: Fostering Multidisciplinary Perspectives*. Rockville: National Institutes of Health.

Collins, J. J. & Messerschmidt, P. M. (1993). Epidemiology of alcohol related violence. *Alcohol & Health Research World*, 17, 93–100.

Comer, M. J. (1985). *Corporate Fraud*. Aldershot: Gower.

Conklin. J. E. (1972). *Robbery and the Criminal Justice System*. Philadelphia: J. B. Lippincott.

Connolly, J., Pepler, D., Craig, W. & Taradash, A. (2000). Dating experiences of bullies in early adolescence. *Child Maltreatment*, 5, 299–310.

Cook, P. J. (1980). Research in Criminal Deterrence: *Laying the Groundwork for the Second Decade. Crime and Justice: An Annual Review of Research*. Chicago: University of Chicago Press.

Cooper, A. (1989). Sexuality and the Internet: Surfing into the new millennium. *Cyberpsychology and Behaviour*, 1, 181–187.

Copello, A. G. & Tata, P. R. (1990). Violent behaviour and interpretative bias: An experimental study of the resolution of ambiguity in violent offenders. *British Journal of Clinical Psychology*, 29, 417–428.

Cornish, D. & Clarke, R. V. (1986). *Introduction in the Reasoning Criminal*. New York: Springer-Verlag. pp 1–16.

Cornish, D. B. (1994). The procedural analysis of offending and its relevance for situational offending. In R. V. Clarke (Ed.) *Crime Prevention Studies* (Volume 3). Monsey, NY: Criminal Justice Press.

Cornish, D.B. & Clarke, R.V. (Eds.) (1986). *The Reasoning Criminal: Rational Choice Perspectives on Offending*. New York, NY: Springer-Verlag.

Corrin, C. (Ed.) (1996). *Women in a Violent World: Feminist Analyses and Resistance across 'Europe'*. Edinburgh University Press, Edinburgh.

Cortoni, F. & Marshall, W. L. (2001). Sex as a coping strategy and its relationship to juvenile sexual history and intimacy in Sexual Offenders. *Sexual Abuse: A Journal of Research and Treatment*, 13 (1), 27–43.

Cortoni, F., Nunes, K. L. & Latendresse, M. (2006). An examination of the effectiveness of the violence prevention programming. Research Report R-178. Ottawa, ON: Correctional Service of Canada.

Coughlin, B. C. & Venkatesh, S. A. (2003). The Urban Street Gang after 1970. *Annual Review of Sociology*, 29, 41–64.

Cox, D. J. & Maletzky, B. M. (1980). Victims of exhibitionism. In Cox, D. J. & Daitzman, R. J. (Eds.), *Exhibitionism: Description, Assessment and Treatment*. New York: Garland Press.

Craissati, J. (2005). Sexual violence against women: A psychological approach to the assessment and management of rapists in the community. *Probation Journal*, 52 (4), 401–422.

Craissati, J., Webb, L. & Keen, S. (2005). *Personality Disordered Sex Offenders. Report of Research across the London Probation Area*. Oxleas NHS Trust and Home Office.

Craissati, J., Webb, L. & Keen, S. (2008) The relationships between developmental variables, personality disorder, and risk in sex offenders. *Sexual Abuse: A Journal of Research and Treatment*, 20 (2), 119–138.

Crawford, A. (1998). *Crime Prevention and Community Safety: Politics, Policies and Practices*. Harlow: Longman.

Creeden, K. (2009). How Trauma And Attachment Can Impact Neurodevelopment: Informing Our Understanding And Treatment Of Sexual Behaviour Problems. *Journal of Sexual Aggression*, 15 (3), 261–273.

Cressey, D. R. (1953). *Other People's Money: A Study in the Social Psychology of Embezzlement*. Glencoe, Illinois: Free Press.

Crick, N. R. & Dodge, K. A. (1994). A review and reformulation of social information-processing mechanisms in children's social adjustment. *Psychological Bulletin, 115*, 74–101.

Criminal Justice Act (1988). Available at http://www.opsi.gov.uk/acts/acts1988/Ukpga_19880033_en_1.htm, accessed on 13 November 2009.

Criminal Justice and Court Services Act (2000). Available at http://www.opsi.gov.uk/acts/acts2000/20000043.htm, accessed on 13 November 2009.

Croall, H. (2001a). *Understanding White Collar Crime*. Buckingham: Open University Press.

Croall, H. (2001b). The victims of white collar crime. In S. Lindgren (Ed.), *White Collar Crime Research: Old Views and Future Potentials* (pp. 35–51). Stockholm: National Council for Crime Prevention.

Cromwell, P. F., Olson, J. N. & Avery, D'Aunn (1991). *Residential Burglary: An Ethnographic Analysis. Studies in Crime Law and Justice, 8*. London: Sage.

Crown Prosecution Service (2009). *CPS Policy for Prosecuting Cases of Domestic Violence*. London: CPS. Available at http://www.cps.gov.uk/publications/docs/domesticviolencepolicy.pdf, accessed on 30 November 2011.

Cullen, E. & Newell, T. (1999). *Murderers and Life Imprisonment: Containment, Treatment, Safety and Risk*. Winchester: Waterside Press.

Cuthber, M. (1991). Investigation of the incidence and analysis of cases of alleged violence reporting to St Vincent's Hospital. In D. Chappel, P. Grabowsky and H. Strang (Eds.), *Australian Violence: Contemporary Perspectives* (pp. 135–146). Canberra: Australian Institute of Criminology.

D'Cruze, S., Walklate, S. & Pegg, S. (2006). *Murder*. Cullompton: Willan.

Dalby, J. T. (1988). Is telephone scatologia a variant of exhibitionism? *International Journal of Offender and Comparative Criminology, 1*, 45–49.

Daly, M. & Wilson, M. (1988). Homicide, New York: De Gruyter.

Dandescu, A. & Wolfe, R. (2003). Considerations on fantasy use by child molesters and exhibitionists. *Sex Abuse, 15*, 297.

Davia, H. R. (2000). *Fraud 101: Techniques and Strategies for Detection*. New York: John Wiley and Sons, Inc.

Davies, D. (2000). *Fraud Watch* (2nd edition). London: ABG Professional Information.

De Young, M. (1988). The indignant page: Techniques of neutralization in the publications of pedophile organizations. *Child Abuse and Neglect, 12*, 583–591.

DeKeseredy, W. S. (2000). Current controversies on defining nonlethal violence against women in intimate heterosexual relationships: Empirical implications. *Violence against Women, 6*, 728–774.

DeKeseredy, W. S. & Schwartz, M. D. (2001). Definitional issues. In C. M. Renzetti, J. L. Edleson & R. K. Bergen (Eds.), *Sourcebook on Violence against Women* (pp. 23–34). Thousand Oaks, CA: Sage.

Dennis, I. (2006). Sentencing shoplifting. *Criminal Law Review*, December, 1017–1018.

Dennison, S. M. (2007). Interpersonal relationships and stalking: Identifying when to intervene. *Law and Human Behavior, 31*, 353–367.

Dennison, S. M. & Stewart, A. (2006). Facing rejection: New relationships, broken relationships, shame, and stalking. *International Journal of Offender Therapy and Comparative Criminology, 50*, 324–337.

Dennison, S. M. & Thomson, D. M. (2005). Criticisms or plaudits for stalking laws? What psycholegal research tells us about proscribing stalking. *Psychology, Public Policy, and Law,* 11, 384–406.

Department for Communities (no date) *Fire Statistics,* United Kingdom 2000. Available at http://www.communities.gov.uk/archived/publications/fire/firestatisticsunited4, accessed on 30 November 2010.

DeVoe, E. R. & Coulborn Faller, K. (1999). The characteristics of disclosure who may have been sexually abused. *Child Maltreatment,* 4 (3), 217–227.

Di Placido, C., Simon, T. L., Witte, T. D., Gu, D. & Wong, S. C. P. (2006). Treatment of gang members can reduce recidivism and institutional misconduct. *Law and Human Behavior,* 30, 93–114.

Dickens, G., Sugarman, P., Edgar, S. Hofberg, K., Tewari, S. & Ahmad, F. (2009). Recidivism and dangerousness in arsonists. *The Journal of Forensic Psychiatry and Psychology,* 20 (5), 621–639.

Dill, K. E., Anderson, C. A., Anderson, K. B. & Deuser, W. E. (1997). Effects of aggressive personality on social expectations and social perceptions. *Journal of Research in Personality,* 31, 272–292.

DirectGov (2010). Gangs and Gang Crime: The facts. Available online at http://www.direct.gov.uk/en/Parents/Yourchildshealthandsafety/WorriedAbout/DG_171314, accessed on 01 August 2010.

Dobash, R. E. & Dobash, R. P. (1978). Wives: The 'appropriate' victims of marital violence. In R. K. Bergen, J. L. Edleson & C. M. Rengetti (Eds.) (reprint 2005) *Violence against Women: Classic Papers.* Boston: Pearson and Ablongman.

Dobash, R. E., Dobash, R. P., Cavanagh, K. & Lewis R. (2000). *Changing Violent Men.* London: Sage Publications.

Dodd, T., Nicholas, S., Povey, D. & Walker, A. (2004). *Crime in England and Wales 2003/4.* (Statistical Bulletin 10/04). London: HMSO.

Dodge, K. A. (1980). Social cognition and children's aggressive behavior. *Child Development,* 51, 162–170.

Dodge, K. A. & Frame, C. L. (1982). Social cognitive biases and deficits in aggressive boys. *Child Development,* 53, 620–635.

Doig, A. (2006). *Fraud.* Cullompton: Willan Publishing.

Dollard, J., Doob, L., Miller, N., Mowrer, O. H. & Sears, R. R. (1939). *Frustration and Aggression.* New Haven, CT: Yale University Press.

Dorling, D. (2006). Prime suspect: Murder in Britain. *Prison Service Journal,* 166, 3–10.

Dorn, N., Murji, K. & South, N. (1992). *Trafficking: Drug Markets and Law Enforcement.* London: Routledge.

Douglas, J., Burgess, A.W., Burgess, A.G. & Ressler, R. (1992). *Crime Classification Manual.* Lexington, MA: Lexington.

Downes, D. & Rock, P. (1998). *Understanding Deviance.* Oxford: Oxford University Press.

Doyle, T. (2009). Privacy and Perfect Voyeurism. *Ethics and Information Technology Archive,* 11 (3), 181–189.

Dressing, H., Gass, P. & Kuehner, C. (2007). What can we learn from the first community-based epidemiological study on stalking in Germany? *International Journal of Law and Psychiatry,* 30, 10–17.

Duffield, G. & Grabosky, P. (2001). The psychology of fraud. *Australian Institute of Criminology: Trends and Issues in Crime and Criminal Justice,* 199 (March), 1–6.

Dunseith, N. W., Nelson, E. B., Brusman-Lovins, L. A., Holcomb, J. L., Beckman, D., Welge, J. A., Roby, D., Taylor, B., Soutullo, C. A. & McElroy, S. L.

(2004). Psychiatric and legal features of 113 men convicted of sexual offences. *Journal of Psychiatry*, 65, 293–300.

Dupéré, V., Lacourse, É., Willms, J. D., Vitaro, F. & Tremblay, R. E. (2007). Affiliation to youth gangs during adolescence: The interaction between childhood psychopathic tendencies and neighborhood disadvantage. *Journal of Abnormal Child Psychology*, 35, 1035–1045.

Dutton, D. G. (2007a). *The Abusive Personality* (2nd ed). New York. The Guildford Press.

Dutton, D.G. (2007b). Caveat assessor: Potential pitfalls of generic assessment for intimate partner violence. In A. Baldry (Ed.) *Intimate Partner Violence Prevention and Intervention: The Risk Assessment and Management Approach*. New York: Nova Press.

Dutton, L. B. & Winstead, B. A. (2006). Predicting unwanted pursuit: Attachment, relationship satisfaction, relationship alternatives, and break-up distress. *Journal of Social and Personal Relationships*, 23, 565–586.

Dye, M. G. W., Green, C. S. & Bavelier, D. (2009). The development of attention skills in action video game players. *Neuropsychologia*, 47 (8–9), 1780–1789.

Eagly, A. H. & Steffen, V. J. (1986). Gender and aggressive behavior: A meta-analytic review of the social psychological literature. *Psychological Bulletin*, 100, 309–330.

Ecclestone, L. & Owen, K. (2007). Cognitive treatment 'Just For Rapists': Recent developments. In T. A. Gannon, T. Ward, A. R. Beech, and D. Fisher (Eds.), *Aggressive Offenders' Cognition: Theory, Research and Practice* (pp. 135–151). Chichester: John Wiley.

Edwards, D., Ashmore, M. & Potter, J. (1995). Death and furniture: The rhetoric, politics and theology of bottom line arguments against relativism, *History of the Human Sciences*, 8, 26–35.

Edwards, S. S. (2000). Prosecuting 'child pornography': Possession and taking of indecent photos of children. *Journal of Social Welfare and Family Law*, 22, 1–21.

Ehrensaft, M. K. (2008). Intimate partner violence: Persistence of myths and implications for interventions. *Children and Youth Services Review*, 30, 276–286.

Ekblom, P., Law, H. & Sutton, M. (1996). *Domestic Burglary Schemes in the Safer Cities Programme* (Home Office Research Study 164). London: HMSO. Available at http://www.popcenter.org/library/scp/pdf/66-Ekblom_el_al.pdf, accessed 12 Feb 2012.

e-lawresources.co.uk. (2010). Common assault. Available at http://www.e-lawresources.co.uk/Assault.php, accessed 21 August 2010.

Elliot, I. A. & Beech, A. R. (2009). Understanding online child pornography use: Applying sexual offense theory to Internet offenders. *Aggression and Violent Behaviour*, 14, 180–193.

Epps, K., Haworth, R. & Swaffer, T. (1993). Attitudes toward women and rape among male adolescents convicted of sexual versus nonsexual crimes, *The Journal of Psychology*, 127 (5) 501–506.

Ernst & Young (2000). *Fraud: Risk and Prevention*. London: Caspian Publishing Ltd.

Esbensen, F. A., Winfree, L. T., Jr., He, N. & Taylor, T. J. (2001). Youth gangs and definitional issues: When is a gang a gang, and why does it matter? *Crime and Delinquency*, 47, 105–130.

Eytan, A., Paoloni-Giacobino, A., Thorens, G., Eugster, N. & Graf, I. (2002). Firesetting behaviour associated with Klinefelter syndrome. *International Journal of Psychiatry in Medicine*, 32 (4), 395–399.

Farrington, D. P. & Lambert, S. (1997). Predicting offender profiles from victim and witness descriptions. In J. L. Jackson and D. A. Bekerian (Eds.), *Offender Profiling: Theory, Research and Practice*. Chichester: Willey.

Fawcett Society. (2007). Rape: The Facts. Available at http://www.fawcettsociety.org.uk/documents/Rape%20-%20The%20Facts.doc, 13 January 2010.

Feeney, F. (1986). Robbers as decision-makers. In D. B. Cornish & R. V. Clarke (Eds.), *The Reasoning Criminal: Rational Choice Perspectives on Offending* (pp. 53–71). New York: Springer-Verlag.

Fein, R. A. & Vossekuil, B. (1998). Protective intelligence and threat assessment investigations: A guide for state and local law enforcement officials. NIJ/OJP/DOJ Publication No. 170612. Washington, DC: U.S. Department of Justice.

Feldman, P. (1993). *The Psychology of Crime*. Cambridge: Cambridge University Press.

Fellstrom, C. (2008) *Hoods: The Gangs of Nottingham – A Study in Organized Crime*. England: Milo books.

Felson, R. B., Baumer, E. P. & Messner, S. F. (2000). Acquaintance robbery. *Journal of Research in Crime and Delinquency, 37*, 284–305.

Fergusson, D. M. & Horwood, L. J. (2000). Alcohol abuse and crime: A fixed-effects regression analysis. *Addiction, 95*, 1525–1536.

Festinger, L. (1957). *A Theory of Cognitive Dissonance*. Stanford: Stanford University Press.

Finch, E. & Munro, V. E. (2005). Juror stereotypes in blame attribution in rape cases involving intoxicants. *British Journal of Criminology, 45*, 25–38.

Fineman, K. R. (1995). A model for the qualitative analysis of child and adult fire deviant behaviour. *American Journal of Forensic Psychology, 13* (1), 31–60.

Finkelhor, D. (1984). *Child Sexual Abuse: New Theory and Research*. New York, US: The Free Press, Collier Macmillan Publishers.

Finkelhor, D. (1994). Current information on the scope and nature of child sexual abuse. *The Future of Children, 4* (2), 31–53.

Finkelhor, D. & Araji, S. (1985). Explanations of pedophilia: Review of empirical research. *Bulletin American Academy Psychiatry Law, 13*, 17–37.

Finkelhor, D. & Araji, S. (1986). Explanations of pedophilia: A four factor model. *Journal of Sex Research, 22*, 145–161.

Finkelhor, D., Mitchell, K. J. & Wolak, J. (2000). *Online Victimization: A Report on the Nation's Youth*. Washington, D. C.: National Center for Missing and Exploited Children.

Finkelhor, D., Ormrod, R. K., Turner, H. A. & Hamby, S. L. (2005). Measuring poly-victimization using the JVQ. *Child Abuse & Neglect, 29* (11), 1297–1312.

Finney, A. (2006). *Domestic Violence, Sexual Assault and Stalking: Findings from the 2004/5 British Crime Survey*. Home Office Online Report 12/06.

Fire statistics monitor (2010). Communities and Local Governments Fire Statistics Monitor April 2009 to March 2010, Issue No. 03/10. Available from http://www.communities.gov.uk/documents/statistics/pdf/1693248.pdf.

Firestone, P. Kingston, D. A., Wexler, A. & Bradford, J. M. (2006). Long-Term follow up of exhibitionists: Psychological, phallometric and offense characteristics. *The Journal of the American Academy of Psychiatry and the Law, 34*, 3.

Fisher, D. & Beech, A. R. (2007). The implicit theories of rapists and sexual murderers in Gannon, T. A., Ward, T., Beech, A. R. and Fisher, D. (Eds.) *Aggressive Offenders' Cognition: Theory, Research and Practice*. Chichester: John Wiley.

Fisher, D., Beech, A. & Browne, K. (1999). Comparison of sex offenders to nonoffenders on selected psychological measures, *International Journal of Offender Therapy and Comparative Criminology, 43,* 473–491.

Fiske, S. T. & Taylor, S. E. (1991). *Social Cognition* (2nd ed). New York: McGraw-Hill.

Flatley, J., Kershaw, C., Smith, K., Chaplin, R. & Moon, D. (Eds.) (2010). *Crime in England and Wales 2009/2010.* London: Home Office.

Forrester, D., Frenz, S., O'Connor, M. & Pease, K. (1990). *The Kirkholt Burglary Prevention Project Phase II* (Crime Prevention Unit Paper 23). London: Home Office.

Fraud Act (2006). Chapter 35. London: HMSO.

Fraud Advisory Panel (2000). *Annual Report 1999–2000.* London: Fraud Advisory Panel.

Fraud Advisory Panel (2006). *Victims of Fraud.* London: Fraud Advisory Panel.

Fraud Advisory Panel (2008). *Fraud Facts Issue 1 October 2008.* London: Fraud Advisory Panel.

Fraud Advisory Panel (2009). *Annual Report 2008–2009.* London: Fraud Advisory Panel.

Freud, S. (1920). *A General Introduction to Psychoanalysis.* New York: Boni & Liveright.

Freud, S. (1932). The acquisition of power over fire. *The International Journal of Psychoanalysis,* 12, 405–410.

Freund, K. & Blanchard, R. (1989). Phallometric diagnosis of pedophilia. *Journal of Consulting and Clinical Psychology,* 57, 100–105.

Freund, K. & Kuban, M. (1993). Toward a testable developmental model of pedophilia: The development of erotic age preference. *Child Abuse and Neglect,* 17, 315–324.

Freund, K. & Seto, M. C. (1998). Preferential rape in the theory of courtship disorder. *Archives of Sexual Behaviour,* 27, 5.

Freund, K. (1990). Courtship disorder. In W. L. Marshall, D. R. Laws & H. E. Barbaree (Eds.), *Handbook of Sexual Assault.* New York: Plenum Press.

Freund, K., Watson, R. & Reinzo, D. (1988). The value of self-reports in the study of voyeurism and exhibitionism. *Sexual Abuse: A Journal of Research and Treatment,* 1 (2), 243–262.

Friedrichs, D. O. (2003). *Trusted Criminals: White Collar Crime in Contemporary Society.* Belmont: Wadsworth.

Friendship, C., Mann, R. E. & Beech, A. (2003). Evaluation of a national prison-based treatment program for sexual offenders in England and Wales. *Journal of Interpersonal Violence,* 18, 744–759.

Fruzzetti, A. E. & Levensky, E. R. (2000). Dialectical behavior therapy for domestic violence: Rationale and procedures. *Cognitive and Behavioral Practice,* 7, 435–446.

Fullerton, A. R. (2007). Psychoanalysing kleptomania. *Marketing Theory,* 7 (4), 335–352.

Fullerton, A. R. & Punj, G. N. (2004). Shoplifting as moral insanity: Historical perspectives on kleptomania. *Journal of Macromarketing,* 24, 8–16.

Furby, L., Weinrott, M. R. & Blackshaw, L. (1989). Sex offender recidivism: A review. *Psychological Bulletin,* 105 (1), 3–30.

Galbreath, N., Berlin, F. & Sawyer, D. (2002). Paraphilias and the internet. In A. Cooper (Ed.), *Sex and the Internet: A Guidebook for Clinicians* (pp. 187–205). Philadelphia: Brunner-Routledge.

Garot, R. (2007). "Where You From!": Gang Identity as Performance. *Journal of Contemporary Ethnography, 36*, 50–84.

Gaylor, D. (2002). *Getting Away with Murder: The Re-Investigation of Undetected Homicide.* London: Crown

Gaynor, J. (1996). Firesetting. In M. Lewis (Ed.), *Child and Adolescent Psychiatry: A Comprehensive Textbook* (2nd ed., pp. 591–603). Baltimore: Williams & Wilkins.

Gaynor, J. & Hatcher, C. (1987). *The Psychology of Child Firesetting: Detection and Intervention.* Philadelphia, PA, US: Bruner/Mazel Inc.

Geller, J. L. (1992). Pathological fire-setting in adults, *International Journal of Law and Psychiatry, 15*, 283–302.

Genders, E. & Player, E. (1995) *Grendon: A Study of a Therapeutic Prison.* Oxford: Oxford University Press.

Gilbert, F. & Daffern, M. (2010). Integrating contemporary aggression theory with violent offender treatment: How thoroughly do interventions target violent behavior? *Aggression and Violent Behavior, 15* (3), 167–180.

Gilchrist, E. & Blissett, J. (2002). Magistrates' attitudes to domestic violence and sentencing options. *The Howard Journal of Criminal Justice, 4*, 348–363.

Gilchrist, E., Johnson, R., Takriti, R., Beech, A., Kebbell, M. & Weston, S. (2003). *Domestic Violence Offenders: Characteristics and Offending Related Needs.* Findings No. 217. London: Home Office.

Gilfus, M. E., Trabold, N., O'Brien, P., & Fleck-Henderson, A. (2010). Gender and intimate partner violence: Evaluating the evidence. *Journal of Social Work Education, 46*, 2.

Gill, M. L. & Loveday, K. (2003). What do offenders think about CCTV? *Crime Prevention and Community Safety: An International Journal, 5*, 17–25.

Gill, M. L. & Pease, K. (1998). Repeat robbers: How are they different? In M. Gill (Ed.), *Crime at Work: Studies in Security and Crime Prevention.* Leicester: Perpetuity Press.

Gill, R. (1995). Relativism, reflexivity and politics: Interrogating discourse analysis from a feminist perspective. In S. Wilkinson and C. Kitzinger (Eds.), *Feminism and Discourse* (pp. 165–186). London: Sage Publications.

Gillespie, A. (2005). Tackling child pornography: The approach in England and Wales. In E. Quayle and M. Taylor (Eds.), *Viewing Child Pornography on the Internet: Understanding the Offence, Managing the Offender, Helping the Victims.* Lyme Regis: Russell House Publishing.

Gilligan, J. (2000). *Violence: Reflections on Our Deadliest Epidemic.* London: Jessica Kingsley.

Gilyeat, D. (1994). *A Companion Guide to Offence Seriousness.* Ilkley: Owen Wells Publishers.

Girard, A. L. & Senn, C.Y. (2008). The role of new 'date rape drugs' in attributions about date rape. *Journal of Interpersonal Violence, 23* (1), 3–20.

Glasser, M., Kolvin, I., Campbell, D., Glasser, A., Leitch, I. & Farrelly, S. (2001). Cycle of child sexual abuse: Links between being a victim and becoming a perpetrator. *British Journal of Psychiatry, 179*, 482–494.

Gold, L. (1962). Psychiatric profile of the firesetter. *Journal of Forensic Sciences, 7*, 404–417.

Golding, J. M. (1999). Intimate partner violence as a risk factor for mental disorders: A meta-analysis. *Journal of Family Violence, 14*, 99–132.

Goldstein, P. (1985). The drugs-violence nexus; a tripartite framework. *Journal of Drug Issues, 39*, 143–174.

Gondolf, E. W. (2002). *Batter Intervention Systems: Issues, Outcomes and Recommendations*. Thousand Oaks, CA: Sage Publications.

Goode, E. (1997). *Between Politics and Reason*. New York: St Martin's Press.

Goodey, J. (2005). *Victims and Victimology: Research, Policy and Practice* Maidenhead: Open University Press.

Gordon, L., Tinsley, L., Godfrey, C. & Parrott, S. (2006). The economic and social costs of class a drug use in England and Wales, 2003/04. In N. Singleton, R. Murray & L. Tinsley (Eds.), *Measuring Different Aspects of Problem Drug Use: Methodological Developments*. London: Home Office.

Gouze, K. R. (1987). Attention and social problem solving as correlates of aggression in preschool males. *Journal of Abnormal Child Psychology*, 15, 181–197.

Grant, B. F., Stinson, F. S., Dawson, D., Chou, S. P., Ruan, M. A. & Pickering, R. P. (2004). Co-occurrence of 12-month alcohol and drug use disorders and personality disorders in the United States. *Archives of General Psychiatry*, 61, 361–368.

Grant, J. E. (2004). Co-occurrence of personality disorders in persons with Kleptomania: A preliminary investigation. *Journal of American Academy of Psychiatry Law*, 32 (4), 395–8.

Grant, J. E. (2006). Understanding and treating Kleptomania: New models new treatments. *Journal of Psychiatry Science*, 43 (2), 81–87.

Grant, J. E. & Kim, S.W. (2002a). Clinical Characteristics and Associated Psychopathology of 22 Patients with Kleptomania. *Comprehensive Psychiatry*, 43 (5): 378–84.

Grant, J. E. & Kim, S.W. (2002b). An open label study of Naltrexone in the treatment of Kleptomania. *Journal of Clinical Psychiatry*, 63(4), 349–356.

Grant, J. E. & Odlaug, B. L. (2007). Kleptomania: Clinical characteristics and treatment. *Rev. Bras. Psiquiatr*, 30, 1.

Grant, J. E. & Polenza, M. N. (2004). Impulse control disorders: Clinical characteristics and pharmalogical management. *Annals of Clinical Psychiatry*, 16 (4), 27–34.

Gray, J. M. (2006). Rape myth beliefs and prejudiced instructions: Effects on decisions of guilt in a case of date rape. *Legal and Criminological Psychology*, 11, 75–80.

Greenberg, J. (1997). A social influence model of employee theft. In J. R. Lewicki, B. H. Sheppard and R. J. Bies (Eds.), *Research on Negotiation in Organizations* (pp. 29–51). Greenwich, CT: JAI Press.

Greenburg, D. M. & Bradford, J. M. W. (1997). Treatment of the paraphilic disorders: A review of the role of the selective serotonin reuptake inhibitors. *Sexual Abuse: A Journal of Research and Treatment*, 9 (4), 349–360.

Greenfeld, L. A. & Henneberg, M. A. (2001). Victim and offender self-reports of alcohol involvement in crime. *Alcohol Research and Health*, 25, 20–31.

Griffiths, M. (2000). Excessive Internet use: implications for sexual behaviour, *Cyberpsychology and Behavior*, 3, 537–551.

Groth, A. N. & Birnbaum, H. J. (1978). Adult sexual orientation and attraction to underage persons. *Archives of Sexual Behavior*, 7 (3), 175–181.

Groth, A. N. & Birnbaum, H. J. (1979). *Men Who Rape: The Psychology of the Offender*. New York: Plenum.

Gruenewald, P. J., Freisthler, B., Remer, L., LaScala, E. A. & Treno, A. (2006). Ecological models of alcohol outlets and violent assaults: Crime potentials and geospatial analysis. *Addiction*, 101, 666–677.

Guay, D.R.P (2009). Drug Treatment of Paraphilic and Nonparaphilic Sexual Disorders. *Clinical Therapeutics,* 31 (1), 1–31.

Gudjonsson, G. H. & Sigurdsson, J. F. (2004). Motivation for offending and personality. *Legal and Criminological Psychology,* 9, 69–81.

Haggert, M. (2001). A typology study of mentally disordered arsonists. *Unpublished MSc. Disssertation. University of Sheffield.* Cited in The Burning Issue.

Häkkänen, H., Hagelstam, C. & Santtila, P. (2003). Stalking actions, prior offender-victim relationships and issuing of restraining orders in a Finnish sample of stalkers. *Legal and Criminological Psychology,* 8, 189–206.

Hall, G. C. N. & Hirschman, R. (1991). Toward a theory of sexual aggression: a quadripartite model. *Journal of Consulting and Clinical Psychology,* 59, 662–669.

Hall, G. C. N. & Hirschman, R. (1992). Sexual aggression against children: A conceptual perspective of etiology. *Criminal Justice and Behavior,* 19, 8–23.

Hall, G.C.N. (1995). Sex offender recidivism revisited: A meta-analysis of recent treatment studies. *Journal of Consulting and Clinical Psychology,* 63, 802–809.

Hall, R. C. W. & Hall, R. C. W. (2007). A profile of pedophilia: Definition, characteristics of offenders, recidivism, treatment outcomes, and forensic issues. *Mayo Clinical Proceedings,* April 82 (4), 457–471.

Hamel, J. & Nicholls, T. L. (2006). *Family Interventions in Domestic Violence: A Handbook of Gender-Inclusive Treatments.* New York: Springer Publishing.

Hamilton, L. (2010). Boundary seesaw model: Good fences make for good neighbours. In A. Tennant & K., Howells (Eds.), *Using Time, Not Doing Time: Practitioner Perspectives on Personality Disorder & Risk* (pp. 181–194). Chichester: Wiley-Blackwell.

Hamilton-Smith, N. & Kent, A. (2005). The prevention of domestic burglary. In N. Tilley (Ed.), *Handbook of Crime Prevention and Community Safety.* Collumpton: Willan.

Hammersley, R. (2008). *Drugs and Crime.* Cambridge: Polity Press.

Hanson, R. & Bussiere, M. (1998). Predicting relapse: A meta-analysis of sexual offender recidivism studies. *Journal of Consulting and Clinical Psychology,* 86: 348–362.

Hanson, R. K., Gordon, A., Harris, A J. R., Marques, J. K., Murphy, W., Quinsey, V. L. & Seto, M. C. (2002). First report of the collaborative outcome data project on the effectiveness of psychological treatment for sex offenders. *Sexual Abuse: A Journal of Research and Treatment,* 14 (2), 169–194.

Harrison, P and Wilson, D (2008). *Hunting Evil: Inside the Ipswich Serial Murders.* London: Sphere.

Harwin, N. (2006). Putting a stop to domestic violence in the United Kingdom. *Violence against Women,* 12, 556–567.

Hatcher, R. M., Palmer, E. J., McGuire, J., Hounsome, J. C., Bilby, C. A. L. & Hollin, C. R. (2008). Aggression replacement training with adult male offenders within community settings: A reconviction analysis. *Forensic Psychiatry and Psychology,* 19, 517–532.

Hayslett-Mccall, K. L. & Bernard, T. J. (2002). Attachment, masculinity, and self-control: A theory of male crime rates. *Theoretical Criminology,* 6 (1), 5–33.

Heal, K. & Laycock, G. (Eds.) (1986). *Situational Crime Prevention: From Theory to Practice.* London. HMSO.

Healy, M. (1997). Child pornography: An international perspective. Prepared as a working document for the World Congress against Commercial Sexual Exploitation of Children. Available at http://www.usis.usemb.se/children/csec/215e.htm, accessed on 5 November 2009.

Heerden, J. H. van, Blignaut, J. N. & Groenendijk, N. S. (1999). On the shady side of economics. *South African Journal of Economics and Management,* 2 (2), 207–221.

Heise, L. L (1998). Violence against women: An integrated ecological framework. *Violence against Women,* 4, 262–290.

Henry, S. & Lanier, M. M. (2006). *The Essential Criminology Reader.* Boulder: Westview Press.

Hepburn, A. (2000). On the alleged incompatibility between Relativism and Feminist Psychology. *Feminism and Psychology,* 10 (1), 91–106.

Hester, M. & Westmarland, N. (2005). *Tackling Domestic Violence: Effective Interventions and Approaches, HORS 290.* London, Home Office. Available at http://rds.homeoffice.gov.uk/rds/pdfs05/hors290.pdf, accessed on 30 November 2011.

Hester, M., Pearson, C. Harwin, N. & Abrahams, H. A. (2007). *Making an Impact: Children and Domestic Violence: A Reader* (2nd ed). London: Jessica Kingsley Publishers.

Hester, M., Westmarland, N., Pearce, J. & Williamson E. (2008). *Early Evaluation of the Domestic Violence, Crime and Victims Act 2004.* Ministry of Justice Research Series 14/08: London, Ministry of Justice. Available at http://dro.dur.ac.uk/5093/1/5093.pdf?DDD34+dssonw, accessed 12 Feb 2012.

Higson, A. (1998). *Why Is Management Reticent to Report Fraud? An Exploratory Study.* Loughborough: Loughborough University Business School.

Hildebrand, M., De Ruiter, C. & De Vogel, V. (2004). Psychopathy and sexual deviance in treated rapists: Association with sexual and nonsexual recidivism. *Sexual Abuse: A Journal of Research and Treatment,* 16, 1–24.

HMIC (2000). *Policing London: 'Winning Consent'. A Review of Murder Investigation and Community and Race Relations Issues in the Metropolitan Police Service.* London: HMIC.

Holland, G. (2005). Identifying victims of child abuse images: an analysis of successful identifications. In E. Quayle and M. Taylor (Eds.), *Viewing Child Pornography on the Internet: Understanding the Offence, Managing the Offender, Helping the Victims.* Lyme Regis: Russell House Publishing.

Hollinger, R. C. & Davis, J. L. (2003). 2002 National Retail Security Survey Final Report. University of Florida, Gainesville, Florida.

Holtzworth-Munroe, A. & Stuart, G. L. (1994) Typologies of male batterers: Three subtypes and the differences among them. *Psychological Bulletin,* 116 (3), November, 476–497.

Holtzworth-Munroe, A., Meehan, J. C., Herron, K., Rehman, U. & Stuart, G. L. (2003). Do subtypes of maritally violent men continue to differ over time? *Journal of Consulting and Clinical Psychology,* 71, 728–740.

Home Office (2000). *Fire Statistics: United Kingdom, 1999 (issue number 20/00).*

Home Office (2001). *The Joint Prison Probation Accreditation Panel.* London: HMSO.

Home Office (2002). *Information Relating to Offences and Prosecutions under the 1971 Criminal Damage Act Supplied by the Home Office.*

Home Office (2003). *Official Statistics.* Offending and Criminal Justice Group (RDS). Ref: IOS 503-03 and IOS 164-05.

Home Office (2005). Recorded Crime Stats 1989 – 2004/05. Recorded crime datasets, available at http://www.homeoffice.gov.uk/science-research/research-statistics/crime/crime-statistics-internet/, accessed 12 Feb 2012.

Home Office (2006). *Statistics on Race and the Criminal Justice System 2005*. London: Home Office.

Home Office (2007). *Sentencing Statistics*. London: HMSO.

Home Office (2008a). Consultation on the British Crime Survey extension to cover under 16s. Available at http://rds.homeoffice.gov.uk/rds/pdfs08/consult-bcsu16-response08.pdf, accessed 12 Feb 2012.

Home Office (2008b). *Drugs: Protecting Families and Communities*. London: Home Office.

Home Office (2008c). *Tackling Drugs Changing Lives: Evidence of the Impact of the Drug Interventions Programme – Summaries and Sources*. Available at http://drugs.homeoffice.gov.uk/publication-search/dip/DIP-impact-evidence-round-up-v22835.pdf?view=Binary.

Home Office (2009). *Criminal Statistics England and Wales 2008/2009*. London, HMSO Available at http://www.homeoffice.gov.uk/rds/pdfs09/hosb1109vol1.pdf, accessed on 13 January 2009.

Home Office (2010a). *Crime in England and Wales 2009/10*. Available at http://www.homeoffice.gov.uk/rds/pdfs10/hosb1210.pdf, accessed 12 Feb 2012.

Home Office (2010b). Crime in England and Wales: Quarterly update to June 2010. Home Office Statistical Bulletin. Available at http://rds.homeoffice.gov.uk/rds/pdfs10/hosb1610.pdf, accessed on 30 October 2010.

Home Office (2010c). *Criminal Statistics England and Wales 2009/2010*. London, HMSO.

Home Office (2010d). *Recorded Crime Statistics 1898–2010* [online]. Research Development & Statistics, Home Office. Available at homeoffice.gov.uk/rds/recordedcrime1.html accessed 7 September 2010.

Home Office (2010e). *Home Office Statistical Bulletin, Crime in England and Wales 2009/10; Findings from the British Crime Survey and Police Recorded Crime.*

Homel, P., Nutley, S. N., Tilley, N. & Webb, B. (2004). *Investing to Deliver. Reviewing the Implementation of the UK Crime Reduction Programme* (Home Office Research Study 281). London: HMSO.

Hope, T. (2002). The road taken: Evaluation, replication and crime reduction. In G. Hughes, E. McLaughlin and J. Muncie (Eds.), *Crime Prevention and Community Safety: New Directions*. London: Sage.

Horvath, M. & Brown, J. (2007). Alcohol as drug of choice: Is drug assisted rape a misnomer? *Psychology, Crime and Law, 13* (5), 417–429.

Hough, M. (1996). *Drug Misusers and the Criminal Justice System: A Review of the Literature*. London: Home Office.

Howells, K. (1981). Adult sexual interest in children: Considerations relevant to theories of aetiology. In M. Cook and K. Howells (Eds.), *Adult Sexual Interest in Children* (pp. 55–94). London: Academic Press.

Howitt, D. (1995). *Paedophiles and Sexual Offences against Children*. Chichester: John Wiley and Sons.

Howitt, D. (2002). *Forensic and Criminal Psychology*. Harlow, Essex: Pearson Education.

Howitt, D. (2004). Just what is the role of fantasy in sex offending? *Criminal Behaviour and Mental Health, 14*, 182–188.

Howitt, D. (2008). *Introduction to forensic and criminal psychology* (3rd edition). Harlow, Essex: Pearson Education.

Howitt, D. & Sheldon, K. (2007). The role of cognitive distortions in paedophilic offending; Internet and contact offenders compared. *Psychology, Crime and Law*, 13, 469–486.

Howlett, C. (2003). The way forward: A law enforcement perspective. In A. MacVean, and P. Spindler (Eds.), *Policing Paedophiles on the Internet*. John Grieve Centre for Policing and Community Safety. Bristol: The New Police Bookshop.

Hucker, S. (2009). *Exhibitionism*. Available at www.forensicpsychiatry.ca/paraphilia/exhibition.htm, accessed on 04 September 2009.

Hudson, S. & Ward T. (1997). Rape: Psychopathology and theory. In R. D. Laws and W.T. O.Donohue (Eds.), *Sexual Deviance: Theory, Assessment and Treatment*. New York: Guilford Press.

Huesmann, L. R. (1988). An information processing model for the development of aggression. *Aggressive Behavior*, 14, 13–24.

Hughes, C. E. & Stevens, A. (2010). What can we learn from the Portuguese decriminalization of illicit drugs. *British Journal of Criminology*, 50, 999–1022.

Huntington, I. and Davies, D. (1994). *Fraud Watch: A Guide for Business*. London: Institute of Chartered Accountants in England and Wales.

Hyde, L. W., Shaw, D. S. & Moilanen, K. L. (2010). Developmental Precursors of Moral Disengagement and the Role of Moral disengagement in the Development of Antisocial Behavior. *Journal of Abnormal Child Psychology*, 38 (2), 197–209.

Inciardi, J. A. (1970). The adult firesetter. A typology. *Criminology*, 8, 145–155.

Internet Watch Foundation (2008). 2007 annual and charity report. Available at http://www.iwf.org.uk/assets/media/IWF%20Annual%20Report%202007.pdf, accessed 12 Feb 2012.

Interpol (2008). Databases. Interpol Fact Sheet, COM/FS/2008-07/GI-04. Available at http://www.interpol.int/Public/ICPO/FactSheets/GI04.pdf, accessed on 3 October 2008.

Itzin, C. (2000). Gendering domestic violence: The influence of feminism on policy and practice. In J. Hamner and C Itzin (Eds.), *Home Truths about Domestic Violence: Feminist Influences on Policy and Practices: A Reader*. London: Routledge.

Jackson, H. F. (1994). Assessment of fire setters. In M. McMurran and J. Hodge (Eds.), *The Assessment of Criminal Behaviours of Clients in Secure Settings*. London: Jessica Kingsley.

Jackson, H. F., Glass, C. A. & Hope, S. (1987a). A functional analysis of recidivist arson. *British Journal of Clinical Psychology*, 26, 175–185.

Jackson, H. F., Hope, S. & Glass, C. (1987b). Why Are Arsonists Not Violent Offenders? *International Journal of Offender Therapy and Comparative Criminology*, 31, 143–152.

Jagessar, J. D. H. & Sheridan, L. P. (2004). Stalking perceptions and experiences across two cultures. *Criminal Justice and Behavior*, 31, 97–119.

Jewkes, Y. & Andrews, C. (2005). Policing the filth: The problems of investigating online child pornography in England and Wales, *Policing and Society*, 15 (1), 42–62.

Johnson, G. M. & Knight, R.A. (2000). Developmental antecedents of sexual coercion in juvenile sexual offenders. *Sexual Abuse: A Journal of Research and Treatment*, 12, 165–178.

Johnson, M. P. (2008). *A Typology of Domestic Violence: Intimate Terrorism, Violent Resistance, and Situational Couple Violence*. Boston: Northeastern University Press.

Joint Prison Probation Accreditation Panel (2002). *What Works 2001–2002: Third Report from the Joint Prison/ Probation Accreditation Panel*. London: HMSO.

Joint statement on the impact of entertainment violence on children: Congressional Public Health Summit (2000, July 26). Available at http://www.aap. org/advocacy/releases/jstmtevc.htm, accessed on 28 January 2010.

Jones, A., Donmall, M., Millar, T., Moody, A, Weston, S., Anderson, T., Gittins, M., Abeywardana, V. & D'Souza, J. (2009). *The Drug Treatment Outcomes Research Study (DTORS): Final Outcome Report*. London: Home Office.

Jones, J. S., Alexander, C., Wynn, B. N., Rossman, L. & Dunnuck, C. (2009). Why women don't report sexual assault to the police: The influence of psychosocial variables and traumatic injury, *Journal of Emergency Medicine*, 36 (4), 417–424.

Jones, S., Lewis, D. & Maggs, P. (2002). *The Economic Cost of Fraud: A Report for the Home Office and the Serious Fraud Office*. London: NERA Economic Consultants.

Jones, T. (2003). Child abuse or computer crime? The proactive approach. In A. MacVean, and P. Spindler (Eds.), *Policing Paedophiles on the Internet* (pp. 41–48). John Grieve Centre for Policing and Community Safety. Bristol: The New Police Bookshop.

Jones, T. & Wilson, D. (2009). When thinking leads to doing: The relationship between fantasy and reality in sexual offending. In J. L. Ireland, C. A. Ireland and P. Birch (Eds.), *Violent and Sexual Offenders: Assessment, Treatment and Management*. Devon: Willan Publishing.

Kafka, M. P. (1991). Successful anti-depressant treatment of non paraphilic sexual addictions and paraphilias in men. *Journal of Clinical Psychiatry*, 52 (2), 60–65.

Kafka, M. P. (1994). Sertraline pharmacotherapy for paraphilias and paraphilia-related disorders: An open trial. *Annals of Clinical Psychiatry*, 6, 189–195.

Kafka, M. P. (1997). A monoamine hypothesis for the pathophysiology of paraphillic disorders. *Archives of Sexual Behaviour*, 26, 343–358.

Kafka, M. P. & Prentky, R. (1992). A comparative study of nonparaphilic sexual addictions and paraphilias in men. *Journal of Clinical Psychiatry*, 53 (10), 345–350.

Kafka, M. P. & Prentky, R. (1994). Preliminary observations of DSM-III-R axis I comorbidity in men with paraphilias and paraphilia-related disorders. *Journal of Clinical Psychiatry* 55 (11), 481–487.

Kafka, M. P. & Hennen, J. (2003). Hypersexual desire in males: Are males with paraphilias different from males with paraphilia related disorders. *Sexual Abuse: A Journal of Research and Treatment*, 4, 307–321.

Kahn, A. (1984). *Victims of Violence: Final report of the APA Taskforce on the Victims of Crime*. Washington, DC: American Psychological Association.

Kamphuis, J. H., Emmelkamp, P. M. G. & de Vries, V. (2004). Informant personality descriptions of postintimate stalkers using the Five Factor Profile. *Journal of Personality Assessment*, 82, 169–178.

Kaplan, H. B. (1975). Increase in self-rejection as an antecedent of deviant responses. *Journal of Youth and Adolescence*, 4 (3), 281–292.

Katz, J. (1988). *The Seductions of Crime: The Moral and Sensual Attractions of Doing Evil*. New York: Basic Books.

Kelly, L., Lovett, J. & Regan, L. (2005). *A Gap or Chasm? Attrition in Reported Rape Cases* London: Home Office.

Kemshall, H. et al. (2010). *Child Sex Offender Review (CSOR) Public Disclosure Pilots: A Process Evaluation – 2nd Edition.* London: Home Office.

Kennedy-Souza, B. L. (1998). Internet addiction disorder. *Interpersonal Computing and Technology: An Electronic Journal for the 21st Century,* 6, 1–2.

Kienlen, K. K. (1998). Developmental and social antecedents of stalking. In J. R. Meloy (Ed.), *The Psychology of Stalking: Clinical and Forensic Perspectives* (pp. 52–67). Toronto: Academic Press.

Kienlen, K. K., Birmingham, D. L., Solberg, K. B., et al. (1997) A comparative study of psychotic and non-psychotic stalking. *Journal of the American Academy of Psychiatry and Law,* 25 (3), 317–334.

Kirsh, S. J. & Olczak, P. V. (2002). The effects of extremely violent comic books on social information processing. *Journal of Interpersonal Violence,* 17, 1160–1178.

Klein, M. W. (1995). *The American Street Gang.* New York: Oxford University Press.

Klein, M. W., Weerman, F. M. & Thornberry, T. P. (2006). Street gang violence in Europe. *European Journal of Criminology,* 3, 413–437.

Kleptomaniacs and Shoplifters Anonymous (no date). Available at http://www.kleptomaniacsanonymous.com/, accessed on 30 November 2011.

Klostermann, K. C. & Fals-Stewart, W. (2006). Intimate partner violence and alcohol use: Exploring the role of drinking in partner violence and its implications for intervention. *Aggression and Violent Behavior,* 11, 587–597.

Knight, R. A. & Prentky, R. A. (1990). Classifying sexual offenders: The development and corroboration of taxonomic models. In W. L. Marshall, D. R. Laws and H. E. Barbaree (Eds.), *Handbook of Sexual Assault: Issues, Theories, and Treatment of the Offender* (pp. 23–52). New York: Plenum.

Knust, S. & Stewart, A. L. (2002). Risk-taking behaviour and criminal offending: An investigation of sensation seeking and the Eysenck personality questionnaire. *International Journal of Offender Therapy and Comparative Criminology,* 45, 586–602.

Kocsis, R. N. (2002). Arson: Exploring Motives and Possible Solutions. *Australian Institute of Criminology, Trends and Issues in Crime and Criminal Justice,* 236, 1–6.

Kohn, C. S. (2006). Conceptualization and treatment of Kleptomania behaviours using cognitive and behavioural strategies. *The International Journal of Behavioural Consultation and Therapy,* 2 (4), 553–559.

Kohn, C. S. & Antonuccio, D. O. (2002). Treatment of kleptomania using cognitive and behavioural strategies. *Clinical Case Studies,* 1, 25–38.

Koson, D. F. & Dvoskin, J. (1982). Arson: A diagnostic study. *Bulletin of the American Academy of Psychiatry and Law,* 10, 39–49.

Krahé, B. (2001). *The Social Psychology of Aggression.* East Sussex: Psychology Press.

Krasnovsky, T. & Lane, R. (1998). Shoplifting: a review of the literature. *Aggression and Violent Behaviour,* 3 (3), 219–235.

Kropp, P. R., Hart, S. D. & Lyon, D. R. (2002). Risk assessment of stalkers: Some problems and possible solutions. *Criminal Justice and Behavior,* 29, 590–616.

Kropp, P. R., Hart, S. D. & Lyon, D. R. (2008). *Guidelines for Stalking Assessment and Management (SAM).* Vancouver, Canada: ProActive Resolutions Inc.

Kuehner, C., Gass, P. & Dressing, H. (2007). Increased risk of mental disorders among lifetime victims of stalking – Findings from a community study. *European Psychiatry, 22,* 142–145.

Lacourse, E., Nagin, D. S., Vitaro, F., Côté, S., Arseneault, L. & Tremblay, R. E. (2006). Prediction of early-onset deviant peer group affiliation: A 12-year longitudinal study. *Archives of General Psychiatry, 63,* 562–568.

Lamontagne, Y., Boyer, R., Hetu, C. & Lacerte- Lamontagne (2000). Anxiety, Significant Losses, Depression, and Irrational Beliefs in First Offense Shoplifters. *Journal of Psychiatry, 45* (1), 64–66.

Lane, J. (2002). Fear of Gang Crime: A Qualitative Examination of the four Perspectives. *Journal of Research in Crime and Delinquency, 39,* 437–471.

Lang, R. A., Checkley, K. L, Langevin, R. & Pugh, G. (1987). Genital exhibitionism: Courtship disorder or narcissism? *Canadian Journal of Behavioural Sciences,* 19, 2.

Langevin, R. (1983). *Sexual Strands: Understanding and Treating Sexual Anomolies in Men.* Hillsdale, NJ: Lawrence Erlbaum Associates.

Langevin, R. & Lang, R. A. (1987). The courtship disorders. In G. D. Wilson (Ed.), *Variant Sexuality, Research and Theory.* Kent: Croom Helm Ltd.

Langevin, R., Paitich, D., Freeman, R., Mann, K. & Handy, L. (1978). Personality characteristics and sexual anomalies in males. *Canadian Journal of Behavioural Sciences,* 10, 3.

Langevin, R., Paitich, Hucker, S., Newman, S., Ramsay, G., Pope, S., Geller, G. & Anderson, C. (1979). The effect of assertiveness training, provera and sex of therapist in the treatment of genital exhibitionism. *Journal of Behaviour Therapy and Experimental Psychiatry,* 10 (4), 275–282.

Långström, N. & Hanson, R. K. (2006). High rates of sexual behaviour in the general population: Correlates and risk factors. *Archives of Sexual Behaviour,* 35, 37–52.

Långström, N. & Seto, M. (2006). Exhibitionistic and voyeuristic behaviour in a Swedish national population survey. *Archives of Sexual Behaviour,* 35, 427–435.

Langton, C. M. (2007). Rape related cognition: Current research. In T. A. Gannon, T. Ward, A. R. Beech and D. Fisher (Eds.), *Aggressive Offenders' Cognition: Theory, Research and Practice.* Chichester: John Wiley.

Langton, C. M. & Marshall, W. L. (2001). Cognitions in rapists: Theoretical patterns by typological breakdown. *Aggression and Violent Behaviour,* 6, 499–518.

Lanning, K. (2001 4th Edition). *Child Molesters: A Behavioural Analysis.* National Center for Missing and Exploited Children, Washington, D. C.

Laroche, D. (2005). *Aspects of the Context of Domestic Violence: Situational Couple Violence and Intimate Terrorism in Canada 1999.* Quebec: Institut de la statistique du Québec. Available at http://www.stat.gouv.qc.ca/publications/conditions/pdf/AspectViolen_an.pdf, accessed on 30 November 2011.

Laulik, S., Allam, S. & Sheridan, L. (2007). An investigation into maladaptive personality functioning in internet sex offenders, *Psychology, Crime and Law,* 13 (5), 523–535.

Laville, Sandra (2009). Rape investigations unit launched as Met aims to target serial attackers. Available at http://www.guardian.co.uk/uk/2009/dec/01/met-launches-rape-investigations-unit, accessed on 13 January 2010.

Laws, D. R. & Marshall, W. L. (1990). In W. L. Marshall, D. R. Laws and H. E. Barbaree (Eds.), *Handbook of Sexual Assault: Issues, Theories and Treatment of the Offender,* A conditioning theory of the etiology and maintenance of deviant sexual preference and behaviour. pp. 209–229. New York: Plenum Press.

Laycock, G. (1991). Operation identification or the power of publicity? *Security Journal*, 2, 67–71.

Lea, S. & Auburn, T. (2001). The social construction of rape in the talk of a convicted rapist. *Feminism and Psychology*, 11 (1), 11–33.

Lee, J. K., Pattison, P., Jackson, H. J. & Ward, T. (2001). The general, common and specific features of psychopathology for different types of paraphilias. *Criminal Justice and Behaviour*, 28, 227.

Lee, J. K. P., Jackson, H. J., Pattison, P. & Ward, A. (2002). Developmental risk factors for sexual offending. *Child Abuse & Neglect*, 26 (1), 73–92.

Leitenberg, H. & Henning, K. (1995). Sexual fantasy. *Psychological Bulletin*, 117, 469–496.

Levi, M. (1991). Sentencing white-collar crime in the dark?: Reflections on the Guinness Four. *The Howard Journal*, 30 (4), 257–279.

Levi, M. & Pithouse, A. (1992). The victims of fraud. In D. Downes (Ed.), *Unravelling Criminal Justice* (pp. 229–247). Basingstoke and London: Macmillan Press Ltd.

Levi, M., Burrows, J., Fleming, M. H. and Hopkins, M. (2007). *The Nature, Extent and Economic Impact of Fraud in the UK*, Report for the Association of Chief Police Officers' Economic Crime Portfolio.

Levin, B. (1976). Psychological characteristics of fire setters. *Fire Journal*, 70 (2), 36–41.

Lewis, N. D. C. & Yarnell, H. (1951). Pathological fire setting (pyromania). *Nervous and Mental Disease Monograph*, 82.

Lindberg, N., Holi, M. M., Tani, P. & Virkkunen, M. (2005). Looking for pyromania: Characteristics of a consecutive sample of Finnish male criminals with histories of recidivistic fire-setting between 1973 and 1993. *BMC Psychiatry*, 5 (47), doi:10.1186/1471-244X-5-47.

Linehan, M. M. (1993). *Cognitive Behavioral Treatment of Borderline Personality Disorder*. New York: Guilford Press.

Lo, L. (1994). Exploring teenage shoplifting behaviour: A choice & constraint approach. *Environment & Behaviour*, 26 (5), 613–639.

Lochman, J. E. & Dodge, K. A. (1994). Social-cognitive processes of severely violent, moderately aggressive, and nonaggressive boys. *Journal of Consulting and Clinical Psychology*, 62, 366–374.

Logan, T. K. & Cole, J. (2007). The impact of partner stalking on mental health and protective order outcomes over time. *Violence and Victims*, 22, 546–562.

Logan, T. K. & Walker, R. (2008). Civil protective order outcomes: Violations and perceptions of effectiveness. *Journal of Interpersonal Violence*, 24, 675–692.

Logie, R. H., Wright, R. T. & Decker, S. (1992). Recognition memory performance and residential burglary. *Applied Cognitive Psychology*, 6, 109–123.

Longo, R. E. & Groth, N. A. (1983). Juvenile sexual offenses in the histories of adult rapists and child molesters. *International Journal of Offender Therapy and Comparative Criminology*, 27, 150.

Losel, F. & Schmucker, M. (2005). The effectiveness of treatment for sexual offenders: A comprehensive meta-analysis. *Journal of Experimental Criminology*, 1 (1), 117–146.

Lucy Faithfull Foundation (2008). 'Inform+' treatment manual. Available on request from the Lucy Faithfull Foundation, Nightingale House, 46–48 East Street, Epsom, U.K., KT17 1HB.

Lynam, D. R., Piquero, A. R., & Moffitt, T. E. (2004). Specialization and the propensity to violence: Support from self-reports but not official records. *Journal of Contemporary Criminal Justice*, 20, 215–228.

Macht, L. B. & Mack, J. E. (1968). The firesetter syndrome. *Psychiatry*, 31, 277–288.

MacKenzie, R., Mullen, P., Ogloff, J. & McEwan, D. (2008). Parental bonding and adult attachment styles in different types of stalkers. *Journal of Forensic Sciences*, 53, 1443–1449.

MacKinnon, C. A. (1987). *Feminism Unmodified: Discourses on Life and Law*. Cambridge: Harvard University Press.

Maguire, M. (1980). The impact of burglary on victims. *British Journal of Criminology*, 20, 197, 175.

Maguire, M. (1982). *Burglary in a Dwelling: The Offence, the Offender and the Victim: Cambridge Studies in Criminology*. London: Heinmann.

Malamuth, N. M. & Brown, L. M. (1994). Sexually aggressive men's perceptions of women's communications. *Journal of Personality and Social Psychology*, 67 (4), 699–712.

Maletzky, B. M. (1991). *Treating the Sexual Offender*. Newberry Park, CA: Sage Publications

Maletzky, B. M. (1997). Exhibitionism: Assessment and treatment. In D. R. Laws and W. T. O'Donahue (Eds.), *Sexual Deviance Theory, Assessment, and Treatment*. New York: Guilford.

Mann, K. (1985). *Defending White-Collar Crime: A Portrait of Attorneys at Work*. New Haven and London: Yale University Press.

Mann, R. E. & Shingler, J. (2006). Schema-driven cognition in sexual offenders: Theory, assessment and treatment. In W. L. Marshall, Y. M. Fernandez, L. E. Marshall, and G. A. Serran (Eds.), *Sexual Offender Treatment: Controversial Issues* (pp. 173–185). Chichester, UK: Wiley.

Mann, R. E., Ainsworth, F., Al-Attar, Z. & Davies, M. (2008). Voyeurism: Assessment and treatment. In D. R. Laws and W. T. O'Donahue (Eds.), *Sexual Deviance Theory, Assessment, and Treatment* (2nd ed). New York: Guilford.

Marcus-Newhall, A., Pedersen, W.C., Carlson, M. & Miller, N. (2000). Displaced aggression is alive and well: A meta-analytic review. *Journal of Personality and Social Psychology*, 78, 670–689.

Marshall, B., Webb, B. & Tilley, N. (2005). *Rationalisation of Current Research on Guns, Gangs and Other Weapons: Phase One*. London: UCL.

Marshall, P. (1997). A Reconviction Study of HMP Grendon Therapeutic Community, Research Findings No. 53, London: Home Office Research and Statistics Directorate.

Marshall, W. L. (2006). Ammonia aversion with an exhibitionist: A case study. *Clinical Case Studies*, 5, 15.

Marshall, W. L. & Barbaree, H. E. (1990). An integrated theory of the etiology of sexual offending. In W. L. Marshall, D. R. Laws and H. E. Barbaree (Eds.), *Handbook of Sexual Assault: Issues, Theories and Treatment of the Offender* (pp. 257–275). London: Plenum Press.

Maruna, S. (2001). *Making Good: How Ex-convicts Reform and Rebuild Their Lives*. Washington: APA.

Maruna, S. & Mann, R. E. (2006). A fundamental attribution error? Rethinking cognitive distortions. *Legal and Criminological Psychology*, 11, 155–177.

Marziano, V., Ward, T., Beech, A. R. & Pattison, P. (2006). Identifiction of five fundamental implicit theories underlying cognitive distortions in child abusers: A preliminary study *Psychology, Crime and Law*, 12 (1), 97–105.

Matek, O. (1988). Obscence phone callers. *Journal of Social Work and Human Sexuality*, 7, 113–130.

Matrix Knowledge Group (2007). *The Economic Case for and against Prison: Technical Appendix*. London: Matrix Knowledge Group. Available at http://www.matrixknowledge.com/wp-content/uploads/technical-appendix.pdf, accessed on August 2010.

Matsumura, E. M. & Tucker, R. R. (1992). Fraud detection: A theoretical foundation. *The Accounting Review*, 67 (4, October), 753–782.

Matthews, R. (1996). *Armed Robbery: Two Police Responses. Crime Detection and Prevention Series Paper 78*. Home Office Police Research Group.

Matza, D. (1964). *Delinquency and Drift*. New York: John Wiley and Sons Inc.

McCann, J. (2001). The development of stalking. *Stalking in Children and Adolescents: The Primitive Bond* (pp. 79–117). Washington, DC: American Psychological Association.

McCann, R., Ball, E. M. & Ivanoff, A. (2000). DBT with an inpatient forensic population: The CMHIP Forensic Model. *Cognitive and Behavioral Practice*, 7, 447–456.

McCulloch, H. (2005). Interpol and Crimes against children. In E. Quayle and M. Taylor (Eds.), *Viewing Child Pornography on the Internet: Understanding the Offence, Managing the Offender, Helping the Victims*. Lyme Regis: Russell House Publishing.

McElroy, K., McElrath, K. & Higgins, K. (1998). Does Ulster still say no? Drugs, politics, and propaganda in Northern Ireland. *Journal of Drug Issues*, 28, 122–154.

McElroy, S. L., Pope, H. G. Jr., Hudson, J. I., Keck, P. E. Jr. & White, K. L. (1991). Kleptomania: A report of 20 cases. *American Journal of Psychiatry*, 148 (5), 652–657.

McEwan, T., Mullen, P. E. & Purcell, R. (2007). Identifying risk factors in stalking: A review of current research. *International Journal of Law and Psychiatry*, 30, 1–9.

McKeganey, N. (2007). The challenge to UK drug policy. *Drugs: Education, Prevention and Policy*, 14, 559–571.

McKeganey, N. & Barnard, M. (1992). *AIDS, Drugs and Sexual Risk: Lives in the Balance*. Buckingham: Open University Press.

McMurran, M. (2008). Substance abuse. In K. Soothill, P. Rodgers & M. Dolan (Eds.), *Handbook of Forensic Mental Health*. Devon: Willan Publishing.

McVie, S. (2010). Gang Membership and Knife Carrying: Results from the Edinburgh Study of Youth Transitions and Crime. Scottish Government Social Research. Available online at http://www.scotland.gov.uk/Resource/Doc/324153/0104312.pdf, accessed on 29 October 2010.

Mead, B. T. (1975). Coping with obscene phone calls. Medical aspects of human sexuality, 9, 127–128.

Meloy, J. R. (1996). Stalking (obsessional following): A review of some preliminary studies. *Aggression and Violent Behavior*, 1, 147–162.

Meloy, J. R. (1998). *The Psychology of Stalking*. San Diego, CA: Academic Press.

Meloy, J. R. (2007). Stalking: The state of the science. *Criminal Behaviour and Mental Health*, 17, 1–7.

Meloy, J. R. & Boyd, C. B. (2003). Female stalkers and their victims. *Journal of American Academic Psychiatry and Law*, 31, 211–219.

Melton, H. C. (2007). Predicting the occurrence of stalking in relationships characterized by domestic violence. *Journal of Interpersonal Violence*, 22, 3–25.

Menard, S., Mihalic, S. & Huizinga, D. (2001). Drugs and crime revisited. *Justice Quarterly*, 18, 269–299.

Merton, Robert K. (1938). Social structure and anomie. *American Sociological Review*, 3, 672–82.

Metropolitan Police (2010). Gangs Group Violence and the Law. Available online at http://www.safe.met.police.uk/gangs_and_violence/consequences_and_the_law.html, accessed on 25 October 2010.

Meyer, W. J. Collier, C. & Evangeline, E. (1992). Depo provera treatment for sex offending behavior: An evaluation of outcome. *Bulletin of the American Academy of Psychiatry & the Law*, 20 (3), 249–259.

Michaels, Sean. (2009). *N-Dubz members to assist police after DJ's rape arrest*. Available at http://www.guardian.co.uk/music/2009/nov/18/n-dubz, accessed on 13 January 13 2010.

Middleton, D., Beech, A. & Mandeville-Norden, R. (2005). What sort of person could do that? Psychological profiles of internet pornography users. In E. Quayle and M. Taylor (Eds.), *Viewing Child Pornography on the Internet: Understanding the Offence, Managing the Offender, Helping the Victims*. Lyme Regis: Russell House Publishing.

Middleton, D., Elliott, I. A., Mandeville-Norden, R. & Beech, A. (2006). An investigation into the applicability of the ward and siegert pathways model of child sexual abuse with internet offenders. *Psychology, Crime and Law*, 12 (6), 589–603.

Miller, N. (2001). *Stalking Laws and Implementation Practices: A National Review for Policymakers and Practitioners*. Institute for Law and Justice, Alexandria, VA.

Miller, N. E. (1948). Theory and experiment relating psychoanalytic displacement to stimulus-response generalization. *Journal of Abnormal and Social Psychology*, 43, 155–178.

Miller, T. R., Cohen, M. A. & Rossman, S. B. (1993). Victim costs of violent crime and resulting injuries. *Health Affairs*, Winter, 186–197.

Millie, A. (2010). Moral politics, moral decline and antisocial behaviour. *People, Place and Policy Online*, 4, 6–13.

Miner, M. H. & Dwyer, S. M. (1997). The psychosocial development of sex offenders: Differences between exhibitionists, child molesters and incest offenders. *International Journal of Offender Therapy and Comparative Criminology*, 41 (1), 36–44.

Ministry of Justice (2008a). *Criminal Statistics: England and Wales 2007, Statistics Bulletin*. Available at http://www.justice.gov.uk/publications/docs/crim-stats-2007-tag.pdf, accessed on 30 November 2011.

Ministry of Justice (2008b). The Blakey review: Disrupting the supply of illegal drugs into prisons. Available at http://www.csc-scc.gc.ca/text/pblct/gangsdrugssympsm/docs/blakey-Sympsmgds-eng.pdf, accessed on 30 November 2011.

Ministry of Justice (2009). *Sentencing Statistics, 2007 England & Wales: Ministry of Justice Statistics Bulletin*. Available at http://www.justice.gov.uk/publications/docs/sentencing-statistics-2007-revised.pdf, accessed on 30 November 2011.

Ministry of Justice (2010a). Criminal Statistics: England and Wales 2008. Available at http://www.justice.gov.uk/publications/docs/criminal-stats-2008.pdf, accessed 12 Feb 2012.

Ministry of Justice (2010b). *Sentencing Statistics: England and Wales 2008 Statistics Bulletin*. London: HMSO.

Ministry of Justice (2010c). Reoffending of Adults: Results from the 2008 Cohorts. England and Wales. Ministry of Justice Statistics Bulletin.

Mitchell, I. & Gilchrist, E. (2006). Domestic violence and panic attacks – common neural mechanisms? *Legal and Criminological Psychology*, 11, 267–282.

Mitchell, J. & Palmer, E. J. (2004). Evaluating the 'reasoning and rehabilitation' program for young offenders. *Journal of Offender Rehabilitation*, 39 (December), 31–45.

Moffitt, T. E. (1993). Adolescent-limited and life-course-persistent antisocial behavior: A developmental taxonomy. *Psychological Review*, 100, 674–701.

Moffitt, T. E., Robbins, R. W. & Caspi, A. (2001). A couples analysis of partner abuse with recommendations for treatment. *Criminal Justice and Policy*, 1, 5–36.

Money, J. (1986). *Love Maps – Clinical Concepts of Sexual/Erotic Health and Pathology, Paraphilia, and Gender Transposition in Childhood, Adolescence, and Maturity*. New York: Prometheus Books.

Morahan-Martin, J. & Schumacher, P. (2000). Incidence and correlates of pathological Internet use among college students. *Computers in Human Behavior*, 16 (1) 13–29.

Morin, J. W. & Levenson, J. S. (2008). Exhibitionism: Assessment and treatment. In D. R. Laws and W. T. O'Donahue, (Eds.), *Sexual Deviance Theory, Assessment, and Treatment* (2nd ed). New York: Guilford.

Morrison, K. A. (2008). Differentiating between physically violent and nonviolent stalkers: An examination of Canadian cases. *Journal of Forensic Science*, 53, 742–751.

Muir, D. (2005). *Violence against Children in Cyberspace*. Bangkok: ECPAT International.

Mullen, P. E., Mackenzie, R., Ogloff, J. R. P., Pathé, M., McEwan, T. & Purcell, R. (2006). Assessing and managing the risks in the stalking situation. *Journal of American Academic Psychiatry and Law*, 34, 439–450.

Mullen, P. E., Pathé, M., Purcell, R. & Stuart, G. W. (1999). Study of stalkers. *American Journal of Psychiatry*, 155, 1244–1249.

Murphy, R. & Eder, S. (2010). Acquisitive and other property crime. In J. Flatley, C. Kershaw, K. Smith, R. Chaplin and D. Mood (Eds.), *Crime in England and Wales 2009/10: Findings from the British Crime Survey and Police Recorded Crime (Home Office Report 12/10)*. London: HMSO.

Murphy, G. H. & Clare, C. H. (1996). Analysis of motivation in people with mild learning disabilities (mental handicap) who set fires. *Psychology, Crime and Law*, 2, 153–164.

Murphy, W. D. (1990). Assessment and modification of cognitive distortions in sex offenders. In W. L. Marshall, R. D. Laws and H. Barbaree (Eds.), *Handbook of Sexual Assault: Issues, Theory and Treatment of the Offender*. New York: Plenum.

Murphy, W. D. (1997). Exhibitionism, psychopathology and theory. In D. R. Laws and W. T. O'Donahue (Eds.), *Sexual Deviance Theory, Assessment, and Treatment* (pp. 22–39). New York: Guilford.

Murphy, W. D. & Page, I. J. (2008). Exhibitionism: Psychopathology and theory. In D. R. Laws and W. T. O'Donahue (Eds.), *Sexual Deviance Theory, Assessment, and Treatment* (2nd ed) (pp. 61–75). New York: Guilford.

Mustaine, E. E. & Tewksbury, R. (1999). A routine activity theory explanation for women's stalking victimizations. *Violence against Women*, 5, 43–62.

National Archive (no date) Criminal Damage Act 1971. Available at http://www.legislation.gov.uk/ukpga/1971/48/contents, accessed 30 November 2011.

National Association for Shoplifting Prevention (NASP). Available at http://www.shopliftingprevention.org/main.asp, accessed on 30 November 2011.

National Crime Statistic 2008/2009. Available at http://www.justice.gov.uk/publications/docs/criminal-stats-2008.pdf, accessed on 30 November 2011.

National Economic Research Associates (2000). *The Economic Cost of Fraud: A Report for the Home Office and the Serious Fraud Office.* London: National Economic Research Associates (NERA).

National Gang Intelligence Centre (2009). National Gang Assessment Threat. Washington USA: National Gang Intelligence Centre. Available at http://www.fbi.gov/stats-services/publications/national-gang-threat-assessment-2009-pdf, accessed 12 Feb 2012.

NCPE (2005). *Guidance on Investigating Child Abuse and Safeguarding Children.* Hook, UK: National Centre for Policing Excellence.

Nee, C. (2010a). Residential burglary: Methodological and theoretical underpinnings. In J. Brown and E. Campbell (Eds.), *Cambridge Handbook of Forensic Psychology.* Cambridge: University of Cambridge Press.

Nee, C. (2010b). Research on residential burglary: Ways of improving validity and participants' recall when gathering data. In W. Bernasco (Ed.), *Offenders on Offending: Learning about Crime from Criminals.* Cullumpton: Willan.

Nee, C. & Meenaghan, A. (2006). Expert decision-making in burglars. *British Journal of Criminology, 46,* 935–949.

Nee, C. & Taylor, M. (1988). Residential burglary in the Republic of Ireland. In M. Tomlinson, T. Varley and C. McCullagh (Eds.), *Whose Law and Order.* The Sociological Association of Ireland: Galway.

Nee, C. & Taylor, M. (2000). Examining burglars' target selection: interview, experiment, or ethnomethodology? *Psychology, Crime and Law, 6,* 45–59.

Nelken, D. (2002). White-collar crime. In M. Maguire, R. Morgan and R. Reiner (Eds.), *Oxford Handbook of Criminology* (pp. 355–392). Oxford: Oxford University Press.

NSPCC (2009). NSPCC research shows fifty recorded child sex offences a day. Press release, 19 January. Available at http://www.nspcc.org.uk/whatwedo/mediacentre/pressreleases/2009_19_january_fifty_recorded_child_sex_offences_a_day_wdn62997.html, accessed on 29 August 2009.

NSPCC (2010). Child Homicides. Available at http://www.nspcc.org.uk/Inform/research/statistics/child_homicide_statistics_wda48747.html, accessed on 15 October 2010.

Nutt, D., King, L. A., Saulsbury, W. & Blakemore, C. (2007). Development of a rational scale to assess the harm of drugs of potential misuse. *The Lancet, 369,* 1047–1053.

O'Connell, R. (2004). From fixed to mobile Internet: The morphing of criminal activity on-line. In M. Calder (Ed.), *Child Sexual Abuse and the Internet: Tackling the New Frontier* (pp. 37–55). Lyme Regis: Russell House Publishing.

Office of the Deputy Prime Minister (2005). *Arson Terminology.* London: Office of the Deputy Prime Minister Publications.

Office of the Deputy Prime Minister (2006). *The Economic Cost of Fire: Estimates for 2004.* London: ODPM. Available at http://www.communities.gov.uk/documents/fire/pdf/144524.pdf, accessed on 30 November 2011.

Okami, P. & Goldberg, A. (1992). Personality correlates of pedophilia: Are they reliable indicators? *Journal of Sex Research, 29,* 297–328.

Olweus, D. (2005). A useful evaluation design, and effects of the Olweus bullying prevention program. *Psychology, Crime & Law, 11,* 389–402.

Orth, U. (2002). Secondary victimisation of crime victims by criminal proceedings. *Social Justice Research, 15* (4), 313–325.

Pakes, F. & Winstone, J. (2007). *Psychology and Crime: Understanding and Tackling Offending Behaviour.* Devon: Willan.

Pakhomou, S. M. (2006). Methodological aspects of telephone Scatologia: A case study. *International Journal of Law and Psychiatry, 29,* 178–185.

Palmer, E. J., Caulfield, L. S. & Hollin, C. R. (2007). Interventions with arsonists and young fire setters: A survey of the national picture in England and Wales. *Legal and Criminological Psychology, 12,* 101–116.

Palmer, E. J., Holmes, A. & Hollin, C. R. (2002). Investigating burglars' decisions factors influencing target choice, method of entry, reasons for offending, repeat victimization of a property and victim awareness. *Security Journal, 15,* 7–18.

Palmer, T. (2005). Behind the screen: Children who are the subjects of abusive images. In E. Quayle and M. Taylor (Eds.), *Viewing Child Pornography on the Internet: Understanding the Offence, Managing the Offender, Helping the Victims.* Lyme Regis: Russell House Publishing.

Palmeri, T. J., Wong, A. C. & Gauthier, I. (2004). Computational approaches to the development of expertise. *Trends in Cognitive Sciences, 8,* 378–386.

Paradine, K. & Wilkinson, J. (2004). *Research and Literature Review: Protection and Accountability – The Reporting, Investigation and Prosecution of Domestic Violence cases.*

Pathé M. & Mullen, P. E. (1997). The impact of stalkers on their victims. *British Journal of Psychiatry, 170,* 12–17.

Pearson, F. & Lipton, D. (1999). A meta-analytic review of the effectiveness of corrections-based treatments for drug abuse. *Prison Journal, 79,* 384–410.

Pease, K. (1985). Obscene telephone calls to women in England and Wales. *Howard League Journal of Criminal Justice, 24,* 275–281.

Pease, K. (1998). *Repeat Victimization: Taking Stock.* (Crime Detection and Prevention Series Paper 90) London, UK: Home Office Police Research Group.

Pence, E. & Paymar, M. (1993). *Education Groups for Men who Batter.* New York: Springer Publishing.

Perry, A., McDougall, C. & Farrington, D. P. (Eds.) (2006). *Reducing Crime: The Effectiveness of Criminal Justice Interventions.* Chichester: Wiley.

Peters, C. (2005). *Harold Shipman: Mind Set on Murder.* London: Carlton Books.

Petersen, R. D. (2000). Definitions of a gang and impacts on public policy. *Journal of Criminal Justice, 28,* 139–149.

Phelan, J. (2002). Childhood Kleptomania: Two Clinical Case Studies with Implications for Further Research. *Psychology and Education an Interdisciplinary Journal, 39,* 19–21.

Pithers, W. D. (1990). Relapse prevention with sexual aggressors. In W. L. Marshall, D. R. Laws, and H. E. Barbaree (Eds.), *Handbook of Sexual Assault* (pp. 343–361). New York: Plenum Press.

Pitts, J. (2007). *Reluctant Gangsters: Youth Gangs in Waltham Forest.* University of Bedfordshire London: Waltham Forest Council. Available at http://www.walthamforest.gov.uk/reluctant-gangsters.pdf, accessed on 30 November 2011.

Polaschek, D. L. L. (2006). Violent offender programmes: Concept, theory, and practice. In C. R. Hollin, and E. J. Palmer (Eds.), *Offending Behaviour*

Programmes: Development, Application and Controversies (pp. 113–154). Chichester: Wiley.

Polaschek, D. L. L. (2010a). High-intensity rehabilitation for violent offenders in New Zealand: reconviction outcomes for high- and medium-risk prisoners. *Journal of Interpersonal Violence,* 26 (4) 664–482.

Polaschek, D. L. L. (2010b). Rehabilitating violent offenders. In J. Brown & E. Campbell (Eds.), *Handbook of Forensic Psychology: Theory, Assessment, Research and Practice.* Cambridge UK: Cambridge University Press.

Polaschek, D. L. L. & Dixon, B. G. (2001). The violence prevention project: The development and evaluation of a treatment programme for violent offenders. *Psychology, Crime, and Law,* 7, 1–23.

Polaschek, D. L. L. & Gannon, T. A. (2004). The implicit theories of potential rapists: What convicted offenders tell us. *Sexual Abuse: A Journal of Treatment and Research,* 16 (4), 299–314.

Polaschek, D. L. L. & Ward, T. (2002). The implicit theories of potential rapists: What our questionnaires tell us. *Aggression and Violent Behaviour,* 7 (4), 385–406.

Polaschek, D. L. L., Collie, R. M. & Walkey, F. H. (2004). Criminal attitudes to violence: Development and preliminary validation of a scale for male prisoners. *Aggressive Behavior,* 30, 484–503.

Polaschek, D. L. L., Hudson, S. M., Ward, T. & Siegert, R. J. (2001). Rapists' offense processes: A preliminary descriptive model. *Journal of Interpersonal Violence,* 16, 523–544.

Polaschek, D. L. L., Wilson, N. J., Townsend, M. A. & Daly, L. R. (2005). Cognitive-behavioral rehabilitation for high-risk violent offenders: An outcome evaluation of the Violence Prevention Unit. *Journal of Interpersonal Violence,* 20, 1611–1627.

Police and Criminal Evidence Act (PACE) (1984). Available at http://www.legislation.gov.uk/ukpga/1984/60/contents, accessed 30th November 2011, accessed on 30 November 2011.

Polvi, N., Looman, T., Humphries, C. & Pease, K. (1991). The time course of repeat burglary victimization. *British Journal of Criminology,* 31, 411–414.

Price, M., Kafka, M., Commons, M. L., Gutheil, G. T. & Simpson, W. (2002). Telephone scatologia comorbidity with other paraphilias and paraphilia related disorders. *International Journal of Law and Psychiatry,* 25, 37–49.

PricewaterhouseCoopers (2009). Global Economic Crime Survey 2009.

Prins, H. (1995). Adult fire-raising: Law and psychology. *Psychology, Crime and Law,* 1, 271–281.

Prins, H. (1980). *Offenders, Deviants or Patients?* London: Tavistock Publications.

Prins, H. (1994). *Fire-Raising. Its Motivation and Management.* London: Routledge.

Prins, H. (1999). The motivation of arsonists – Reflections on research and practice. *The British Journal of Forensic Practice,* 1 (1), 6–11.

Prins, H. (2001). Arson – a brief review. *Prison Service Journal,* 133, 2–5.

Prins, H., Tennant, G. & Trick, K. (1985). Motives for Arson (Fire-setting), *Medicine, Science and the Law,* 25, 275–278.

Prins, H. A. (2005). *Offenders, Deviants and Patients?* (3rd edn). London: Psychology Press.

Prison Reform Trust (2001). *Life Sentenced Prisoners – 'Lifers'.* London: HM Prison Service.

Protection of Children Act (1978). Available at http://www.legislation.gov.uk/ukpga/1978/37, accessed 12 Feb 2012.

Purcell, R., Pathé, M. & Mullen, P. E. (2002). The prevalence and nature of stalking in the Australian community. *Australian and New Zealand Journal of Psychiatry, 36*, 114–120.

Purcell, R., Pathé, M. & Mullen, P. E. (2004). Editorial: When do repeated intrusions become stalking? *The Journal of Forensic Psychiatry and Psychology, 15*, 571–583.

Purcell, R., Flower, T., Mullen, P. & Moller, B. (2009) Stalking among juveniles. *The British Journal of Psychiatry, 194*, 451–455.

Puri, B. K., Baxter, R. & Cordess, C. C. (1995). Characteristics of firesetters: A study and proposed multiaxial psychiatric classification. *British Journal of Psychiatry, 166*, 393–396.

Putnam, D. E. (2000). Initiation and maintenance of online sexual compulsivity: Implications for assessment and treatment. *CyberPsychology and Behavior, 3*, 553–563.

Putwain, D. & Sammons, A. (2002). *Psychology and Crime.* Hove: Routledge.

Quayle, E. (2004). The impact of viewing on offending behaviour. In M. Calder (Ed.), *Child Sexual Abuse and the Internet: Tackling the New Frontier* (pp. 25–36). Lyme Regis: Russell House Publishing.

Quayle, E. & Taylor, M. (2002). Child pornography and the Internet: Perpetuating a cycle of abuse. *Deviant Behavior: An Interdisciplinary Journal, 23* (4), 331–361.

Quayle, E., Vaughan, M. & Taylor, M. (2006). Sex offenders, Internet child abuse images and emotional avoidance: The importance of values. *Aggression and Violent Behavior, 11*, 1–11.

Rachman, S. & Hodgson, R. (1980). *Obsessions and Compulsions.* New Jersey: Prentice Hall.

Rader, N. E. (2004). The threat of victimization: A theoretical reconceptualization of fear of crime. *Sociological Spectrum, 24*, 689–704.

Raine, A. (1993). *The Psychopathology of Crime: Criminal Behaviour as a Clinical Disorder.* San Diego: Academic Press.

Ramage, S. (2005) *Serious Fraud and Current Issues.* New York: iUniverse, Inc.

Rape Crisis (2007). *Rape Crisis – England and Wales: Myths.* Available at http://www.rapecrisis.org.uk/mythsampfacts2.php, accessed 12 Feb 2012.

Rape Crisis Scotland (2008). This is not an invitation to rape me. Available at http://www.thisisnotaninvitationtorapeme.co.uk/dress/, accessed on 24 February 2010.

Rasmussen, D.W. & Benson, B.L. (1999). Reducing the harms of drug policy: An economic perspective. *Substance Use and Misuse, 34*, 49–67.

Ray, J. H. & Briar, K. (1988). Economic motivators for shoplifting US. *Journal of Sociology & Social Welfare, 15* (4), 177–189.

Reed, E., Raj, A., Miller, E. & Silverman, J.G. (2010). Losing the 'Gender' in Gender-based violence: The mis-steps of research on dating and intimate partner violence. *Violence against Women, 16*, 348–354.

Reid, L. & Konrad, M. (2004). The gender gap in fear: Assessing the interactive effects of gender and perceived risk on fear of crime. *Sociological Spectrum, 24* (4), 399–425.

Renold, E., Creighton, S. J., Atkinson, C. & Carr, J. (2003). *Images of Abuse: A Review of the Evidence on Child Pornography.* The National Society for the Prevention of Cruelty to Children. London.

Repo, E., Virkkunen, M., Rawlings, R. & Linnolia, M. (1997). Criminal and psychiatric histories of Finnish arsonists. *Acta Psychiatrica Scandinavica, 95*, 318–323.

Reppetto, T.A. (1974). *Residential Crime*. Massachusetts: Ballinger.

Resnick, P. (2007). Stalking risk assessment. In Debra Pinels (Ed.), *Stalking: Psychiatric Perspectives and Practical Approaches* (pp. 61–84). New York, NY: Oxford University Press.

Response from the Home Office. Available at http://rds.homeoffice.gov.uk/rds/pdfs08/consult-bcsu16-response08.pdf, accessed on 30 October 2010.

Rice, M. & Harris, G.T. (1991). Predicting the recidivism of mentally disordered firesetters. *Journal of Interpersonal Violence*, 11 (3), 364–375.

Rider, A. (1980). The fire-setter: A psychological profile, pt.1. *FBI Law Enforcement Bulletin*, 49 (7), 7–17.

Rights of Women (2008). *From Report to Court: A handbook for adult survivors of sexual violence*. Available at www.rightsofwomen.org.uk, accessed on 13 January 2010.

Riordan, S. (1999). Indecent exposure: The impact on the victims fear of sexual crime. *Journal of Forensic Psychiatry*, 10, 309–316.

Ritchie, E. C. & Huff, T. G. (1999). Psychiatric aspects of arsonists. *Journal of Forensic Sciences*, 44 (4), 733–740.

Robbins, P. & Darlington, R. (2003). The role of industry and the internet watch foundation. In A. MacVean, and P. Spindler (Eds.), *Policing Paedophiles on the Internet* (pp. 79–86). John Grieve Centre for Policing and Community Safety. Bristol: The New Police Bookshop.

Roberts, J. V. & Hough, J. M. (2005). *Understanding Public Attitudes to Criminal Justice*. Maidenhead, Berkshire: Open University Press.

Robinson, A.L., Hudson, K. & Brookman, F. (2009). *A Process Evaluation of Ynys Saff, the Sexual Assault Referral Centre in Cardiff: Final Evaluation Report*. Cardiff: School of Social Sciences, Cardiff University.

Roe, S. (2010). Domestic violence. In K. Smith, J. Flatley, K. Coleman, S. Osborne, P. Kaiza & S. Roe. (Eds.), *Homicides, Firearm Offences and Intimate Violence 2008/09. Supplementary Volume 2 to Crime in England and Wales 2008/09 (2nd Ed)*. London: Home Office. .

Roizen, J. (1997). Epidemiological issues in alcohol-related violence. In M. Galanter (Ed.), *Recent Developments in Alcoholism: Alcohol and Violence* (Vol. 13, pp. 7–39). New York: Plenum Press.

Romero, J. J. & Wiliams, L. M. (1985). Recidivism among convicted sex offenders: A ten year follow up study. *Federal Probation*, 49, 58–64.

Romero, R. J. & Williams, L. (1983). Group psychotherapy and intensive probation supervision with sex offenders: A comparative study. *Federal Probation*, 47(4), 36–42.

Romney, M. B., Albrecht, W. S. & Cherrington, D. J. (1980). Red-flagging the white-collar criminal. *Management Accounting*, March, 51–57.

Rosenfeld, B. (2003). Recidivism in stalking and obsessional harassment. *Law and Human Behavior*, 27, 251–265.

Rosenfeld, B. (2004). Violence risk factors in stalking and obsessional harassment: A review and preliminary meta-analysis. *Criminal Justice and Behavior*, 31, 9–36.

Rosenfeld, B. & Harmon, R. (2002). Factors associated with violence in stalking and obsessional harassment cases. *Criminal Justice and Behavior*, 29, 671–691.

Rosenfeld, B. & Lewis, C. (2005). Assessing violence risk in stalking cases: A regression tree approach. *Law and Human Behavior*, 29, 343–357.

Rosenfeld, B., Fava, J. & Galietta, M. (2009). Working with the stalking offender: Considerations for risk assessment and intervention. In J. Werth, E. Welfel, &

A. Benjamin (Eds.), *The Duty to Protect: Ethical, Legal, and Professional Considerations for Mental Health Professionals* (pp. 95–109). Washington, DC, US: American Psychological Association. doi: 10.1037/11866-007.

Rosenfeld, B., Galietta, M. & Ivanoff, A., Garcia-Mansilla, A., Martinez, R., Fava, J., Fineran, V. & Green, D. (2007). Dialectical behavior therapy for the treatment of stalking offenders. *The International Journal of Forensic Mental Health, 6*, 95–103.

Rosenkoetter, L. I., Rosenkoetter, S. E. & Acock, A. C. (2009). Television violence: An intervention to reduce its impact on children. *Journal of Applied Developmental Psychology, 30*, 381–397.

Roskill, Lord (1986). *Fraud Trials Committee Report*. London: HMSO.

Ross, J. M. & Babcock, J. C. (2009). Gender differences in partner violence in context: Deconstructing Johnson's control-based typology of violent couples. *Journal of Aggression, Maltreatment & Trauma, 18*, 604–622.

Ross, R. R., Fabiano, E. A. & Ewles, C. D. (1988). Reasoning and rehabilitation. *International Journal of Offender Therapy and Comparative Criminology, 32*, 29–36.

Rossi, L. (2006). Obsessive compulsive disorder and related conditions. *Psychiatric Annals, 36* (7), 514–517.

Rowson, D. (2009). The Problem with Fraudulent Solicitors: Issues of Trust, Investigation and the Self-Regulation of the Legal Profession. PhD Dissertation.

Sacco, V. (1985). Shoplifting prevention: The role of communication-based intervention strategies. *Canadian Journal of Criminology, 27* (1), 15–29.

Sachs, A. (1978). The myth of male protectiveness and the legal subordination of women: An historical analysis. In C. Smart and B. Smart (Eds.), *Women, Sexuality and Social Control* (pp. 27–41). London: Routledge and Kegan Paul.

Salter, A. C. (2001). *Predators: Pedophiles, Rapists and Other Sex Offenders*. New York: Basic Books.

Samuels, J., Bienvenu, O. J., Cullen, B., Costa, P. T., Eaton, W. W. & Nestadt, G. (2004). Personality dimensions and criminal arrest. *Comprehensive Psychiatry, 45*, 275–280.

Sarasalo, E., Bergman, B. & Toth, J. (1996). Personality Traits and Psychiatric and Somatic Morbidity Among kleptomaniacs. *Acta Psychiatry Scandinavia, 94* (5), 358–364.

Scarr, H. A. (1973). *Patterns of Burglary*. Washington, D.C.:Government Printing Office.

Schank, R. C. & Abelson, R. P. (1977). *Scripts, Plans, Goals and Understanding*. Hillsdale, New Jersey: Lawrence Erlbaum Associates.

Schewe, P.A. (1997). Paraphilia not otherwise specified. In D. R. Laws and W. T. O'Donahue (Eds.), *Sexual Deviance Theory, Assessment, and Treatment*. New York: Guilford.

Schlueter, G. R., O'Neal, F. C., Hickey, J. & Sellers, G. L. (1989). Rational vs. Non-Rational shoplifting types: Implications for loss prevention. *International Journal of Offender Therapy and Comparative Criminology, 33*, 227–239.

Scully, D. (1990). *Understanding Sexual Violence: A Study of Convicted Rapists* London: Unwin Hyman Ltd.

Scully, D. & Marolla, J. (1985). 'Riding the Bull at Gilleys': Convicted rapists describe the rewards of rape, *Social Problems, 32* (3), 251–263.

Segal, Lynne (1990). *Slow Motion: Changing Masculinities, Changing Men*. London: Virago.

Sentencing Advisory Panel (2002). Advice to the Court of Appeal – 10. Offences Involving Child Pornography. Home Office Communications Directorate. Available at http://sentencingcouncil.judiciary.gov.uk/, accessed 12 Feb 2012.

Sentencing Guidelines Council (2004). Overarching Principles: Seriousness. Available at http://www.sentencingcouncil.org.uk/docs/web_seriousness_guideline.pdf, accessed on 24 October 2010.

Sentencing Guidelines Council (2008a). Assault and Offences against the Person. Available at http://www.sentencingcouncil.org.uk/docs/Assault_and_other_offences_against_the_person_accessible.pdf, accessed on 24 October 2010.

Sentencing Guidelines Council (2008b). Magistrates Court Sentencing Guidelines. Available at http://sentencingcouncil.judiciary.gov.uk/, accessed 12 Feb 2012.

Sentencing Guidelines Council (2008c). New Guidelines for Judges and Magistrates on Theft, Burglary and Breach of ASBOs. Available at http://sentencingcouncil.judiciary.gov.uk/, accessed 12 Feb 2012.

Sentencing Guidelines Council (2009a). Attempted Murder. Available at http://www.sentencingcouncil.org.uk/docs/Attempted_Murder_-_Definitive_Guideline_(web)accessible.pdf, accessed on 24 October 2010.

Sentencing Guidelines Council (2009b). Magistrates' Court Sentencing Guidelines: Definitive Guideline. Available at http://sentencingcouncil.judiciary.gov.uk/docs/Magistrates_Guidelines_including_update_1__2__3_4_web.pdf, accessed on 30 November 2011.

Serbin, L. A., Stack, D. M., De Genna, N., Grunzeiwieg, N., Temcheff, E. C. Schwartzman, A. E. & Leddingham, J. (2004). When aggressive girls become mothers. Problems in parenting, health, and development across two generations. In M. Putallaz & K. L. Bierman (eds). *Aggression, Antisocial Behavior, and Violence among Girls.* New York: Guilford Press.

Serious Organised Crime Agency (SOCA) (2010). *Asset Recovery.* Available at http://www.soca.gov.uk/about-soca/how-we-work/asset-recovery, accessed on 30 November 2011.

Seto, M. C. & Eke, A. W. (2005). The criminal histories and later offending of child pornography offenders. *Sexual Abuse: A Journal of Research and Treatment,* 17 (2), 201–210.

Seto, M. C. & Lalumiere, M. (2001). A brief screening scale to identify pedophilic interests among child molesters. *Sexual Abuse,* 13 (1), 15–25.

Sexual Assault Referral Centres (no date). Available at http://webarchive.nationalarchives.gov.uk/+/http:/www.homeoffice.gov.uk/crime-victims/reducing-crime/sexual-offences/sexual-assault-referral-centres/index.html, accessed 12 Feb 2012.

Sexual Offences Act 2003 (c.42). Available at http://www.opsi.gov.uk/Acts/acts2003/ukpga_20030042_en_1, accessed on 14 January 2010.

SFO (Serious Fraud Office) (2010) [online] Available at http://sfo.gov.uk, accessed on 30 November 2011.

Sharp, C., Aldridge, J. & Medina, J. (2006). Delinquent youth groups and offending behaviour: Findings from the 2004 offending. *Crime and Justice Survey* (Home Office).

Sheldon, K. and Howitt, D. (2007). *Sex Offenders and the Internet.* Chichester: John Wiley and Sons Ltd.

Sheldon, K. & Howitt, D. (2008). Sexual fantasy in paedophile offenders: Can any model explain satisfactorily new findings from a study of Internet and contact sexual offenders? *Legal and Criminological Psychology*, 13 (1), 137–158.

Sher, K. J., Bartholow, B. D., Wood, M. D. (2000). Personality and substance use disorders: A prospective study. *Journal of Consulting and Clinical Psychology*, 68, 818–829.

Sheridan, L., Gillett, R., Davies, G. M., Blaauw, E. & Patel, D. (2003). 'There's no smoke without fire': Are male ex-partner perceived as more 'entitled' to stalk than acquaintance or stranger stalkers? *British Journal of Psychology*, 94, 87–98.

Shover, N. (1973). The Social organisation of burglary, *Social Problems*, 20, 499–514.

Shover, N. & Honaker, D. (1992). The socially bounded decision making of persistent property offenders. *Howard Journal of Criminal Justice*, 31, 276–293.

Shover, N. & Wright, J. P. (2001). Victims and costs: Introduction. In N. Shover and J. P. Wright (Eds.), *Crimes of Privilege: Readings in White-Collar Crime* (pp. 49–51). Oxford: Oxford University Press.

Shury, J., Speed, M., Vivian, D., Kuechel, A. & Nicholas (2005). Crime against Retail and Manufacturing Premises: Findings from the 2002 Commercial Victimisation Survey, Home Office Online Report 37/05. London: HMSO.

Silberman, C. (1978). *Criminal Violence, Criminal Justice*. New York: Vintage.

Simmons, J. & Dodd, T. (2003) *Crime in England and Wales 2003/4* (Home Office Statistical Bulletin 07/03). London: HMSO.

Simon, L. M. J. (1997). Do criminal offenders specialize in crime types? *Applied and Preventative Psychology*, 6, 35–53.

Singleton, N., Farrell, M. & Meltzer, H. (1999). *Substance Misuse among Prisoners in England & Wales*. London: Office for National Statistics.

Smith, J. (2003). *The Nature of Personal Robbery*. Home Office Research Study 254. London: Home Office.

Smith, M. D. & Morra, N. N. (1994). Obscene and threatening telephone calls to women: Data from a Canadian national survey. *Gender and Society*, 8 (4), 584–596.

Smith, P. & Waterman, M. (2004). The role of experience in processing bias for aggressive words in forensic and non-forensic populations. *Aggressive Behavior*, 30, 105–122.

Smith, P., Waterman, M. & Ward, N. (2006). Driving aggression in forensic and non-forensic populations: Relationships to self-reported levels of aggression, anger and impulsivity. *British Journal of Social Psychology*, 97, 387–403.

Snyder, H. (2000). Sexual assault of young children as reported to law enforcement: Victim, incident, and offender characteristics. Retrieved September, 2010, from American Bureau of Justice Statistics Clearinghouse, http://bjs.ojp.usdoj.gov/content/pub/pdf/saycrle.pdf.

SOCA (Serious Organised Crime Agency) (2010). The United Kingdom Threat Assessment of Organised Crime. Available at http://www.soca.gov.uk/threats, accessed 12 Feb 2012.

Soothill, K. & Pope, P. (1973). Arson: A twenty-year cohort study. *Medicine, Science, and the Law*, 13 (2), 127–138.

Soothill, K., Ackerley, E. & Francis, B. (2004). The criminal careers of arsonists. *Medicine, Science and the Law*, 44, 27–40.

Soothill, K., Francis, B., Sanderson, B. & Ackerley, E. (2000). Sex offenders: Specialists, generalists or both? A 32-year criminological study. *British Journal of Criminology*, 40, 56–67.

South, N. (2007). Drugs, alcohol, and crime. In M. Maguire, R., Morgan & R. Reiner, R. (Eds.), *The Oxford Handbook of Criminology* (pp. 810–838).Oxford: Oxford University Press.

Spitzberg, B. H. & Cupach, W. R. (2007). The state of the art of stalking: Taking stock of the emerging literature. *Aggression and Violent Behavior,* 12, 64–86.

Stanko, E. (2001). The day to count: Reflections on a methodology to raise awareness about the impact of domestic violence within the UK. *Criminology and Criminal Justice,* 1, 215–226.

Stevens, J. A. (1997). Standard investigatory tools and offender profiling. In J. L. Jackson and D. A. Bekerian (Eds.), *Offender Profiling: Theory, Research and Practice.* Chichester: Wiley.

Stinson, J. D., Sales, B. D. & Becker, J. V. (2008). *Sex offending: Casual Theories to Inform Research, Prevention and Treatment.* Washington: APA.

Stith, S. M., Smith, D. B., Penn, C. E., Ward, D. B. & Tritt, D. (2004). Intimate Partner physical abuse perpetration and victimisation risk factors: A meta-analytic review. *Aggression and Violent Behavior,* 10, 65–98.

Storey, J. E., Hart, S. D., Meloy, J. R. & Reavis, J. A. (2009). Psychopathy and stalking. *Law and Human Behavior,* 33, 237–246.

Stotland, E. (1977). White collar criminals. *Journal of Social Issues,* 33, 179–196.

Stott, C. (2009). Crowd Psychology & Public Order: An Overview of Scientific Theory and Evidence. Submission to the HMIC Policing of Public Protest Review Team.

Stover, C. S., Meadows, A. L. & Kaufman, J. (2009). Interventions for intimate partner violence: Review and implications for evidence-based practice. *Professional Psychology: Research and Practice,* 40, 223–233.

Straus, M. A. (1979). Measuring intrafamily conflict and violence: The Conflict Tactics Scales. *Journal of Marriage and the Family,* 41, 75–88.

Straus, M. A., Hamby, S. L., Boney-McCoy, S. & Sugarman, D. B. (1996). The revised Conflict Tactics Scales (CTS2): Development and preliminary psychometric data. *Journal of Family Issues,* 17, 283–316.

Sullivan, J. & Beech, A. (2003). Are collectors of child abuse images a risk to children? In A. MacVean, and P. Spindler (Eds.), *Policing Paedophiles on the Internet* (pp. 49–60). John Grieve Centre for Policing and Community Safety. Bristol: The New Police Bookshop.

Sullivan, M. L. (2005). Maybe we shouldn't study 'Gangs': Does reification obscure youth violence? *Journal of Contemporary Criminal Justice,* 21 (2), 170–190.

Sumnall, H., McGrath, Y., McVeigh, J., Burrell, K., Wilkinson, L. & Bellis, M. (2006). *Drug Use Prevention among Young People.* London: NICE.

Svedin, C. G. & Back, K. (1996). *Children Who Don't Speak Out.* Sweden: Radda Barnen Swedish Save the Children.

Swaffer, T., Haggett, M. & Oxley, T. (2001). Mentally disordered firesetters: A structured intervention programme. *Clinical Psychology and Psychotherapy,* 8, 468–475.

Tajfel, H. (1972). La catégorisation sociale (English Translation). In S. Moscovici (Ed.), *Introduction à la psychologie sociale* (Vol. 1). Paris: Larousse.

Tate, T. (1990). *Child Pornography.* London: Methuen.

Taylor, M. & Nee, C. (1988). The Role of Cues in Simulated Residential Burglary. *British Journal of Criminology,* 28, 105–116.

Taylor, M. & Quayle, E. (2003). *Child Pornography: An Internet Crime.* Hove: Brunner-Routledge.

Taylor, M. & Quayle, E. (2006). The Internet and abuse images of children: search, precriminal situations and opportunity. In R. Wortley and S. Smallbone (Eds.), *Situational Prevention of Child Sexual Abuse*. New York: Criminal Justice Press/Willan Publishing.

Taylor, M., Holland, G. & Quayle, E. (2001a). Typology of paedophile picture collections, *The Police Journal*, 74 (2), 97–107.

Taylor, M., Quayle, E. & Holland, G. (2001b). Child pornography, the Internet and offending, ISUMA. *The Canadian Journal of Policy Research*, 2 (2), 94–100.

Taylor, R. (2000). A Seven-Year Reconviction Study of HMP Grendon Therapeutic Community, Research Findings No. 115, London: Home Office.

Taylor Thorne & Slavkin (2004). Treatment of fire setting behaviour. In W. L. Lindsay, J. L. Taylor and P. Sturmey (Eds.), *Offenders with Developmental Disabilities* (pp. 221–240). London: Wiley.

Thakker, J., Ward, T. & Navathe, S. (2007). The cognitive distortions and implicit theories of child sexual abusers in Gannon, T. A., Ward, T., Beech, A. R. and Fisher, D. (2007) *Aggressive Offenders' Cognition: Theory, Research and Practice* Chichester: John Wiley

The Observer (2002). Gangland Britain. *The Observer for the Guardian*. Issue 17 November 2002. Available at http://www.guardian.co.uk/uk/2002/nov/17/drugsandalcohol.ukcrime, accessed on 10 November 2010.

Theft Act (1968). The UK Statute Law Database. Available at http://www.legislation.gov.uk/ukpga/1968/60/section/24, accessed on April 2011.

Thibaut, F., De La Barra, F., Gordon, H., Cosyns, P., Bradford, J. M. W & the WFSBP Task Force on Sexual Disorders (2010) The World Federation of Societies of Biological Psychiatry (WFSBP) Guidelines for the biological treatment of paraphilias. *The World Journal of Biological Psychiatry*, 11, 604–655.

Thomas, S. D. M., Purcell, R., Pathé, M. & Mullen, P. E. (2008). Harm associated with stalking victimization. *Australian and New Zealand Journal of Psychiatry*, 42, 800–806.

Thornberry, T. P., Krohn, M. D., Lizotte, A. J. & Chard-Wierschem, D. (1993). The role of juvenile gangs in facilitating delinquent behavior. *Journal of Research in Crime and Delinquency*, 30, 55–87.

Thornton, D. (14 February 2000). *Impact of the Early SOTP on Reconviction Rates*. Unpublished correspondence to Ken Sutton, Director of Regimes, Her Majesty's Prison Service.

Tjaden, P. & Thoennes, N. (1998). *Stalking in America: Findings from the National Violence against Women Survey* (National Institute of Justice report 169592). Washington, DC: U.S.

Tomak, S., Weschler, F. S. Ghahramanlou-Holloway, M., Virden, T. Nademin, M. E. (2009). An empirical study of the personality characteristics of Internet sex offenders. *Journal of Sexual Aggression*, 15 (2), 139–148.

Tonglet, M. (2002). Consumer misbehaviour: An exploratory study of shoplifting. *Journal of Consumer Behaviour*, 1 (4), 336–354.

Tonin, E. (2004). The attachment styles of stalkers. *Journal of Forensic Psychiatry and Psychology*, 15 (4), 584–590.

Topalli, V., Wirgy, R. & Fornanfo, R. (2002). Drug-dealers, robbery and retaliation: Vulnerability, deterrence and the contagion of violence. *British Journal of Criminology*, 42, 337–351.

Tseloni, A. & Pease, K. (1998). 'Nuisance' Phone calls to women in England and Wales. *European Journal on Criminal Policy and Research*, 6, 91–111.

Turnbull, P. J., McSweeney, T., Webster, R., Edmunds, M. & Hough, M. (2000). Drug Treatment and Testing Orders: Final Evaluation Report, Home Office Research Study No. 212. London: Home Office.

U.K. National Probation Service (2005). Internet Sex Offender Treatment Programme (i-SOTP) Treatment Manual. Available on request from the Interventions and Substance Misuse Group, National Offender Management Service, Ministry of Justice, 102 Petty France, London, SW1H 9AJ, U.K.

U.S. Department of Justice, Bureau of Justice Statistics (2006). National Crime Victimization Survey 2006. Available at http://bjs.ojp.usdoj.gov/index.cfm?ty=pbdetail&iid=765, accessed on 30 November 2011.

UK Drug Policy Commission (2008). *Reducing Drug Use, Reducing Reoffending.* Available at http://www.ukdpc.org.uk/publications.shtml#RDURR_report.

UNICEF (1990). United Nations Convention on the Rights of the Child. Available at http://www.unicef.org/crc/, accessed 12 Feb 2012.

Department for Transport, Local Government and the Regions (DTLR) (2000). *Fire Statistics, United Kingdom, 2000.* DTLR: London.

Valdez, A., Kaplan, C. D. & Codina, E. (2000). Psychopathy among Young Mexican American Gang Members: A comparative study. *International Journal of Offender Therapy and Comparative Criminology*, 44, 46–58.

van Honk, J., Tuiten, A., de Haan, E., van den Hou, M. & Stam, H. (2001). Attentional biases for angry faces: Relationships to trait anger and anxiety. *Cognition and Emotion*, 15, 279–297.

Vandiver, D. M. & Kercher, G. (2004). Offender and victim characteristics of registered female sexual offenders in Texas: A proposed typology of female sexual offenders. *Sexual Abuse: A Journal of Research and Treatment*, 16, 121–137.

Vold, G. & Bernard, T. (1986). *Theoretical Criminology* (3rd edition). Oxford: Oxford University Press.

Vreeland, R. G. & Waller, M. B. (1979). *The Psychology of Fire Setting: A Review and Appraisal.* Washington, DC: U.S. Department of Commerce National Bureau of Standards.

Wachman, R. (2005). Corporate fraud loses UK business £72bn each year. *The Observer*, 20 November, p. 1.

Walby, S. (2004). *The Cost of Domestic Violence.* London: Women & Equality Unit.

Walby, S. & Allen, J. (2004). *Domestic Violence, Sexual Assault and Stalking: Findings from the British Crime Survey.* Home Office Research Study 276. London: Home Office.

Walker, L. E. (1979). *The Battered Woman.* New York: Harper and Row.

Walsh, D. (1978). *Shoplifting: Controlling a Major Crime.* London: Macmillan Press Ltd.

Wang, A. Y. (1994). Pride and prejudice in high school gang members. *Adolescence*, 29 (114), 279–291.

Ward, R. W. & Bird, R. (2005). *Domestic Violence, Crime and Victims Act 2004 – A Practitioners' Guide.* Bristol: Jordan's Publishing

Ward, T. (2000a). Child molesters cognitive distortions as implicit theories, *Aggression and Violent Behaviour*, 5 (5), 491–507.

Ward, T. (2000b). Sexual offenders' cognitive distortions as implicit theories. *Aggression and Violent Behavior*, 5, 491–507.

Ward, T. & Beech, A. R. (2006). An integrated theory of sexual offending. *Aggression and Violent Behavior*, 11, 44–63.

Ward, T. & Hudson, S. M. (1998). The construction and development of theory in the sexual offending area: a meta-theoretical framework. *Sexual Abuse: A Journal of Research and Treatment*, 10, 47–63.

Ward, T. & Hudson, S. M. (2000). Sexual offenders' implicit planning: A conceptual model. *Sexual Abuse: A Journal of Treatment and Research*, 12 (3), 189–202.

Ward, T., & Keenan, T. (1999). Child molesters' implicit theories. *Journal of Interpersonal Violence*, 14 (8), 821–838.

Ward, T. & Siegert, R. (2002). Toward a comprehensive theory of child sexual abuse: A theory of knitting perspective. *Psychology, Crime and Law*, 8, 319–351.

Ward, T., Polaschek, D. L. L. & Beech, A. R. (2006). *Theories of Sexual Offending*. Chichester: John Wiley.

Ward, T., Hudson, S. M., Siegert, R. J. & Marshall, W. L. (1995). Attachment style and intimacy deficits in sexual offenders: A theoretical framework. *Sexual Abuse: A Journal of Research and Treatment*, 7, 317–335.

Warren, L. J., Mackenzie, R., Mullen, P. E. & Ogloff, J. R. P. (2005). The Problem Behavior Model: The development of a stalkers clinic and a threateners clinic. *Behavioral Sciences and the Law*, 23, 387–397.

Waterhouse, L. & Carnie, J. (1992). Assessing child protection risk. *British Journal of Social Work*, 22, 47–60.

Watt, B. D. & Howells, K. (1999). Skills training for aggression control: Evaluation of an anger management programme for violent offenders. *Legal and Criminological Psychology*, 4, 285–300.

Webb, L. Craissati, J. & Keen, S. (2007). Characteristics of Internet child pornography offenders: A comparison with child molesters, *Sex Abuse*, 19, 449–465.

Webber, C. (2010). *Psychology and Crime*. London: Sage.

Weerman, F. M., Maxson, C. L., Esbensen, F., Aldridge, J., Medina, J. & van Gemert, F. (2009). EUROGANG PROGRAMME MANUAL Background, development, and use of the Eurogang instruments in multi-site, multi-method comparative research. Available at http://www.umsl.edu/~ccj/eurogang/EurogangManual.pdf, accessed 12 Feb 2012.

Weiner, M. (2001). *The Economic Costs of Fire*. Home Office Research Study 229. Home Office: London.

Weir, E. (2001). Drug-facilitated date rape. *Canadian Medical Association Journal*, 165, 80.

Welsh, B. & Farrington, D. (1999). Value for money? A review of the costs and benefits of situational crime prevention. *British Journal of Criminology*, 39, 345–368.

Westmarland, N. (2004). Rape Law Reform in England and Wales, *School for Policy Studies Working Paper Series, Paper Number 7*.

White, H. R. (1990). The drug use-delinquency connection in adolescence. In R. Weisheit (Ed.) *Drugs, Crime, and Criminal Justice*. Cincinnati: Anderson Publishing Company.

White, H. R. & Gorman, D. M. (2000). Dynamics of the drug crime relationship. *Criminal Justice*, 1, 151–218.

White, J., Kowalski, R. M., Lyndon, A. & Valentine, S. (2000). An integrative contextual developmental model of male stalking. *Violence and Victims*, 15, 373–388.

Whyte, S., Petch, E., Penny, C. & Reiss, D. (2008). Who stalks? A description of patients at a high security hospital with a history of stalking behaviour. *Criminal Behaviour and Mental Health*, 18, 27–38.

Wiersma, E. (1996). Commercial burglars in the Netherlands: Reasoning decision-makers? *International Journal of Risk, Security and Crime Prevention*, 1, 217–225.

Wigman, S. A. (2009). Male victims of former-intimate stalking: A selected review. *International Journal of Men's Health*, 8, 101–115.

Wiles, P. & Costello, A. (2000). *The 'Road to Nowhere': The Evidence for Travelling Criminals* (Home Office Research Study 207). London: HMSO.

Wilkinson, J. (2005). Evaluating evidence for the effectiveness of the reasoning and rehabilitation programme. *The Howard Journal of Criminal Justice*, 44, 70–85.

Williams, R. (2008). *'I did my bit in reporting a rapist, the authorities didn't do theirs'*. Available at http://www.guardian.co.uk/uk/2008/aug/16/rape.police, accessed on 1 February 2010.

Wilson, D. (2007). *Serial Killers: Hunting Britons and Their Victims*. Winchester: Waterside Press.

Wilson, D. (2009). *A History of British Serial Killing*. London: Sphere.

Wilson, D. (2010). Blinded by the micro-science. *Tribune*, 20 February.

Wilson, G. I. & Sullivan, J. P. (2007). On gangs, crime and terrorism. *Special to Defense and the National Interest*. Available at http://www.draco securityconsultants.com/draco_docs/GANGS%20CRIME%20TERRORISM. pdf, accessed on 12 August 2010.

Wilson, J. S., Ermshar, A. L. & Welsch, R. K. (2006). Stalking as paranoid attachment: A typological and dynamic model. *Attachment & Human Development*, 8, 139–157.

Wilson, N. J. (2002). *Montgomery House VPP Re-imprisonment Analysis. Internal Memorandum*, Department of Corrections Psychological Service, Wellington, New Zealand.

Wilson, R. J., Huculak, B. & McWhinnie, A. (2002). Restorative justice innovations in Canada. *Behavioral Sciences & the Law*, 20, 1–18.

Winder, B. & Grayson, A. (in prep.) Exploring the barriers and catalysts for paedophilic offending through the case study of a serial contact child sex offender.

Wolak, J., Finkelhor, D. & Mitchell, K.J. (2005). Child pornography possessors arrested in Internet-related crimes; findings form the National online Victimization study. Available at http://www.missingkids.com/en_US/publications/ NC144.pdf, accessed 5 November 2009.

Wolfe, D. T. & Hermanson, D. R. (2004). The Fraud Diamond: Considering the Four Elements of Fraud [online]. *CPA Journal Online*, December 2004. Available at nysscpa.org/cpajournal/2004/1204/essentials/p38.htm, accessed on 7 September 2010.

Wolhuter, L., Olley, N. & Denham, D. (2009). *Victimology: Victimisation and Victims' Rights*. London: Routledge.

Wong, D. S. W. (2005). A study of children's shoplifting behaviour: Implications to preventive measures. *International Journal of Adolescence & Youth*, 12 (1–2), 49–68.

Wood, J. & Alleyne, E. (2010). Street gang theory and research: Where are we now and where do we go from here? *Aggression and Violent Behaviour*, 15 (2), 100–111.

Wood, J., Wheelwright, G. & Burrows, J. (1997). *Crime against Small Businesses: Facing the Challenge*. Swindon: Crime Concern.

Woolnough, A. (2009). Fear of crime on campus: Gender differences in use of self-protective behaviours at an urban university. *Security Journal*, 22 (1), 40–55.

World Health Organization (WHO) (2002a). *Sexual Violence*. Available at http://www.who.int/violence_injury_prevention/violence/world_report/factsheets/en/index.html, accessed on 13 January 2010.

World Health Organization (WHO) (2002b). *WHO Multi-country Study on Women's Health and Domestic Violence against Women: Initial Result on Prevalence, Health Outcome and Women's Responses*. Available at http://www.who.int/gender/violence/who_multicountry_study/en/index.html, accessed on 30 November 2011.

World Health Organization (WHO) (2009). *Violence against Women: Fact Sheet 239*. Available at http://www.who.int/mediacentre/factsheets/fs239/en/,accessed on 30 November 2011.

Wright, R. T. & Decker, S. H. (1994). *Burglars on the Job: Street Life and Residential Break-Ins*. Boston, MA: Northeastern University Press.

Wright, R. T. & Decker, S. H. (1997). *Armed Robbers in Action: Stickups and Street Culture*. Boston, MA: Northeastern University Press.

Wright, R., Logie, R. H. & Decker, S. H. (1995). Criminal expertise and decision making: An experimental study of the target selection process in residential burglary. *Journal of Research in Crime and Delinquency*, 32, 39–53.

Yablonsky, Lewis (1962). *The Violent Gang*. New York: Macmillan.

Yüksel, G. E., Taşkin, E. O., Ovali, Y. G., Karaçam, M. & Danaci, E. A. (2007). Case report: kleptomania and other psychiatric symptoms after carbon monoxide intoxication. *Turkish Journal of Psychiatry*, 18 (1), 80–86.

Zhang, L., Welte, J. W. & Weiczorek, W. F. (1999). Youth gangs, drug use, and delinquency. *Journal of Criminal Justice*, 27 (2), 101–109.

Zillman, D. (1979). *Hostility and Aggression*. Hillsdale, NJ: Erlbaum.

Zona, M. A., Palarea, R. E. & Lane, J. C. (1998). Psychiatric diagnosis and the offender-victim typology of stalking. In J. Reid Meloy (Ed.), *The Psychology of Stalking: Clinical and Forensic Perspectives* (pp. 69–84). San Diego, CA: Academic Press.

NAME INDEX

SUBJECT INDEX

technological addiction, 130
technology and fraud, 81
Telecommunications Act 1984, 245
telephone scatologia, defined, 245
The Theft Act 1968, 198, 202, 226
thematic pornography, 118
theory knitting, 168
traditional sex-role ideology, 44
trauma and drug use, 66
treatment
    arson, 12, 15
    domestic violence, 48
    drug use, 72–3
    internet sex offences, 127–8
    non-contact sexual offences, 252–3
    paedophilia, 163–5
    rape, 187
    shoplifting and kleptomania,
        204–5
    and stalking, 216, 221–2
types
    arson, 17–19
    burglars, 26
    domestic violence, 57–8
    murder, 139–40
    rapists, 180
    stalking offenders, 210–11

victim data, 3–4
victim responses, burglary, 32
victims
    drug use, 75
    fraud, 92–4
    gangs, 105, 111
    internet sex offences, 129
    non-contact sexual offences, 255

paedophilia, 166–7
stalking, 217
violent crime, 233–4
Victim Support, 39
video games and violence, 228
violence
    arson, 15
    instrumental and expressive, 144–5
    stalking, 214–15, 221–2
violent crime, 225–42
    alcohol, 227
    cognitive neo-association theory,
        237
    conviction, 230–1
    defined, 226
    demographics, 226–7
    detection, 231
    frustration-aggression hypothesis,
        236–7
    key debate, 228–9
    media violence, 241
    psychodynamic theory, 236
    recidivism, 232
    sentencing, 231–2
    social learning theory, 237–8
    statistics, 229–30, 233–4
    victims, 233–4
voyeurism, 243–6
    defined, 243–4

Walker's cycle of abuse, 59–60
WHO, 41
Women's Aid: domestic violence
        defined, 43

XYY Theory, 144